Exponential Random (

Exponential random graph models (ERGMs) are increasingly applied to observed network data and are central to understanding social structure and network processes. The chapters in this edited volume provide the theoretical and methodological underpinnings of ERGMs, including models for univariate, multivariate, bipartite, longitudinal, and social influence–type ERGMs. Each method is applied in individual case studies illustrating how social science theories may be examined empirically using ERGMs. The authors supply the reader with sufficient detail to specify ERGMs, fit them to data with any of the available software packages, and interpret the results.

Dr. Dean Lusher is Lecturer in Sociology at Swinburne University of Technology. He works closely with leading methodologists to develop an intuitive understanding of exponential graph models, how they link to broader network theory, and how to fit them to real-life data. His research applications are directed at issues of social norms and social hierarchies.

Dr. Johan Koskinen is Lecturer in Social Statistics at the University of Manchester. He is a statistician working with modeling and inference for Social Science data. Focusing on social network data, Dr. Koskinen deals with generative models for different types of structures, such as longitudinal network data, networks nested in multilevel structures, and multilevel networks classified by affiliations.

Garry Robins is Professor in the School of Psychological Sciences at the University of Melbourne. Robins is a mathematical psychologist whose research deals with quantitative and statistical models for social and relational systems. His research has won international awards from the Psychometric Society, the American Psychological Association, and the International Network for Social Network Analysis.

Structural Analysis in the Social Sciences

Mark Granovetter, Editor

The series *Structural Analysis in the Social Sciences* presents studies that analyze social behavior and institutions by reference to relations among such concrete social entities as persons, organizations, and nations. Relational analysis contrasts with both reductionist methodological individualism and macrolevel determinism, whether based on technology, material conditions, economic conflict, adaptive evolution, or functional imperatives. In this more intellectually flexible structural middle ground, analysts situate actors and their relations in a variety of contexts. Since the series began in 1987, its authors have variously focused on small groups, history, culture, politics, kinship, aesthetics, economics, and complex organizations, creatively theorizing how these shape, and in turn are shaped by, social relations. Their style and methods have ranged widely, from intense, long-term ethnographic observation to highly abstract mathematical models. Their disciplinary affiliations have included history, anthropology, sociology, political science, business, economics, mathematics, and computer science. Some have made explicit use of social network analysis, including many of the cutting-edge and standard works of that approach, whereas others have kept formal analysis in the background and used "networks" as a fruitful orienting metaphor. All have in common a sophisticated and revealing approach that forcefully illuminates our complex social world.

Other Books in the Series

1. Mark S. Mizruchi and Michael Schwartz, eds., *Intercorporate Relations: The Structural Analysis of Business*
2. Barry Wellmann and S. D. Berkowitz, eds., *Social Structures: A Network Approach*
3. Ronald L. Brieger, ed., *Social Mobility and Social Structure*
4. David Knoke, *Political Networks: The Structural Perspective*
5. John L. Campbell, J. Rogers Hollingsworth, and Leon N. Lindberg, eds., *Governance of the American Economy*
6. Kyriakos M. Kontopoulos, *The Logics of Social Structure*
7. Philippa Pattison, *Algebraic Models for Social Structure*
8. Stanley Wasserman and Katherine Faust, *Social Network Analysis: Methods and Applications*
9. Gary Herrigel, *Industrial Constructions: The Sources of German Industrial Power*
10. Philippe Bourgois, *In Search of Respect: Selling Crack in El Barrio*
11. Per Hage and Frank Harary, *Island Networks: Communication, Kinship, and Classification Structures in Oceana*
12. Thomas Schweitzer and Douglas R. White, eds., *Kinship, Networks, and Exchange*
13. Noah E. Friedkin, *A Structural Theory of Social Influence*
14. David Wank, *Commodifying Communism: Business, Trust, and Politics in a Chinese City*

Continued after the index

Exponential Random Graph Models for Social Networks

Theory, Methods, and Applications

Editors

DEAN LUSHER

JOHAN KOSKINEN

GARRY ROBINS

CAMBRIDGE
UNIVERSITY PRESS

32 Avenue of the Americas, New York NY 10013-2473, USA

Cambridge University Press is part of the University of Cambridge.

It furthers the University's mission by disseminating knowledge in the pursuit of education, learning, and research at the highest international levels of excellence.

www.cambridge.org
Information on this title: www.cambridge.org/9780521141383

© Cambridge University Press 2013

First published 2013
Reprinted 2013

A catalog record for this publication is available from the British Library.

Library of Congress Cataloging in Publication data
Exponential random graph models for social networks : theory, methods, and applications / [edited by] Dean Lusher, Swinburne University of Technology, Johan Koskinen, University of Manchester, Garry Robins, University of Melbourne, Australia.
    pages   cm. – (Structural analysis in the social sciences ; 35)
Includes bibliographical references and index.
ISBN 978-0-521-19356-6 (hardback) – ISBN 978-0-521-14138-3
(paperback) 1. Social networks – Mathematical models.   2. Social networks – Research – Graphic methods.   I. Lusher, Dean, editor of compilation.
II. Koskinen, Johan, editor of compilation.   III. Robins, Garry, editor of compilation.
HM741.E96   2012
302.3–dc23   2012021034

ISBN   978-0-521-19356-6   Hardback
ISBN   978-0-521-14138-3   Paperback

For

Jo, Massimo, and Priscilla

Pirkko

Jane, and Olivia

THANKS

We thank our chapter contributors for their knowledge, dedication, and patience in producing this book. Thanks also to our colleagues in the Melnet social network group and elsewhere who have collaborated with us and provided advice in our research on exponential random graph models. Additionally, we are indebted to MelNet SNA course participants whose questions and inquisitiveness have directed the content of this edited volume. We are grateful to colleagues at the Defence Science and Technology Organization (DSTO) in Australia, and Nuffield College and the Mitchell Center in the UK for valuable comments and feedback. In particular, thanks to Nectarios Kontoleon, Jon Fahlander, and Bernie Hogan for comments on selected parts of the book. Finally, thank you to Sarah Craig and Claudia Mollidor for preparing the book for publication.

Contents

List of Figures   *page* xvii

List of Tables   xxi

1. Introduction   1
    1.1   Intent of This Book   2
    1.2   Software and Data   2
    1.3   Structure of the Book   3
          1.3.1 Section I: Rationale   3
          1.3.2 Section II: Methods   3
          1.3.3 Section III: Applications   4
          1.3.4 Section IV: Future   5
    1.4   How To Read This Book   5
    1.5   Assumed Knowledge of Social Network Analysis   6

SECTION I: RATIONALE
2. What Are Exponential Random Graph Models?   9
    2.1   Exponential Random Graph Models: A Short
          Definition   9
    2.2   ERGM Theory   10
    2.3   Brief History of ERGMs   12
    2.4   Network Data Amenable to ERGMs   14

3. Formation of Social Network Structure   16
    3.1   Tie Formation: Emergence of Structure   16
          3.1.1 Formation of Social Ties   16
          3.1.2 Network Configurations: Consequential
                Network Patterns and Related Processes   17
          3.1.3 Local Network Processes   19
          3.1.4 Dependency (and Theories of Network
                Dependence)   19

3.1.5 Complex Combination of Multiple and Nested
Social Processes   21
3.2   Framework for Explanations of Tie Formation   23
3.2.1 Network Self-Organization   23
3.2.2 Individual Attributes   26
3.2.3 Exogenous Contextual Factors: Dyadic
Covariates   28

4. Simplified Account of an Exponential Random Graph Model
as a Statistical Model   29
4.1   Random Graphs   30
4.2   Distributions of Graphs   31
4.3   Some Basic Ideas about Statistical Modeling   34
4.4   Homogeneity   35

5. Example Exponential Random Graph Model Analysis   37
5.1   Applied ERGM Example: Communication in "The
Corporation"   37
5.2   ERGM Model and Interpretation   41
5.2.1 Multiple Explanations for Network Structure   45

SECTION II.   METHODS

6. Exponential Random Graph Model Fundamentals   49
6.1   Chapter Outline   49
6.2   Network Tie-Variables   49
6.3   Notion of Independence   51
6.4   ERGMs from Generalized Linear Model Perspective   52
6.5   Possible Forms of Dependence   56
6.5.1 Bernoulli Assumption   56
6.5.2 Dyad-Independent Assumption   56
6.5.3 Markov Dependence Assumption   57
6.5.4 Realization-Dependent Models   57
6.6   Different Classes of Model Specifications   58
6.6.1 Bernoulli Model   58
6.6.2 Dyadic Independence Models   59
6.6.3 Markov Model   60
6.6.4 Social Circuit Models   69
6.7   Other Model Specifications   75
6.8   Conclusion   76

7. Dependence Graphs and Sufficient Statistics   77
7.1   Chapter Outline   77
7.2   Dependence Graph   78
7.2.1 Hammersley-Clifford Theorem and Sufficient
Statistics   82
7.2.2 Sufficient Subgraphs for Nondirected Graphs   83

7.3	Dependence Graphs Involving Attributes	88
7.4	Conclusion	89
8.	**Social Selection, Dyadic Covariates, and Geospatial Effects**	**91**
8.1	Individual, Dyadic, and Other Attributes	91
8.2	ERGM Social Selection Models	93
	8.2.1 Models for Undirected Networks	95
	8.2.2 Models for Directed Networks	96
	8.2.3 Conditional Odds Ratios	97
8.3	Dyadic Covariates	98
8.4	Geospatial Effects	99
8.5	Conclusion	101
9.	**Autologistic Actor Attribute Models**	**102**
9.1	Social Influence Models	102
9.2	Extending ERGMs to Distribution of Actor Attributes	103
9.3	Possible Forms of Dependence	106
	9.3.1 Independent Attribute Assumption	106
	9.3.2 Network-Dependent Assumptions	107
	9.3.3 Network-Attribute–Dependent Assumptions	107
	9.3.4 Covariate-Dependent Assumptions	108
9.4	Different Model Specifications and Their Interpretation	109
	9.4.1 Independence Models	109
	9.4.2 Network Position Effects Models	109
	9.4.3 Network-Attribute Effects Models	111
	9.4.4 Covariate Effects Models	112
9.5	Conclusion	113
10.	**Exponential Random Graph Model Extensions: Models for Multiple Networks and Bipartite Networks**	**115**
10.1	Multiple Networks	115
	10.1.1 ERGMs for Analyzing Two Networks	116
	10.1.2 ERGM Specifications for Two Networks	116
10.2	Bipartite Networks	120
	10.2.1 Bipartite Network Representation and Special Features	121
	10.2.2 ERGM Specifications for Bipartite Networks	122
	10.2.3 Additional Issues for Bipartite Networks	128
11.	**Longitudinal Models**	**130**
11.1	Network Dynamics	130
11.2	Data Structure	130
11.3	Model	131
	11.3.1 Continuous-Time Markov Chain	131
	11.3.2 Tie-Oriented Dynamics	132
	11.3.3 Definition of Dynamic Process	133

	11.3.4 Stationary Distribution	134
	11.3.5 Estimation Based on Changes	135
	11.3.6 Configurations for Networks	136
11.4	Relations to Other Models	137
	11.4.1 Reciprocity Model as Precursor	137
	11.4.2 Stochastic Actor-Oriented Models as Alternatives	138
11.5	Conclusion	139

12. Simulation, Estimation, and Goodness of Fit — 141

12.1	Exploring and Relating Model to Data in Practice	141
12.2	Simulation: Obtaining Distribution of Graphs for a Given ERGM	142
	12.2.1 Sampling Graphs Using Markov Chain Monte Carlo	142
	12.2.2 Metropolis Algorithm	146
12.3	Estimation	147
	12.3.1 Maximum Likelihood Principle	147
	12.3.2 Curved ERGMs	147
	12.3.3 Bayesian Inference	148
12.4	Solving the Likelihood Equation	149
	12.4.1 Importance Sampling: Geyer-Thompson Approach	149
	12.4.2 Stochastic Approximation: Robbins-Monro Algorithm	151
	12.4.3 Modifications for Longitudinal Model	154
12.5	Testing Effects	156
	12.5.1 Approximate Wald Test	157
	12.5.2 Alternative Tests	158
	12.5.3 Evaluating Log-Likelihood	160
12.6	Degeneracy and Near-Degeneracy	160
12.7	Missing or Partially Observed Data	162
12.8	Conditional Estimation from Snowball Samples	163
12.9	Goodness of Fit	165
	12.9.1 Approximate Bayesian GOF	166

13. Illustrations: Simulation, Estimation, and Goodness of Fit — 167

13.1	Simulation	167
	13.1.1 Triangulation	168
	13.1.2 Degrees	171
	13.1.3 Stars and Triangles Together	172
13.2	Estimation and Model Specification	174
	13.2.1 Some Example Model Specifications	176
13.3	GOF	179

13.3.1 How Do You Know Whether You Have a
Good Model? 179
13.3.2 What If Your Model Does Not Fit a Graph
Feature? 184
13.3.3 Should a Model Explain Everything? 184

SECTION III. APPLICATIONS

14. Personal Attitudes, Perceived Attitudes, and Social
Structures: A Social Selection Model 189
14.1 Perceptions of Others and Social Behavior 189
14.2 Data and Measures 191
14.2.1 Social Network Questions 191
14.2.2 Attribute Measures 192
14.2.3 Analyses 193
14.2.4 Goodness of Fit 193
14.3 Model Specification 194
14.3.1 Purely Structural Effects 194
14.3.2 Actor-Relation Effects 194
14.3.3 Covariate Network Effects 194
14.4 Results 195
14.4.1 Example 1: Schoolboys 196
14.4.2 Example 2: Football Team 199
14.5 Discussion 200

15. How To Close a Hole: Exploring Alternative Closure
Mechanisms in Interorganizational Networks 202
15.1 Mechanisms of Network Closure 202
15.2 Data and Measures 205
15.2.1 Setting and Data 205
15.3 Model Specification 207
15.4 Results 208
15.5 Discussion 210

16. Interdependencies between Working Relations: Multivariate
ERGMs for Advice and Satisfaction 213
16.1 Multirelational Networks in Organizations 213
16.2 Data, Measures, and Analyses 215
16.3 Descriptive Results 216
16.4 Multivariate ERGM Results 219
16.4.1 Low-AS Bank 219
16.4.2 High-AS Bank 222
16.5 Discussion 224

17. Brain, Brawn, or Optimism? Structure and Correlates of
Emergent Military Leadership 226
17.1 Emergent Leadership in Military Context 226

17.1.1 Antecedents to Emergent Leadership   226
17.1.2 Structure of Emergent Leadership   228
17.1.3 Setting and Participants   229
17.2 Model Specification   231
17.2.1 Modeling Issues   231
17.2.2 Purely Structural Effects   231
17.2.3 Actor-Relation Effects   232
17.3 Results   232
17.3.1 Results for Purely Structural Effects   232
17.3.2 Results for Actor-Relation Effects   234
17.4 Dicussion   235

18. Autologistic Actor Attribute Model Analysis of
Unemployment: Dual Importance of Who You Know and
Where You Live   237
18.1 Unemployment: Location and Connections   237
18.2 Data, Analysis, and Estimation   239
18.2.1 Data   239
18.2.2 Analysis   242
18.2.3 Estimation   243
18.3 Results   244
18.4 Discussion   246

19. Longitudinal Changes in Face-to-Face and Text
Message–Mediated Friendship Networks   248
19.1 Evolution of Friendship Networks, Communication
Media, and Psychological Dispositions   248
19.2 Data and Measures   251
19.2.1 Social Network Questions   251
19.2.2 Actor-Relation Measures   251
19.2.3 Analyses   252
19.3 Model Specification   252
19.4 Results   252
19.4.1 Results for Face-to-Face Superficial Networks   253
19.4.2 Results for Face-to-Face Self-Disclosing
Networks   254
19.4.3 Results for Text Message–Mediated Superficial
Networks   255
19.4.4 Results for Text Message–Mediated
Self-Disclosing Networks   255
19.5 Discussion   256

20. Differential Impact of Directors' Social and Financial Capital
on Corporate Interlock Formation   260
20.1 Bipartite Society: The Individual and the Group   260
20.1.1 Director Capital and Interlock Formation   261

20.2 Data and Measures 262
   20.2.1 Social Network Data 262
   20.2.2 Actor-Relation Measures 263
   20.2.3 Analyses 264
20.3 Model Specification 266
   20.3.1 Independent Bivariate Attribute Analysis 266
   20.3.2 Purely Structural Effects 266
   20.3.3 Models with Attributes: Actor-Relation Effects 266
20.4 Results 267
   20.4.1 Results for Independent Bivariate Analysis 267
   20.4.2 Results for Purely Structural Effects 267
   20.4.3 Results for Models Including Purely Structural
      and Actor-Relation Effects 268
20.5 Discussion 270

21. Comparing Networks: Structural Correspondence between
   Behavioral and Recall Networks 272
21.1 Relationship between Behavior and Recall 272
21.2 Data and Measures 273
   21.2.1 Description of Networks 273
   21.2.2 Data Transformations 274
   21.2.3 Model Specification 274
21.3 Results 275
   21.3.1 Visualization 275
21.4 Preliminary Statistical Analysis 277
21.5 Univariate Models 277
21.6 Models of Recall Networks with Behavioral Networks
   as Covariates 278
21.7 Multivariate Models 280
21.8 Discussion 282

SECTION IV. FUTURE
22. Modeling Social Networks: Next Steps 287
22.1 Distinctive Features of ERGMs 287
22.2 Model Specification 289
   22.2.1 Dependence Hierarchy 291
   22.2.2 Building Model Specifications 296
   22.2.3 Models with Latent Variables: Hybrid Forms 297
   22.2.4 Assessing Homogeneity Assumptions 299
22.3 General Issues for ERGMs 299

References 303
Index 327
Name Index 331

List of Figures

3.1.   Some network configurations and their underlying social
        processes.   *page* 18
3.2.   Nested configurations for a transitive triad.   22
3.3.   Conceptual framework for processes of social tie
        formation discussed in this book.   24
3.4.   Examples of network configurations for actor-relation
        effects.   27
3.5.   Example of network configurations for dyadic covariates.   28
4.1.   (a) Simple random network and (b) empirical
        communication network.   30
4.2.   Distribution of reciprocated arcs from sample of 1,000
        random graphs.   32
5.1.   Communication network of The Corporation.   38
5.2.   Mutual ties only (asymmetric ties removed) in
        communication network.   39
5.3.   Communication network with employee experience
        represented by size.   40
5.4.   Communication network with seniority.   40
5.5.   Communication network with office membership
        represented by shape.   41
5.6.   Multiplex communication and advice ties (all other ties
        removed).   42
6.1.   (a) Network variables of X and (b) a realization x for
        network on four vertices.   50
6.2.   Social circuit dependence.   58
6.3.   Configurations in 2-star model.   60
6.4.   Configurations with three edges: 3-star and triangle.   61
6.5.   Expected and 95% intervals for number of edges and
        triangles as function of triangle parameter in Markov
        model.   63

6.6.   Number of triangles for Markov model.   65
6.7.   Directed star configurations on three nodes.   67
6.8.   Configurations on three vertices with exactly one tie for
        each dyad.   68
6.9.   (a) Alternating triangles on base (i, j) and (b) independent
        2-paths.   70
6.10.   Configurations for directed graphs in alternating forms
        (a) AT-T and (b) A2P-T.   72
6.11.   Additional triadic configurations for directed graphs in
        alternating forms (a) AT-U, (b) AT-D, and (c) AT-C.   73
6.12.   Additional 2-path configurations for directed graphs in
        alternating forms (a) A2P-U and (b) A2P-D.   73
6.13.   Configurations associated with brokerage.   75
7.1.   Tie-variables of (a) four-node graph and (b) associated
        Bernoulli dependence graph.   78
7.2.   Tie-variables of (a) four-node graph and (b) associated
        Markov dependence graph.   79
7.3.   Tie-variables of social circuit graph and its dependence
        graph and dependence graph conditional on some
        tie-variables being zero.   80
7.4.   Singleton clique in dependence graph and corresponding
        configuration in X.   84
7.5.   Three-clique in dependence graph and corresponding
        3-star configuration in X.   84
7.6.   Three-clique in dependence graph and corresponding
        triangle configuration in X.   85
7.7.   Tie-variables for directed graph on four vertices with
        corresponding Markov dependence graph.   88
7.8.   Sufficient subgraphs for directed Markov graph on four
        vertices.   89
10.1.   Cross-network dyadic configurations.   117
10.2.   Cross-network 2-star effects.   118
10.3.   Cross-network triangle effects.   119
10.4.   Cross-network social circuit effects.   119
10.5.   Cross-network dyadic attribute effects.   120
10.6.   A $(5, 6)$ bipartite network.   121
10.7.   Bipartite 3-path and 4-cycle.   122
10.8.   Bipartite star configurations.   123
10.9.   Four-cycle dependence assumption.   124
10.10. Three-path dependence assumption.   124
10.11. Alternating 2-paths.   125
10.12. Attribute activity effects.   125
10.13. Two-star attribute effects.   126
10.14. Four-cycle attribute effects.   127

10.15. Dyadic between-set configurations. 128
12.1. Distribution of edges and alternating triangles for Kapferer's (1972) data. 143
12.2. Number of edges in sequence of graphs in Markov chain. 144
12.3. Number of edges against alternating triangles for sequence of graphs in Markov chain. 145
12.4. Robbins-Monro algorithm for network on $n = 20$ actors. 153
12.5. Graph on seven vertices with five edges. 161
12.6. Zones of order 0 through 3 for seed node a. 164
13.1. Simple random graph with thirty nodes and forty-three edges. 168
13.2. Graphs from simulations with different triangulation parameters. 169
13.3. Example graph for massive alternating triangle parameter. 170
13.4. Example graphs for alternating triangle parameters with different λs. 171
13.5. Simulation results for alternating star parameter. 172
13.6. Example graphs from simulations with both alternating and Markov star parameters. 173
13.7. Example graph from simulation with positive triangle and negative star parameters. 173
15.1. Local configurations of network ties representing different closure mechanisms: (a) path closure, (b) activity closure, (c) popularity closure, and (d) cyclic closure. 204
15.2. Network structure of interhospital patient mobility. 206
16.1. Advice-giving and satisfaction network in Low-AS bank branch. 217
16.2. Advice-giving and satisfaction network in High-AS bank branch. 217
18.1. Process of constructing augmented network. 240
18.2. Employment status and social connections. 242
18.3. Geographic distribution of employed and unemployed individuals. 243
18.4. Number of participants by wave. 244
19.1. Triadic configurations used in models. 252
21.1. Visualization of four pairs of networks. 276
22.1. Hierarchy of dependence structures. 293

List of Tables

4.1.	Selected network statistics for networks in Figure 4.1	*page* 31
5.1.	ERGM parameter estimates (and standard errors) for communication relations in The Corporation	43
6.1.	Two independent tie-variables	51
6.2.	Two dependent tie-variables	52
8.1.	Some social selection configurations for undirected networks	94
8.2.	Some social selection configurations for directed networks	95
8.3.	Dyadic covariate configurations for ERGMs	99
9.1.	Network position configurations, statistics, and parameters	110
9.2.	Network-attribute configurations, statistics, and parameters	111
9.3.	Covariate effects configurations, statistics, and parameters	112
13.1.	Suggested starting set of parameters for ERGM for positive affect networks	175
13.2.	Three models for The Corporation communication network	177
13.3.	Selected goodness-of-fit (GOF) details for communication network	180
14.1.	Two models for positive affect relations among schoolboys	195
14.2.	Two models for aggression relations among the footballers	196
15.1.	ERGM estimates of structural and actor-relation effects on the presence of patient transfers between hospitals	209
16.1.	Descriptive statistics of two bank branches	218
16.2.	Model estimates for Low-AS bank advice-giving and satisfaction network	220

16.3.   Model estimates for High-AS bank advice-giving and
         satisfaction network   223
17.1.   Parameter estimates for two models examining emergent
         leadership among recruits in military training   233
18.1.   Descriptive statistics   241
18.2.   ALAAM estimates (and SEs) for predicting unemployment
         using network, geospatial, and actor attribute effects   245
19.1.   Parameter estimates and standard errors in face-to-face
         friendship networks   253
19.2.   Parameter estimates and standard errors in text
         message–mediated friendship networks   254
20.1.   Summary statistics for attributes and attribute interactions   265
20.2.   Results of two bipartite ERGMs of directorships
         including only purely structural effects   268
20.3.   Two bipartite ERGM of directorships, with structural,
         actor relation, and actor relation interaction effects   269
21.1.   Overview of four different networks   274
21.2.   Descriptive statistics of four networks for behavior and
         recall   277
21.3.   Univariate ERGM parameter estimates (SEs) for four data
         sets   278
21.4.   Parameter estimates (SEs) for four recall networks (with
         behavioral network included as covariate network)   279
21.5.   Multivariate ERGM parameter estimates (SE) for four
         data sets   280

1

Introduction

Dean Lusher, Johan Koskinen, and Garry Robins

[handwritten marginalia: So ERGMs assume analytic build up perhaps moderated by very local conditions. Can social strs at a higher level be wrought thr of data are right?]

Exponential random graph models[1] (ERGMs) are a class of statistical
model for social networks. They account for the presence (and absence)
of network ties, and so provide a model for network structure. An ERGM
models a given network in terms of small local tie-based structures, such
as reciprocated ties and triangles. A social network can be thought of
as being built of these local patterns of ties, called "network configurations," which correspond to the parameters in the model. Moreover,
these configurations can be considered to arise from local social processes, whereby actors in the network form connections in response to
other ties in their social environment. ERGMs are a principled statistical
approach to modeling social networks. They are theory driven in that
their use requires the researcher to consider the complex, intersecting,
and, indeed, potentially competing theoretical reasons why the social ties
in the observed network have arisen. For instance, does a given network
structure occur due to processes of homophily, reciprocity, transitivity,
or a combination of these? By including such parameters together in the
one model, a researcher can test these effects one against the other, and so
infer the social processes that have built the network. Being a statistical
model, an ERGM permits inferences about whether, in our network of
interest, there are significantly more (or less) reciprocated ties, or triangles
(for instance), than we would expect.

ERGMs are fast becoming recognized as one of the central approaches
in analyzing social networks. In this short introductory chapter, we
describe the intent of this book, how it is structured, how it may be
read, the software resources available, and the knowledge that we expect
readers to have before following our text.

---

[1] Throughout this book, we use this now-established convenient term instead of the more
correct (but cumbersome) "exponential family random graph models."

1

1.1   Intent of This Book

In this book, we aim to introduce ERGMs in a way that takes the reader from the basic theoretical assumptions underlying the models, through the technical specifications and statistical detail, to applied examples illustrating how various substantive research questions may be investigated and tested empirically. The goals of this book are twofold: to describe ERGMs and to demonstrate how recent methodological developments allow us to address social network research questions in new and powerful ways. A specific target audience is the growing number of social scientists who are interested in statistical models for social networks and network-based social processes. We aim to provide an intuitive understanding of these models for those readers who may be unfamiliar with ERGMs. We also focus on delivering sufficient technical detail for those with a social network methodological background and who are interested in a deeper understanding of the modeling and estimation. We hope to lay bare the value of a statistical modeling approach in answering core questions about interactive social processes.

1.2   Software and Data

The book includes references to data and software that can be downloaded so that readers can reproduce some of the applications in a "hands-on" fashion. Some parts of this book make explicit use of the PNet suite of programs for ERGMs (Wang, Robins, & Pattison, 2009), and we tend to use PNet terminology for parameters and the like, but the exposition is in no way contingent on the software used (as long as the software does deal with ERGMs, naturally). The estimation algorithms used in PNet and in the R package statnet (Handcock et al., 2003; Handcock et al., 2008) are both described in Chapter 12, as is the principle of Bergm (Caimo & Friel, 2011). SIENA 3 can be used for fitting ERGMs to cross-sectional data (indeed, the main parts of PNet draw heavily on SIENA) and longitudinal models can be analyzed in RSIENA (or SIENA 4). Models for multiple networks, longitudinal networks, and bipartite networks can be estimated from the PNet suite of programs, XPNet, LPNet, and BPNet, respectively. The autologistic actor attribute models require iPNet. PNet and the example data used in this book can be downloaded to help you work through the chapters in a practical, hands-on fashion (http://www.sna.unimelb.edu.au). The package statnet is an ERGM estimation program in the R environment and can be installed from CRAN in standard R fashion. A useful introduction to the statnet package is given in a special issue of *Journal of Statistical*

Software (Hunter et al., 2008), and the worked-through examples of Goodreau et al. (2008) are particularly helpful.

1.3 Structure of the Book

This book is divided into four main sections that broadly map onto the rationale and theory, method, and application of ERGMs, with a fourth overview section discussing future directions. We consider that theory, method, and empirical work are fundamentally intertwined and interdependent. Thus, you will note that the first section, despite its flavor of conceptual discussion, still addresses methodological issues and provides empirical examples, whereas theoretical concepts permeate the methods section.

1.3.1 Section I: Rationale

Section I of this book provides an intuitive introduction to ERGMs by connecting to various aspects of social network (and social science) theory, the thinking behind the methods, and the empirical examination of research questions. Chapter 2 provides a very general initial description of ERGMs, including some broad definitions and a discussion of some central elements of the ERGM approach. Chapter 3 introduces some important network ideas about the formation of social ties and social structure more generally, and explains how these relate to an ERGM analysis. Chapter 4 introduces some central methodological details of ERGMs in intuitive terms for readers unfamiliar with the models, with more technical details delayed until Section II on methods. Finally, in this section, Chapter 5 provides an early and simple example of applying an ERGM to network data (an example we explore in greater detail in Chapter 13). In this way, we illustrate the type of inferences and interpretations that can be made about network structure using ERGMs. Our aims in this first section are not only to describe theoretical issues important to ERGMs but also to build intuitions for those coming to this modeling approach for the first time, before they encounter the more technical detail in Section II.

1.3.2 Section II: Methods

Section II of this book presents the basic statistical framework of ERGMs. Throughout the book, the case of a single observation on a (binary, unipartite) network is taken as a standard point of reference, and the technical details of ERGMs are introduced in the context of such a case in Chapter 6. Chapter 7 seeks to give a deeper understanding of ERGMs by way of the notion of the dependence graph. From here, a range of more specific ERGMs are presented, beginning with models that include social selection, dyadic covariate, and geospatial effects in Chapter 8. Chapter 9 covers autologistic actor attribute models (ALAAMs), which are a version of social influence models, for the attributes of the actors. The next chapters describe models for multiple networks and bipartite networks (Chapter 10) as well as longitudinal network data (Chapter 11). The section concludes with descriptions of simulation, estimation, and goodness-of-fit procedures (Chapter 12), together with some illustrations (Chapter 13).

1.3.3   Section III: Applications

Section III of this book demonstrates how ERGMs can be applied empirically to answer social network research questions. In this section, we present an application for each of the different types of ERGMs presented previously. The chapters illustrate to the reader the range of possibilities, issues, and general frame of reference a researcher engages in when using ERGMs. The chapters are presented as separate self-contained case studies, but together they cover a set of network theoretical issues and features of the modeling framework.

In these chapters, we seek to show why and how the models can be used to answer novel and theoretically important questions, formulated in a relational framework. The range of issues covered gives some indication of the breadth of approach that ERGMs offer. For instance, Lusher and Robins (Chapter 14) note how the individual perceptions of attitudes held by others in the network have an independent association on the formation of network ties in two different contexts. They draw on theory from social psychology in their exposition. Lomi and Pallotti (Chapter 15) examine various path closure effects and, ultimately, show the importance of structural equivalence–type patterns in the transfer of patients among hospitals. Zhao and Rank (Chapter 16) examine how multiple types of relations within the one organization relate to each other. Drawing on various leadership theories, Kalish and Luria (Chapter 17) construe leadership as a relational phenomenon and show how leadership networks differ from many other types of social networks. Daraganova and Pattison (Chapter 18) test competing hypotheses about the impact of spatial factors and social ties on unemployment. Igarashi (Chapter 19) demonstrates the importance of homophily in a longitudinal analysis of networks involving different methods of communication. Using bipartite network models, Harrigan and Bond (Chapter 20) show how different forms of capital lead to different types of linking behavior. In the final applications chapter, Quintane

(Chapter 21) examines differences in self-reported ties and observed relational behaviors.

1.3.4 Section IV: Future

There is ongoing methodological development: this book is by no means the last word on ERGMs. To conclude this book, Pattison and Snijders look to future directions for ERGM research and methods.

1.4 How To Read This Book

We suggest that a cover-to-cover reading may not be the best way to approach the book for all readers. Readers with less statistical knowledge might begin with all four chapters in Section I: Rationale, which provides the general basis of ERGMs. Following this, the introductory methods chapter on the fundamentals of ERGMs (Chapter 6) is important, although it could be tackled later if need be. At the very least, the social selection models (Chapter 8) and the illustrations chapter (Chapter 13) in Section II: Methods should be read before moving to relevant chapters of Section III: Applications, and Section IV: Future.

Some readers, however, may want to understand ERGMs from the point of view of the statistical model. Thus, they may want to jump straight to the methods section, especially Chapters 6 and 7, and then work their way through Chapter 12 before returning to the conceptual issues of Section I.

For some readers whose interests are principally directed to fitting models empirically, the chapter on dependency (Chapter 7), which details important conceptual issues with regard to ERGMs, may be skipped at the first or first few readings. For those interested in the theoretical underpinning of the statistical model, however, this chapter is important.

For readers with some familiarity with the ERGM framework and an interest in a specific type of model, it is probably good to have skimmed through Section I first (and perhaps the first chapter of Section II). From there, the reader may go on to the applications chapter of choice, and then work him- or herself back to the relevant chapters in Section II, for clarification of details. You may, for example, have a particular interest in social influence–type models, in which case you might want to start with Chapter 18 and refer back to Chapter 9 in Section II, when necessary.

If you intend to fit your own ERGMs, it is necessary to understand how the models are fitted, whether as introduced in Chapters 4 and 5 of Section I and then Chapter 13, or more in-depth as in Chapter 12 (simulation, estimation, and goodness of fit). Specific applications chapters in Section III may also prove quite useful as a guide. Finally, once you have fitted a model, or several, you may want to delve deeper into the details of Section II.

1.5   Assumed Knowledge of Social Network Analysis

We assume basic familiarity with social network analysis and that the reader understand the general concepts and terminology used in network and graph theory. For this purpose, we refer the reader to one of the many introductory texts, including Wasserman and Faust (1994), Prell (2011), Knoke and Yang (2008), Scott (2000), de Nooy, Mrvar and Batageli (2005), van Duijn and Vermunt (2006), and Hanneman and Riddle (2005), for a more detailed introduction. We assume that the reader is familiar with standard statistical techniques such as regression analysis and logistic regression. Kolaczyk (2009) and Knoke and Yang (2008) both have sections introducing ERGMs. The former provides a good technical and comprehensive treatment of statistical models for networks, which might be useful as further reading for the purposes of introducing alternative models. Reference is occasionally made to more advanced issues in statistics that the interested reader can follow-up on if a more comprehensive picture is desired.

Section I

Rationale

2

What Are Exponential Random Graph Models?

Garry Robins and Dean Lusher

2.1 Exponential Random Graph Models: A Short Definition

Exponential random graph models (ERGMs) are statistical models for network structure, permitting inferences about how network ties are patterned. Put another way, ERGMs are tie-based models for understanding how and why social network ties arise. This focus aligns ERGMs with a principal goal of much empirical social network research, which is to understand a given "observed" network structure (i.e., a network on which a researcher has collected data), and so to obtain insight into the underlying processes that create and sustain the network-based social system.

Much of social network analysis has been concerned with representing the network, a graph G, through various summary measures. From the literature, the reader may be familiar with summary measures $z(G)$ such as the number of edges in G, the number of mutual ties, centrality measures, triad census, and so on. We call these summary measures "network statistics," and in mathematical terms, the ERGM assigns probability to graphs according to these statistics:

$$P_\theta(G) = ce^{\theta_1 z_1(G) + \theta_2 z_2(G) + \cdots + \theta_p z_p(G)}.$$

The probability of a given network G is given by a sum of network statistics (the zs in this expression) weighted, just as in a regression, by parameters (the θs) inside an exponential (and where c is a normalizing constant). The network statistics are counts of the number of network configurations in the given network G, or some function of those counts. These configurations are small, local subgraphs in the network. In short, the probability of the network depends on how many of those configurations are present, and the parameters inform us of the importance of each configuration.

9

This expression is explained in much more detail in Section II. However, because the mathematical features are not important for our purposes here, we hope to explain ERGMs in a relatively intuitive way in this introductory section.

To put it as simply as possible, a researcher specifies an ERGM by choosing a set of configurations of theoretical interest. As we will see, there are many sets of plausible configurations that can be used. Then, by applying this particular model to an observed social network, parameters are estimated. This permits inferences about the configurations – the network patterns – in the data, and this in turn allows inferences about the type of social processes that are important in creating and sustaining the network. Thus, ERGMs provide a methodology to investigate network structures and processes empirically.

Note that there is not just one ERGM – there are whole classes of them. The researcher has to choose the specification of an ERGM for the data (just as a researcher has to choose the variables to include in a regression). For an ERGM, the specifications involve choices of configurations that the researcher believes are relevant to the network structure. Although there are some standard ways to do this, the choices are ultimately based on theories about how ties come into being and appear in regular patterns. We discuss some of these theories in greater length in Chapter 3. However, an ERGM itself carries some metatheory about networks, a conceptualization of a social network, and how it is created.

2.2   ERGM Theory

The use of an ERGM is consistent with some basic theoretical assumptions about social networks:

- Social networks are locally emergent.
- Network ties not only self-organize (i.e., there are dependencies between ties), but they are also influenced by actor attributes and other exogenous factors.
- The patterns within networks can be seen as evidence for ongoing structural processes.
- Multiple processes can operate simultaneously.
- Social networks are structured, yet stochastic.

Each idea is discussed more extensively in the following chapters. What is evident is that ERGMs are not "theory free." The preceding list details certain claims consistent with the use of ERGMs that may shape the sort of social network questions that can be asked. Yet many of these claims are not exclusive to ERGMs and overlap with other thinking about social networks. For instance, an ERGM views social tie formation as locally constructed, and much social network theory refers to local processes (e.g., reciprocity, transitivity, homophily – see Chapter 3). On the issue of multiple processes, Monge and Contractor (2003) argued that network research should be multitheoretical – that is, research should examine multiple theoretical perspectives at the same time, and, indeed, ERGMs can do this (see Section 3.1.5).

An explicit and particularly important feature of ERGMs is that network ties depend on one another (i.e., there is network self-organization); thus, the presence of one tie may affect the presence of others (see Sections 3.1.4 and 3.2.1 for general details, and Chapters 6 and 7 for more specific details). Of course, it is well understood that within a social network, individuals are by definition interdependent. In a seminal social networks article, White, Boorman, and Breiger (1976) famously lamented the divergence of theoretical and methodological perspectives on social interaction. On the one hand, they argued, theories are largely concerned with interaction; however, on the other hand, in empirical practice, researchers revert to aggregating individuals by categories. Thus, it is insufficient when we analyze such networks to consider individuals as unrelated "units of analysis" and instead more realistic to consider them as "actors in social relations" (Abbott, 1997, 1152). ERGMs take interdependency one step further by supposing that there is interdependence between network ties. It is in this way that network ties are construed as forming important patterns – the "configurations" parameterized in an ERGM. It is a theoretical and empirical task to delineate the various forms of dependence that are exhibited in actual social structures. We regard this as social network theory at a fundamental level.[1] Dependency among network ties is discussed at many stages of this book, particularly in Chapter 7.

Although there are certain assumptions that one engages when using ERGMs, there is also considerable freedom available to the researcher. As noted previously, there is not just one ERGM, but many. A researcher chooses which model to use by selecting which network structures are important. The utility, as well as the challenge, of ERGMs is the specification of a particular theory (or theories) into social network terms – specifically, in articulating network configurations that, in isolation or combination, reflect a relevant theoretical concept. We hope it is clear

---

[1] We are referring here to the particular way in which dependence is modeled for cross-sectional data. There are a number of other cross-sectional statistical models that also cater to dependency-related issues such as the random effects $p2$ model (van Duijn, Snijders, & Zijlstra, 2004) and latent social space/variable models (Airoldi et al., 2008; Handcock, Raftery, & Tantrum, 2007; Hoff, Raftery, & Handcock, 2002; Schweinberger & Snijders, 2007). The ERGM approach to dependency, however, is arguably the first and most explicit. See Snijders (2011) for an overview of statistical approaches to network analysis.

from Section III how this might be done. The process of theory translation requires the alignment of theoretical concepts with network configurations. As examples of how this is done, Chapters 14 and 17 focus on the actor attributes that are associated with receiving many network ties, whereas Chapter 15 considers endogenous network processes – specifically, on different closure mechanisms. Yet the attribute-network tie associations in Chapters 14 and 17 are modeled while controlling for endogenous (i.e., self-organizing) network processes, including closure. Likewise, Chapter 15 models endogenous network processes while controlling for network effects related to actor attributes. There are commonalities in the network structures examined in all three chapters (e.g., reciprocity and in-degree effects), demonstrating that many theoretical concepts relating to social tie formation are being analyzed simultaneously in different studies and highlighting that multiple theories need to be considered simultaneously. However, the analyses across the three chapters by no means engage with identical theories. Many theories may be examined in an ERGM, but some may be more important to the particular question in which a researcher is interested. In summary, an ERGM is a relatively open framework that is amenable to the testing of a range of network theories, depending on the interest of the researcher. Once a researcher has translated social theory into hypotheses in relational, quantitative terms, the ERGM provides a framework within which these hypotheses can be statistically examined.

2.3   Brief History of ERGMs

Moreno and Jennings (1938) introduced statistical network approaches by comparing observed network data to that expected under a null distribution. Although their method was simple enough, it did provide the insight that structural effects introduce "bias" into randomness. Some years later, this was picked up quite explicitly in the biased net theory of Rapoport (1953, 1957). Models for randomness itself were provided by the Erdös-Rényi graph (Erdös & Rényi, 1959) or, equivalently, the uniform Bernoulli graph distribution (Frank, 1981). (A number of refinements of null distributions have since been proposed in the literature – see Pattison et al., 2000.)

Holland and Leinhardt (1981) introduced a dyadic independence statistical model called the "p_1 model," which was the first ERGM to extend these simple random graph distributions. Although they set the grounds for future work, they did not go beyond dyads. Their simple model could be estimated using standard log-linear models; however, once triadic formations came into play, the independence assumptions necessary for log-linear models were expressly undermined. (More sophisticated dyadic-based models, with extradyadic dependence, have since been proposed by van Duijn et al. (2004).)

The crucial work from which all else flows, including this book, was that of Frank and Strauss (1986). They decided that rather than searching for new clever methods based on independence, a proper approach to network dependence was required. Translating and extending spatial statistical approaches into a network context, they proposed Markov random graph models that became the mainstay of ERGMs for nearly two decades. This was indeed a landmark paper in the history of ERGMs.

Yet the Markov random graph approach was slow to be adopted by network researchers. It was not until the 1990s that an influential article by Wasserman and Pattison (1996) popularized this type of network modeling as p^* models (with the nomenclature p^* following p_1 – see also Rennolls, 1995). The emphasis put on the log-linear form of the p^* facilitated extensions of the basic Markov graph framework that resulted in models for multivariate (Pattison & Wasserman, 1999), valued (Robins, Pattison, & Wasserman, 1999), and bipartite (Skvoretz & Faust, 1999) network data. Actor attributes were incorporated in social selection (Robins, Elliott, & Pattison, 2001) and social influence (Robins, Pattison, & Elliott, 2001) models. ERGMs were proposed as an effective vehicle for investigating theories in network social science (Contractor, Wasserman, & Faust, 2006; Monge & Contractor, 2003).

These developments, however, were limited by the estimation procedure (maximum pseudolikelihood estimation) that did not properly deal with the assumed dependencies in data. In the past decade, nevertheless, the pace of new development for, and the popularity of, ERGMs has grown dramatically. Various groups worked on algorithms to calculate (or, more precisely, approximate) maximum likelihood estimates, all being based on computer-intensive simulation (Corander, Dahmström, & Dahmström, 1998, 2002; Crouch, Wasserman, & Trachtenberg, 1998; Handcock, 2002, 2003; Snijders, 2002). What at first seemed to be algorithmic difficulties were suspected by Handcock (2002) and Snijders (2002) to be deficiencies of the Markov specification of the ERGM, which up to then was considered the natural default specification capturing tendencies toward transitivity, as proposed by Frank and Strauss (1986) (for model deficiencies, see Section 6.6.3 on the Markov model and Section 12.6 on degeneracy and near-degeneracy). As a remedy to these deficiencies, and building on the realization-dependent conditional independence assumptions developed by Pattison and Robins (2002), the Markov specification was generalized to specifications satisfying the social circuit model in Snijders et al. (2006). This proposal was a breakthrough in improving the capacity of ERGMs to fit real data (Robins et al., 2007).

A number of simulation-based algorithms for approximating the maximum likelihood estimate were implemented in software. This led to three publicly available computer programs: SIENA (Snijders et al., 2005), in which the ERGM estimation was included as an extension and algorithmic analogue of the previously available estimation methods for longitudinal actor-oriented models; the `statnet` software suite (Handcock et al., 2008), which used a different algorithm to produce the same estimates; and the PNet package (Wang, Robins, & Pattison, 2005), which used the same algorithm as SIENA.

There were ensuing steps in model formulation and estimation (Hunter & Handcock, 2006) and in novel goodness-of-fit approaches (Hunter, 2007; Hunter, Goodreau, & Handcock, 2008; Robins et al., 2007). As described later in this book, new developments have since begun to proliferate. These include approaches to estimation under varying circumstances – such as Bayesian inference and models for missing data and snowball sampling – as well as new models for directed, bipartite, multivariate, longitudinal, selection, and influence data. These extensions are described in Section II of this book.

2.4   Network Data Amenable to ERGMs

An ERGM is designed to be used with empirical network data. As we will see, it is possible to simulate networks using ERGMs (see Chapters 12 and 13), but the strength of the method comes to the fore with observed network data, the data that researchers have collected and are keen to understand.

Section III of this book highlights a number of different types of networks that are amenable to analysis using ERGMs. Networks can be directed or undirected,[2] and all networks used with ERGMs are binary. Valued network ties are typically not used except as covariate, exogenous networks to predict the binary network. ERGMs have been formulated for ordinal ties (e.g., strong/weak – Robins et al., 1999), but this has yet to be implemented in current estimation software.

An ERGM is typically used with completely observed networks; however, this is not to say that it could not be used with ego or personal networks. As noted in Chapter 12, network data derived from snowball sampling can also be estimated with ERGMs, and estimation can proceed even when some network data are missing.

The number of nodes is an important consideration because estimation processes can be computationally intensive (and assumptions of homogeneity may be tenuous in large networks). With current computing capability, estimation of networks of more than 1,000 to 2,000 nodes

---

[2]   Throughout the book, we use the terms "undirected" and "nondirected" interchangeably.

is possible (Goodreau, 2007). The new snowball sampling techniques, however, open future possibilities of estimating very large networks.

Most ERGMs to date have been applied to cross-sectional data, but longitudinal ERGMs are available as described in Chapter 11. Typically, ERGMs examine one type of network tie, although multiple networks can be estimated simultaneously (Chapter 10), and models can include other networks as exogenous covariates (Chapter 8). ERGMs are also available for bipartite network data (Chapter 10) and, in principle, can be developed for any sort of relational data.

Multilevel analyses can be performed with ERGMs (Lubbers & Snijders, 2007), whereby ERGMs can be estimated for a number of similar networks (e.g., networks in several school classrooms), and then multilevel post hoc analyses conducted to assess significant parameters across the entire data set.

It is possible to focus solely on the examination of network ties (and thus to disregard actor attributes) with ERGM models. However, ERGMs can also incorporate any number of binary, categorical, and continuous actor attributes to determine whether actor attributes are associated with the formation of network ties (Chapter 8), and geospatial variables can also be included in an ERGM (Chapter 8). Finally, it is possible to use the general ERGM approach for models that predict the presence of binary actor attributes given the presence of network ties. These autologistic actor attribute models (ALAAM) can be used to examine a variety of social influence and related effects (Chapter 9).

3

Formation of Social Network Structure

Dean Lusher and Garry Robins

3.1 Tie Formation: Emergence of Structure

It is not always recognized that an exponential random graph model (ERGM) carries theory in the form of assumptions about networks, network processes, and social structures. We can think of "ERGM theory" as network metatheory because it is not specific to a particular network process. It is a theoretical perspective within which more specific network theories may be investigated. The essence of ERGM theory is the formation of social structure through the accumulation of small local substructures and, ultimately, through the formation of individual ties into the patterns of those substructures.

3.1.1 Formation of Social Ties

ERGMs are first and foremost concerned with explaining the patterns of ties in a social network. This tie-based approach of ERGMs permits answers to some questions but not others. A standard ERGM is *not* a model focused on predicting outcomes for individuals in the network (so called diffusion or social influence models[1]); instead, it is about revealing patterns that may enable inferences on tie formation processes, including social selection processes where network ties are predicted from the attributes of the network actors.

Of course, there are many network theories about tie formation or tie patterning that can be drawn on in specifying an ERGM for a given network. For instance, reciprocity or exchange is seen as a basic and universal human activity (Blau, 1964), so that, generally, in human social networks we expect ties to be reciprocated. Beyond dyads, the importance

---

[1] An ERGM-type approach can be used for social influence models, however (see Chapter 9).

of triadic relations was proposed by Simmel (1950). Following Heider (1958), Cartwright and Harary (1956) introduced structural balance theory, providing a graph theoretical approach to triangulation among social network ties, otherwise known as "path closure" or "network closure." Since then, network closure has become a central theme in social network research. Granovetter (1973) contrasted closure of strong ties with nonclosure of weak ties. Burt (1992) examined network brokerage and structural holes, suggesting that the person in the center of a nonclosed structure is advantaged. In contrast to closure, theories of prominence in networks also suggest that people who are socially well connected may be advantaged or have distinctive status (Bavelas, 1950; Freeman, 1977, 1979). Preferential attachment describes how network popularity may induce further popularity (Barabási & Albert, 1999; Merton, 1968; Yule, 1925), resulting in some high-degree actors in the network. In regard to actor attributes, the importance of homophily has been well documented (McPherson, Smith-Lovin, & Cook, 2001) as a means to explain the presence of network ties. For multiple networks with different types of tie, Nadel (1952) and White (2008) suggested one social network could provide a context for another, so that there may be interdependencies *across* different networks, whereby ties in one network might encourage the formation of ties in another.

3.1.2   Network Configurations: Consequential Network Patterns and Related Processes

These theories and ideas provide explanations as to why ties might be present in a network, how ties might come to form particular local network patterns, and how ties might be associated with actor attributes. In terms of an ERGM, we call such local network patterns "network configurations." A network configuration is a possible small subgraph that may represent a local regularity in social network structure. It is an empirical question whether a particular configuration is present in a given network, but configurations embody some ideas about how networks may be patterned locally.

Some illustrative examples of network configurations for directed graphs are given in Figure 3.1. In the first example on the left, the double-headed arrow between two nodes represents the reciprocation of ties between two actors. The next configuration represents transitive closure in the form of a particular triadic structure (note that there are other directed triadic forms depending on the direction of the arrows and whether some of the ties in the triad might also be reciprocated). The next configuration (labeled "Activity") is termed an "out-2-star": it is a starlike structure with two outgoing ties from the central node. Outgoing starlike structures are often used to represent activity-based configurations, where

Reciprocity   Transitive closure   Activity   Popularity   Homophily

Figure 3.1. Some network configurations and their underlying social processes.

an actor directs ties to many network partners. These configurations obviously relate to the out-degree distribution of the graph. There are also in-star configurations, often described in terms of network "popularity," that relate to the in-degree distribution. Finally, the fifth configuration is a structure where two actors with the same attribute (e.g., gender – hence the similar coloring on the nodes) have a reciprocated tie. This is often used to represent reciprocated homophily, whereby ties are associated with similar actor attributes.

Social networks are often seen as emerging from various social processes or mechanisms (Hedström & Swedberg, 1998), in which case the patterns of network ties can be revealing about the processes that give rise to them. The idea of process invokes the dynamics of the system, perhaps suggesting that we need longitudinal observations (as discussed in Chapter 11). Yet, structural processes will result in network patterns that are evident even in cross-sectional data. The presence of these configurations (such as in Figure 3.1) might be thought of as akin to archeological traces that are etched into network structure by social mechanisms operating across time. For instance, suppose that people tend to collaborate more if they share (say) the same profession, the well-known network process of "homophily". If we observed the system at multiple time points, we would see a series of collaborations forming between pairs of individuals who share professions. At the last (cross-sectional) observation point, we will see more of these same-profession collaboration links than we expect to see by chance, regardless of whether we take heed of the earlier observational points. The final cross-sectional observation in itself provides evidence for homophily because we will see more of the homophily configuration of Figure 3.1 than we would expect just by chance. So, even using cross-sectional network data, by examining appropriate network patterns we can obtain insight about the social mechanisms that drive the structure of the network.

The importance of a network configuration is that it is a consequential pattern that may represent an underlying social process.[2] This

---

[2] Of course, there are some networks for which this statement is not applicable, especially those that are not social networks. ERGMs can still be applied to these networks, but the interpretation of network configurations will then differ.

explanation maintains a distinction argued by Harrison White (2008) between a network structure and the process by which it has arisen, implying that "a network structure is the consequence of a dynamic process".[3] Of course, this distinction between pattern and process is not limited to ERGMs, but relating static structures to social processes is particularly important to ERGMs even though it is often cross-sectional data that are modeled. (Mathematically, it can indeed be shown that the ERGM is the end product of a process of tie formation and deletion – see Section 11.3.4.)

3.1.3 Local Network Processes

In ERGMs, the configurations we study are local. A network tie is between a pair of individuals. If we ask how network ties come into being, we need to focus on pairs, not on individuals one at a time. So, an ERGM is a "tie-based" model for social networks.[4] A tie comes into place in response to the existing local social environment within which the two individuals operate. This social neighborhood contains other pairs of actors and their ties. Thus, we are not concentrating only on pairs of individuals, even if that is our starting point. We may have quite complex local network structures involving several ties in the local social environment. The patterning of these other ties, in addition to the properties of actors in the local neighborhood, may influence the presence of a new tie. In this way, network configurations can come into being.

3.1.4 Dependency (and Theories of Network Dependence)

A fundamental concept underpinning an ERGM is of the dependency between network ties. Without some form of dependence among ties, it is impossible to argue for tendencies for certain patterns of ties to form. So, to postulate configurations as consequential network patterns is to postulate dependence among network ties. If ties do not depend on each other – in the sense that the presence of some ties influences the presence of others – then there is no impetus for them to form configurations.

Importantly, to make the local configuration approach work, we need a theory of what counts as "local" and what specific configurations to look for. Perhaps surprisingly, it turns out that the answer to these two questions is one and the same. To formulate an ERGM, we need a theory

---

[3] It is also true that process can be constrained by structure.

[4] Although an ERGM is not an "actor-based" model where decisions of individual actors are modeled explicitly in terms of preferences and constraints, as in the stochastic actor – oriented models for longitudinal networks of Snijders (2002), an ERGM is not inconsistent with an actor-based theory. In Chapter 7, we see also how ties depend on each other through individual actors. For explicit links between actor-oriented and edge-based processes, see Section 11.4.2 and Snijders (2006, 2010).

of "dependence," and fortunately, there are now several available for a researcher to consider. Once we adopt a theory of dependence, it turns out that we automatically have a definition of "local," and the types of patterns to consider are then constrained. However, if we believe that certain network patterns are important based on more specific social science/social network theory, we are adopting (implicitly or explicitly) a particular dependence hypothesis and a consequent definition of "local."

There are a number of possible dependence assumptions that are set out more fully in Chapters 6 and 7. Each has a different definition of what counts as a local social neighborhood, and so implies a different family of ERGMs. Recent work on how to understand these different definitions, as well as the relationships among them, is described in Chapter 22 of this book.

As a simple example, suppose someone in your workplace often confides in you about important issues. This is likely to increase your tendency to communicate with that person. We know this as reciprocity, an important feature of social life. Reciprocity is a form of dependency, whereby the two possible directed ties within a dyad are dependent on each other. In other words, the presence of tie from Fred to Mary increases the chances of a tie from Mary to Fred (and vice versa). This is known as "dyadic dependence." The reciprocal tie configuration was presented in Figure 3.1. Here, a dependence hypothesis (dyadic dependence) naturally leads to a decision about a configuration to apply in an ERGM (reciprocity).

Previously, we described dependence in terms of local social neighborhoods that affect the presence of network ties. If dyadic dependence is the only applicable dependence assumption, then the definition of "local" is simply the dyad. There are no other effects outside the dyad that affect the presence of ties (hence, it is sometimes referred to as "dyadic independence" because the dyads are independent of each other).

Of course, there can be more complex dependencies instead of, or in addition to, dyadic dependence. As a second example, the chances of any one individual being a friend of President Barack Obama are small. However, if you are friends with Michelle Obama, then your chances of striking up a friendship with Barack substantially increase. We know of this as transitivity or path closure, or "a friend of a friend is a friend." In later chapters, we see how this configuration (along with others) arises from "Markov dependence," where ties are assumed dependent if they share a node.

Still other dependency assumptions are possible. Consider, for example, the presence of two couples at a party. Because one partner from each couple may be friends and start talking away, their previously unacquainted partners may strike up a conversation with one another and over time become friends. The presence of existing relationships creates the conditions whereby an old friendship tie affects the chances of a new friendship. We know this pattern of relations as a "4-cycle," and it can be an important configuration arising from "social circuit dependence."

In addition, there are particular types of dependence assumptions relating to actor attributes and dyadic and extradyadic covariates of network ties.

In these cases, we see how dependency among social ties can give rise to network configurations. Reciprocity, transitive closure, and four-cycles can come about because the formation of a tie depends on the presence of other ties in certain ways. Dependence helps us define what is local, but it also gives us an implied explanation of dynamics.

However, standard statistical approaches assume *independence of observations*. From an independence perspective, if someone communicates with you, this will have no bearing on whether you communicate back. From an independence of observations perspective, you assume that being friends with Michelle Obama does not affect your chances of being friends with Barack, and previously unacquainted husbands have no greater chance of coming to know each other, even if their wives are already friends. These do not seem reasonable descriptions of social life. So, if we are to understand systems based on some form of dependence between ties, we cannot rely on standard statistical methods such as *t*-tests, analysis of variances (ANOVAs), and regressions that assume independence. Because an ERGM can incorporate dependence, it is a more principled approach to understand the patterning of network ties.

3.1.5 Complex Combination of Multiple and Nested Social Processes

It is important to note that the tie-based approach of ERGMs permits an understanding of the "complex combination" of social processes by which network ties are formed. We point to multiple and nested processes.

Multiple Origins of Social Network Structure. Previously in this chapter, we presented a number of theories about the formation of network ties, without attempting a complete list. However, it would be a brave person who would suggest that one and only one of these processes explains *all* there is to know about the organization of a social network. The totality of ties in a network is not likely to be explained only by homophily, or only by reciprocity, but it is certainly feasible that both processes may be at play at the same time within the one network. By incorporating a number of configurations simultaneously into a model (such as one for homophily and one for reciprocity), an ERGM can test the evidence as to which processes contribute to the formation of the network structure (Monge & Contractor, 2003).

Transitive triad

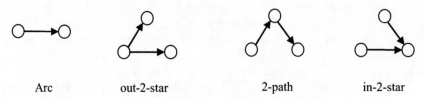

Arc   out-2-star   2-path   in-2-star

Figure 3.2. Nested configurations for a transitive triad.

In the one social network, there is no a priori reason why multiple social processes should not be present. Because humans are intentional beings with multiple motivations for and multiple expressions of social action, it is especially in human social networks that we expect that multiple processes will occur simultaneously. Of course, we do need to be guided by theory, and we certainly need to be empirical, but expecting a simple explanation for a complex human social system is naive.

Nested Configurations. It is important to realize that configurations are often nested within one another. The simplest network configuration is a single network tie. Every other configuration obviously contains this configuration, and possibly others. Consider a transitive triad. This configuration includes within it three single arcs: one 2-path, one out-2-star, and one in-2-star (see Figure 3.2 for a depiction of these configurations).

Because configurations are nested in one another, it is not enough, for instance, to observe many triangles to infer an effect for network closure. There may be many triangles because there are many ties (i.e., the network is dense), or because there are many 2-paths or 2-stars (i.e., in- and out-2-stars for directed networks). To have solid evidence of network closure, we need to observe more than expected triangles given (i.e., taking into consideration) the number of 2-paths (and arcs and 2-stars) in the data.

Given an average baseline propensity to form arcs, if that propensity is strong enough, we will see some transitive triads simply by chance. The stronger the baseline effect, the more transitive triads. The same applies if there are propensities to form 2-stars and 2-paths. Thus, we can only infer a specific process of transitive closure by considering the propensities for the four lower-order configurations and a transitivity effect *simultaneously*. We ask, do we see more transitive triads in the network data than we expect to see *given* the average tendency to form arcs, 2-stars, and 2-paths? If so, we have evidence for a transitive closure effect. If not, then the presence of transitive triads in the network can be explained more simply by the presence of the lower-order configurations, and we do not need to postulate a closure effect to explain this network structure.

In summary, when we talk of multiple processes, it is not just that there are many choices. Rather, local, multiple, and nested network effects combine into a complex combination of processes. ERGMs are about understanding the complexity of a social system – its multiplicity, its interconnectedness, and its dependencies.

3.2   Framework for Explanations of Tie Formation

In this book, we discuss three broad categories of tie formation processes, represented in Figure 3.3: self-organizing network processes, attribute-based processes, and exogenous dyadic covariates. More specific effects can be identified under each of these three broad categories. Figure 3.3 does not claim to be exhaustive or exclusive because, of course, there are many possible tie formation processes. For instance, exogenous contextual factors could include categories for culture or settings and so on. Rather, Figure 3.3 is a schematic that focuses on topics of interest in the ensuing chapters. Each process here, however, has a well-established basis in social network or social science theory. Each results in networks with particular types of configurations.

3.2.1   Network Self-Organization

Network ties can organize themselves into patterns because the presence of some ties encourages others to come into existence. We often refer to these as "purely structural" effects because they do not involve actor attributes or other exogenous factors. They are "endogenous" effects in that the network patterns arise solely from the internal processes of the system of network ties.

Network self-organization can arise through degree-based effects. For instance, individuals – by being popular – may attract even more popularity. In that case, we expect diversity in popularity across the actors, which translates into higher dispersion in the degree distribution, or equivalently, into greater network centralization with network ties directed to a few highly central nodes. In social network theory, such processes are often referred to as "preferential attachment" (Barabási & Albert, 1999) or the "Matthew effect" (de Solla Price, 1976). There are several different versions of degree-based processes: for instance, in directed networks,

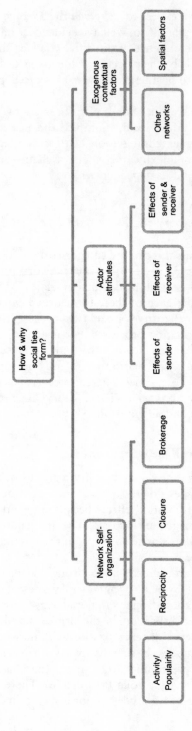

Figure 3.3. Conceptual framework for processes of social tie formation discussed in this book.

24

it is possible to have effects related to both in-degree ("popularity") and out-degree ("activity"). An example configuration relating to in- and out-degrees are the in- and out-2-stars depicted in Figure 3.2. A node with high out-degree is centered on many out-2-stars, so networks that are highly centralized in terms of out-degrees (activity) will have a high number of out-2-stars; similarly for in-2-stars and in-degrees (popularity) (the number of 2-stars is directly related to degree variance and centralization (Hagberg, 2004; Snijders, 1981a, 1981b). A "2-path" or "mixed-2-star" is also possible where a node has one network tie directed toward it and one directed away from it (Figure 3.2), reflecting correlations between in- and out-degrees (e.g., good listeners who do not talk too much). These variations are possible in directed networks; in undirected networks, we have only the 2-star configuration because the difference between the three types of directed 2-stars disappears. Of course, it is also possible to have higher-order star configurations – 3-stars, 4-stars, and so on – with three or more ties centered on the one node (these are, in fact, moments of the degree distribution and reflect skewness and kurtosis, respectively).

A third important self-organizing effect involves network closure. Especially in networks invoking some form of positive affect or collaboration, as we discussed previously, there are often tendencies for 2-paths of actors to "close the path" by forming a third tie that produces a triangle (Davis, 1970). This is also referred to as "network clustering," or in directed networks, "transitivity" (when the tendency is for the formation of transitive triads).

Triangulation reflects the human social propensity to operate in group-like structures. A network triangle involving three ties can be viewed as a simple archetypal expression of a small group, in the sense that a group is likely to appear as a subset of actors with many ties among them. In that case, we will see many triangles among that subset. Thus, over and above the formation of individual triangles, there is often a process of "multiple triangulation," where triangles occur together among larger subsets of actors in clique-like structures rather than as separated features spread evenly across the network (akin to *community structure* – see Newman and Park (2003) – or other long-standing definitions of cohesive subgroups – see Wasserman and Faust (1994)).

There are several different versions of triangulation and network closure. A "transitive triad" configuration for directed networks is in Figure 3.2. A transitive triad represents network closure of a particular type because it implies a local hierarchy, with one node receiving two ties and sending none, one node receiving no ties and sending two, and one node receiving and sending a tie. Depending on the content of the network relationship, in the right circumstances this may be interpreted as the receiving node being the most popular within the group-like triangular structure. If instead we have a "cyclic triad," where the direction of all ties is consistent so that they form a "3-cycle," then none of the three nodes would be singled out. Of course, in undirected networks, there is no distinction between a transitive triad and a cyclic triad: only an undirected triangle is possible.

Under network self-organization, Figure 3.3 also includes provision for "network brokerage," which has been a major theme in social network research in recent years (e.g., Burt, 1992). This has been the topic of recent ongoing work in the specification of ERGMs and is presented briefly in Chapter 6 (see Section 6.7).

3.2.2 Individual Attributes

Individuals bring their own capacities, capabilities, and predispositions to a social system. The qualities of individuals in networks can be very important to the formation of network ties (Emirbayer & Goodwin, 1994; Kilduff & Krackhardt, 2008; Parkhe, Wasserman, & Ralston, 2006). Depending on the domain of research, many types of individual-level variables – basic demographics such as age or gender, expertise or profession, and psychological motivations and attitudes – may be relevant. In network terms, these individual measures are termed "actor attributes." For ERGMs, we often use the terminology of "actor-relation effects," which refers to "the association of a particular attribute with a social tie," representing the propensity of actor attributes to affect tie formation.

An actor attribute may operate by affecting the involvement of the actor in the network. For instance, in directed networks, an attribute might encourage that individual to be more *active* (i.e., express more ties) or make that actor more *popular* (i.e., receive more ties). We call these the "sender effect" and the "receiver effect," respectively. Importantly, these effects are different to preferential attachment mentioned previously. Preferential attachment suggests that new ties occur because of the presence of other ties. A sender or receiver effect suggests, however, that actors send or receive more ties because of their attributes. So, in an ERGM, we can delineate popularity (and/or activity) as resulting from network self-organization or actor attributes.

Because ties involve pairs of actors, attributes of both parties can also come into play in the formation of network ties. For instance, an individual might select a partner because their attributes match. This process of homophily arises when people tend to be connected to others who are in some way similar to themselves.

Thus, there are several distinct processes whereby attributes may affect network ties, operating at the level of a single actor or across two actors. There is a need to consider processes together to make the right inference from the data. Suppose that, in a school, girls tend to be more active

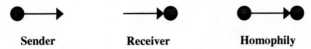

Sender   **Receiver**   **Homophily**

Figure 3.4. Examples of network configurations for actor-relation effects.

than boys in having friends. Then, simply by chance, there will be a higher proportion of friendship ties between pairs of girls because girls are implicated in more ties anyway. If all we do is to observe the many ties between girls, we cannot conclusively infer that there is a tendency for homophily over and above a simpler activity or popularity effect. It is only by considering effects simultaneously that we can disentangle whether there is a predisposition for girls specifically to select other girls as friends.

In an ERGM, actor attributes are treated as exogenous or explanatory variables that affect the presence of social ties. These are discussed as social selection models in Chapter 8. (It is also possible to have models that predict attribute status, with network ties as exogenous predictors – see Chapter 9.) Network self-organization, in contrast, is treated as an endogenous process. The distinction between endogenous and exogenous explanations for the presence of social ties is important. We need to account for purely structural tendencies for tie formation in order to make the right inferences about actor attribute effects. If, for instance, we predict the presence of a network tie from actor attributes and assume that ties arise only through those individual qualities, we are not taking into account possible dependencies among network ties, and so we are ignoring network self-organization. As such, we may overestimate (or underestimate) the importance of attributes in the network.

Examples of network configurations for actor-relation effects are presented in Figure 3.4. Here, a colored node represents an actor with a particular attribute status (e.g., "female"). Thus, in this example, the sender configuration represents a female expressing ties to other actors (irrespective of whether these other actors are male or female), the receiver configuration represents a female actor receiving ties from other actors, and the homophily configuration represents a tie between two females. Although this example presents configurations for a binary attribute variable, as explained in Chapter 8, there are counterparts for continuous or categorical attributes.

Whether one specifically examines networks for actor-relation effects (as in Chapter 14) or uses them as controls when looking for network self-organization (as in Chapter 15), such effects are nonetheless important, and their addition to ERGMs is a significant advantage for testing network theory.

Entrainment

Figure 3.5. Example of network configurations for dyadic covariates.

3.2.3   Exogenous Contextual Factors: Dyadic Covariates

Finally, other exogenous contextual factors may be important to tie formation. In this book, we often treat these as dyadic tie covariates, although they do not necessarily have to be in only dyadic form. An instance of a dyadic covariate may be another social network considered to be fixed and exogenous to the model. An ERGM can then investigate whether the presence of the covariate tie predicts the corresponding tie in our network of interest (see Chapter 8). A good example is the importance of the formal organizational hierarchy on the presence of actual communication ties within an organization. Ties from the two types of network may co-occur (or be *entrained*), in which case, for instance, a worker may communicate with his or her boss. In that sense, an ERGM may help understand the extent to which top-down, centrally decreed structures relate to bottom-up informal networks.

A network configuration representing the dyadic covariate effect of entrainment is presented in Figure 3.5. Here, the dotted arc represents the covariate network. The presence of these configurations in the network indicates the extent to which the network ties of interest co-occur with the covariate network ties. More elaborate dependencies on covariate networks may also be formulated, such as the multiplex configurations of Chapter 10. As explained further in Chapter 8, other covariates may also be relevant, including geospatial factors, shared affiliations, and contexts, and they can enter the models in distinctive ways.

In summary, the framework of Figure 3.3 takes into account some of the many network ideas about tie formation and presents them to permit their understanding in terms of network configurations. This is the general structure whereby we formulate specific ERGMs to answer precise research questions about the origins of social network structure.

4

Simplified Account of an Exponential Random Graph Model as a Statistical Model

Garry Robins and Dean Lusher

This chapter provides a simplified overview of some methodological aspects of exponential random graph models (ERGMs), with the technical detail presented in Section II, specifically in Chapters 6 and 7. To begin, it is worthwhile to consider the value of a statistical model in understanding social network structure.

Harrison White made the important observation that "sociology has to account for chaos and normality together" (2008, 1). Social life is stochastic, and social networks are not predetermined or invariant. We do not expect that in a human social network, reciprocity will apply (strictly) in all situations; rather, there may be a tendency toward reciprocity in the sense that more reciprocation will be present than otherwise expected over and above what would result from other processes. In a sense, if we do not allow for "tendencies" with some variation, in the extreme, a nonstochastic model requires one unique explanation for each tie, present or absent.

Accordingly, it makes sense to use a statistical model such as an ERGM to investigate network structure. By incorporating randomness, statistical models deal with expected values, so we are then able to draw inferences about whether observed data are consistent with expectations.

The balance between randomness and order is an important issue in much social network research. For instance, in considering the "small world" nature of many social networks, Watts (1999) showed that adding a small amount of randomness to a highly structured graph could dramatically shorten path lengths. In an ERGM context, a configuration represents the ordered nature of local structure. If effects for configurations in a model are minimal (e.g., a tendency for reciprocity might be weak), then the resulting networks will be close to purely random. In contrast, if an effect is strong (e.g., a strong tendency for reciprocity), then the resulting networks will appear as highly structured (e.g., most ties will be reciprocated). Because an ERGM is stochastic, the model does

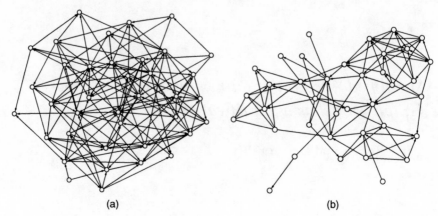

(a)   (b)

Figure 4.1. (a) Simple random network and (b) empirical communication network.

not imply just one network. The result is a "probability distribution of graphs," which we discuss in more detail later in this chapter.

4.1   Random Graphs

We noted in Chapter 3 that a given dependence assumption picks out certain configurations as important to the structure of the network. We have also noted that some configurations will occur just by chance, even in a network where ties are formed independently of one another (i.e., no dependence). Figure 4.1a presents a random graph of 38 nodes and 146 arcs generated by scattering the 146 arcs purely randomly among the nodes (to be precise, the graph comes from a uniform random graph distribution conditional on the presence of 146 arcs – see Section 4.2). The number of nodes and arcs has been chosen to match those of an empirical communication network in Figure 4.1b. (This communication network is presented in more detail later in this chapter.) From the visualization, it seems that the random network is quite different from the empirical network. This also seems apparent from the selected network statistics for both networks in Table 4.1.

From Table 4.1, however, some network configurations still occur, even in the random network. When the 146 ties are distributed among the nodes by chance, there are still *some* reciprocated ties and *some* transitive triads but not nearly as many as in the communication network (although the in- and out-stars are not so different between the two networks). Nevertheless, although there are undoubtedly less reciprocated ties and transitive triads in the random network, how do we judge whether

Table 4.1. *Selected network statistics for networks in Figure 4.1*

	Random network	Communication network
Actors	38	38
Arcs	146	146
Reciprocated arcs	6	44
Transitive triads	53	212
In-2-stars	292	313
Out-2-stars	254	283

there are *significantly more* in the communication network than we might expect?

4.2 Distributions of Graphs

A statistical (nonparametric) technique to address whether there are significantly more particular network structures than expected by chance is to simulate a large sample of random (directed) graphs of 146 arcs on 38 nodes. This can be considered a sample of graphs from a "graph distribution" where every (di)graph is equally probable if it has 146 arcs (and has 0 probability otherwise). A graph distribution is simply the set of all possible graphs (in this case, on 38 nodes), with a probability assigned to each graph. The graph distribution we just described is called the U|L distribution (the uniform distribution of digraphs on 38 nodes given the number of arcs L = 146). (For further discussion of U|L, see Wasserman and Faust (1994).) It is a uniform distribution because each graph of 146 arcs has equal probability. Such approaches reflect the early history of statistical network methods, which was dominated by techniques relying on testing a hypothesis using a simplistic null distribution, going back to Moreno and Jennings (1938).

Having produced a large sample of graphs, we can then calculate the number of reciprocated arcs and transitive triads for each sampled graph. We did this for 1,000 simple random graphs with the results for reciprocated arcs presented in Figure 4.2. The mean of this sampled distribution is 7.5, and the number of reciprocated arcs ranges from around 0 to 15 across the 1,000 graphs. Accordingly, based on this information, if we had a network from this random graph distribution, we would expect to see around 7 to 8 reciprocated ties just by chance, and it would be very unusual to see more than 15 reciprocated ties. The communication network, however, has 44 reciprocated ties (represented in Figure 4.2 by the dotted vertical line), many more than expected by chance from a distribution of simple random graphs. This is evidence for a number of

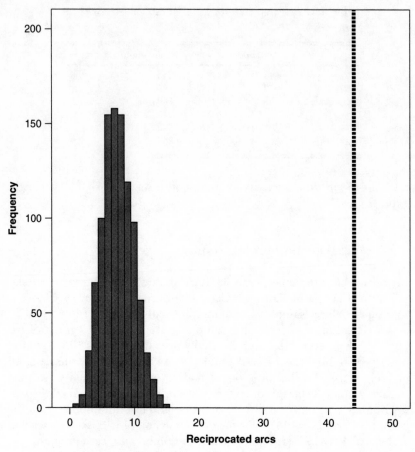

Figure 4.2. Distribution of reciprocated arcs from sample of 1,000 random graphs.

conclusions: (1) the observed network is not just a random graph (2) there is dependence among network ties, and (3) there are reciprocity processes active in this network.

To put the results more succinctly, the probability of observing 44 reciprocated ties in a random network is very close to 0. This is less than 5% (if we choose that as an alpha level); thus, in accord with standard null hypothesis significance testing, we can say that the number of observed reciprocated arcs is significantly above what is expected from the null distribution (U|L), and so there is significant reciprocation in this network.

We can draw a similar conclusion about transitive triads. From the sample of 1,000 simple random graphs, the mean number of transitive triads is 55, with a standard deviation of 7.8. The observed number in the data of 212 is significantly greater.

However, there are two (related) limitations to this type of inference. First, our comparison is only to a distribution of random graphs (i.e., those with 146 arcs). Perhaps if we had another type of graph distribution (e.g., graphs with 146 arcs and 44 reciprocated ties), the number of transitive triads in the observed data would not be extreme. Second, in a related fashion, we only consider each effect one at a time, and we ignore the nesting of configurations. For instance, we can say that there are significantly more transitive triads, but we do not know whether that arises because there are an increased number of stars or because of a triangulation process. When we say that there are significantly more reciprocated ties and transitive ties than in the U|L distribution, we are rejecting the null hypothesis (the observed graph was generated by a U|L model), but we are not saying anything about the alternative – whether reciprocation or transitivity are significant processes.

What an ERGM tries to do, however, is to model the effects of interest (e.g., reciprocated ties, transitive triads) and, in relation to an observed network, to find a distribution of graphs where the observed data are central in that distribution. (More technically, we *fit* the model by *estimating parameters*.) In fact, for the communication network, an ERGM tries to find a distribution of graphs on 38 nodes, which have *an average* of 146 arcs, 44 reciprocated ties, and 212 transitive triads (and, indeed, also 313 in-2-stars and 283 out-2-stars to cater for nested effects). This might seem like a complex task and indeed it is. Fortunately for researchers, there is software for this purpose, so we do not necessarily need to know precisely how the algorithms work (although Chapter 12 enlightens those who want to know). Later in this chapter, we demonstrate how to find this distribution of graphs for this particular network. In doing so, we discover which configurations are important in the network, which effects have independent explanatory value, and which can be explained by other effects.

In one sense, what an ERGM does is compare an observed network to the other possible ways it could be arranged. In all networks, there are a finite number of ways that ties can be arranged. This is called the "sample space," and in large networks, this number of possible arrangements can be incredibly large. For a directed network, the number of possible network states is $2^{n(n-1)}$, where n is the number of nodes: this is a (very) large number for even a 38-node graph.[1] Then, for a distribution of graphs, we have to assign a probability to each of this really

---

[1] In fact, already for $n = 17$, the number of possible directed graphs exceeds what has frequently been quoted as the number of atoms in the observable universe, as $2^{17(17-1)} \approx 10^{80}$ (Wikipedia, 2012).

large number of graphs. Model estimation assigns probabilities so that an observed network is central, not extreme, in terms of the effects being modeled.

4.3   Some Basic Ideas about Statistical Modeling

It is important to understand why we *model* a network. Models represent theories we may have about observed data, and fitting a model permits us to see if our theoretical conception about the data can be validated. A desirable goal of a model is to best represent our observed data – to reproduce the structures we witness in our observed network. In an ERGM, our model represents the combination of structures of which our observed network is composed, permitting inferences about the processes of network tie formation. As noted, when applying an ERGM to observed data we are in fact estimating a model for that data, just as we do when we apply a regression model to non-network data.

Outdated (and unreliable) methods of estimating an ERGM used standard logistic regression procedures. Any comparison with logistic regression breaks down decidedly once network dependencies are introduced because logistic regression assumes independent observations. However, there are some analogies that may be helpful to readers who are new to ERGMs. In a logistic regression, we predict a binary variable from a number of predictor variables, with model parameters (regression coefficients) indicating how important a predictor variable is in that prediction. Similarly, with an ERGM, we predict the presence of a network tie (a binary variable) from several predictor variables (the types of network configurations in which that tie is involved), with model parameters indicating the importance of a configuration to the presence of a tie.

By predicting individual ties in this way, however, the ERGM assigns a probability to each graph in the sample space and hence produces a graph distribution. The following are some terms to understand:

Statistic: An ERGM statistic always relates to a particular configuration. The statistic is typically the count of configurations of different types in the network (e.g., the number of reciprocated ties), although in some cases it may be complex combination of counts or other functions of the configurations.

Parameter: The parameter is the weight applied to the statistic (just as in a logistic regression with predictor variables and regression coefficients). In that sense, it indicates the importance of a statistic, and thereby the importance of a configuration in the network.

An ERGM then assigns a probability to a graph by a (function of a) sum of statistics weighted by parameters, as described at the beginning of Chapter 2. For the moment, it suffices to understand that in the graph distribution, a positive parameter assigns higher probability to those graphs with many of the relevant configurations. For instance, if a transitive triad parameter is large and positive, then graphs with many transitive triads are more probable (in the graph distribution for that model). If our model is a good explanation for real networks, then the observed graph has more transitivity than a random graph. This fits in nicely with a graph distribution where highly transitive graphs are more probable. However, if a transitive triad parameter is large and negative, then graphs with fewer transitive triads become more probable under our model. Throughout, we are assuming that the data we see are very likely, not unlikely (and so the method of estimation is called "maximum likelihood").

Simulation: One can formulate an ERGM and then simply select some parameter values to simulate the model to see the type of graphs produced. In Figure 4.2, we learned from a simulation that graphs generated by U|L with 38 nodes and 146 arcs tend to have less than 15 reciprocated arcs. Thus, a simulation tells us what to expect from a particular model with parameter values that we choose. We can study any graph feature of interest in this way, not just reciprocated arcs.

Estimation: However, we also know that for the purposes of understanding reciprocity, the communication network in Figure 4.1, with 44 reciprocated arcs, has significantly more reciprocity. So, for observed data, instead of merely choosing values for the parameters in an ad hoc way, we can systematically search through possible parameter values until we find the right *estimates* so that observed statistics are not extreme, but are central, in the distribution of graph statistics from the resulting ERGM.

Standard error (SE): Each parameter estimate has a SE, which is a measure of the precision, or how certain we are, of the parameter estimate. A small SE indicates greater precision and certainty, whereas a large SE indicates less certainty. We know that a large and positive parameter estimate indicates that more of the associated configurations are likely to be seen in the network. The SE can give us an indication of what to consider as "large." In this book, we typically use the rule that a significant parameter is one with an absolute value more than twice its SE (see Section 12.5.1 for more detail).

4.4 Homogeneity

When considering reciprocation in the communication network in Figure 4.1b, we are not interested in knowing specifically if there is a reciprocated tie for each pair of actors. Rather, we are interested in the overall tendency for reciprocity in the network. Typically, an ERGM produces one estimate of reciprocity for *all pairs* of actors across the network. Of course, some individuals may be more inclined than others to reciprocate network ties, but we can consider the estimate as indicative of an average effect across the network. Inherent here is the assumption that local network configurations occur homogeneously across the observed network.[2] The use of actor attributes is one way to relax homogeneity. Boys and girls in a school may have different levels of average reciprocity, and so we could have different reciprocity parameters for each.

With a basic understanding of the methodological details of ERGMs in hand, we now proceed to show a simple example application of an ERGM to a social network of interest. In doing so, we demonstrate how competing explanations about how network ties arise can be statistically compared within a single model.

---

[2] Homogeneity assumptions are not something particular to ERGM. All general linear model techniques assume homogeneity. For instance, in a regression, a case is only identified up to the values of the variables that represent it.

5

Example Exponential Random Graph Model Analysis

Dean Lusher and Garry Robins

Exponential random graph models (ERGMs) permit us to examine competing theories regarding the formation of network ties, all within a single analysis. This means that a researcher can test one network theoretical concept for tie formation against another (e.g., Does homophily explain this network, or is it reciprocity?) for their network of interest.

This chapter aims to make the ERGM framework clearer through a simple illustrative example. We only use the terminology introduced in the previous chapters, and leave a full description of the parameters and so on to later chapters in Section II. A more detailed analysis of this example is found in Chapter 13.

5.1   Applied ERGM Example: Communication in "The Corporation"

As a practical example of the issues facing social network researchers, we now present the application of ERGMs to the following organizational case study. This example network draws together a number of issues presented so far. The organization of interest is called "The Corporation," a fictitious name for a real organization in the entertainment industry, which consists of thirty-eight executives. The network under investigation (our "observed network" on which we have collected data) is the "communication network," which is binary and directed. A tie here represents a response from an actor to a survey item about other executives with whom it was important to communicate to get work completed effectively. The network is depicted in Figure 4.1b. Some basic statistics of the network were presented in Table 4.1.

The Corporation is in competition with other organizations for market dominance. We are interested in understanding the structure of informal communication ties. We also have information on the executives

37

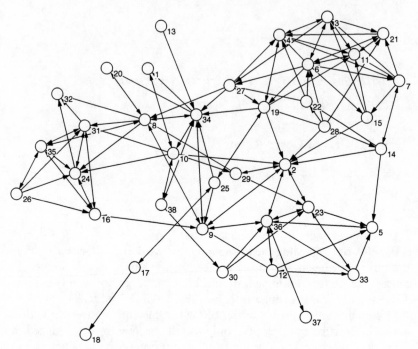

Figure 5.1. Communication network of The Corporation ($n = 38$ actors).

themselves, such as the number of projects they have been involved with, their level of seniority in The Corporation, and their office membership. Finally, we also have information about advice relations within the organization, a binary, directed network of relations with ties pointing toward executives from whom advice is received. The following visualizations display the structure of communication ties within The Corporation in isolation and also in relation to both actor attributes and the covariate network.

This data set can be downloaded in its entirety from MelNet (http://www.sna.unimelb.edu.au/) so that readers can fit the models themselves and gain experience in how ERGMs can be applied to real data. The models here are fit with PNet which can be downloaded from the same website.

Network self-organization may be responsible for communication ties. What is evident from Figure 5.1 is the number of triads in the network. With the exception of a few individuals, most employees are within some form of triadic structure. In fact, some regions of the network are very densely clustered. Furthermore, it appears that some nodes (e.g., twenty-four and thirty-four) act as hubs and receive more ties than others in the network.

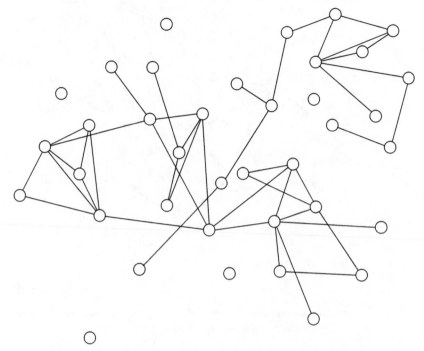

Figure 5.2. Mutual ties only (asymmetric ties removed) in communication network.

Figure 5.2 presents the mutual ties in the network (i.e., undirected ties derived from reciprocated ties in the original data), of which there are many, so it is possible that communication is at least partially explained by reciprocity.

Actor attributes may be important to network structure. For instance, Figure 5.3 depicts node sizes as varying according to the number of projects completed by the executives, with larger nodes indicating more projects. It suggests that there may be a homophily effect based on number of projects (experience).

Figures 5.4 and 5.5 represent seniority of the executives and the branch office of each executive, respectively. It seems that there could be homophily due to seniority, but branch office effects are not so clear from the visualization.

Communication ties may be affected by the presence of advice relations among these executives. Figure 5.6 presents those ties that align (i.e., are entrained) between communication and advice networks. There are twenty-four aligned ties between these networks, although it is difficult to say from the visualization whether this is due to mere chance or whether there is a distinct entrainment effect.

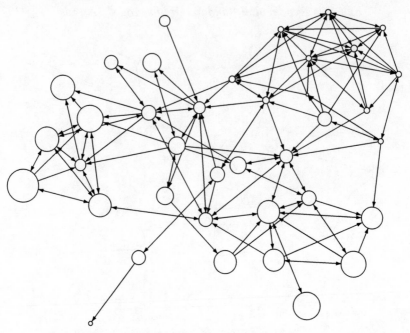

Figure 5.3. Communication network with employee experience represented by size (larger = more experience).

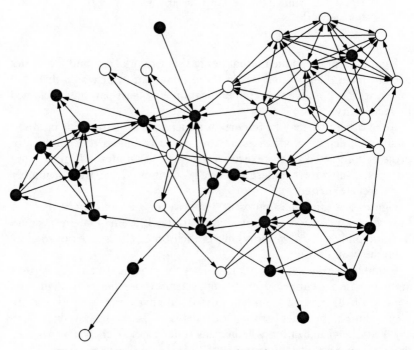

Figure 5.4. Communication network with seniority (black = senior, white = other).

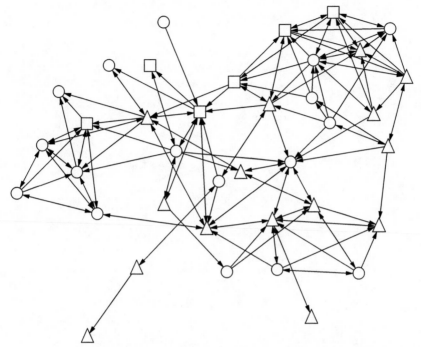

Figure 5.5. Communication network with office membership represented by shape.

So, there are many possible competing explanations for the network structure of communication ties. If we examine only one process at a time, then we may overestimate its worth. With an ERGM, we can infer whether there are independent tendencies for a particular configuration to occur in the network, or whether the presence of that configuration can be more parsimoniously explained by the combined presence of other effects in the model.

5.2   ERGM Model and Interpretation

The model produces parameter estimates that indicate the strength and direction of network patterns. The parameter estimates (and standard errors) for one model of the communication network are presented in Table 5.1. Significant parameters[1] are designated by an asterisk (*). A positive (negative) estimate indicates more (less) of the configuration in the network than expected (given the other effects in the model). We

---

[1]   See Section 12.5.1 for an explanation of significant effects.

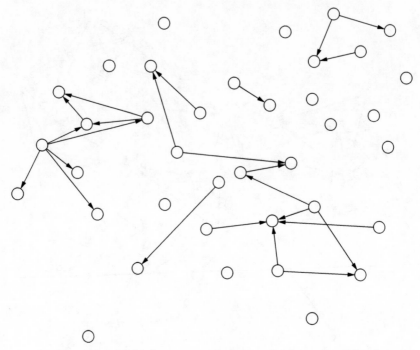

Figure 5.6. Multiplex communication and advice ties (all other ties removed).

include visualizations of each network effect for clarity. The magnitudes of parameter estimates are not directly comparable across different effects because the scaling of the statistics is different. In presenting this model, we have used simplified parameter names based on the general terminology used in this chapter. This model, as well as comparative models for this data, are presented in much more detail in Chapter 13.

Arc: First, we have a negative *arc* effect. The arc effect is like an intercept effect in a linear regression and can be interpreted as the baseline propensity for the occurrence of ties.[2]

Reciprocity: The reciprocity estimate is positive and significant. Employees are likely to reciprocate communication.

Popularity and activity (in- and out-degree effects): These effects represent tendencies for centralization in the in- and out-degree distributions, respectively. The in-degree parameter estimate is negative but nonsignificant, suggesting no distinctively popular employees in this company, net of other effects in the model. The out-degree effect is negative and significant, indicating an absence of centralization in network activity,

---

[2] The arc parameter *is not* a direct measure of network density.

Table 5.1. *ERGM parameter estimates (and standard errors) for communication relations in The Corporation*

Network effect		Estimate (SE)
Purely structural effects (endogenous)		
Arc	○——▶○	−1.96 (0.73)*
Reciprocity	○◀——▶○	2.88 (0.46)*
Popularity (in-degree)		−0.27 (0.32)
Activity (out-degree)		−0.34 (0.34)
Simple 2-path[3]		−0.06 (0.08)
Multiple 2-paths		−0.06 (0.09)
Transitivity (transitive path closure of multiple 2-paths)		1.22 (0.19)*
Cyclic closure (cyclic closure of multiple 2-paths)		−0.37 (0.17)*
Actor relation effects (exogenous) (black nodes indicates actor with attribute)		
Sender (seniority)	●——▶	−0.56 (0.29)
Sender (projects)	●——▶	0.01 (0.02)
Receiver (seniority)	——▶●	0.08 (0.23)
Receiver (projects)	——▶●	−0.02 (0.02)
[4] Homophily (seniority)	●——▶●	0.64 (0.26)*
Heterophily (projects)	●——▶●	−0.08 (0.02)*
Homophily (office)	●——▶●	−0.01 (0.17)
Covariate network (exogenous)		
Advice entrainment (covariate arc)	○┄┄▶●	1.76 (0.30)*

* = parameter estimate is greater than two times the standard error in absolute value, indicating the effect is significant (see Section 12.5.1 for details).

---

[3] The term "simple 2-path" is used to contrast the single 2-path (simple connectivity) with the multiple 2-paths (multiple connectivity) noted in Table 5.1. To be clear, a simple 2-path parameter is also known as a 2-path or mixed 2-star parameter.

[4] Homophily (and heterophily, its logical opposite) works differently for binary, continuous, and categorical variables. This is taken up in detail in Chapter 8, and explained again in Section III. For binary and categorical variables, we measure homophily – that is the choice of similar others. For continuous variables, we measure the difference between the attributes of actors. As such, a positive parameter estimate would indicate heterophily (i.e., large differences in scores), and a negative estimate would indicate homophily (i.e., small differences in scores).

so that people tend to be rather uniform in the number of choices of communication partners.

Simple 2-path: This parameter is not significant, indicating that we see neither more nor less 2-paths than we might expect given the other effects in the model. That is, there is no evidence that people who send more ties also receive them. If this parameter were significantly positive, for instance, it would suggest that actors who were the most popular were also the most active (i.e., a positive correlation between the in- and out-degree distributions).

Multiple 2-paths: In addition to the single 2-path, it is often desirable to have a multiple 2-paths parameter in the model to indicate the "depth" of local connectivity between pairs of nodes. Notice our contrasting interpretations: the simple 2-path interpretation focuses on the node at the center of the two path (with both an incoming and outgoing tie), whereas the multiple 2-path parameter is best considered as explaining connectivity between pairs of nodes at the end of the paths. Here, this parameter is not significant, indicating that local connectivity is neither stronger nor weaker than we expect given the other effects in the model.

Transitivity: There is a significant and positive effect for transitivity, indicating a tendency for hierarchical path closure in this network. Notice from the diagram that we do not use single triangles to model this effect, but multiple transitive triads based on multiple 2-paths. As is seen later, there are important technical reasons why single triangle parameters are problematic for ERGMs and typically do not result in coherent models.[5] This reflects an important feature of many empirical social networks: triangles tend to occur together in denser regions of the network. Multiple 2-paths are nested within multiple triangles, so the combination of the two parameter estimates provides an important elaboration of our previous interpretation of the multiple 2-path parameter. When multiple 2-paths occur, they tend to be closed in transitive form (positive transitivity estimate).

Cyclic closure: There is a significant and negative effect for cyclic closure, indicating a lack of nonhierarchical (or generalized exchange) network closure in this network. Again, the cyclic closure form is associated with multiple 2-paths, so we can further elaborate our interpretation of the parameters together. When multiple 2-paths occur, they tend to be closed in transitive form and tend not to be closed in cyclic form; once these two closure processes are taken into account, there are no other evident tendencies for multiple 2-paths to be present or absent. In other words, local connectivity is explained by tendencies for transitive closure and tendencies against cyclic closure.

---

[5] Technically, models with single triangle parameters very often do not converge. This is discussed in Chapter 6.

Sender effects: The sender effect measures the degree to which actors with a specific attribute send more ties compared to others in the network. The negative but not quite significant sender effect for the binary attribute seniority means that managers who are not senior (i.e., those who have a score of zero) have a tendency to send ties. In contrast, the number of projects was measured as a continuous attribute variable. However, there were no sender effects for number of projects completed, so there is no evidence here that experience in projects affects tendency to communicate. Finally, note that there is no sender effect (or receiver effect) for the variable "office" because it is a categorical variable.

Receiver effects: The receiver effect measures the degree to which actors with a specific attribute have the propensity to receive ties. There were no significant receiver effects for the variables of seniority and number of projects.

Homophily: There is a significant and positive estimate for homophily for seniority and the number of projects. Actors tend to communicate with others of the same seniority and with others of similar experience in terms of the number of projects. We note that the effect is negative for projects, here measured as the (absolute) difference, and thus a negative value indicates small differences. The estimate for the categorical variable office homophily was not significant.

Covariate advice network: The covariate advice network has been treated as exogenous to the communication network, and so is fixed in the modeling process. Theoretically, this means that we assume advice may have an effect on communication (the network we are modeling) but that communication has no effect on advice (for an extended discussion on this, see Chapter 21). More to the point, we seek to understand how advice ties might explain communication ties but not the other way around. The significant and positive parameter of the covariate network indicates that advice and communication ties co-occur, or are entrained.

5.2.1   Multiple Explanations for Network Structure

First and foremost, when examining the estimates in Table 5.1, we highlight the fact that there are significant effects for purely structural, actor-relation, *and* covariate network effects. That is, each subtype of network effects has an independent explanatory capacity for the presence of ties in the communication network. This emphasizes a number of points. If we were to believe that social network ties were not dependent on the individual characteristics of actors, we would miss important information, specifically, how communication occurs around similarity on a number of characteristics in The Corporation. Furthermore, exogenous relational structures (i.e., advice) also have a unique impact on communication ties. The purely structural effects by themselves do not wipe out the actor-relation effects, and thus this highlights the importance of examining the qualities of actors in the network. Conversely, the inclusion of attributes does not erase the purely structural effects found for the network, indicating that attributes alone are insufficient for explaining the formation of network ties.

We hope that the example in this chapter gives an early illustration of how an ERGM may be applied to understand network structure. With this motivation behind us, we now turn to more precise methodological details about how ERGMs are formulated and implemented in Section II.

Section II

Methods

6

Exponential Random Graph Model Fundamentals

Johan Koskinen and Galina Daraganova

6.1   Chapter Outline

This chapter provides a more detailed description of exponential random graph models and aims at answering the following questions:

- What do the different notions of independence and interdependence imply for the modeling of tie-variables?
- What are exponential random graph models? What can they tell us?
- Why and when should we use exponential random graph models?
- What different model specifications are available? How may these be interpreted?

After presenting some necessary notation, we revisit the concept of statistical independence in order to move to an understanding of interdependence. A network approach implies some level of dependence among the observations. We then explain the exponential random graph model (ERGM) framework akin to more familiar generalized linear models, emphasizing that we now have dependence, not independence, of observations. Next, the exact nature of these departures from independence is explained, and the implications for model specifications are presented. We begin by explaining individual ties because this illustrates the snug fit between individual ties, endogenous dependencies, and the model expressed in terms of the entire graph.

6.2   Network Tie-Variables

For a given undirected graph, a set of n nodes is represented as $N = \{1, \ldots, n\}$, and $i \in N$ means that "i belongs to the set N." This set is assumed to be fixed and predetermined. Let J be the set of all possible relational

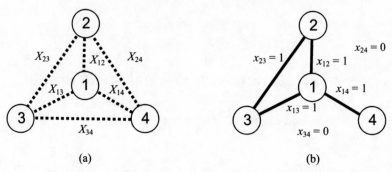

Figure 6.1. (a) Network variables of X and (b) a realization x for network on four vertices.

ties for the node set N, $J = \{(i,j) : i,j \in N, i \neq j\}$. This set excludes pairs (i,i) because self-ties are disallowed. The number of elements[1] in J is $\binom{n}{2} = \frac{n(n-1)}{2}$. For any observed network, some edges in J may be present and some absent. For a stochastic model, the set of ties E that are present is a random subset of J. If $(i,j) \in E$, then the edge between i and j is present. For any element $(i,j) \in J$, a random variable X_{ij} can be defined where $X_{ij} = 1$ if $(i,j) \in E$ and $X_{ij} = 0$ if $(i,j) \notin E$. This description is for an undirected graph: the same ideas applies to a directed graph with some slight variation in details (e.g., the number of elements in J is then $n(n-1)$).

These variables are called "tie-variables." The tie-variables can be collected in a stochastic adjacency matrix $X = [X_{ij}]$, where the entry in row i and column j pertains to the tie from i to j. The space of all possible adjacency matrices is denoted by $\mathbf{X}$. A realization of the stochastic adjacency matrix X is denoted by $x = [x_{ij}]$, a realization being a particular instance of the stochastic adjacency matrix – here, a matrix of actual zeros and ones rather than variables. Any observed network, then, is a realization.

The collection of network tie-variables and a particular realization for a network on four nodes is represented in Figure 6.1. The left panel of Figure 6.1 schematically represents the collection of six tie-variables that constitute a random graph on four vertices. The dotted line between nodes 2 and 3, for example, represents the tie-variable X_{23}. One realization of the random graph is depicted in the right-hand panel. Here, the tie between 2 and 3 is present, indicated by a solid line, but the tie between

---

[1] In general, the number of ways in which one may choose k-subsets out of n elements is given by

$$\binom{n}{k} = \frac{n(n-1)\cdots(2)(1)}{k(k-1)\cdots(2)(1)(n-k)(n-k-1)\cdots(2)(1)} = \frac{n(n-1)\cdots(n-k+2)(n-k+1)}{k(k-1)\cdots(2)(1)}$$

Table 6.1. *Two independent tie-variables*

		Tie (i,j)	
		Prob absent: .5	Prob present: .5
Tie (h,m)	Prob absent: .5	Prob $(h,m),(i,j) \notin E$: .25	Prob $(h,m) \notin E,(i,j) \in E$: .25
	Prob present: .5	Prob $(h,m) \in E,(i,j) \notin E$: .25	Prob $(h,m),(i,j) \in E$: .25

vertices 2 and 4 is absent – the realizations of the corresponding tie-variables are $x_{23} = 1$ and $x_{24} = 0$, respectively.

The main focus is on modeling a process of network tie formation. As mentioned in Chapter 3, the presence of a tie between any two individuals may be explained by a combination of actor attribute variables and by patterns of ties among other members of the network. In other words, the likelihood of a tie may not only be a function of individual characteristics of actors who share the tie, but also a function of presence or absence of other network ties in the network. This possible dependence between tie-variables creates the main difficulty in formulating a stochastic model for a network.

6.3   Notion of Independence

To understand statistical dependence, let us begin with the idea of independence (see, e.g., Newbold, Carlson, and Thorne (2007) for an introduction to statistical concepts). The assumed independence of two tie-variables, X_{ij} and X_{hm}, may be compared to coin tosses. If we assume that the ties (h,m) and (i,j) are equally likely to be present and absent, we may think of a model for these ties as two coins, coins I and II, so that when we flip them separately, each has the probability of .5 of coming up heads and tails. If a coin is heads, we deem the corresponding tie to be present, and if it is tails, we deem the tie absent.

If the coinflips are independent, this means that the probability that they will both come up heads is just the product of the individual probabilities of coming up heads, as in Table 6.1. This is a statistical model for a network where the density is expected to be .5.

Suppose instead that the tie-variables behaved as in Table 6.2, where multiplying the probabilities of "heads" does not produce the joint probabilities. In this case, the variables are not independent. The marginal probabilities are the same as in Table 6.1; the probability of (h,m) being present is still .5 (= .1 + .4).

An equivalent definition of independence of two variables, X_{ij} and X_{hm}, is that the information that $X_{hm} = x_{hm}$ does not alter the probability that $X_{ij} = x_{ij}$. In other words, information regarding the realization of one variable does not help us predict the value of the other variable – the

Table 6.2. *Two dependent tie-variables*

		Tie (i,j)	
		Prob absent: .5	Prob present: .5
Tie (h,m)	Prob absent: .5	Prob $(h,m),(i,j)\notin E$: .4	Prob $(h,m)\notin E,(i,j)\in E$: .1
	Prob present: .5	Prob $(h,m)\in E,(i,j)\notin E$: .1	Prob $(h,m),(i,j)\in E$: .4

unconditional (or marginal) probability is still our best guess for the second variable.

Most standard statistical approaches such as logistic regression require independence, as in Table 6.1, whereas for networks we generally expect dependence of some sort, as in Table 6.2. For instance, if we know that Mary talks to John and that John talks to Peter, we expect that the chance of Mary talking to Peter is greater than just the marginal probability of two randomly selected people in the whole world talking to each other (which is very small indeed). In a directed network, it does not seem plausible that a coin flip for X_{ij} is independent of a coin flip for X_{ji} because these variables relate to the same dyad. Thus, if John invites Jack to dinner, the chances of Jack inviting John to dinner are likely to increase. Furthermore, for a directed or undirected graph, it does not seem plausible that a coin flip for X_{ij} is independent of a coin flip for X_{ih}, because both tie-variables pertain to the same actor, i (this is the reasoning underlying the Markov dependence assumption explained later in this chapter).

In these cases, there is dependence among tie-variables, and the presence of some ties affects the probability that other ties may be observed. Ignoring dependence among observations has major consequences for the statistical conclusions we draw, and this is well documented in related fields (Snijders & Bosker, 1999). Exponential random graph models have the explicit aim to relax the assumption of independence between network tie-variables and to incorporate possible dependencies among tie-variables. Conditioning – "knowing that Mary knows John" – is a central part of model formulation, interpretation, and simulation. ERGMs do not aim at predicting the probability of a tie in a social vacuum, as in the case of a logistic regression, but rather the "conditional probability" of a tie, given what is observed in the rest of the network.

6.4 ERGMs from Generalized Linear Model Perspective

Although ERGMs have some similarities to generalized linear models (GLMs), especially standard log-linear models and logistic regressions, an ERGM *does not* (except in trivial cases) reduce to logistic regression. Yet, because some fundamental concepts are common to GLMs and ERGMs, it is instructive to illustrate these in the familiar language of logistic regression. This also serves to emphasize how the main departure of ERGMs from logistic regression, namely, the assumptions of dependence between observations, play out. Although logistic regression assumes independence of observations as in Table 6.1, ERGMs do not make this assumption, rather the opposite.

Suppose that we are primarily interested in explaining observed ties as a function of a collection of covariates, or predictor variables. The covariates for the tie-variable X_{ij} could, for example, relate to the individual characteristics of the two actors i and j, such as the difference in age between i and j, and a variable indicating whether i and j have the same gender. Denote these dyadic covariates by $w_{ij,1}, w_{ij,2}, \ldots, w_{ij,p}$, for p covariates. For a GLM, we would try to find a function η of w and unknown parameters $\theta_1, \theta_2, \ldots, \theta_p$ that best describe the expected value $E(X_{ij}) = \eta(w, \theta)$ (the probability that $X_{ij} = 1$). For dichotomous response variables such as X_{ij}, a logistic regression estimates a set θ of unknown parameters $\theta_1, \theta_2, \ldots \theta_p$ (logistic regression coefficients) that best predict the probability that the tie is present. The logistic regression function is

$$
\begin{aligned}
\Pr(X_{ij} = 1 | \theta) &= \eta(w, \theta) \\
&= \frac{\exp\{\theta_1 w_{ij,1} + \theta_2 w_{ij,2} + \cdots \theta_p w_{ij,p}\}}{1 + \exp\{\theta_1 w_{ij,1} + \theta_2 w_{ij,2} + \cdots \theta_p w_{ij,p}\}}.
\end{aligned}
$$

If a covariate, say, $w_{ij,2}$, indicated whether i and j were of the same gender, a positive value of the corresponding parameter θ_2 indicates a higher probability of a tie between people of the same gender. It is usually easier to interpret the model in terms of the logit or log-odds, which is the natural logarithm of $\Pr(X_{ij} = 1 | \theta) / \Pr(X_{ij} = 0 | \theta)$:

$$
\text{logit} \Pr(X_{ij} = 1 | \theta) = \log \frac{\Pr(X_{ij} = 1 | \theta)}{\Pr(X_{ij} = 0 | \theta)} = \theta_1 w_{ij,1} + \theta_2 w_{ij,2} + \cdots + \theta_p w_{ij,p}.
$$

Anyone familiar with linear and/or logistic regression will be comfortable with the expression on the right-hand side. The parameters (θ) weight the relative importance of their corresponding predictors (w) for the probability of a tie. Positive parameters correspond to effects that increase the probability of a tie, whereas negative parameters relate to effects that decrease the probability of a tie.

The difference in the log-odds for two pairs (i, j) and (h, m), the covariates of whom only differ in that i and j are of the same gender $(w_{ij,2} = 1)$

and h and m are of different gender ($w_{hm,2} = 0$), is

$$\frac{\text{logit} \Pr(X_{ij} = 1|\theta)}{\text{logit} \Pr(X_{hm} = 1|\theta)} = \theta_1(w_{ij,1} - w_{hm,1}) + \theta_2(w_{ij,2} - w_{hm,2}) + \cdots$$

$$+ \theta_p(w_{ij,p} - w_{hm,p}) = \theta_2.$$

This ratio (of being of the same gender) is the well-known odds ratio. The larger the value of θ_2, the greater the probability of a tie for same-gender pairs as compared to different-gender pairs, everything else being equal. We can think of θ_2 as relating to the *change* in going from a situation of a different gender to a same-gender pair with everything else the same.

For ERGMs, in addition to the exogenous covariates used in logistic regression such as the w variables, we include as covariates counts of "network configurations" in the linear predictor. Configurations were introduced in Chapter 3, and examples include edges, 2-stars, and triangles (see Section 3.1.2). In addition, we provide details of other possible configurations later in this chapter. The interpretation of the parameters corresponding to these configurations is similar to those of exogenous covariates; for example, a positive parameter corresponding to the number of triangles means that a tie is more likely to occur if it closes a 2-path than if it does not. In the example of the triangle, as the reader will notice, whether a tie closes a 2-path depends on whether the other two ties of the triangle are present.

Consequently, the second departure from logistic regression is that we have to formulate the model for each tie-variable conditional on the rest of the graph: that is, in predicting a tie X_{ij}, we need to take into account the other ties that might be present. In other words, ERGMs predict the probability for X_{ij}, conditional on all other ties observed in the network (which we denote as X_{-ij}). This conditional probability is written as $\Pr(X_{ij} = 1|X_{-ij} = x_{-ij}, \theta)$. Leaving aside the dyadic covariates (the w variables previously mentioned), and concentrating only on the configuration counts as predictors, the (conditional) logit then becomes

$$\log \frac{\Pr(X_{ij} = 1|X_{-ij} = x_{-ij}, \theta)}{\Pr(X_{ij} = 0|X_{-ij} = x_{-ij}, \theta)} = \theta_1 \delta^+_{ij,1}(x) + \theta_2 \delta^+_{ij,2}(x) + \cdots$$

$$+ \theta_p \delta^+_{ij,p}(x). \tag{6.1}$$

The functions $\delta^+_{ij,k}(x)$ are called the "change statistics" for the kth configuration. They are not just counts of the configurations in the graph (e.g., the number of triangles) but the change in going from a graph for which $X_{-ij} = x_{-ij}$ and $X_{ij} = 0$ to a graph for which $X_{-ij} = x_{-ij}$ and $X_{ij} = 1$. For example, if one covariate is the number of edges, then adding the edge (i, j) to $X_{-ij} = x_{-ij}$ will result in an increase in the number of edges by one, say, $\delta^+_{ij,edge}(x) = 1$. Adding the edge (i, j) to $X_{-ij} = x_{-ij}$ when $x_{ik} = x_{kj} = 1$ will result in an increase in the number of triangles by (at least) one because this would create a new triangle $x_{ij} = x_{ik} = x_{kj} = 1$. If the parameter corresponding to the number of triangles is positive, then the fact that the triangle count increases would contribute positively to the probability for $X_{ij} = 1$.

Note here the important fact that we need to know the rest of the graph $X_{-ij} = x_{-ij}$ in order to calculate the $\delta_{ij,k}^+(x)$ and the conditional logits. This is a direct consequence of the assumption that ties may be interdependent – the probability of a tie depends on whether other ties are present. The probabilities (or probability distributions) presented in this chapter may be interpreted conditionally – an ERGM prescribes how likely it is to add or delete a tie for a pair of actors given everything else. These probabilities are based on the weighted contributions of changes in configurations that adding or deleting the tie in question would yield.

Why are the predictors the change statistics of configurations rather than the raw count of configurations? In Equation (6.1), we have an expression for the log-odds for the presence of a tie on X_{ij} compared to the absence of a tie on X_{ij}. In that case, the correct predictor is the change from the graph, when $x_{ij} = 0$, to the graph, when $x_{ij} = 1$.

There is an equivalent form of the model as a probability expression for all tie-variables simultaneously, where the predictors are then the counts of configurations. This is known as the joint form of the model:

$$\Pr(X = x|\theta) \equiv P_\theta(x) = \frac{1}{\kappa(\theta)} \exp\{\theta_1 z_1(x) + \theta_2 z_2(x) + \cdots + \theta_p z_p(x)\}. \tag{6.2}$$

Equation (6.2) is the general form of the ERGM that we stick to throughout the book. The functions $z_k(x)$ are counts of configurations in the graph x, such that the corresponding change statistic for $z_k(x)$ would be $\delta_{ij,k}^+(x) = z_k(\Delta_{ij}^+ x) - z_k(\Delta_{ij}^- x)$, where $\Delta_{ij}^+ x$ ($\Delta_{ij}^- x$) denotes a matrix x for which x_{ij} is constrained to be equal to one (zero). The parameters weight the relative importance of their respective configurations, and the normalizing term $\kappa(\theta) = \sum_{y \in X} \exp\{\theta_1 z_1(y) + \theta_2 z_2(y) + \cdots + \theta_p z_p(y)\}$ ensures that the sum of the probability mass function, $P_\theta(x)$, over all graphs is one.

Equation (6.2) describes a probability distribution for all graphs with n nodes. Let us suppose that we have only one configuration represented in a model for the network – the number of edges. Then there will be a parameter θ_1 for edges and a statistic $z_1(x)$ that is simply the count L of the number of edges in the graph x. So, for any and every graph x with n nodes, Equation (6.2) with a given edge parameter θ_1 will assign a probability to x based on the number of edges. We can then think of a graph from this probability distribution as a random graph, and due to the form of Equation (6.2), we term it an "exponential (family) random graph distribution." Because Equation (6.2) is based on certain network configurations, we can think of graphs in this distribution as built up by the presence and absence of those particular configurations, combining together in ways represented by the parameter values to create the total graph structure.

As the ERGM gives us a distribution of graphs over **X**, the model also implies a distribution of statistics. This offers a convenient way of studying various properties of a model through inspecting the various implied distributions of statistics (as is done in Chapter 4; the use of simulated distributions of statistics is described in more detail in Chapter 12 (simulation, estimation, and goodness of fit) and further illustrated in Chapter 13). As an example, we frequently make use of the expected values $E_{x|\theta}\{z(x)\} = \sum_{x \in X} z(x) P_\theta(x)$ of these implied distributions.

Of course, this description is still quite abstract. To obtain a particular model, we first need to decide which configurations are relevant. We are guided here by hypotheses about possible dependencies among tie-variables.

6.5   Possible Forms of Dependence

We now introduce the different forms of dependence among tie-variables that have been proposed in the literature and briefly note the different types of models that result. With this quick summary of dependence in place, we go on to describe each form of the model in more detail. A more detailed discussion of dependence is provided in Chapter 7.

6.5.1   Bernoulli Assumption

The simplest form of dependence is represented by the Bernoulli graph (e.g., Bollobás, 1985; Frank, 1981; Frank & Strauss, 1986; Karońsky, 1982) in which the tie-variables are assumed to be independent. The Bernoulli graph is called "homogeneous" if the tie-variables are independent and identically distributed Bernoulli variables (in other words, just like a coinflip, although perhaps biased with unequal probabilities for heads and tails). The Bernoulli dependence assumption defines the class of Bernoulli graphs, where the (log-) probability of a graph is proportional to the weighted sum of number of edges. This assumption is quite unrealistic for social networks but can serve as a baseline for comparison.

6.5.2   Dyad-Independent Assumption

For directed graphs, an intuitive form of dependence is to allow for the tie *from* person i to person j to be dependent of the tie *to* person i from person j. Hence, the model is no longer a model for the ties of the network but for pairs of ties of the network, and the pairs of tie-variables are called "dyads."

6.5.3 Markov Dependence Assumption

Frank and Strauss (1986) proposed a "Markov dependence assumption," the simplest assumption that goes beyond a dyad. Two tie-variables are assumed to be independent unless they share a node. If instead of considering the edges of a graph as connecting nodes, we think of the nodes of the graph as connecting the edges, the Markov dependence assumption suggests itself. Because node i connects the possible edges (i,j) and (i,h), we say that the tie-variables corresponding to (i,j) and (i,h) are *dependent* conditional on the rest of the graph.

This assumption accounts for the fact that whether Mary talks to John may depend on whether Mary talks to Peter because both ties pertain to Mary. In addition, the probability that John talks to Peter may be affected by whether both John and Peter talk to Mary (a possible tie between John and Peter is conditionally dependent on ties between Mary and John and between Mary and Peter under the Markov assumption – note the triangle!). The Markov dependence assumption leads to the class of Markov random graphs, where the (log-) probability of a graph is proportional to the weighted sum of counts of different structural features such as edges, stars, and triangles. How these features are derived is summarized in Chapter 7, and the structural features themselves and how they may be interpreted is dealt with in the next section.

6.5.4 Realization-Dependent Models

Pattison and Robins (2002) suggested that in some circumstances, two tie-variables, X_{ij} and X_{hm}, may be conditionally dependent given the presence of other network tie-variables even when they do not share a node. This is a "partial conditional independence assumption" that is a generalization of the more familiar notion of conditional independence, which refers to the situation of statistical independence of two variables given the state of a third variable (Dawid, 1979, 1980). In the case of partial conditional independence for tie-variables, two tie-variables are statistically independent if and only if a third tie-variable is in a particular state.[2]

An example of a partial conditional independence assumption is the "social circuit dependence assumption," where two tie-variables, X_{ij} and

---

[2] This approach is similar in form to that used by Baddeley and Möller (1989) for spatial models, which is why Pattison and Robins (2002) adopted the same term referring to these models as "realization-dependent models."

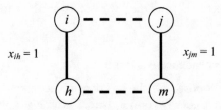

Figure 6.2. Social circuit dependence.

X_{hm}, that do not share a vertex are conditionally dependent if ties exists between i and h and between j and m. In this case, if the two-variables are observed (i.e., $x_{ih}x_{jm} = 1$), then a 4-cycle is created as in Figure 6.2. This dependence may be typified in collaborative ties, when i works with h and j works with m. Then the presence of collaboration between i and j is likely to affect whether h and m also collaborate.

This assumption in combination with the Markov dependence assumption gives rise to a set of additional configurations in the network model, including sets of 2-paths with common starting and ending nodes, and sets of triangles with a common base.

6.6   Different Classes of Model Specifications

A dependence assumption constrains the types of configurations among network tie-variables in the model. This point is argued more fully in Chapter 7, which presents technical details of dependence at greater length. For the moment, it suffices to know that a particular dependence assumption implies that the conditional probability of a tie is affected by certain network configurations. In other words, based on the nature of the dependence, a tie is more (or less) probable if it features in some of these configurations. Counts of these subgraphs in the observed graph then become the statistics in the model that permit us to move beyond logistic regression and take dependence into account. Different model specifications involve different combinations of statistics. We now describe a number of commonly used models based on different dependence assumptions, although this is not a complete list of possible models.

6.6.1   Bernoulli Model

Undirected Graphs. The simplest ERGM is the Bernoulli model. As noted previously, for the homogeneous Bernoulli model, each possible tie can be modeled as the independent flip of a $(p\text{-})$ coin. The interpretation is that for each possible tie, we flip a $(p\text{-})$ coin, where the probability of heads is p: if this coin comes up heads, we deem a tie present; otherwise, it is absent. The conditional probability is then

$$\Pr(X_{ij} = 1 | X_{-ij} = x_{-ij}, \theta) = \Pr(X_{ij} = 1 | \theta) = \frac{e^\theta}{1 + e^\theta}.$$

The logit of the probability of a tie is given simply by θ, the edge parameter. The joint ERGM probability mass function for the adjacency matrix according to the general formula (Equation (6.2)) is

$$P_\theta(x) = \frac{1}{\kappa(\theta)} \exp\{\theta_L L(x)\}. \tag{6.3}$$

The parameter θ_L is called the "edge parameter," and the corresponding statistic for this is the number of edges $L(x) = \sum_{i < j} x_{ij}$. There is only one network configuration relevant to this model: the single edge.

Directed Graphs. The homogeneous Bernoulli model for directed graphs follows the same principles as for undirected graphs with the difference that there are twice as many tie-variables.

6.6.2 Dyadic Independence Models

An obvious limitation of the Bernoulli model for directed graphs is that it does not allow for tendencies toward reciprocation, a well-known tendency in human social relations. This prompted the development of the dyad-independent (or p_1) class of exponential family distributions by Holland and Leinhardt (1981) and Fienberg and Wasserman (1981). For two actors $i, j \in N$, the Bernoulli model assumes that the probability that $X_{ij} = x_{ij}$ and $X_{ji} = x_{ji}$ is the product of the two marginal probabilities as in Table 6.1, akin to two independent coin tosses (with biased coins). The dyad-independent model, in contrast, allows for these variables to be dependent as in Table 6.2. Nevertheless, the dependence assumption is limited: the model assumes that dyads are independent of each other, so that the probability of $X_{ij} = 1$ depends only on x_{ji}. Hence, the tie-variables (X_{ij}, X_{ji}) may be treated as independent observations for each pair (i, j) of nodes. Because of the simple dependence assumption, a dyad-independent model may still be fitted using standard statistical techniques (more specifically, multinomial logistic regression).

The simplest form of a dyad-independent model is what Snijders (2002) called the "reciprocity p^* model":

$$P_\theta(x) = \frac{1}{\kappa(\theta)} \exp\{\theta_L L(x) + \theta_M M(x)\},$$

where $L(x)$ is now the number of arcs and $M(x) = \sum_{i < j} x_{ij} x_{ji}$ is the number of reciprocated (or mutual) arcs in the graph. Here, there are

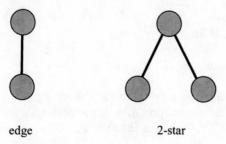

edge   2-star

Figure 6.3. Configurations in 2-star model.

two configurations relevant to the model: arcs and reciprocated arcs. For each dyad, there are four possible outcomes for which the associated probabilities are easily seen to be

$$
\Pr(X_{ij} = x_{ij}, X_{ji} = x_{ji} \mid \theta) = \begin{cases} \dfrac{1}{\kappa_{ij}(\theta)} & x_{ij} = x_{ij} = 0 \\ \dfrac{1}{\kappa_{ij}(\theta)} \exp\{\theta_L\} & x_{ij} = 1, x_{ji} = 0 \\ \dfrac{1}{\kappa_{ij}(\theta)} \exp\{\theta_L\} & x_{ij} = 0, x_{ji} = 1 \\ \dfrac{1}{\kappa_{ij}(\theta)} \exp\{2\theta_L + \theta_M\} & x_{ij} = x_{ji} = 1 \end{cases},
$$

where $\kappa_{ij}(\theta) = 1 + 2e^{\theta_L} + e^{2\theta_L + \theta_M}$, obtained from adding the probabilities of the four outcomes.

In the original p_1 class of models, the parameter θ_L was assumed to be a function of sender and receiver effects to reflect an actor's propensity to establish ties to others and to receive ties. In subsequent elaborations of the p_1, Bayesian smoothing has been employed (Wong, 1987), and more recently, more complicated dependencies have been introduced through random effects in the p_2 model (van Duijn, Snijders, & Zijlstra, 2004).

Although reciprocity is typically not the only type of interdependency encountered in social network data, it is an integral part of most realistic models for directed networks.

6.6.3   Markov Model

Nondirected Markov Random Graph Models. The Markov dependenceassumption gives rise to a model whose statistics in Equation (6.2) are the number of edges; the numbers of k-stars $S_k(x) = \sum_{i \in N} \binom{x_{i+}}{k}$ of different sizes ($2 \leq k \leq (n-1)$), where $x_{i+} = \sum_j x_{ij}$ (see Figures 6.3 and 6.4 for depictions of 2- and 3-stars, respectively); and the number of triangles $T(x) = \sum_{i<j<k} x_{ij} x_{jk} x_{ki}$. The Markov dependence assumption supposes that two tie-variables are conditionally dependent if they share a node.

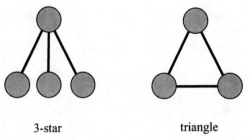

3-star   triangle

Figure 6.4. Configurations with three edges: 3-star and triangle.

What this means is that any configuration in the model must have ties that all share nodes with each other. A little thought will show that the only way that this can occur is if a configuration is a single edge, if all ties in the configuration share the one node (i.e., a star of different sizes, depending on how many ties there are), or if there are three ties with three nodes (a triangle). (This argument is presented in more detail in Chapter 7.)

The full Markov model then becomes

$$\Pr(X = x) = \frac{1}{\kappa} \exp(\theta_L L(x) + \theta_{S_2} S_2(x) + \theta_{S_3} S_3(x) + \cdots$$
$$+ \theta_{S_{n-1}} S_{n-1}(x) + \theta_T T(x)). \qquad (6.4)$$

Subsets of models nested in the full Markov model are obtained by setting some parameters to be zero. Recall (see Figure 3.2 in Section 3.1.5) that the higher-order configurations contain lower-order configurations, so that the statistics are nested. The count of 2-stars (Figure 6.3) is not just a count of nodes with degree 2: a 3-star contains three 2-stars, as does a triangle (Figure 6.4). Similarly, a triangle contains three edges, and so on. Thus, statistically, the higher-order configurations represent statistical interactions involving lower-order configurations. This has the effect of permitting inferences about, for instance, the relevance of 2-star configurations given the number of edges in the graph, or the importance of triangles given the number of 2-stars. We want to make inferences about whether there is a distinct process of network ties forming into triangles, over and above the chance accumulation of edges and 2-stars.

Setting different statistics to zero gives rise to different model specifications. As explained later in this chapter, it turns out that most Markov models alone do not represent social network data well and have now generally been superseded by social circuit models. Nevertheless, a more detailed discussion of a few simple Markov models will assist understanding of the general modeling approach.

The simplest Markov model is the "2-star model," where the higher-order star and triangle parameters are set to zero: $\theta_{S_3} = \theta_{S_4} = \cdots = \theta_{S_{n-1}} = \theta_T = 0$. The configurations in the model are then simply edges and 2-stars.

The 2-star statistic may equivalently be written in terms of the degree distribution as $S_2(x) = \sum_{i<j} \sum_{k \neq i,j} x_{ik} x_{kj} = \sum_{j \geq 2} \binom{j}{2} d_j(x)$, where d_j is the number of nodes of degree j. For a given number of edges, a positive 2-star parameter increases the probability of graphs with more 2-stars. For a given number of edges, the simplest way to get many 2-stars is to have some high-degree nodes, thereby leading to a skewed-degree distribution. The degree variance $S = \frac{1}{n} \sum_{i=1}^{n} (x_{i+} - \bar{x})^2$ has been used as a measure of centralization (Hagberg, 2004; Snijders, 1981a, 1981b), and expanding this expression, the first term is a sum of 2-stars centered on node i, $x_{i+}^2 = \sum_{j,h} x_{ij} x_{ih}$. So, in fitting a 2-star model, we are modeling the average number of ties per node (the edge parameter) and the variation in the number of ties of each node (the 2-star parameter), that is, the mean and variance of the degree distribution. Some technical aspects of the 2-star model are studied more closely by Handcock (2003) and Park and Newman (2004).

Although this model accounts for degree variation, it rarely fits observed network data because it is unable to capture network closure (clustering or triangulation). However, the model can be extended by including triangle configurations. Frank and Strauss (1986) called this the "triad model." Again, this model is of limited empirical value because it can only be fit to data under very limited circumstances. However, a brief discussion illustrates a number of important points. The model may equivalently be formulated in terms of triad counts (Frank & Strauss, 1986), that is, in counts of induced subgraphs consisting of three vertices with no, one, two, or three edges. Triad counts of undirected graphs have been extensively used to test hypothesis by comparing them against various null distributions (Frank, 1979; Frank & Harary, 1982; Holland & Leinhardt, 1971, 1976; Karlberg, 1997, 2002).

A positive triangle parameter indicates network closure or clustering. In friendship networks, for example, there may be a tendency for friends to meet through other friends (i.e., a friend of a friend is a friend). Because the 2-star configuration is a subgraph of the triangle, a lower-order interaction, it is desirable to include the 2-star parameter whenever the triangle parameter is included. Without a 2-star parameter, we cannot tell whether the prevalence of triangles was due to accumulation of 2-stars or a distinct effect of closure.

The triad model may be extended by including a 3-star parameter (Figure 6.4). Then, the edge, 2-star parameter, and 3-star parameter model the mean, standard deviation, and skew of the degree distribution,

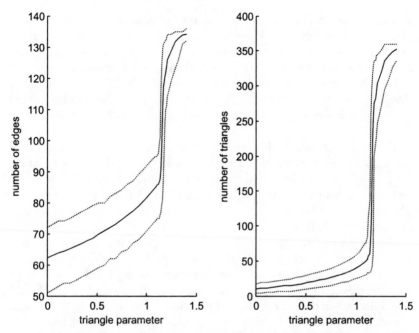

Figure 6.5. Expected and 95% intervals for number of edges and triangles as function of triangle parameter in Markov model on thirty nodes
with edges (−3), 2-stars (0.5), 3-stars (−0.2), and triangles.

respectively. In terms of interpretation, positive 2-star and negative 3-star
parameters indicate some centralization through high-degree nodes but
with a cap on the level of that centralization (through the negative 3-star
parameter). In other words, a positive 2-star parameter suggests a tendency to have multiple ties, but the negative 3-star parameter indicates
that there is a point beyond which additional ties are not desirable (we
cannot be friends with everyone!).

A fundamental property of an ERGM is that parameters regulate how
many of their corresponding configurations are expected on average. As
an illustrative example, consider how the triangle parameter θ_T controls
the number of triangles in a model that also includes parameters for
edges, 2-stars, and 3-stars, with parameter values fixed at −3.0, 0.5,
and −0.2 respectively,[3] for undirected graphs with thirty nodes. The
expected number of triangles and the range of the likely number of triangles for different values of the triangle parameter is graphed in Figure
6.5. If there is no effect for triangulation (i.e., $\theta_T = 0$) from the right-hand

---

[3] For the purpose of simple illustration, we have chosen these numbers as parameter values
based on experience.

panel, we expect around 10 triangles on average, and with probability
.95, we observe between 4 and 17 triangles. As we increase the triangle parameter, the number of triangles we expect to see steadily rises:
for example, when $\theta_T = 1$, we get 40 triangles on average, and 95% of
the graphs generated from this model have between 25 and 59 triangles.
Roughly after $\theta_T = 1.11$, there is a dramatic rise in the number of triangles, and when $\theta_T = 1.15$, the 95% interval extends from 38 to 293
triangles.

The statistics are highly interdependent: we cannot increase the
expected number of triangles without also increasing the expected number of edges as in the left-hand panel. Hence, although we get between 51
and 72 edges when $\theta_T = 0$, we get between 71 and 92 edges when $\theta_T = 1$.
The explosion in the number of triangles after $\theta_T = 1.11$ is mirrored in
the steep rise in edges.

The transition from low-density graphs to high-density graphs in Figure
6.5 illustrates one of the difficulties with Markov models. For models
with a triangle parameter (all other parameters being fixed) in the range
0 to roughly 1.11, the increase in the number of triangles is small and
gradual as a function of increases in the triangle parameter. In that range,
the increase in the probability of a graph for an additional triangle is
counteracted by the negative edge parameter (and also the negative 3-star
parameter).

Compare two graphs, x and y, where y has one triangle more than
x through the addition of an edge that closes a 2-path. Then y has an
additional θ_T in the (exponent for the) probability compared to x, mean-
ing that the triangle contributes positively to favoring y over x. However,
an additional edge in y also contributes negatively to the probability of the
graph given that the edge parameter is negative. Hence, leaving aside the
star parameters for the moment, increasing the number of triangles contributes positively to the likelihood of observing that graph through the
triangle parameter but contributes negatively through the edge parameter. In Figure 6.5, we see that there is a balance between the positive
triangle and negative edge effect until roughly $\theta_T = 1.11$. From roughly
$\theta_T = 1.18$, the balance is upset in favor of graphs with many triangles.
This dramatic change is known as a phase transition from low-density
graphs to high-density graphs, characterized by high uncertainty with a
very wide 95% interval.

Figure 6.6 depicts the number of triangles across graphs when $\theta_T =$
1.1524. The high variability occurs because the model places half the
probability on low-density graphs and half on high-density graphs, and
very little on graphs in-between. Bimodality as in Figure 6.6 is problematic for both inference and interpretation of parameters. Researchers
have found that observed data often fall in between two such humps
for Markov graphs, when it is impossible to find combinations of

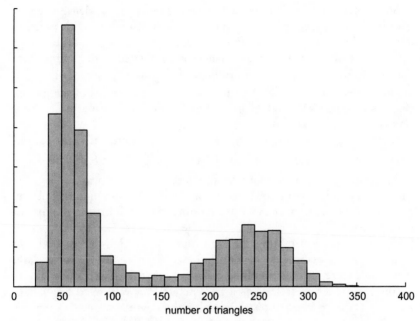

Figure 6.6. Number of triangles for Markov model with edges (−3), 2-stars (0.5), 3-stars (−0.2), and triangles (1.1524).

parameter values such that the observed combination of graph statistics is central in the distribution of graph statistics (see, e.g., Snijders et al., 2006).

Similar phase transitions can be observed for the star parameters, so although the triad model models the degree distribution and recognizes network closure, it has been demonstrated to be inadequate for reproducing the forms of degree heterogeneity and clustering commonly observed in empirical social networks (Handcock, 2003; Robins & Pattison, 2005; Snijders et al., 2006). It is perhaps not surprising given that social relationships are potentially complex phenomena that they cannot be described only at the dyadic and/or triadic levels implied by the Markov dependence assumption.

Alternating Star Parameters. One parameterization that helps considerably with phase transitions involving star parameters is that of "alternating star parameters" or (equivalently) "geometrically weighted degree parameters." The alternating star statistic is a weighted sum of all star counts (with alternating signs on the counts – see the next paragraph) and dampens the effects of higher-order stars to help avoid a dramatic phase transition from low-density to high-density graphs.

When fitting models to real data, the combination of density, 2-star parameter, and 3-star parameter in the triad model often yields parameters with alternating signs (as do indeed models with higher-order stars). The alternating sign of star parameters is associated with the fact that the k-star counts are nested: every k-star contains $\binom{k}{j}$ j-stars, for $j \leq k$. Higher-order stars are higher-order statistical interactions in the model: changes in signs with higher-order interaction effects are familiar from standard general linear model approaches.

Frank and Strauss (1986) proposed to reparameterize the star parameters in terms of the degree distribution $\theta_{d(j)} = \sum_{k \geq j} \binom{j}{k} \theta_{S(k)}$, where $\theta_{d(j)}$ and $\theta_{S(k)}$ are parameters for nodes of degree j- and k-stars, respectively. This is a complete parameterization of the degree distribution but creates too many free parameters to be estimated. To limit the number of parameters, Snijders et al. (2006) suggested the restriction $\theta_{d_j} = \theta_{d_{j-1}} e^{-\alpha}$, for $\alpha > 0$, down-weighting the contributions of high-degree nodes in a geometrically decreasing fashion (see also Hunter (2007) for a slight variation). Here, α is a smoothing constant either fixed at a value chosen by the researcher or treated as a parameter to be estimated (see Chapter 12). These parameter restrictions for the degree parameters may be translated back to the parameters for the stars. With some minor modifications, $\theta_{d_j} = \theta_{d_{j-1}} e^{-\alpha}$ is equivalent to the constraint $\theta_{S(k)} = -\frac{\theta_{S(k-1)}}{\lambda}$ on the star parameters, where $\lambda = \frac{e^{\alpha}}{e^{\alpha} - 1}$. Treating λ as a fixed constant, this constraint implies that we have one alternating star parameter θ_S, with an associated statistic:

$$z_s(x; \lambda) = S_2(x) - \frac{S_3(x)}{\lambda} + \cdots + (-1)^k \frac{S_k(x)}{\lambda^{k-2}} + \cdots$$
$$+ (-1)^{n-1} \frac{S_{n-1}(x)}{\lambda^{n-3}}. \tag{6.5}$$

Because of the special properties of the stars of order 2 and 3, and their relation to degree variance and skew, it is sometimes useful to include effects for stars of order 2 and 3 in addition to the alternating star effects. It is almost always recommended to include the edge parameter θ_L in addition to the alternating star statistic (unless using fixed density models – see later in this chapter). The alternating star statistic differs from the geometrically weighted degree (GWD) statistic (Snijders et al., 2006) (and the subtly different GWD statistic of Hunter (2007)) in the treatment of 1-star (i.e., edges) (the exact relation is given in formula 14 of Snijders et al., 2006).

The general interpretation of the alternating star parameter θ_S is as follows. A positive parameter value with $\lambda > 1$ indicates centralization based on high-degree nodes. The value of λ controls the amount of that

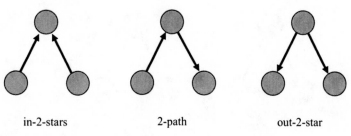

in-2-stars   2-path   out-2-star

Figure 6.7. Directed star configurations on three nodes.

centralization, with a larger λ encouraging higher-degree nodes. Thus, a large λ may assist with modeling graphs with more highly skewed degree distributions. When θ_S is negative, however, the reverse will be true, so that the degree distribution is relatively more equal among nodes. For many empirical data sets, $\lambda = 2$ is a reasonable value for this smoothing constant for alternating statistics (Robins & Morris, 2007), although λ may also be considered a free parameter to be estimated (Hunter & Handcock, 2006; Snijders et al., 2006).[4]

Directed Markov Models. For directed graphs, there are many more configurations than for undirected graphs, too many to fit all of them in one model (see Figure 7.8 in Chapter 7 for the twenty-five configurations with less than four vertices). Some star configurations with special status in directed graph Markov models are in-2-stars, 2-paths, and out-2-stars, given by $IS_2(x) = \sum_i \binom{x_{+i}}{2}$, $P_2(x) = \sum_i \sum_{j,h,j \neq h} x_{ji} x_{ih}$, and $OS_2(x) = \sum_i \binom{x_{i+}}{2}$, respectively (shown in Figure 6.7). These are the configurations of three (non-isolate) nodes with two arcs (Snijders, 2002). Directed graphs have two degree distributions: the in-2-star parameter controls variation of in-degrees, whereas the out-2-star controls variation of out-degrees. So, in principle, the in-2-star and out-2-star parameters model the heterogeneity in a graph with respect to popularity and activity. The 2-path parameter controls for the correlation between in- and out-degree.

The full Markov model for directed graphs parameterizes the entire triad census (Holland & Leinhardt, 1970), although again this is generally too many parameters. If we limit the triangle parameters to those that consist of three vertices with exactly one arc between any pair of nodes,

---

4   As Snijders et al. (2006) point out, if λ is considered a free parameter, the model no longer belongs to the exponential family of distributions but to the curved exponential family of distributions. Hunter and Handcock (2006) show how λ may be estimated using maximum likelihood, and Koskinen, Robins, and Pattison (2010) estimate the smoothing constant using Bayesian inference (see Chapter 12). This also holds for smoothing constants in the other alternating statistics presented here.

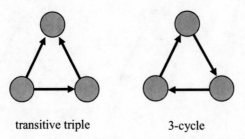

transitive triple   3-cycle

Figure 6.8. Configurations on three vertices with exactly one tie for each dyad.

the configurations correspond to the 3-cycle and the transitive triple (Figure 6.8). The 3-cycle can be seen to consist of three distinct 2-paths, and the transitive triple consists of a 2-path, in-2-star, and out-2-star. These are effects that should be controlled for when 3-cycle and transitive triadic parameters are included in a model. In addition, a directed Markov model should include the arc and reciprocity parameters familiar from the dyadic dependence directed model, as well as star-based parameters to control for the degree distribution.

Transitivity and cyclicity represent different forms of network closure. They have interesting differences in regard to local hierarchies in the network. Consider the case when the network represents the flow of orders, so that a node may only send ties to other nodes of lower status. In that case, there can be no cycles, but there may be transitive triples. (Local hierarchy, however, does not necessarily imply global hierarchy.) It is quite common in friendship networks to see a negative effect for 3-cycles and a positive effect for transitive triads, suggesting that friendship is quite strongly organized in terms of local hierarchies. Sometimes cyclicity is also interpreted as a form of generalized exchange.

Even though the family of Markov models covers a variety of different models and is able to produce many different types of graphs (Robins, Pattison, & Woolcock, 2005), difficulty in fitting models to real data as described previously (Corander et al., 1998; 2002; Frank & Strauss, 1986; Handcock, 2003; Snijders, 2002) prompted the introduction of statistics that were not derived exclusively from Markov dependence.

We have already introduced alternating star statistics for undirected models, motivated by these issues. Alternating in- and out-star parameters can be used in directed models in an analogous way. Two alternating counts of in- and out-degrees suggested by Snijders et al. (2006) were

$$z_{d,out}(x;\alpha) = \sum_{j=0}^{n-1} e^{-\alpha j} d_j^{out}(x) = \sum_{i=0}^{n} e^{-\alpha x_{i+}} \qquad (6.6)$$

and

$$z_{d,in}(x;\alpha) = \sum_{j=0}^{n-1} e^{-\alpha j} d_j^{in}(x) = \sum_{i=0}^{n} e^{-\alpha x_{+i}}. \tag{6.7}$$

These are referred to as "geometrically weighted out-degrees" and "geometrically weighted in-degrees," respectively. In the same fashion as we may express the geometrically decreasing degrees statistic as alternating star statistics, geometrically weighted out- and in-degrees have an alternate representation as alternating out- and in-stars, respectively (Robins, Pattison, & Wang, 2009). As $z_{d,out}(x;\alpha)$ models the shape of the out-degree distribution, the corresponding effect may be called "activity spread." Analogously, we term the effect corresponding to $z_{d,in}(x;\alpha)$ "popularity spread," referring to the way in which differences in number of ties received (for positive relations) reflect differences in popularity. A large positive value on the in- or out-star parameter indicates a network with high- (in- and out-) degree nodes (i.e., a network more centralized in terms of popularity or activity, respectively). The parameter α is usually treated as a smoothing constant for alternating statistics (as described previously).

The social circuit dependence assumption permits further extensions to address the problems associated with fitting Markov models.

6.6.4 Social Circuit Models

Undirected Models. The social circuit dependence assumption, in combination with Markov dependence, leads to the following configurations: edges, k-stars of different order, k-triangles, and k-independent 2-paths. These are the most commonly used social circuit configurations in model fitting (although the social circuit assumption also permits other possible configurations, such as cliques of different sizes, that are not often used).

A k-triangle consists of two connected nodes that are also jointly connected to k other distinct nodes. A k-independent 2-path consists of two nodes jointly connected to k other distinct nodes. These are depicted in Figure 6.9a (k-triangles) and Figure 6.9b (k-independent 2-paths), where we refer to (i,j) as the *base* and (i,h_k) and (j,h_k) as the *sides* of the k-triangle. Note that these configurations are consistent with the combined social circuit/Markov dependence assumptions because they are counts of 4-cycles (social circuit) with – for k-triangles – a base that is accounted for by Markov dependence.

The motivation for using k-triangle configurations relates to the difficulty in modeling triangles in Markov models as noted previously. A Markov model, in effect, assumes that triangles are distributed evenly

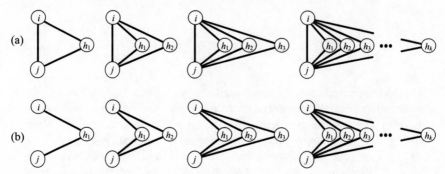

Figure 6.9. (a) Alternating triangles on base (i,j) and (b) independent 2-paths.

throughout the graph. For many observed networks, however, triangles are clumped together in denser regions of multiple triangulation, which the higher-order k-triangles are better able to model.

Just as a 2-star and 3-star model the variance and skew of the degree distribution, the 2-triangle and 3-triangle model the variance and skew of the distribution of triangles across the graph – more specifically, the distribution across ties (i,j) of the number of third nodes connected to both i and j (termed the "edgewise shared partner distribution").

The k-2-path configuration is lower order to the counterpart k-triangle configuration, so the inclusion of both parameters permits inference about whether k shared partners encourage the presence of a tie between two nodes. (The distribution of k-2-paths across dyads is often referred to as the "dyadwise shared partner distribution.")

The count of k-triangles in a graph x is $T_k(x) = \sum_{i<j} x_{ij} \binom{S_{2ij}(x)}{k}$, where $S_{2ij}(x) = \sum_{k \neq i,j} x_{ik}x_{kj}$ is the number of 2-paths connecting i and j (except for the 1-triangle, which is counted as the number of triangles, as in the Markov case). As with the alternating star statistic, distinct parameters for each of the k-triangles and k-2-paths give an overdetermined model with too many parameters. Snijders et al. (2006) proposed to combine the counts of k-triangles through the alternating triangle statistic, analogously to the alternating star statistic:

$$z_T(x;\lambda) = 3T_1(x) - \frac{T_2(x)}{\lambda} + \frac{T_3(x)}{\lambda^2} + \cdots + (-1)^{k-1}\frac{T_k(x)}{\lambda^{k-1}} + \cdots$$
$$+ (-1)^{n-3}\frac{T_{n-2}(x)}{\lambda^{n-3}}. \tag{6.8}$$

(The factor of 3 for the T_1 count arises because the 1-triangles are counted as single Markov triangles – see Snijders et al. (2006).) The constraints on the k-triangle parameters implied by the alternating triangle statistic means that edges whose nodes are connected by many indirect paths get differentially weighted. The strength of this effect will depend on the values of the parameter and the damping factor λ. For $\lambda > 1$ and a positive parameter value, the model favors graphs with highly clustered regions. The weight of higher-order k-triangles is smaller the greater the value of λ. For higher values of λ, the highly clustered regions of the graph tend to be larger. So, the alternating triangle statistic represents network closure in dense regions of the network with the size of those regions represented by the value of λ. (In practice, we typically set $\lambda = 2$ and treat it as a smoothing parameter for alternating statistics, as explained previously.) The geometrically weighted edgewise shared partner (GWESP) term in statnet is parameterized in terms of $\log(\lambda)$, so that gwesp(0.693) is the alternating triangle statistic with $\lambda = 2$. The geometrically weighted dyadwise shared partner (GWDSP) statistic (alternating 2-paths) is similarly parameterized, so that gwdsp(0.693) has $\lambda = 2$.

In the Markov model with a positive triangle parameter, the triangles are "evenly" distributed in the graph. In a model with an alternating triangle statistic, however, the presence of one triangle may increase the likelihood of other triangles "attaching themselves" to it. However, the increase in probability for creation of a k-triangle is a decreasing function of k. This can be interpreted as follows: if a social tie between individuals who share many social partners is absent, the increase in a number of shared partners is not likely to increase the probability of the tie greatly. In empirical settings, we may see serious impediments to a tie being formed (e.g., mutual antipathy or geographic distance), and additional shared partners will not alter the situation much.

It is obvious that alternating triangles emerge not only from formation of new bases of k-triangles but also from the formation of new sides. Analogous to the use of 2-paths as a control for triangles that result from accumulated two paths, the alternating independent 2-path statistic can be used as a control for the alternating triangle statistic. As previously, a sequence of alternating and decreasing weights for the counts of independent 2-paths (Figure 6.9b) can be used to create a single aggregate statistic termed the "alternating path statistic" with a damping factor λ.

Note that an independent 2-path of order 2 corresponds to a 4-cycle. The constant λ may be distinct from that for alternating triangles (although we do not make any notational distinctions), but again it is commonly set to 2. There is a functional dependence between alternating 2-paths and alternating triangles, and it is common that the 2-path parameter is negative in combination with a positive triangle parameter. In that case, actors are less likely to have shared partners unless they are themselves connected, a clear indicator for network closure.

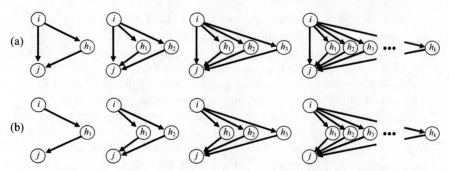

Figure 6.10. Configurations for directed graphs in alternating forms (a) AT-T and (b) A2P-T.

Directed Graphs. Just as with Markov models, the directed equivalent of the social circuit specifications has more variety in possible configurations. We have already mentioned parameters for alternating in- and out-stars.

For a directed version of the alternating triangle configuration, Snijders et al. (2006) proposed the transitive version shown in Figure 6.10a. The vertices at the base, i and j, are connected to each other and also indirectly through 2-paths via k others. The lower-order k-2-path counterparts are depicted in Figure 6.10b. As in the undirected case, the number of parameters can be reduced by using alternating parameter constraints. These alternating statistics are denoted AT-T and A2P-T, respectively, where T signifies "transitive." (For directed networks, the GWESP and GWDSP terms in statnet, gwesp(), and gwdsp() are equivalent to these transitive configurations AT-T and A2P-T with the log(λ) parameterization.) The counterpart parameters are referred to as the "path closure" and "multiple 2-path" parameters, respectively.

Considering the way the directed k-triangles are built on the directed 1-triangle (i.e., the transitive triple), we note that there are other possible choices of base. In an undirected triangle, the three vertices are structurally equivalent, so that the subgraph stays the same even if the labels of the nodes are rearranged. In a transitive triple, however, the three nodes have distinct positions: one sends two ties, one receives two ties, and one receives and sends one tie. In the directed 1-triangle in Figure 6.10a, these roles are occupied by i, j, and h_1, the center of an out-2-star, an in-2-star and a 2-path, respectively. Different directed k-triangles may be formed by adding out-2-stars, in-2-stars, and 2-paths to a suitable base. In addition to the AT-T structure in Figure 6.10 (formed by adding 2-paths to a base), Robins et al. (2009) proposed the directed k-triangles in Figure 6.11: (1) AT-U, by adding 2-out-stars to the base; (2) AT-D, by adding 2-in-stars; and (3) AT-C to form cyclic patterns. The 2-path "controls" for the latter two are given by the alternating 2-paths in Figure 6.12: A2P-U ("shared activity") and A2P-D ("shared popularity").

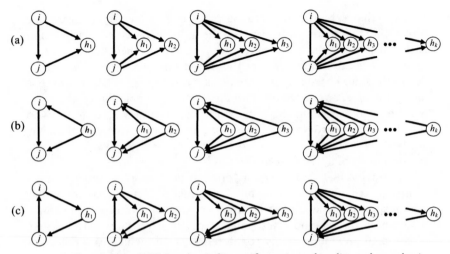

Figure 6.11. Additional triadic configurations for directed graphs in alternating forms (a) AT-U, (b) AT-D, and (c) AT-C.

These four different forms of alternating triangle effects relate to different forms of network closure. (The notation in Figure 6.11 of AT-D and AT-U derives from the classic triad census, with the D and U referring to "down" and "up"; the AT-C notation refers to "cycle." See Chapter 15 for an example of the application of such configurations.)

We may think of AT-T in terms of transitive path closure. In terms of friendship, i tends to choose those j who are friends of their friends h_u. Following Robins, Pattison, and Wang (2009), a positive AT-T parameter, the "path closure" parameter, can be interpreted as a tendency for structural holes to close when there are multiple independent paths between i and j.

A positive AT-U parameter – referred to as an "activity closure" parameter – suggests that if two actors i and j are similar with respect to

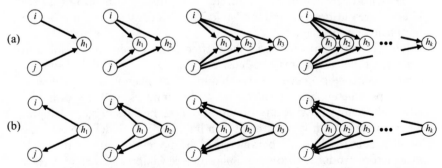

Figure 6.12. Additional 2-path configurations for directed graphs in alternating forms (a) A2P-U and (b) A2P-D.

activity – that is, they send ties to the same people – then this increases the probability that there is a tie between them. Implicit in this interpretation is that if individuals send ties to the same others, then they are either doing this because they are faced with the same conditions or embedded in the same social neighborhoods or social settings. These conditions may, of course, be created or reinforced by repeated similarity of action. For example, we could think of two individuals new to a group who therefore send ties to popular people and, in doing so, recognize that they are both in a similar position, something that is acknowledged by the establishment of a tie between them.

A positive AT-D parameter – a "popularity closure" parameter – may be interpreted in similar terms, but in this case for actors who are similar with respect to popularity rather than activity. One interesting example would be if the relation investigated is positive, yet there was a degree of competition among highly connected nodes, in which case this competitiveness might act against the prevalence of AT-D counts. A positive AT-C parameter – a "cyclic closure" parameter – indicates the presence of many 3-cycles in the network. This represents nonhierarchical network closure.

Robins, Pattison and Wang (2009) also proposed that equating the three transitive triadic parameters – path, activity, and popularity closure – to create one *general transitivity* parameter might also be useful and parsimonious in certain circumstances (we label the associated statistic "AT-TDU"). A positive general transitivity parameter indicates a general tendency for hierarchical network closure without differentiating among the three effects. Of course, it is an empirical question whether a particular network exhibits this general effect or whether one or other of the individual transitive closure effects is paramount.

Robins, Pattison and Wang (2009) also suggested inclusion of three parameters that can help control the degree distributions of directed graphs. These were parameters for the number of "isolated nodes" (i.e., nodes with degree zero), for "sources" (i.e., nodes with zero in-degree but positive out-degree), and for "sinks" (i.e., nodes with zero out-degree but positive in-degree).

Interpreting parameters and their effects independently in isolation from the other effects may be hazardous in light of the high degree of interdependence between different counts. The magnitudes of the estimated parameters are typically hard to interpret as well. Accordingly, although we may provide interpretations along the lines suggested in previous paragraphs, it is often helpful to interpret the model – that is, the simultaneous results of the parameters in the model – in terms of the kinds of structure produced through simulation (see Chapter 12). Sometimes it is helpful to use conditional log-odds and odd ratios, especially when we include actor attributes in models, as we illustrate in Chapter 8.

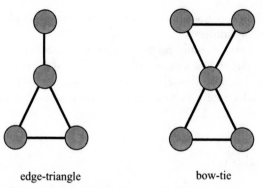

edge-triangle   bow-tie

Figure 6.13. Configurations associated with brokerage.

6.7 Other Model Specifications

Whether a particular model specification is appropriate in a given context is in part an empirical question, regardless of how coherent the underpinning theoretical framework. Almost certainly, therefore, we will come to entertain different dependence assumptions and different models within the broad ERGM class as we work with new forms of network data, and as we gain experience in understanding the strengths and limitations of particular model specifications.

Butts (2006) proposed a form of dependence termed "reciprocal path dependence," the idea that two tie-variables are conditionally dependent if their presence creates a directed cycle of any length in the graph. Statistics for the resulting homogeneous model are the counts of cycles of each length in the graph, the so-called cycle census.

Although closure is testified as being a central mechanism in tie formation, we saw that too much closure is responsible for the instabilities of the pure Markov model (Figures 6.5 and 6.6). Robins, Pattison, Snidjers, and Wang (2009) also argued that as there are costs associated with establishing and maintaining relationships with people, there may be additional costs associated with maintaining big groups. Consequently, both from the perspective of creating models that generate realistic graphs and based on theoretical considerations, tendencies for nonclosure might be considered. Robins, Pattison, Snijders, and Wang (2009) proposed configurations such as edge-triangles and bow ties, representing particular mechanisms that counteracted closure (Figure 6.13). The edge-triangle configuration is interpreted as a form of brokerage from the central node (the one with three ties). Similarly, the bow tie may be seen to represent partially overlapping group membership, where there is one node that belongs to two triangles. Here, the triangle is interpreted as the simplest form of a group. There is ongoing work examining the complexities of these additional configurations.

In these cases, a means of building model specifications from a particular construal about dependencies has provided a valuable path to model building. Equally important, though, in an empirical setting, is the means of evaluating how adequately a model has been specified. This is an issue that is taken up in Chapter 12.

6.8   Conclusion

The central premise of the ERGM modeling endeavor is its dual interpretation as a model for ties and for the graph. This duality mirrors both theoretical considerations – the way individuals form ties but at the same time are constrained and affected by structure – and technical considerations – we provide a model for tie-variables but conditional on the rest of the graph. In this chapter, we define different model specifications in terms of localized structures and attempt to interpret these in terms of substantively interesting effects. In Chapter 7, we show how the dual consideration for ties and overall structure give rise to and motivate the inclusion of the subgraph counts presented in this chapter. We explain how the dependence assumptions relate to subgraphs and how the probability of a tie is informed by neighboring structures.

7

Dependence Graphs and Sufficient Statistics

Johan Koskinen and Galina Daraganova

7.1   Chapter Outline

This chapter is written for those interested in a more detailed under-standing of how assumptions regarding various forms of dependence can be formalized. What is treated here is not essential for applying expo-nential random graph models (ERGMs) and may be skipped at a first reading. The general idea, laid down by Frank and Strauss (1986), is nevertheless crucial to the formulation of statistical models treated in this book.

Important key points in this chapter are as follows:

- Subgraph counts are not arbitrarily chosen in ERGMs but corre-spond to specific dependency structures.
- The subgraph counts in ERGMs are intricately nested and inter-dependent, so care has to be taken in interpreting parameters in isolation.
- An ERGM is akin to a log-linear model where the subgraph counts are represented by interactions of tie-variables.
- ERGMs try to reduce the complexity of observed networks into systematic underlying principles and stochastic components.
- A homogeneous ERGM assigns equal probability to graphs that are structurally identical.

In this chapter, we focus on models for undirected graphs. Dependence graphs for directed models are a natural extension of what we describe here, but we only discuss them briefly.

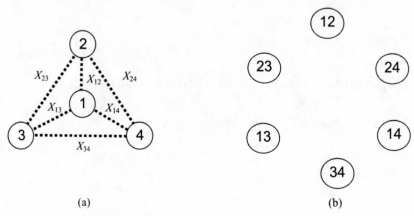

(a)   (b)

Figure 7.1. Tie-variables of (a) four-node graph and (b) associated Bernoulli dependence graph.

7.2   Dependence Graph

Frank and Strauss (1986) proposed a dependence graph D to represent the dependence assumptions for tie-variables.[1] The dependence graph is a representation of the way in which tie-variables may depend on one another.

Formally, a dependence graph D for a (random) graph G is defined using the tie-variables X_{ij} from G. D has as its node set the tie-variables X_{ij} so that there are $n(n-1)/2$ and $n(n-1)$ nodes in D according to whether G is undirected or directed. The edges of D, however, represent the conditional dependencies among the tie-variables of G. That is, (X_{ij},X_{kl}) is an edge of D if and only if X_{ij} and X_{kl} are assumed to be conditionally dependent given the values of all remaining tie-variables. Hence, the dependence graph indicates which random variables are conditionally dependent on (or conditionally independent of) each other. It is worth emphasizing that the dependencies among random variables are indeed a matter of assumption. They reflect the basic hypotheses that the researcher assumes underpin the model.

Take as a simple example possible networks on only four nodes. With four nodes, there are exactly six tie-variables (Figure 7.1a). Thus, the dependence graph will have six nodes, one for each tie-variable. For instance, the tie-variable X_{23} in Figure 7.1a is represented by node 23 in the dependence graph.

---

[1]   Frank and Strauss derived their dependence graph from similar notions in the graphical modeling literature (see Lauritzen, 1996). In that literature, the same construct is termed an "independence graph."

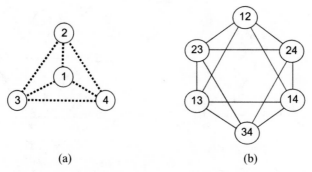

Figure 7.2. Tie-variables of (a) four-node graph and (b) associated Markov dependence graph.

Suppose we want D to represent the Bernoulli dependence assumption, where tie-variables are independent of each other. An edge in the dependence graph indicates a conditional dependence between two tie-variables, so in this case there are no edges in D. The dependence graph for the Bernoulli assumption is an empty graph as in Figure 7.1b.

Suppose, instead, that the dependence graph D represents Markov graph dependence. Then two tie-variables X_{ij} and X_{hm} are dependent, given the rest of X, if the intersection of $\{i,j\}$ and $\{h,m\}$ is nonempty. Edges in D are between tie-variables that share a node as in Figure 7.2b (e.g., there is an edge between nodes 12 and 24 because they have node 2 in common).

A very important feature of this dependence graph is that although there are edges between many nodes in Figure 7.2b, D is not complete (e.g., there is no edge between nodes 12 and 34). What this means is that, for a given graph G, once we know the rest of the graph (i.e., the values of the tie-variables X_{ij} for every pair of nodes excluding 12 and 34), then knowing X_{12} does not help us determine X_{34}: the two variables are conditionally independent (i.e., conditional on the rest of the graph). There must be some level of independence or else the models will not be identifiable and cannot be estimated from data.

For the social circuit model, the dependence assumption states that, in addition to Markov dependencies, two tie-variables X_{ij} and X_{hm} are conditionally dependent even when the intersection of $\{i,j\}$ and $\{h,m\}$ is empty, as long as ties between i and h and between j and m exist in the observed graph G. This assumption may be described in terms of the 4-cycle as explained in previous chapters. This complicates the representation of a dependence graph because some edges may appear due to the values of tie-variables in G. Note, however, that the social circuit models also presuppose Markov dependence, so the dependencies in Figure 7.2b at the least are present. In Figure 7.2b, there is no edge

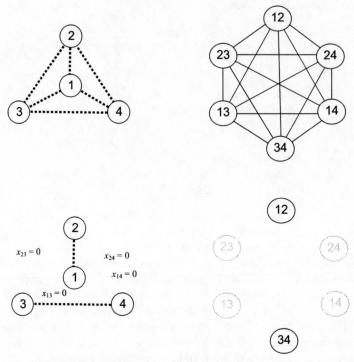

Figure 7.3. Tie-variables of social circuit graph and its dependence graph (top) and dependence graph conditional on some tie-variables being zero (greyed out vertices not in partial dependence graph).

between 12 and 34, but in social circuit dependence there may be an edge between 12 and 34 if, for example, $x_{13} = x_{24} = 1$ because then a 4-cycle can be created. If, however, all tie-variables other than X_{13} and X_{24} are zero, we know that the ties $\{1,2\}$ and $\{3,4\}$ could not create a 4-cycle, and in that scenario X_{13} and X_{24} are independent. So, there is some level of independence available for an identifiable model; this may be specified in the "partial dependence graph" conditional on some variables being zero, $x_{13} = x_{14} = x_{23} = x_{24} = 0$ (in Figure 7.3). In this dependence graph, if we know that $x_{13} = x_{14} = x_{23} = x_{24} = 0$ – represented in Figure 7.3 by the lighter shading of the nodes 13, 14, 23, and 24 – then X_{13} and X_{24} are independent, and hence there is no edge between 12 and 34. In principle, there is a partial dependence graph describing the dependencies that exist when each possible subset of tie-variables is set to zero, so that the complex social circuit dependence structure (for any G) can – again, in principle – be represented by a series of partial dependence graphs. Once again, we see that, as for the Markov dependence graph, there are pairs of tie-variables in the partial dependence graph that are not tied. Consequently, there are instances of conditional independence. Partial conditional dependence was introduced for a number of different conditions for ERGMs in Pattison and Robins (2002), where further technical details can be found.

We have now constructed dependence graphs for three dependence assumptions. Frank and Strauss (1986) showed that the dependence graph is a conceptual link between the dependence assumptions and how they are expressed in the data. Although the dependence assumption implies that a network can be characterized by a limited number of subgraphs, the corresponding dependence graph delineates the subgraphs of particular importance.

In summary, the link between the dependence graph and the model is that collections of nodes in D that are mutually connected to each other – that is, cliques of tie-variables in D – can be represented in the model by the corresponding interaction effects among tie-variables. Each clique in the dependence graph represents a possible configuration and hence a possible parameter in the model. More important, if there is no clique in D for a set of nodes, then there should not be a configuration involving that set of nodes in the model.

For example, if the two tie-variables X_{12} and X_{13} are linked in D, then a model for the network that respects the dependence assumption underlying D may include the interaction effect $X_{12}X_{13}$. If X_{12} and X_{13} are linked in D, then X_{12} and X_{13} are conditionally dependent given the rest of G. By the definition of dependence, $\Pr(X_{12} = x_{12}, X_{13} = x_{13}|rest) \neq \Pr(X_{12} = x_{12}|rest)\Pr(X_{13} = x_{13}|rest)$, so that the ties 12 and 13 would co-occur with a probability different from expected under the marginal probabilities for 12 and 13. The implication is that there may be an interaction effect $X_{12}X_{13}$. Furthermore, suppose that X_{12}, X_{13}, and X_{23} were all jointly dependent given the rest of the graph (as they would be under a Markov assumption), then the extent of the co-occurrence of these three tie-variables would be measured by the interaction $X_{12}X_{13}X_{23}$.

Note that if $x_{12} = x_{13} = 1$, then $x_{12}x_{13} = 1$, and there is a 2-star on node 1. Thus, the interaction effect $x_{12}x_{13}$ represents a possible 2-star, a Markov configuration, and so a parameter in the Markov model. Furthermore, if $x_{12} = x_{13} = x_{23} = 1$, then $x_{12}x_{13}x_{23} = 1$, and there is a triangle on nodes 1, 2, and 3. Hence, the interaction effect $X_{12}X_{13}X_{23}$ represents a possible triangle, another Markov configuration, and so another parameter in the Markov model. It is in this way that the cliques of the dependence graph come to identify possible effects in the model. Suppose, however, that $x_{12} = x_{34} = 1$, then although it is true that $x_{12}x_{34} = 1$, there is no clique for 12 and 34 in D because there is no edge between them. So, *for a Markov model*, it would be improper to include a parameter for this configuration of ties.

7.2.1   Hammersley-Clifford Theorem and Sufficient Statistics

The important link between the probability of a graph and the dependence graph is provided by the Hammersley-Clifford theorem (Besag, 1974). The theorem is an important basis for the graphical modeling literature (e.g., Lauritzen, 1996) and was introduced into network statistical methodology by Frank and Strauss (1986). The main points are the following (we have left out the details, which can be found in Frank and Strauss (1986) and Robins and Pattison (2005)).

The probability distribution function for any graph distribution may be written $\Pr(X = x) = \kappa^{-1} \exp Q(x)$ for some real-valued function Q (where κ is a normalizing constant and assuming $\Pr(X = x) > 0$ for all $x \in X$). By writing $Q(x) = \log\{\Pr(X = x)/\Pr(X = x^{(0)})\}$ with reference to the empty graph $x^{(0)}$, we can use the inclusion–exclusion principle to write $Q(x) = \sum \lambda_A(x_A)$ for functions λ_A defined on subsets $A \subseteq J$. For a ratio $\Pr(X = \Delta_{ij}^+ x)/\Pr(X = \Delta_{ij}^- x)$, it follows from the definition of conditional probability that $Q(\Delta_{ij}^+ x) - Q(\Delta_{ij}^- x)$ may be a function only of $x_{k\ell}$ that x_{ij} is *conditionally dependent on* – these $x_{k\ell}$ are given by D. Hence, it can be seen (although this may require some thought) that $\lambda_A(x_A) \neq 0$ only for A that are cliques of D.

To arrive at the sufficient statistics, note first that for a binary graph we may write $\lambda_A(x_A) = \theta_A \prod_{\{i,j\} \in A} x_{ij}$. Because $\prod_{\{i,j\} \in A} x_{ij}$ is a product of binary variables, it can only take two values: 1 if all the variables in the index set A are equal to one, and 0 if at least one of the variables in the index set A is equal to zero. We may call A a configuration because it corresponds to a subset of potential ties, and $\lambda_A(x_A) = \theta_A$ when all ties of the configuration A are present. If, for example, A is equal to $\{i,j\},\{j,h\},\{h,i\}$, A is present if the triangle involving nodes i, j, and h is present (i.e., if $x_{ij}x_{jh}x_{hi} = 1$ or x_{ij}, x_{jh}, and x_{hi} are all equal to one). The function λ_A is called the A interaction in X.

The model thus expressed in terms of $\lambda_A(x_A) = \theta_A \prod_{\{i,j\} \in A} x_{ij}$ has the form of an exponential random graph model as presented in Chapter 6 (Equation 6.2). In other words, the Hammersley-Clifford theorem completely determines the general form of the model once a dependence assumption is adopted. In these network terms, the theorem can be expressed as

$$\Pr(X = x) = \kappa^{-1} \exp \sum_{A \subseteq J^*} \theta_A \prod_{\{i,j\} \in A} x_{ij}$$
$$= \kappa^{-1} \exp \sum_{A \subseteq J^*} \theta_A z_A(x), \tag{7.1}$$

where J^* is the set of all cliques of the dependence graph, θ_A is a parameter associated with the clique (configuration) A, and $z_A(x)$ is an indicator variable that has value 1 if configuration A is observed in graph x, and is 0 otherwise.

It is worth noting that any single tie-variable is also a clique in the dependence graph, and any subgraph of a clique is also a clique (except for certain partial dependence structures). Hence, if A is a clique of D, then so is every subset of A; consequently, if A is a possible configuration in the model, so are subgraphs of A.

7.2.2 Sufficient Subgraphs for Nondirected Graphs

Bernoulli Model. For the Bernoulli model, the dependence graph (Figure 7.1b) is an empty graph, and hence the only cliques are those comprising a single node from D, each of which relates to an edge in the graph x. So, a model given by Equation (7.1) has a unique parameter for each tie-variable, a large number of parameters. For example, for a network with 20 nodes, the model has $\binom{20}{2} = 190$ parameters to be estimated.

One way of reducing the number of distinct configurations, A, and corresponding parameters, θ_A, is to assume that all structurally identical graphs are equally probable (i.e., that only the structure is relevant). This homogeneity assumption is a central ingredient in modeling networks using ERGMs.

For example, let the parameter θ_{ij} correspond to the edge configuration $A = \{i,j\}$. For a homogeneous model, we equate the parameters $\theta_{ij} = \theta_L$ for all i,j. From Equation (7.1), we then have that

$$\Pr(X = x) = \kappa^{-1} \exp \sum_{A \subseteq J^*} \theta_A \prod_{(i,j) \in A} x_{ij}$$

$$= \kappa^{-1} \exp \sum_{(i,j)} \theta_{ij} x_{ij} = \kappa^{-1} \exp \theta_L L(x),$$

where $L(x) = \sum_{i<j} x_{ij}$ is the number of edges in x. Having imposed the homogeneity assumption for the case where $n = 20$ vertices, instead of the previous 190 configurations, we only need to consider counts of the edges. Once we impose homogeneity in this way (irrespective of the particular dependence assumption used), the statistics, $z_A(x)$, in Equation (7.1) become more than indicator variables for individual configurations. Rather, they rather reduce to counts in x of configurations of particular types, and then Equation (7.1) takes on the familiar form of an ERGM presented in Chapter 6.

For the Bernoulli model, the number of edges is *sufficient* information for the parameter θ_L, and hence sufficient information about the model defined by the Bernoulli dependence graph and the interactions. We say that the subgraph is a "sufficient subgraph" because its count is a sufficient

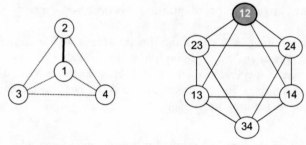

Figure 7.4. Singleton clique in dependence graph and corresponding configuration in X.

statistic in the same way that the number of heads in n flips of a (biased) coin is a sufficient statistic for the probability of heads – letting "1" denote "heads," we do not need to know if the sequence was (1,0,0,1,0) or (0,1,0,0,1), only that the total was 2. Hence, the probability of observing a particular graph is dependent on the graph statistic $z(x)$ for x and corresponding parameter θ.

Markov Model. For the Markov model, just as in the Bernoulli model, the singleton cliques correspond to the individual tie-variables, such as 12 in Figure 7.4.

As described previously, the clique 12, 23 in D corresponds to X_{12} and X_{23}, a configuration in X that is a 2-star centered on vertex 2 whenever $x_{12} = x_{23} = 1$. In contrast, the subgraph in D that is induced by 12 and 34 is not complete because these two vertices are not tied. Cliques of size 3 in D correspond to two different configurations in X. For example, the 3-clique in Figure 7.5, consisting of nodes 12, 23, and 24, all have node 2 from G in common, and therefore correspond to a 3-star centered on node 2 in G. The clique 12, 23, 13 in Figure 7.6 corresponds to a triangle configuration in X.

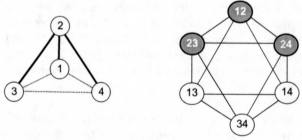

Figure 7.5. Three-clique in dependence graph and corresponding 3-star configuration in X.

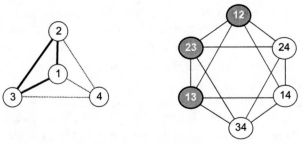

Figure 7.6. Three-clique in dependence graph and corresponding triangle configuration in X.

For Markov graph models, the cliques in *D* correspond to edges, stars, or triangles (Frank & Strauss, 1986). The Hammersley-Clifford theorem informs us that Markov random graphs are completely characterized by their edges, stars, and triangles, the sufficient subgraphs of the Markov random graph model. In other words, for any graph in **X**, its probability, under the Markov assumption, is completely determined by the numbers of edges, stars, and triangles. Whether there is, for example, a complete subgraph with five vertices is not important other than the fact that it contributes ten triangles, ten edges, and so on.

We reiterate that star and triangle configurations correspond to interactions of tie-variables that arise from the Markov dependence assumption. In each case, the interaction term informs us how much more likely (or unlikely) the particular configuration is in comparison to that expected from the probabilities of the respective tie-variables alone. As a result, in a properly hierarchical model, where higher-order interaction effects are included with appropriate lower-order effects, an interaction term gives us information about the presence of a configuration, taking into account the lower-order effects. There is a direct comparison here with a standard log-linear model. So, a 2-star parameter represents a centralization effect, taking into account the lower-order edge effect. In other words, inferences based on a 2-star parameter are conditional on the number of edges, so we can infer whether there are more than expected 2-stars given the number of edges (i.e., more than expected centralization given the density). Similarly, a 3-star parameter permits inferences, taking into account the numbers of 2-stars and edges. Importantly, a triangle parameter represents triangulation conditional on the number of 2-stars and edges. This permits inferences about network closure, given the number of density and the number of 2-paths (i.e., the potential for closure).

This is a remarkable result: given only a simple assumption regarding dependence between the ties, we do not need to know the exact structure of a network in order to know how likely it is, we only need to know some of the subgraphs (edges, stars, triangles) of this network. Let us consider what listing the stars and triangles entail. For each of the n nodes, the other $n - 1$ nodes may have edges that can be combined in $\binom{n-1}{2}$ ways such that the node is the center of a 2-star, and hence there are $n\binom{n-1}{2}$ distinct possible 2-stars. In general, there are $n\binom{n-1}{k}$ distinct possible k-stars, for $k = 2, \ldots, n - 1$. Because a triangle includes three nodes, the number of distinct possible triangles is given by $\binom{n}{3}$. If we were to allow for a separate parameter for each configuration corresponding to a clique in the dependence graph, we would have too many parameters. For example, a Markov graph on twenty vertices would have $\binom{20-1}{2} + 20\binom{20-1}{3} + 20\binom{20-1}{4} + \cdots + 20\binom{20-1}{19} + \binom{20}{3} = 10,486,690$ distinct parameters but only 190 tie-variables.

As before, to reduce the number of distinct configurations and corresponding parameters, we impose homogeneity whereby all structurally identical graphs are equally probable. This means, for instance, that the effect for every 2-star is identical, so that there is one 2-star parameter, with a statistic that is the count of the number of 2-stars. Suppose we apply a Markov dependence assumption to Equation (7.1). Among the possible configurations A are 2-stars with terms $\sum_i \sum_{j < h, j, h \neq i} \theta_{ijh} x_{ij} x_{ih}$ in the equation. We impose homogeneity by letting $\theta_A = \theta_{S(2)}$ for all A corresponding to 2-stars. Then the summation across all 2-star terms reduces to $\theta_{S(2)} S_2(x)$, where $S_2(x)$ is the number of 2-stars in x. Similar results follow for the other configurations (edges, other stars and triangles), so that in the end Equation (7.1) reduces to the Markov model familiar from Chapter 6. Having imposed the homogeneity assumption, with twenty nodes, instead of 10 million subgraphs, we only need to consider counts of edges, of eighteen different star configurations and of triangle configurations. The numbers of edges, of stars of different orders, and of triangles are *sufficient* information for the parameters and hence constitute sufficient statistics for the model. It is worth emphasizing that imposing homogeneity allows us to consider graph topology (the structure of the graph) irrespective of the labeling of the graph nodes.

The homogeneity assumption reduces the model to n parameters, comprising an edge and triangle parameter and $(n - 2)$ star parameters. In most instances, we cannot have unique parameters for all stars. For most data, such a model will not be estimable (e.g., if no node is connected to every other node, the count of $(n - 1)$-stars is zero and the parameter cannot be estimated). In any event, for a large network, n parameters is still not very parsimonious. One way of reducing the number of star parameters is by setting some of them to zero. Setting higher-order parameters to zero is analogous to ignoring higher-order interactions among predictors in a standard logistic regression. For example, Frank and Strauss (1986) suggested (as one possible model) the "triad model" with only an edge, a

2-star, and a triangle parameter. All 3-star and higher-order star parameters are set to zero. Robins, Pattison, and Woolcock (2005) suggested an extension that included a nonzero 3-star parameter. However, for many data sets, these models still cannot be estimated properly, as explained in Chapter 6. An alternative to restricting the number of star parameters is to constrain them into a single alternating star parameter. This is now the preferred way to proceed and helps, although does not eliminate, the problems with estimation. The details are set out in Chapter 6.

We have gone through Bernoulli and Markov dependence at some length because these simpler models illustrate the arguments well. However, we emphasize that for the practical purposes of fitting data, these models will only rarely be used with success. Social circuit models with alternating parameter constraints are by far the preferred option to avoid estimation difficulties.

Social Circuit Dependence. We have already mentioned how the social circuit partial dependence assumption was formalized for the case of random graph models by Pattison and Robins (2002) using partial dependence graphs. Snijders et al. (2006) proposed a model that satisfies the social circuit independence assumption. As described in connection with Figure 7.3, this model means that some tie-variables may be conditionally dependent given the presence of other ties, even if they do not share a node. As explained in Chapter 6, the model consists of all Markov parameters with the addition of parameters for k-triangles and k-independent 2-paths. Other configurations are also consistent with the dependence assumptions but to date have not been widely used (e.g., k-cliques).

Analogous to the case of Markov graphs, allowing for configurations that correspond to all distinct k-triangles would lead to too many statistics, and hence a homogeneity restriction is imposed so that all structurally identical graphs have the same probability under the model. Still, with this homogeneity restriction, the number of triangle parameters will be too large. Using the same rationale as for the introduction of alternating stars, a restriction can be imposed on the k-triangle parameters to produce the alternating triangle parameter, as explained in Chapter 6.

Sufficient Subgraphs for Directed Graphs. Using the same approach as described previously, we can derive sufficient statistics for directed graphs. The important thing to bear in mind is that there are twice as many tie-variables for a directed graph, and thus, there are twice as many nodes in the dependence graph (Figure 7.7). Because there are now two tie-variables for each node pair, there is a greater variety of different star and triangle configurations in Markov dependence. The singleton cliques correspond to a (directed) arc, and cliques 12 and 21 in Figure 7.7 correspond to two distinct configurations.

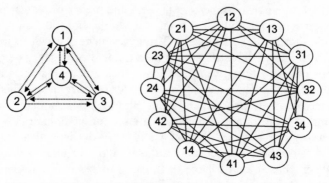

Figure 7.7. Tie-variables for directed graph on four vertices with corresponding Markov dependence graph.

Let us return to the example of a four-node graph using a Markov dependence assumption. Applying the homogeneity restriction as discussed previously, the sufficient subgraphs derived from D in Figure 7.7 are given in Figure 7.8.

In addition to arcs, there is another dyadic configuration, namely, reciprocated arcs (cliques in D of the type {12,21}). There are also various star configurations, as well as seven triangle statistics representing different types of relational closure in a subgroup of three actors. As can be seen, parameters for these configurations essentially parameterize the triad census of a graph (Frank, 1979; Frank & Strauss, 1986; Holland & Leinhardt, 1981; Wasserman & Faust, 1994). If the parameters corresponding to configurations with more than three vertices are set to zero, the directed Markov graph model may be parameterized directly in terms of the triad census.

The social circuit dependence assumption for directed graphs builds naturally on that of the partial dependence approach described previously in this chapter. We do not go into details here. Suffice it to say that the sufficient subgraphs include the directed k-triangle and k-path configurations described in Chapter 6. The alternating or geometrically weighted form of the parameters is the most commonly used in fitting data.

7.3   Dependence Graphs Involving Attributes

Attribute variables can also be introduced into dependence graphs, either as exogenous predictors of network ties (social selection effects) or outcome variables from network structure (social influence effects). These types of models are presented in Chapters 8 and 9. There are some additional complexities in introducing exogenous predictors and different variable types into a dependence graph formulation that are beyond the

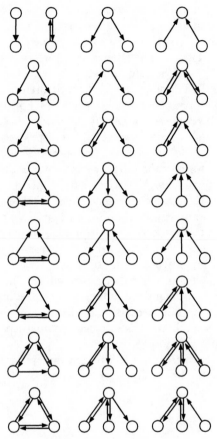

Figure 7.8. Sufficient subgraphs for directed Markov graph on four vertices.

scope of this chapter. Interested readers may consult Robins, Pattison, and Elliott (2001); Robins, Elliott, and Pattison (2001); and Robins and Pattison (2005).

7.4 Conclusion

The ERGM is a stochastic model in which the observed network is regarded as one realization from a probability distribution on the set of possible networks or graphs X on a fixed set of nodes. The probability of any particular realization x depends on parameters and statistics associated with certain configurations of x. These configurations are not arbitrarily chosen; on the contrary, they are seen as the outcomes of particular social processes that give rise to the network.

The process of formulating ERGMs for networks may be seen as comprising the following steps. First, a dependence structure is postulated in the form of dependence graph. Second, cliques are derived from the dependence graphs. Third, the Hammersley-Clifford theorem is applied to provide a factorization with parameters based on cliques. Fourth, some homogeneity constraints are proposed to identify the model. As a result, the general form of the model has parameters and statistics relating to the presence of various types of local network configurations.

Elaborations of this basic form of the model permit different forms of dependence assumptions among network variables to be incorporated in a hierarchy of model forms. In addition, exogenous variables (e.g., node attributes or geographic location) can be built in. This general approach to model building also permits the construction of models for patterns of social influence within a network (i.e., models that allow individual-level attributes to be predicted from network ties).

Work on other possible forms of dependence is ongoing. The advantages of a systematic approach of understanding dependence are more than theoretic: the type of data that need to be collected in a snowball sample to estimate a large-scale ERGM is informed by the dependence structure. Moreover, it is possible to identify a hierarchy of dependence assumptions and so investigate further model elaborations systematically. These issues are taken up in the final chapter of this book.

8

Social Selection, Dyadic Covariates, and Geospatial Effects

Garry Robins and Galina Daraganova

8.1 Individual, Dyadic, and Other Attributes

In this chapter, we introduce models that include effects for actor attributes and dyadic covariates. Actor attributes are individual-level measures on the nodes of the network. Social selection models examine whether attribute-related processes affect network ties (e.g., homophily processes whereby network ties tend to occur between individuals with similar actor attributes) (McPherson, Smith-Lovin, & Cook, 2001). A dyadic covariate, in contrast, is a measure on each dyad, that is, on a pair of actors, and may similarly affect the presence of a tie. For instance, in a study of a trust network within an organization, the formal organizational hierarchy might partly shape the formation of trust ties. In that case, inclusion of the hierarchy as a dyadic covariate permits inferences about whether trust ties tend to align with hierarchical relationships (e.g., Tom is the boss of Fred). A binary dyadic covariate can be used to represent whether people share the same attribute or membership – that is, work at the same place, live in the same household, or attend the same church. Continuous dyadic covariates are also possible. Although spatial embedding of networks, to an extent, can be captured by dyadic continuous covariates, geospatial effects are a distinctive feature, so we provide a separate section in this chapter.

The preceding chapters outline the general ERGM methodology but concentrate exclusively on models for endogenous tie-based effects. The presence or absence of individual ties is affected by a surrounding neighborhood of other ties, with that neighborhood determined by the prevailing dependence assumption. These endogenous effects represent processes of network self-organization.

The inclusion of nodal attributes in a model can be seen as a relaxation of the assumption that endogenous effects are homogeneous across all nodes. However, we prefer to consider attribute effects as indicative of

91

exogenous processes that operate alongside endogenous self-organizing mechanisms. An exogenous effect is assumed to be fixed and hence external to the self-organizing system. For instance, an attribute such as gender can be considered fixed for each actor in the network, although it still varies across actors. The variable *gender* is then exogenous in that it may affect the structure of network ties, but not vice versa (i.e., we may not expect the presence of a network tie to affect an actor's gender). Similarly, the formal organizational hierarchy may be an exogenous dyadic covariate for a network of organizational trust. It is variable in that for each pair of actors, there may or may not be a hierarchical relationship, so that a second network could be defined with ties present when i is the boss of j. This second network of formal hierarchical ties may affect the network of trust (e.g., there may be a tendency for people to trust their bosses), but the hierarchical network *boss of* is exogenous (fixed). Whatever network structure there is to the social system of trust, it does not affect the formal organizational hierarchy.

Actor attributes can be any relevant measures on the nodes. They may include attributes that are genuinely nonchangeable (e.g., birthplace), or attributes that change so slowly or so rarely that in the context of a study they may be taken as fixed in practice (e.g., age in cross-sectional studies). In these cases, there can be little dispute that the attributes should be treated as exogenous. So, the network research question is whether these attributes affect the presence or absence of network ties. This is a question of "social selection": actors may select one another as network partners, depending on the attributes that they have. Akin to a regression, the attributes are predictors of network ties.

However, actor attributes also include variables such as attitudes or behaviors that are liable to change. We can also treat these as exogenous in an ERGM social selection model, but in doing so we are making certain implicit assumptions, principally that the attribute is not changed by the network ties. Of course, this may not always be realistic. Along with social selection, there may also be processes of network "social influence," whereby the presence of a tie may alter an attribute. For instance, people may be influenced by their network partners to change their opinions or behaviors. We cannot readily distinguish influence and selection effects in cross-sectional data (in our next chapter, we discuss this point further when presenting models for social influence). So, in ERGM social selection models, if the attributes are possibly changeable, we are still treating them as predictors of network ties but – again, analogous to a cross-sectional regression – we need to be careful about our inferences. If we see a significant attribute effect, we have evidence for an association between attributes and network ties, but we cannot make confident causal inferences. We do not know whether the attribute leads to the tie, or vice versa, so we cannot be sure whether the observed effect is one of selection or influence. If we want to distinguish selection from influence, we need to collect longitudinal data and use other methods (as discussed in Chapter 11).

In many circumstances, this is not overly problematic. For instance, in a hypothesis testing framework, if the theoretical hypothesis is about homophily, then the use of a social selection ERGM makes sense to examine evidence for the hypothesis. In other instances, inference about an association between ties and attributes, not the causality, may be sufficient for a given study. If the focus of a study is on network structure and not the attributes, it can make sense to treat attributes as predictors, akin to control variables that enable principled inferences about endogenous network structure. These types of decisions are familiar from standard regression analyses, where the associations between predictor and outcome variables are established, but not the direction of causality.

The issue of controlling variables is important. Sometimes we want to make inferences about attribute processes such as homophily. We still need to include endogenous tie-based effects in our model to cater for the dependencies within the data so that we can make sound inferences. Thus, a model with both exogenous attribute effects and endogenous tie effects can be viewed in two ways: if the focus is on the attribute selection effects, the endogenous network tie processes are controlled, and if the focus is on the network structure, the attribute variables operate as controls on selection effects.

Because social selection models investigate associations between ties and attributes, we often refer to attribute-based effects as "actor-relation effects" to emphasize this aspect of association between the two types of variable.

For notation, we continue to use X_{ij} to denote a binary network tie-variable. We denote an attribute variable on node i as Y_i and a dyadic covariate between nodes i and j as W_{ij}. In this chapter, we treat attribute variables and dyadic covariates as binary or continuous, although we make some comments on categorical attributes. The attribute and covariate effects described below can all be fitted using the PNet estimation software.

8.2   ERGM Social Selection Models

An ERGM social selection model involves various forms of dependence between attribute and network tie-variables. The precise details are beyond the scope of this chapter, but, broadly, attribute variables are taken as exogenous predictors of network tie-variables at the same time that there are dependencies among the network variables. Interested readers should consult Robins, Elliott, and Pattison (2001), who set out dependencies for ERGM selection models within the framework

Table 8.1. *Some social selection configurations
for undirected networks*

Configuration		Statistic	Parameter
Binary attributes			
1	●———○	$\sum_{i<j} x_{ij}(y_i + y_j)$	Attribute-based activity
2	●———●	$\sum_{i<j} x_{ij} y_i y_j$	Homophily (interaction)
Continuous attributes			
3	⬤———○	$\sum_{i<j} x_{ij}(y_i + y_j)$	Attribute-based activity
4	⬤———●	$\sum_{i<j} |y_i - y_j| x_{ij}$	Homophily (difference)

of Markov endogenous network processes. Each attribute effect in an ERGM selection model is a statistical interaction between at least one attribute and one tie-variable, so that configurations involve not just patterns of ties but also colors on the nodes (for binary and categorical attribute variables), or size of nodes (for continuous attribute variables).

The general form of an ERGM social selection model is as follows:

$$\Pr(X = x | Y = y) = \frac{1}{\kappa} \exp(\theta^T z(x) + \theta_a^T z_a(x, y)), \qquad (8.1)$$

where θ and z are parameters and statistics for endogenous network effects as discussed in previous chapters, and θ_a and z_a are parameters and statistics for social selection configurations involving an interaction of network (x) and attribute (y) variables.

For binary and continuous attribute variables, the most important social selection configurations are presented in Tables 8.1 and 8.2. In these tables, a filled circle represents a node with attribute value $y_i = 1$. For instance, if the attribute variable *gender* is scored 0 for male and 1 for female, the filled circle represents "female." (For simplicity, we just say that the node "has the attribute"; thus, in the example of *gender*, the attribute can be understood as "being female," given the scoring.) For continuous attribute variables, a larger score on the attribute is represented by a node of larger size. An unfilled circle represents a node, irrespective of attribute status. So, for instance, line 1 of Table 8.1 presents a configuration with a tie from a node with the attribute to another node; that is, the configuration represents the network activity of nodes with the attribute. (In the statistics columns of Tables 8.1 and 8.2, summations are across all nodes i and j, but with the proviso in some cases that $i < j$ to avoid double counting of configurations.)

Table 8.2. *Some social selection configurations for directed networks*

Single arc effects			
Binary attributes			
1	●——▶○	$\sum_{i,j} y_i x_{ij}$	Sender effect (attribute-based activity)
2	○——▶●	$\sum_{i,j} y_j x_{ij}$	Receiver effect (attribute-based popularity)
3	●——▶●	$\sum_{i,j} x_{ij} y_i y_j$	Homophily (interaction)
Continuous attributes			
4	●——▶○	$\sum_{i,j} y_i x_{ij}$	Sender effect (attribute-based activity)
5	○——▶●	$\sum_{i,j} y_j x_{ij}$	Receiver effect (attribute-based popularity)
6	●——▶●	$\sum_{i,j} |y_i - y_j| x_{ij}$	Homophily (single arc difference)
Mutual effects			
Binary attributes			
7	●⇄○	$\sum_{i<j} (y_i + y_j) x_{ij} x_{ji}$	Mutual activity
8	●⇄●	$\sum_{i<j} y_i y_j x_{ij} x_{ji}$	Mutual homophily (mutual difference)

Tables 8.1 and 8.2 present only selection effects related to dyads. It is also possible to have effects relating to stars, triads, and other configurations, with one or more colored (or sized) nodes occupying different positions within the configuration. See Robins, Elliott, and Pattison (2001) for examples.

8.2.1   Models for Undirected Networks

For undirected networks (Table 8.1), dyadic attribute effects are relatively simple. For binary attribute variables, line 1 of Table 8.1 presents a configuration of a node with the attribute sending a tie to another node (irrespective of its attribute status). The statistic is the count of this configuration in the graph. This is an activity effect associated with the attribute. A positive parameter indicates that nodes with the attribute tend to have higher network activity (i.e., more ties) than nodes without the attribute (this may also be called the "main effect" of an attribute). Line 2, however, represents a homophily effect, whereby nodes with the attribute tend to have ties with each other. There are, of course, various ways to implement this effect: in line 2, the statistic indicates an interaction (i.e., a product) between the two attribute variables for nodes i and j, so that it comes into effect when both variables equal 1 (i.e., when both nodes have the attribute).

It is usually helpful to have both activity and homophily effects in the one model. If one type of node (e.g., females) is more active, such nodes will form more ties among themselves as a simple consequence of greater activity, without the necessity of an independent process whereby females specifically select females. With both parameters in the model, the activity effect is controlled and a significant homophily parameter then indicates an independent effect for females selecting females. It is certainly desirable to have both parameters in the model if the research question relates to possible homophily effects.

For categorical attribute variables (e.g., different departments in an organization), homophily could be implemented with a "same category" effect, with statistic $\sum_{i<j} x_{ij} I\{y_i = y_j\}$, where $I\{a\}$ is an indicator that is 1 when the statement is true (0, otherwise), when a positive parameter would indicate homophily (i.e., two nodes in the same category tend to be associated with the presence of a network tie. This effect is referred to as nodematch in statnet; statnet offers a variety of ways of parametrizing different covariate effects, such as nodecov, nodefactor, and nodemix, the latter being a stochastic a priori blockmodel).

Counterpart effects for continuous attributes are in lines 3 and 4 of Table 8.1. Here, the homophily statistic indicates an absolute difference effect, in which case a *negative* parameter indicates homophily (i.e., a *smaller difference* in attribute between the two nodes is associated with the presence of a tie). Of course, other parameterizations of homophily are also possible (e.g., Euclidean instead of absolute distance or interaction). Interaction for continuous covariates captures a different aspect of homophily, namely, where the homophily operates on the basis of extremes – the further the two actors are away from zero (or the mean if the scores are standardized), the more likely they are to choose each other.

8.2.2   Models for Directed Networks

For directed networks, the direction of an arc permits more dyadic effects. In Table 8.2, lines 1 to 3 present single arc effects that include both an activity and a popularity effect, in addition to a homophily parameter. Investigation of homophily for a binary attribute in a directed network should include at least these three parameters. Lines 4 to 6 present counterpart configurations for continuous attributes. Once again, homophily for the binary interaction effect is indicated by a positive parameter value, and a continuous difference effect is indicated by a negative value. Sometimes there may also be interest in studying attribute effects in relation to reciprocated ties in directed networks, in which case the mutual activity and homophily effects for binary attributes (lines 7 and 8) could also be included (and counterpart effects for continuous attribute variables are possible but not presented here).

8.2.3   Conditional Odds Ratios

Just as with a logistic regression, it can sometimes be helpful for interpretation of selection effects to calculate a (conditional) odds ratio. Suppose we have an undirected network with a single binary attribute on the nodes, and we present a model with activity and homophily selection effects drawn from Table 8.1. Equation 8.1 then becomes

$$\Pr(X = x | Y = y) = \frac{1}{\kappa} \exp \left(\theta^T z(x) + \theta_a \sum_{i<j} x_{ij}(y_i + y_j) \right.$$

$$\left. + \theta_b \sum_{i<j} x_{ij} y_i y_j \right), \tag{8.2}$$

where θ_a and θ_b are activity and homophily parameters, respectively. Just as described in Chapter 6, there is an equivalent form of Equation (8.2) in a conditional odds form:

$$\frac{\Pr(X_{ij} = 1 | Y = y, X_{-ij} = x_{-ij})}{\Pr(X_{ij} = 0 | Y = y, X_{-ij} = x_{-ij})} = \exp\left(\theta^T \delta_{ij}^+(x) + \theta_a(y_i + y_j) + \theta_b y_i y_j\right), \tag{8.3}$$

where $\theta^T \delta_{ij}^+(x)$ is the weighted sum of change statistics for endogenous network effects described in Chapter 6 for the conditional logit. Note how the activity statistic becomes a sum of the attribute values for i and j because in predicting the conditional odds of X_{ij} in an undirected network, there are no grounds to privilege either i or j.

For the purposes of interpretation, suppose that we have two nodes, i and j, in a fixed neighborhood of network ties so that $\delta_{ij}^+(x)$ is always the same in what follows. Then let us assign different attribute values to the nodes. Of course, this is purely an abstract thought experiment, but it does help us interpret attribute effects. So, suppose the tie is between nodes without the attribute $(y_i = y_j = 0)$, then the conditional odds of the tie are simply $\exp\{\theta^T \delta_{ij}^+(x)\}$; if the tie is between one node with the attribute and one without $(y_i = 1, y_j = 0)$, then the conditional odds of the tie are $\exp(\theta^T \delta_{ij}^+(x) + \theta_a)$; and if the tie is between nodes with the attribute $(y_i = y_j = 1)$, then the conditional odds of the tie is $\exp(\theta^T \delta_{ij}^+(x) + 2\theta_a + \theta_b)$. The sum inside the exponential function in each case is called the "conditional log-odds."

Let us choose the case of two nodes without attributes (i.e., $y_i = y_j = 0$) as the baseline case. Then the ratio of the odds for one of the other two cases to the odds for the baseline case is called the "odds ratio." Thus, the odds ratio for the case where one node has the attribute is $\exp(\theta_a)$, and for both nodes with the attribute, the odds ratio is $\exp(2\theta_a + \theta_h)$. The interpretation is then straightforward and is analogous to the interpretation of odds ratios in logistic regression. The odds of the tie occurring for the pattern of attributes in the dyad are increased by a factor of the odds ratio over the baseline.

As an example, suppose in a study of gender homophily in schools where female is coded as "1" and male "0", the parameter estimate for activity is -1 and for homophily is 2. Then the odds ratio for a tie between a boy and a girl is $e^{-1} = 0.37$, and between two girls is $e^{-2+2} = e^0 = 1.0$. Remember that these odds ratios use the baseline of a tie between two boys. So, all other things being equal, the odds of a tie between two boys and two girls is the same (odds ratio $= 1$), whereas the odds of a tie between a boy and a girl is only 37% of that of a within-sex tie. The phrase "all other things being equal," of course, supposes that the two ties being compared are in an identical neighborhood of network ties, a situation that may not even occur in the data. The odds ratio analysis does, however, permit us to understand the effect of attribute variables over and above the endogenous processes in the data.

There are equivalent odds ratios calculations for directed models, but in these we need to distinguish between a sender and a receiver having the attribute. Suppose the model includes the three binary attribute single arc effects at the top of Table 8.2, with θ_s, θ_r, and θ_h being the estimates for sender, receiver, and homophily parameters, respectively. Again, let the case of $y_i = y_j = 0$ be the baseline. Then the odds ratio for a node with the attribute sending a tie to a node without the attribute is $\exp(\theta_s)$; the odds ratio for a node without the attribute sending a tie to a node with the attribute is $\exp(\theta_r)$; and the odds ratio for a tie between both nodes with the attribute is $\exp(\theta_s + \theta_r + \theta_h)$.

For continuous attributes, as with logistic regression, it is possible to make an interpretive decision on low and high scores on the attribute (e.g., 1 standard deviation below and above the mean, respectively, or the minimum and maximum values), and then select two low scoring nodes as a baseline and compare that with other patterns of attributes using odds ratios.

8.3   Dyadic Covariates

The use of dyadic covariates in ERGMs is often relatively straightforward. The interest lies in whether the dyadic covariate is associated with the

Table 8.3. *Dyadic covariate configurations for ERGMs*

Configuration	Statistic	Parameter
Undirected networks		
⊂━ ━ ━⊃	$\sum_{i,j} w_{ij} x_{ij}$	Entrainment (covariate edge)
Directed networks		
⊂━ ━ ▶○	$\sum_{i,j} w_{ij} x_{ij}$	Entrainment (covariate arc)

presence of an observed tie. In Table 8.3, we present an "entrainment" effect that captures such an association for both directed and undirected networks. For example, one of the research questions might be to explore whether people from the same department are more likely to form an advice relationship. Here, "same department" is a dyadic covariate. A continuous dyadic covariate might be the amount of time two individuals work together on the same project.

If the dyadic covariate is another network, and something more than a simple control is of interest, then it is possible to extend these effects by using a bivariate ERGM to model the two networks simultaneously, as presented in Chapter 10. Sometimes, of course, a dyadic covariate is not another network but involves a complex conceptualization in its own right. An example is when dyadic covariates are derived from geographic space to which we now turn. (Various triadic effects are also possible as presented in Chapter 10 on multiple networks, such as i is friends with j, j is friends with k, and therefore i trusts k.)

8.4   Geospatial Effects

It has been widely recognized that the presence of a network tie between two individuals might be conditionally dependent on the physical distance between the geographic locations of the corresponding individuals. Spatial embedding of networks may be more complex than simple physical pairwise distance between actors. For instance, there may be a number of possible effects that a researcher may like to consider: closure may be specific to a particular area, distance from centroids may be an alternative to dyadic physical distance, natural spatial barriers or only nearest neighbors may need to be considered, and so on.

To extend ERGM to take into account the geographic arrangement of individuals, let us assume that each individual occupies a particular location in a physical space. This location is fixed and defined in a particular coordinate system (e.g., latitude and longitude coordinates). The preceding interactions between geographic and social space may be incorporated in the ERGM; however, for this initial treatment, we focus on dyadic distance. Based on the spatial locations, we can derive continuous distance variables for all possible physical distances among pairs of individuals in the network. In this form, the geographic arrangement of individuals acts as a dyadic covariate of pairwise distances, but there are a number of challenges associated with employing this approach.

First, a decision should be made regarding a distance measure. Distance between a pair of individuals can be calculated in a number of different ways, and different distance measures may be useful in different contexts. Euclidean distance is commonly used when the focus is on distances in a two-dimensional physical space. For large distances embedded in spherical space (e.g., the Earth's surface), the associated (Riemannian) arc distance could even be calculated.

Because the distance between spatial locations of any nodes i and j is a continuous measure, the second challenge is a choice of distance interaction function (Besag, 1974; Robins, Elliot & Pattison, 2001). The distance interaction function determines a functional relationship between a probability of a network tie between any two nodes and distance between the geographic locations of the corresponding nodes. A wide range of functions can be considered, and a simple curve-fitting exercise can be employed to determine an appropriate functional form. In practice, it is useful to restrict attention to parametric functions with some properties of interest. Butts (2012) defined four such properties: (1) monotonic versus nonmonotonic behavior, (2) behavior of the function when distance between spatial locations equals zero parameterized by a tie probability at the origin, (3) behavior of the function at small distances parameterized by a curvature near the origin, and (4) behavior of the function at large distances parameterized by a tail weight. Interested readers should consult Butts for a detailed description on these properties and corresponding sets of parametric forms. The most commonly used families of spatial interaction functions are exponential decay, $e^{-\alpha d}$, and inverse power law functions, $\frac{1}{1+\alpha d^\gamma}$ (Butts, 2002; Daraganova et al., 2012; Kleinberg, 2000; Latané, 1996). Although these functions are similar in their general model behavior, the main distinction is in tie probabilities at large distances and hence the functional form of the tail. For exponential decay functions, a tie probability at large distances becomes virtually zero beyond some given point, whereas in power law functions a tie probability at large distances is nonnegligible.

A challenge in the ERGM approach is to transform these functions suitably to exponential family form. Although it is quite simple to convert exponential decay functions, the explicit transformation of decreasing power law functions into the ERGM framework leads to a curved exponential family graph model and would require estimation of nonlinear parameters.

Daraganova et al. (2012) showed that in a simple case, when a tie probability between nodes i and j is conditionally independent of other ties in the graph given the distance between i and j, the general inverse power law function can be expressed as a natural logarithm of distance, $\log d$. Although it is always possible that the inclusion of more complex dependence assumptions may lead to changes in the relationship between tie probability and distance, for exploratory purposes one can make a logarithmic transformation of distance for all models and use it as a dyadic covariate in the ERGM formulation.

Extra caution should be given both to zero distances and to very extreme distances. There are two reasons. First, these distance values might lead to instability of model fitting. Second, from theoretical perspectives, different processes may be at work at different scales, and it may be that geospatial effects differ between very small distances, medium distances, and very long distances. There are two possible approaches to deal with zero and very extreme distances. In the first case, zero distances can be transformed to the smallest possible distance in the data set (Preciado et al., 2012), whereas extremely large distances can be disregarded (Daraganova et al., 2012). Daraganova et al. observed that there is a threshold distance after which there are occasional ties, at irregular intervals, and the rate at which these ties occur is seemingly without any dependence on distance. Therefore, it seems to be theoretically appropriate to fit data only for all observations at a distance no greater than the threshold. A second approach might be to derive two dummy variables to indicate zero (or near-zero) and extreme distances.

Hence, to take into account the geographic arrangement of individuals, a researcher should decide on a distance measure between spatial locations and the nature of the distance interaction function that relates distance to marginal tie probability. These decisions are of crucial importance because they determine the form of pairwise distances represented by a dyadic covariate in the ERGMs framework.

8.5   Conclusion

The incorporation of actor-attribute and dyadic covariate parameters is a natural and important element in ERGMs, either as parameters of direct research interest or relating to effects that need to be controlled. When specifying an ERGM for empirical data, any available and relevant actor or dyadic information should be parameterized into the model.

9

Autologistic Actor Attribute Models

Galina Daraganova and Garry Robins

9.1   Social Influence Models

So far, we focused on how a particular network structure may be a product of endogenous network processes (clustering, transitivity, popularity, etc.) and exogenous nodal and dyadic factors (gender, membership, geography, etc.). This chapter presents a class of cross-sectional network models that, rather than modeling network structure, allows us to understand how individual behavior may be constrained by position in a social network and by behavior of other actors in the network. For this purpose, we take network ties to be exogenous and model behaviors of the actors. We use the term "behavior" to refer to whatever nodal attribute we are interested in modeling, but this is understood to also cover, for example, attitudes and beliefs. The behavior is assumed to represent states and, at least in principle, may be liable to change, and possibly to change several times. However, the network ties are treated as exogenous and not changed by the attributes. In this chapter, we deal with binary attribute variables as measures of behavior, and if the variable is 1, we say that the actor displays the behavior, or that the behavior is present for that actor.

Social networks are often important to understand because social processes – such as diffusion of information, exercise of influence, and spread of disease – may be potentiated by network ties. There are relatively few models available for assessing the nature of this association between individual outcomes and network structure. An early instance of a general network approach to model social influence processes originates in network autocorrelation models (Doreian, 1982, 1989, 1990; Doreian, Teuter, & Wang, 1984; Erbring & Young, 1979; Leenders, 2002), based on work in spatial statistics (Anselin, 1982, 1984; Cliff & Ord, 1973, 1981; Ord, 1975). In this approach, network ties are taken to reflect dependencies among individual variables. An explicitly dynamic but deterministic theory of network-mediated social influence was developed by Friedkin (1998), who termed it the structural theory of social influence. This theory has its roots in the work of social psychologists and mathematicians, including DeGroot (1974), Erbring and Young (1979), French (1956), Friedkin and Johnsen (1997), Harary (1959), and others. Friedkin described it as "a mathematical formalization of the process of interpersonal influence that occurs in groups, affects persons' attitudes and opinions on issues, and produces interpersonal agreement, including group consensus, from an initial state of disagreement" (2003, 89). In particular, the structural theory of social influence describes a process in which a group of actors weigh and integrate the conflicting influences of significant others within the context of social structural constraints. Within this tradition, Valente (1995) explicitly modeled the diffusion of innovations across social structures. Modeling the status of the individual as a function of both individual and structural characteristics of the network is also an important approach to understanding the spread of infectious disease (contagion) in network epidemiology (Meyers, 2007; Sander et al., 2002).

These models were developed for social processes, such as influence, contagion, and diffusion, in which a network tie between two actors entails interdependent actor attributes. In other words, the network structure is used to help explain the distribution of attributes/behaviors. The models have enabled important empirical research on the diffusion processes in social networks in a variety of social science fields, including studies by Davies and Kandel (1981) and Epstein (1983) on the peer effect on educational decisions, the study by Gould (1991) on the mobilization in the Paris Commune, and the study by Burt and Doreian (1982) on the perceptions of the significance of journals by sociologists. Influence processes have also generated interest in economics, where they have gone by the general name of "peer effects" (Durlauf, 2001; Jackson, 2008; Manski, 1993). This term has been used to cover a variety of different forms of influence processes and has lately come to include network-mediated influence. Although these models have added substantially to the ability of researchers to understand the nature of the relationship between characteristic of individuals and their social networks, we propose to use the ERGM framework because it offers considerable flexibility in formulating models to examine different types of dependencies among variables.

9.2 Extending ERGMs to Distribution of Actor Attributes

Following the logic of ERGMs and the principled use of the dependence graph, Robins, Pattison, and Elliott (2001) proposed a class of autologistic actor attribute models that they called "social influence models" to distinguish them from social selection models. These models focus on modeling a distribution of attributes across a fixed network of relational ties. They do not attempt to model processes of interpersonal influence explicitly; rather, they are intended to investigate the extent to which a pattern of social relations among individuals (i.e., an individual's structural position and social proximity to others) may be associated with shared opinions and/or similar behavior. As such, these models allow insight into the consequences of diffusion.

In this class of models, an "attribute" of interest is regarded as a dependent stochastic variable measured at the level of an individual, and a network tie-variable is regarded as an independent fixed variable measured at the level of the dyad. The starting point for model development is the idea that the attribute of one individual is potentially dependent on and may potentially influence the attributes of others (Durlauf, 2001).

Let the collection of random variables $Y = [Y_i]$ be a stochastic binary attribute vector where $i = 1, \ldots, n$. This is the dependent attribute of interest. The space of all possible attribute vectors is denoted by $\mathbf{Y}$. A realization of the stochastic attribute vector Y is denoted by $y = [y_i]$, where $y_i = 1$ if the attribute is present, and $y_i = 0$ otherwise. As a reminder, a realization refers to an observed vector of attributes. As in previous chapters, let a collection of network tie-variables be represented by a fixed binary matrix, where $x_{ij} = 1$ if tie is present, and $x_{ij} = 0$ otherwise. There may also be other covariate (predictor) attributes W denoted by $w = [w_i]$, which may be either binary or continuous.

With the network ties treated as exogenous (i.e., explanatory), network-based social influence effects may be inferred when i's attribute is associated with the attributes of the actors who may have social relations with i through the network ties. That is, we assume that the probability of an attribute being present depends on the presence of the attributes in some local network neighborhood of the actor. It is also possible that i may adopt a behavior solely on the basis of i's position in the network, such as greater popularity or activity, or because of other attributes of i. These possibilities need to be built into the model.

Generalizing the ERGM approach, we can specify a probability for observing the attribute for each possible observation:

$$\Pr(Y = y \mid X = x) = \frac{1}{\kappa(\theta_I)} \exp \left\{ \sum_I \theta_I z_I(y, x, w) \right\}, \qquad (9.1)$$

where θ_I and z_I are parameters and statistics for network-attribute configurations involving an interaction of dependent attribute (y), network (x), and covariate (w) variables. Examples of configurations are given in Tables 9.1 to 9.3 later in this chapter.

Equation (9.1) describes a probability distribution of vectors on n nodes in a given graph x. Each possible vector is assigned a specific probability based on the relative number of various configurations present and on the parameter values. When a parameter is large and positive, vectors with many corresponding configurations are more likely to be observed; conversely, for a large negative parameter, such vectors are less probable. The proposed models predict the outcome variable Y while taking the network dependencies between observations into account in a principled way that cannot be addressed in the standard logistic regression. It is worth emphasizing that when the dependence among attributes via network ties is not assumed, the autologistic actor attribute model (ALAAM) is equivalent to standard logistic regression.

The comparison with logistic regression becomes more apparent if we consider the conditional form of the model. We noted in Chapter 6 that ERGMs can be expressed in either a joint form, as in Equation (9.1), or in conditional form as a conditional log-odds. If we take the conditional form of Equation (9.1), and separating out the configurations based on different types as explained here, we have

$$\log \frac{\Pr(Y_i = 1|y_{-i}, x, w)}{\Pr(Y_i = 0|y_{-i}, x, w)} = \theta_1 + \sum \theta_p z_p(x) + \sum \theta_I z_I(x, y)$$
$$+ \sum \theta_C z_C(w) + \sum \theta_{IC} z_{IC}(x, w)$$

Here, θ_1 is an intercept term and is analogous to the edge parameter in a standard ERGM. The θ_P parameters (P for "position") predict Y_i from the network position of i, and the statistics z_P relate to network configurations that involve node i. We term these "network position" effects, and examples are given in Table 9.1. The θ_I parameters (I for "influence") predict Y_i from the Y attribute of other actors j who are connected to i in some way. The statistics z_I relate to network configurations that involve nodes i and j, and their network connections. We term these "network attribute" effects, and examples are shown in Table 9.2. The θ_C parameters (C for "covariate") predict Y_i from covariate attributes of i in some way (top line of Table 9.3). The θ_{IC} parameters predict Y_i from other covariates of other actors j who are connected to i in some way. The statistics z_{IC} relate to network configurations that involve nodes i and j, and their network connections. We term these "covariate" effects, and examples are provided in Table 9.3.

If there is no network diffusion in the system (i.e., if the network is irrelevant), then $\theta_P = \theta_I = \theta_{IC} = 0$, and the model reverts to a standard logistic regression, with the parameters θ_1 and θ_C as the standard logistic regression coefficients. However, when some form of network effect is present, this is quite different from a logistic regression. In that case, when predicting i's attribute status, the attribute variable Y_i is not only considered as a "response" variable, but it is also a predictor variable when predicting j's attribute status. This directly implies the autologistic nature of this class of models. Using a logistic regression will lead to biases in estimation and the risk of improper statistical inference.

Autologistic actor attribute models (ALAAMs) differ from exponential random graph models for social networks in the following way. ERGMs express interdependent tie-variables X_{ij} as a function of endogenous tie-variables and exogenous variables (e.g., attribute variables Y_i or spatial (dyadic) variables), whereas autologistic actor attribute models express interdependent actor attributes Y_i as a function of exogenous tie-variables X_{ij} (as well as, in principle, other exogenous attribute variables and possibly spatial covariates). In other words, ERGMs model ties, given the attributes, and ALAAMs model an attribute, given the ties (and other attributes). Although these models are different in explanatory and response variables, both are models for a class of mutually interdependent variables that may also depend on another class of exogenous variables. An important step for both models is to specify the dependence assumptions appropriately because the proposed dependencies determine the form of the configurations parameterized in the model.

9.3   Possible Forms of Dependence

As emphasized in previous chapters, dependence assumptions among variables may be hypothesized to take a variety of possible forms and to depend on network ties and other attributes in a variety of ways. Appropriate dependence structures are not self-evident, and it is a significant challenge to specify a single set of dependencies as most plausible. In the literature, the following dependence assumptions have been proposed (Daraganova, 2009; Robins, Pattison, & Elliott, 2001). A technical discussion of how dependence assumptions constrain particular network and network-attribute configurations is beyond the scope of this chapter. Interested readers should consult Robins, Pattison and Elliott (2001) and Daraganova (2009) on how statistics may be derived out of directed acyclic graphs (DAGs) and general dependence graphs. The parameters and effects described in this chapter can be fitted using the estimation software IPnet that can be downloaded from the PNet website.

9.3.1   Independent Attribute Assumption

The simplest dependence assumption is the assumption of attribute independence (Robins, Pattison, & Elliott, 2001), where any two attribute variable, Y_i and Y_j, are assumed to be independent of each other. This dependence assumption determines a single node as the only possible configuration. This assumption implies that the network has no effect on the distribution of attributes across the actors, so that there are no social influence effects. It is the assumption that underpins all standard logistic regression models.

9.3.2 Network-Dependent Assumptions

Given that ties are the linkages between people via which influence might be disseminated, a simple notion of influence/dependence can be modeled in terms of individuals' expressed ties (Robins, Pattison, & Elliott, 2001). The simplest form of network dependence assumes that an attribute variable Y_i is conditionally dependent on network tie X_{kj}, if and only if $\{i\} \cap \{k, l\} \neq \emptyset$. Stars (number of connections an individual with the attribute has with others) are important configurations arising from this dependence assumption.

The role of structural position of an individual in the network may be determined not only by an individual's number of connections but also by the level of activity of network partners and whether an individual is involved in transitive relationships (friends of friends are also friends). To represent this form of dependence, an attribute variable Y_i is assumed to be conditionally dependent on network tie X_{jk}, if and only if there is a path of length of 2, $x_{ij} = 1$ and $x_{jk} = 1$, for some j. This leads to the importance of 2-path and triangle configurations. For instance, whether Mary displays a particular behavior may depend on whether she is connected to other people, whether these people are socially active, and whether she is involved in transitive relationships. These assumptions give rise to the class of network-dependent models in which the probability of an attribute is proportional to the weighted sum of counts of different structural characteristics such as actor stars, actor 2-paths, and actor triangles (see Table 9.1 – note that in all tables in this chapter, the statistics presented are those appropriate for the joint form in Equation (9.1), so each contains a summation over all i).

This dependence assumption gives rise to the network position parameters (θ_P in the conditional form of the preceding model).

9.3.3 Network-Attribute–Dependent Assumptions

A more interesting and, from a network perspective, arguably more realistic notion of dependence between attributes arises when two attribute variables are assumed to be conditionally dependent in the presence of ties (Robins, Pattison, & Elliott, 2001).

The simplest network-attribute assumption is the "direct network-attribute assumption," where any two attribute variables Y_i and Y_j are conditionally dependent if and only if they share a tie, $x_{ij} = 1$. As in Chapter 6, this is a "partial conditional independence assumption": two attribute variables are statistically independent if and only if other variables (in this case, the exogenous tie-variable x_{ij}) are in a particular state (see Daraganova (2009) for details).

The direct network-attribute assumption permits modeling of dependence between i's attribute and the attributes of i's network partners. This is a direct contagion effect, akin to an individual catching a disease from people with whom they associate. This assumption conceptualizes microlevel social influence processes at a strictly dyadic level, but it is possible that influence does not always require face-to-face communication. People may be influenced indirectly through their friends (Brock & Durlauf, 2002; Marsden & Friedkin, 1993) in such a way that the overall pattern of friends' connections can substantially affect the individual's attribute status. For example, friends who are socially active by being connected to many others may be considered more influential, and their opinion may be more valuable, than the opinion of friends who are not socially active. In addition, the initial pattern of attributes in a friend's local network can profoundly shape the degree to which each individual is influenced because individuals can be indirectly influenced by their friends' friends or by information about friends of their friends (Bian, 1997; Denrell & Mens, 2007; Mason, Conrey, & Smith, 2007). For example, people may be more likely to possess an attribute if friends of their friends possess the same attribute. To capture indirect influence pathways of these types, the "indirect dependent attribute assumption" has been introduced (Daraganova, 2009). Any two attribute variables Y_i and Y_k are conditionally dependent if and only if they are tied by a path of length 2, $x_{ij} = 1$ and $x_{jk} = 1$, for some j.

These network-attribute assumptions lead to the class of models in which the probability of an attribute vector is proportional to the weighted sum of counts of different characteristics that refer to a combination of node and tie-variables (see Table 9.2). These assumptions give rise to the network-attribute parameters (θ_I in the conditional form of the preceding model).

9.3.4 Covariate-Dependent Assumptions

As in the ERGMs for social networks, exogenous factors – such as spatial locations, memberships, and other individual attributes – can be included in the model as predictors. The simplest dependence assumption is a "covariate dependence assumption," where the actor attribute is assumed to be conditionally dependent on other covariates relating to the same actor. This assumption, on its own, produces models that are equivalent to standard logistic regression, where one variable is predicted from a number of covariates.

Sometimes an individual's characteristics (ego), as well as characteristics of others (alters), can affect the behavior/attribute of an individual.

For example, if we believe that young people do not have many work-related contacts, the probability of an individual being unemployed might be higher if that person is connected to more young people (regardless of the employment status of those young people). To specifically model this hypothesis, we could use the "network covariate dependence assumption" in which the actor attribute Y_i is conditionally dependent on the covariate of another actor w_j if and only if there is a tie between i and j (i.e., $x_{ij} = 1$) (see Table 9.3). These assumptions give rise to the network covariate parameters (θ_C and θ_{IC} in the conditional form of the preceding model).

9.4 Different Model Specifications and Their Interpretation

A particular dependence assumption implies that the conditional probability of an attribute is affected by certain network-attribute configurations that are represented by parameters in the model. To understand the relationship to dependence assumptions, we note that models (just like ERGMs) are constructed using elements of several sets of dependence assumptions: (1) the independence assumption, (2) the network position effects, (3) the network-attribute effects, and (4) the covariate effects. In this section, we discuss four sets of possible configurations constrained by a particular dependence assumption. It should be borne in mind that the combination of these assumptions leads to different model specifications, and in any particular research context, some configurations will prove more interesting than others. The advantage of ALAAM is that some or all assumptions can be combined in one model and tested simultaneously.

9.4.1 Independence Models

The simplest independent attribute assumption constrains the model to only one possible configuration and the corresponding parameter refers to the baseline probability of the attribute being present (i.e., the intercept or attribute frequency). It is not likely to be an adequate model, and it incorporates no influence/diffusion effects, but it may serve as a useful baseline probability model against which more complex models can be compared. If other attribute measures are included as covariate predictors, this model becomes a standard logistic regression.

9.4.2 Network Position Effects Models

The network-dependent assumptions determine a set of different configurations presented in Table 9.1. In all configurations presented here, a black node signifies that the attribute variable is associated with the

Table 9.1. *Network position configurations, statistics, and parameters*

Configuration	Statistic	Parameter
	$\sum_i y_i$	Attribute density
	$\sum_i y_i \sum_j x_{ij}$	Actor activity
	$\sum_i y_i \sum_{i<k} x_{ij} x_{ik}$	Actor 2-star
	$\sum_i y_i \sum_{j<k<l} x_{ij} x_{ik} x_{il}$	Actor 3-star
	$\sum_i y_i \binom{x_{i+}}{k}$	Actor k-star
	$\sum_i y_i \sum_{j,k} x_{ij} x_{jk}$	Partner activity actor 2-path
	$\sum_i y_i \sum_i x_{ij} \binom{x_{j+}}{2}$	Partner 2-star
	$\sum_i y_i \sum_j x_{ij} \binom{x_{j+}}{m}$	Partner m-star
	$\sum_i y_i \sum_{j<k} x_{ij} x_{ik} x_{jk}$	Actor triangle

node included in a configuration statistic. For example, $\sum_i \sum_j y_i x_{ij}$, the statistic corresponding to the actor activity configuration, comprises only the attribute of a focal actor (black node) and her network ties to others, regardless of the attribute of those others (white nodes).

These assumptions give rise to the class of "network position effects," where influence is seen to arise through general levels of interaction activity in a network rather than through interaction with specific others with given attribute status.

If it is assumed that isomorphic configurations have equal parameters, then this model expresses the probability of a vector of attributes as a function of the number of various configurations depicted in Table 9.1 and, hence, allows us to examine how certain local structural positions in a network may affect the distribution of attributes.

As in ERGMs, we can set different statistics to zero to obtain different model specifications. Often parameters corresponding to actor stars of order 4 and higher, as well as partner stars of order 2 and higher, are set to zero. The inclusion of higher-order actor/partner star parameters allows the impact of an individual's level of social activity to be modeled with greater precision, whereas reliance on lower-order parameters alone means that some level of approximation is assumed to suffice.

Table 9.2. *Network-attribute configurations, statistics, and parameters*

Configuration	Statistic	Parameter
●——●	$\sum_{i<j} y_i y_j x_{ij}$	Partner attribute
●——○——●	$\sum_{i<k} y_i y_k \sum_j x_{ij} x_{jk}$	Indirect partner attribute
●——●——○	$\sum_{i,j} y_i y_j x_{ij} x_{j+}$	Partner attribute activity
●——●——●	$\sum_{i,j,k} y_i y_j y_k x_{ij} x_{jk}$	Partner–partner attribute
(triangle, ●●○)	$\sum_{i,j,k} y_i y_j x_{ij} x_{ik} x_{jk}$	Partner attribute triangle
(triangle, ●●●)	$\sum_{i,j,k} y_i y_j y_k x_{ij} x_{ik} x_{jk}$	Partner–partner attribute triangle

The parameters actor activity, actor 2-star and actor 3-star, refer to the dependence of an actor's behavior on the number of network partners of the actor. If the parameter actor activity is positive, it means that an actor with multiple ties is more likely to display the behavior. The actor 2-star and 3-star parameters allow for nonlinear dependence on the number of partners (cf. quadratic and cubic terms in regression). If actor 2-star is positive and actor 3-star is negative, then whereas actors who have multiple partners may be more likely to display the behavior, there may be a decreasing impact of this kind for actors who have accumulated many network partners, depending on the relative magnitude of these parameters. Inclusion of actor 2-path and actor triangle configurations allows us to infer whether the behavior is associated with network closure. If an actor triangle parameter is positive and an actor 2-star parameter is negative, then there is evidence that behavior is more likely to be observed in clustered regions of a network.

9.4.3 Network-Attribute Effects Models

Important network-attribute configurations are presented in Table 9.2.

The "partner attribute" parameter refers to the number of network partners who display the behavior and can be interpreted as a network contagion effect. If this parameter is large and positive, the probability of the behavior is higher if immediate network partners display the behavior.[1] The "indirect partner attribute" parameter refers to structural

---

[1] In the simpler Ising model, the corresponding parameter is called the "interaction of two sites" and "ferromagnetic" or "antiferromagnetic," according to whether the parameter is positive or negative, respectively (Besag, 1972; Cressie, 1993).

Table 9.3. *Covariate effects configurations, statistics,*
and parameters

Configuration	Statistic	Parameter
Continuous or binary exogenous variable		
	$\sum_{i} y_i w_i$	Attribute covariate
	$\sum_{i,j} y_i w_i x_{ij}$	Partner covariate
Categorical exogenous variable		
	$\sum y_i x_{ij} I\{w_i = w_j\}$	Same partner covariate

equivalence between actors with the same behavior. A positive value of
this parameter indicates that the behavior is more probable for two actors
when they are tied to the same people. In loose terms, structurally equivalent actors tend to share attributes (a statistic that obeys a more strict definition of structural equivalence could be easily defined; for a theoretical
motivation, see Burt (1987)). The "partner attribute activity" parameter
can be interpreted in terms of the social activity of network partners with
the behavior, and the "partner–partner attribute" parameter in terms of
the attribute resources of network partners with the behavior. The "partner attribute triangle" can also be thought of as structural equivalence,
but within a cohesive block of equivalent nodes (in contrast to the "indirect partner attribute," where there is no requirement for a tie between
the equivalent nodes). The "partner–partner attribute triangle" refers to
contagion within groups rather than dyads.

9.4.4   Covariate Effects Models

The covariate dependence assumptions extend the effects as in Table 9.3.
In Table 9.3, a box represents another predictor attribute that may pertain
to a node or its network partners.

   The "attribute covariate" parameter controls for other individual-level
predictors in the models and, as explained previously, in the absence of
any network and network-attribute effects represents the model that is
equivalent to standard logistic regression where one variable is predicted
from a number of individual covariates. The "partner covariate" parameter allows us to identify characteristics of network partners that are
more likely to be associated with the behavior. For example, it allows
researchers to test whether being connected to others with high levels of
anxiety affects individuals' drinking behavior, regardless of the drinking
behavior of those others.

The "same partner covariate" parameter allows for testing the hypothesis of whether a person with network partners in the same category on a categorical covariate is more likely to have the behavior. If the parameter is positive, for instance, then an individual is more likely to display the behavior if he or she has more network partners within his or her own category (group, organization, education level). Note that the first two parameters have been developed for the binary and continuous covariates, whereas the third parameter assumes a categorical covariate (however, naturally, as in standard ERGM, we may also use the product or absolute differences in covariates). Effects for continuous dyadic covariates, including geospatial effects, could also be included but are not presented here (see Chapter 8).

In any particular research context, some configurations may be considered more plausible than others. However, it should be borne in mind that if a model includes a parameter for a higher-order configuration (e.g., a triad), it is often helpful that parameters for lower-order configurations (e.g., stars of order 2) are also included in the model (Robins & Pattison, 2005). Such hierarchical models have parameters that are more easily interpreted because they permit us to identify whether the higher-order effect can be explained by the lower-order effect, or whether it has an independent effect in its own right.

9.5   Conclusion

In this chapter, we present a model for attributes of the nodes conditional on the network structure. In general, this class of models aims to identify attribute clustering in the network. The attributes may represent behavior, attitudes, or beliefs. The ALAAM models these outcomes while taking the network dependencies between observations into account in a principled way. In principle, these models can be extended to any plausible relations between individuals whether these relations are represented by network ties, physical proximity, or shared membership. It can be also readily extended from binary relations to valued relations. Of course, for a valued relation, a researcher needs to make a decision of the functional form between strength of the relationship and probability of observing an attribute. An example of how a spatial valued relationship can be incorporated is given in Chapter 18.

The explicit focus of this chapter is on cross-sectional models, but it is important to note that more information about these inherently dynamic social processes may be obtained from longitudinal data. The models presented in this chapter remain to be extended to the longitudinal framework presented in Chapter 11. Furthermore, cross-sectional data give us limited scope to distinguish between social selection and social influence empirically. Whether the processes at work are selection, influence, or a combination of both has to be motivated theoretically. Data that record both network and behavior over time offer increased possibilities for studying the joint dynamics of selection and influence (Snijders, van de Bunt, & Steglich, 2010).

10

Exponential Random Graph Model Extensions: Models for Multiple Networks and Bipartite Networks

Peng Wang

In previous chapters, we presented details of models for univariate one-mode network data. Exponential random graph models (ERGMs), however, can also be applied to other relational data types. In this chapter, we extend ERGM specifications to (1) multivariate analysis of two networks and (2) bipartite (or two-mode) networks. We discuss model specifications and possible parameter interpretations for both classes of models.

10.1 Multiple Networks

Social network analyses are not limited to one type of network, and it is often the case that more than one type of relational tie can be defined among a given set of nodes – for example, we can define both friendship and advice-giving ties among staff of an organization. When we have multiple network ties, we can then ask the research question about how different types of networks interact with each other, and how these interactions affect the structure of each network. For example, do friends seek advice from each other in the organization? We refer to the statistical analysis of multiple networks as "multivariate network analysis."

Several techniques have been developed for the analysis of multiple networks, including blockmodels for multiple networks (White, Boorman, & Breiger, 1976), quadratic assignment procedures (Dekker, Krackhardt, & Snijders, 2007; Krackhardt, 1987), network algebraic models (Pattison, 1993), and ERGMs (Pattison & Wasserman, 1999). In this chapter, we focus on the simplest multivariate ERGM specifications for networks involving two types of ties defined on a common set of nodes.

115

10.1.1 ERGMs for Analyzing Two Networks

As Chapter 6 explains, ERGMs for single network analysis have the following general form:

$$P_\theta(x) = \frac{1}{\kappa(\theta)} \exp\{\theta_1 z_1(x) + \theta_2 z_2(x) + \cdots + \theta_p z_p(x)\}, \qquad (10.1)$$

where x represents a collection of tie-variables $[x_{ij}]$ for a single graph. Pattison and Wasserman (1999) extended ERGMs to multivariate network analysis where a set of M networks are defined on a set of n nodes, x is then a set of tie-variables ($x_{ijm}, m \in M$), and the networks can be represented by an "n by n by M" adjacency array. In directed networks, $x_{ijm} = 1$ if there is a tie sent from node i to j in network m, otherwise, $x_{ijm} = 0$; for undirected networks, $x_{ijm} = x_{jim}$. With the inclusion of M networks in the model, the size of the graph space is many times greater than the single network case. The number of possible graphs is $2^{n(n-1)M}$ for directed networks, and $2^{n(n-1)M/2}$ for undirected networks.

The graph statistics $z_k(x)$ are defined both within and among ties from different types of networks. Thus, they can be more complex than the graph statistics in ERGMs for single networks and have the following general form

$$z_k(x) = \sum_{A \in A_k} \prod_{(i,j,m) \in A} x_{ijm}, \qquad (10.2)$$

where A_k is a collection of isomorphic configurations A of tie-variables.

Following Markov and the social circuit dependence assumptions of single network analysis, we can derive models for ERGMs for multiple networks. The following sections describe some ERGM specifications and possible interpretations for modeling the simplest case of two networks. The models described below can be fitted using the software XPNet that can be downloaded from the PNet website.

10.1.2 ERGM Specifications for Two Networks

Let us consider two networks, A and B, with tie-variables represented as x_{ijA} and x_{ijB}. The model specifications can be divided into two parts: "within-network effects," where graph configurations are defined using ties from one network, and "cross-network effects," which involve ties from both networks. The within-network effects for two-network models can be identical to those for single networks as described in previous chapters so that we can have a set of standard within-graph statistics for each network. Using the Bernoulli model for undirected networks as an example, the within-network effects for networks A and B would then include edge parameters for both A and B (denoted "EdgeA" and "EdgeB" henceforth) with statistics $z_{A,L}(x) = \sum_{i<j} x_{ijA}$ and

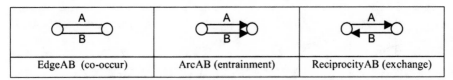

| EdgeAB (co-occur) | ArcAB (entrainment) | ReciprocityAB (exchange) |

Figure 10.1. Cross-network dyadic configurations.

$z_{B,L}(x) = \sum_{i<j} x_{ijB}$, respectively. We could also have Markov or social circuit within-network parameters.

Because these single network effects are covered in previous chapters, we focus here on the cross-network parameters: entrainment, exchange, cross-network activity and popularity, and cross-network clustering. Note that because the ERGMs described in this chapter are for cross-sectional data, the interpretations of the cross-network effect should not infer causality for ties of different types – that is, the existence of ties in one network does not necessarily *lead to* the creation of ties in the other network. Significant cross-network parameters in our models simply indicate that there is an association between the two networks (in the particular form expressed by the parameter). It requires longitudinal data to decide whether one type of tie is likely to lead to the creation of a tie of the other type.

Entrainment and Exchange Effects. The most fundamental cross-network effects are for associations between networks A and B at the dyadic level. Undirected bivariate network models should include a parameter for the "cooccurrence" of ties from the two networks ("EdgeAB"), with the associated statistic

$$z_{LAB}(x) = \sum_{i<j} x_{ijA} x_{ijB}.$$

For directed network models, in contrast, there are two dyadic configurations (Figure 10.1). The "entrainment" parameter ("ArcAB") represents the extent to which the two network ties align within the dyad (i.e., both ties are directed from i to j), whereas the "exchange" parameter ("Reciprocity AB") represents the extent to which the dyad *exchanges* ties of different types (A from i to j, and B from j to i). The relevant statistics can be calculated as

$$z_{\text{Arc}AB}(x) = \sum_{i,j} x_{ijA} x_{ijB}, \quad z_{\text{Reciprocity}\,AB}(x) = \sum_{i,j} x_{ijA} x_{jiB}.$$

These dyadic network effects are the basic configurations for network association and should always be included in a bivariate network model. For many purposes, the inclusion of these parameters may be sufficient

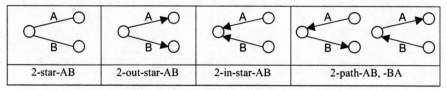

Figure 10.2. Cross-network 2-star effects.

for modeling the association of networks. For instance, for undirected networks A and B, a model might contain parameters for edges, alternating stars, and alternating triangles for each of A and B (i.e., social circuit within-network parameters), as well as the co-occurrence (Edge*AB*) parameter.

A two-network ERGM without cross-network effects is equivalent to two independent single-network ERGMs. By including these cross-network configurations, we can test the dependencies between networks. Comparisons between models with and without these configurations may give us very different within-network effects because strong within-network effects may possibly be explained by the cross-network effects. For instance, triangulation in A may be explained by strong triangulation in B and tendencies for the co-occurrence of A and B.

Cross-Network Activity and Popularity Effects. If a more nuanced understanding of cross-network association is required, then additional effects could be considered. Cross-network Markov activity and popularity effects can be represented by stars of various sizes involving both networks. Figure 10.2 presents 2-star configurations for both directed and undirected networks.

For undirected networks, the *2-star-AB* parameter represents how likely a node will express ties of both types to different partners. For directed networks, *2-in-* and *2-out-star-AB* and *2-path-AB* and *-BA* parameters can be defined. Each represents a different local process. The 2-in- and 2-out-star parameters describe tendencies for nodes to receive and send ties of different types. The 2-path parameter represents tendencies for nodes receiving ties of one type to express ties of the other type.

Cross-Network Clustering Effects. Cross-network clustering effects can be represented by the Markov triangle configurations, as in Figure 10.3 for undirected networks, where the triangles have two ties from one network and one from the other.

Using an enemy network (A) and a friendship network (B) as an example, the "Triangle-*AAB*" configuration represents friendship between pairs of nodes having common enemies. A positive "Triangle-*AAB*"

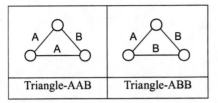

Figure 10.3. Cross-network triangle effects.

parameter estimate shows that the enemy of an enemy is a friend. For directed networks, the number of possible triangle configurations is considerably increased.

Social Circuit Effects. We can extend these cross-network effects in the model using social circuit dependence assumptions and include statistics such as alternating stars, alternating triangles, and alternating 2-paths using ties from both networks (Figure 10.4 gives some examples).

Multivariate Models with Actor Attributes. We can include actor attributes as covariates in multivariate network analyses to form multivariate social selection models in precisely the same way as described in Chapter 8.

The graph statistics are then functions of both network ties and actor attributes. The networks can be directed or undirected, and the actor attributes can be binary, continuous, or categorical. Figure 10.5 gives examples of directed entrainment attribute effects, where ArcAB effects are combined with an attribute labeled as *[Attr]*.

The *[Attr]-SenderAB* effect tests whether nodes with the attribute are sending entrained ties to others in both networks. The *[Attr]-ReceiverAB* configuration is analogous, except that it refers to the receipt of ties. The continuous attribute effect *[Attr]-Sum-ArcAB* tests whether pairs of actors with a higher combined value on an attribute tend to form entrainment ties. Let y_i denote the continuous attribute for node i, then $z_{ASumArcAB}(x) = \sum_{i,j} x_{ijA} x_{ijB}(y_i + y_j)$.

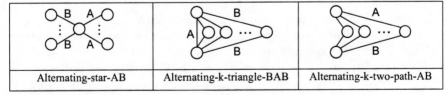

Figure 10.4. Cross-network social circuit effects.

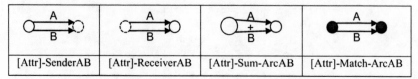

| [Attr]-SenderAB | [Attr]-ReceiverAB | [Attr]-Sum-ArcAB | [Attr]-Match-ArcAB |

Figure 10.5. Cross-network dyadic attribute effects.

The categorical attribute effect *[Attr]-Match-ArcAB* tests whether nodes from the same categories form entrainment ties. The *[Attr]-Match-ArcAB* statistic can be expressed as

$$z_{AMatchArcAB}(x) = \sum_{i,j} x_{ijA} x_{ijB} I(y_i = y_j),$$

where $I(a)$ is an indicator function, with value 1 if the statement inside the brackets is true and 0 otherwise.

The increases in the size of graph space and the complexity of graph statistics can make the modeling of multiple networks a challenge. Compared with models for single networks, multivariate ERGMs usually involve greater number of parameters, and take longer for parameter estimation to converge (see Chapter 12). Our suggestion is for the researcher to start with standard social circuit specifications for within-networks and simple dyadic entrainment and exchange parameters between-networks. Once a suitable model with these simple cross-network effects has been obtained, then the researcher can consider whether it is worthwhile to seek more elaborate cross-network associations. Sometimes it helps to fit univariate models to each network separately, and then to consider using major effects from these models in a combined bivariate model.

Chapter 16 presents an example of multivariate network analysis in an organizational context.

10.2   Bipartite Networks

A bipartite network consists of two sets of nodes, with ties defined only between but not within the two sets of nodes. Breiger (1974) described such networks in terms of "the duality of persons and groups," representing the mutually constitutive relationship between the nodes from the two sets. There are several techniques for analyzing bipartite networks, including correspondence analysis (Faust, 2005), blockmodels (Doreian, Batagelj, & Ferligoj, 2004), and ERGMs (Pattison & Robins, 2004; Skvoretz & Faust, 1999; Wang, Sharpe, Robins, & Pattison, 2009;

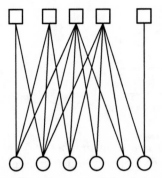

Figure 10.6. A (5,6) bipartite network.

including some social selection models by Agneessens, Roose, & Waege, 2004; Agneessens & Roose, 2008). In this chapter, we describe the special features of bipartite networks and the model specifications of Wang, Sharpe, Robins and Pattison (2009), and introduce some social selection model specifications that have been implemented in the BPNet software (Wang, Robins, & Pattison, 2009).

10.2.1 Bipartite Network Representation and Special Features

We denote a bipartite network with n nodes in set A, and m nodes in set P as a (n,m) bipartite network. Figure 10.6 is an example of a $(5,6)$ bipartite network, where the nodes in set A are represented using squares, and the nodes in set P are represented using circles.

ERGMs for bipartite graphs have the same general form as in Equation (6.1). The network, however, is now represented by an n by m rectangular matrix where the cell $x_{ij} = 1$ if there is a tie between nodes i and j; otherwise, $x_{ij} = 0$. The (n,m) bipartite graph space has the size of 2^{nm}, and the graph statistics can be defined based on tie-variable dependence assumptions introduced in previous chapters.

Because bipartite networks have network ties defined only between the two sets of nodes, configurations involving odd cycles do not exist. The traditional definitions of network closure and triangulation for one-mode networks do not apply in the case of bipartite networks. Several clustering coefficients to measure the extent of closure were proposed by Opsahl (2009), Robins and Alexander (2004), and Skvoretz and Agneessens (2009). For instance, the Robins and Alexander (2004) clustering coefficient $C(x)$ measures the proportion of 3-paths (L_3) closed by another tie to form the smallest bipartite closed structure, a 4-cycle (C_4). The

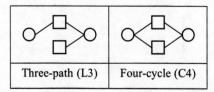

| Three-path (L3) | Four-cycle (C4) |

Figure 10.7. Bipartite 3-path and 4-cycle.

coefficient is calculated as the ratio between the number of 4-cycles and 3-paths, with a factor of 4 to ensure it ranges between 0 and 1:

$$C(x) = \frac{4C_4(x)}{L_3(x)}.$$

Let $t_A(i, k, x) = \sum_j x_{ij} x_{kj}$ denote the number of two-paths between a pair of nodes i and k in node set A, and let $x_{i+} = \sum_j x_{ij}$ denote the degree of node i in A. Then the number of 4-cycle (C4) and 3-paths (L3), shown in Figure 10.7, can be calculated as $z_{C4}(x) = \sum_{i<k} \binom{t_A(i,k,x)}{2}$ and $z_{L3}(x) = \sum_{i<k} t_A(i, k, x)(x_{i+} + x_{k+} - 2)$, respectively.

10.2.2   ERGM Specifications for Bipartite Networks

To accommodate the features of bipartite networks, a special set of ERGM specifications are developed based on various dependence assumptions applied in one-mode networks.

Bernoulli Model. The simplest ERGM for an (n,m) bipartite network is the Bernoulli model, where the tie-variables are conditionally independent. The Bernoulli model has one edge parameter θ_L, with a statistic $z_L(x) = \sum_{i,j} x_{ij}$, the number of edges ($L$) in x. The density of the bipartite network is $d(x) = z_L(x)/nm$. For the Bernoulli model, the maximum likelihood estimate of θ_L can be obtained analytically as $\hat{\theta}_L = \log d(x) - \log[1 - d(x)]$.

Markov Models. Based on Markov dependence, with two tie-variables conditionally independent unless they have a node in common, stars of various sizes, or k-stars, representing network activity can be included in the ERGM specification originally proposed by Skvoretz and Faust (1999). Two types of k-stars can be defined and labeled as S_{Ak} and S_{Pk}, as shown in Figure 10.8. The number of stars S_{Ak} can be calculated as $z_{SAk}(x) = \sum_i \binom{x_{i+}}{k}$.

In a simulation study, Wang, Sharpe, Robins and Pattison (2009) showed that the ERGM specification with only edge and k-star

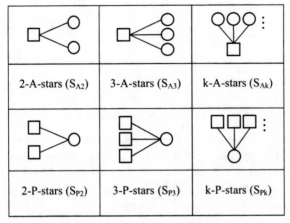

2-A-stars (S_{A2})	3-A-stars (S_{A3})	k-A-stars (S_{Ak})
2-P-stars (S_{P2})	3-P-stars (S_{P3})	k-P-stars (S_{Pk})

Figure 10.8. Bipartite star configurations.

parameters frequently suffered from the type of phase transitions discussed for Markov models in Chapter 6 (see Figures 6.5 and 6.6). For these models, most parameter values generate graph distributions close to empty or complete graphs, or with multiple regions of graphs. As noted in Chapter 6, for unipartite networks, the geometric weighting on the degree distribution introduced by Snijders et al. (2006) alleviates such issues, resulting in the alternating star parameters. Wang, Sharpe, Robins and Pattison (2009) applied the same approach to bipartite networks to introduce alternating k-stars of two types, labeled as *KSA* and *KSP*. The alternating k-stars are measures of the spread of the degree distributions such that a large positive parameter indicates bipartite graphs that are centralized around a few high-degree nodes of either type. Using *KSA* as an example, alternating k-star statistics can be calculated as

$$z_{KSA}(x, \lambda) = \sum_{k=2}^{m} (-1)^k \frac{z_{SAk}(x)}{\lambda^{k-2}}.$$

In addition, the Markov assumption fails to capture the clustering effects in bipartite networks such as the 4-cycles. Social circuit models enable us to model clustering effects in bipartite networks much better.

Realization Dependence Models. Chapter 6 presents realization dependence where two tie-variables become dependent if certain neighboring ties are observed. For bipartite graph models, two types of realization dependence have been used: the 4-cycle (social circuit) assumption and the 3-path assumption, illustrated in Figures 10.9 and 10.10, respectively.

The 4-cycle assumption for bipartite networks assumes that tie-variables X_{ij} and X_{kl} are dependent if $x_{jk} = x_{il} = 1$ such that they become

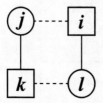

Figure 10.9. Four-cycle dependence assumption.

part of a social circuit (4-cycle). The 4-cycle assumption makes intuitive sense. With a club membership network as an example, suppose we have two members of two different clubs (j is a member of club k and l is a member of club i in Figure 10.9). Then the probability of whether j joins club i is likely to be changed if l is also a member of club k (i.e., l might tell j about club i). In other words, the variables X_{ij} and X_{kl} are conditionally dependent whenever $x_{jk} = x_{il} = 1$. With the 4-cycle assumption, the model can capture bipartite network closure through a 4-cycle parameter. The 4-cycle assumption also implies 2-path configurations of various sizes, or distributions of 2-paths. We define an "h-2-path" as a pair of nodes that is connected by h 2-paths. For bipartite networks, this has a straightforward interpretation as two nodes of one type having ties to h common nodes of the other type. For example, two people may have h common affiliations.

We may apply the alternating form to the 2-path distributions and obtain two parameters with alternating statistics: alternating A cycles (K_{CA}) and alternating P cycles (K_{CP}), as represented in Figure 10.11. Wang, Sharpe, Robins and Pattison (2009) provided further details of these parameters and ways to calculate the associated statistics.

The 3-path assumption further generalizes the 4-cycle assumption such that two tie-variables X_{ij} and X_{kl} are conditionally dependent as long as either $x_{jk} = 1$ or $x_{il} = 1$ (i.e., so that X_{ij} and X_{kl} are part of a 3-path). The 3-path assumption implies a 4-cycle assumption, but not vice versa. Based on the 3-path assumption, a 3-path configuration together with associated statistics (L_3) may be parameterized into the model.

Bipartite Models with Actor Attributes. Actor attributes can be included in bipartite ERGMs as covariates to form social selection models (see Chapter 8). Agneessens et al. (2004) and Koskinen and Edling (2010)

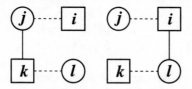

Figure 10.10. Three-path dependence assumption.

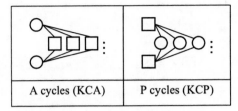

Figure 10.11. Alternating 2-paths.

proposed model specifications for bipartite graphs with actor attributes. In this section, we present some graph configurations involving actor attributes that have been implemented in BPNet. The graph statistics involving actor attributes are based on both the value of the vector of attributes (y) and network ties (x).

There are two ways of categorizing the attribute effects for bipartite models. First, attributes can be binary, continuous, or categorical such that three different types of effects can be defined based on these types. Second, because two sets of nodes are involved in bipartite networks, the effects can be categorized as within- and between-set effects. In terms of these effects, we list some examples of actor attribute configurations for bipartite networks with node sets labeled as A and P.

Within-Node Set Configurations. Within-node set configurations only take attribute values from one set of nodes into account. We use attributes (y) of nodes from set A to demonstrate model specifications of various types. Effects based on attributes of nodes from set P can be derived in similar ways.

Dyadic attribute activity effects can be defined for both binary and continuous attributes (Figure 10.12). In Figure 10.12, a node with the binary attribute is represented as a square containing a "1", and a node with a higher score on the continuous attribute is represented as a square of larger size. Positive parameter values indicate that nodes with the binary attribute, or with a higher continuous attribute, tend to express more ties.

On the 2-star level, several configurations can be defined (Figure 10.13).

Binary attribute activity	Continuous attribute activity
([Attr]-rA (binary))	([Attr]-rA (continuous))

Figure 10.12. Attribute activity effects.

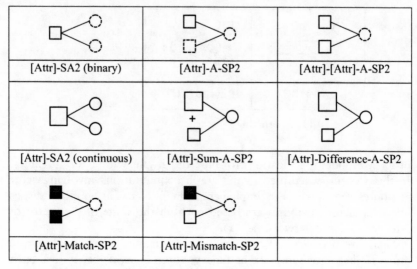

Figure 10.13. Two-star attribute effects.

We can define a 2-star attribute effect based on the attributes of the node at the center of the 2-paths (*[Attr]-SA2*). Both binary and continuous attributes may apply in this case. Because a 2-star parameter expresses variance in the degree distribution, and hence tendencies to network centralization, a binary attribute 2-star parameter with the node at the center of the star reflects tendencies for higher centralization around nodes of that type. Similarly for continuous attributes, the parameter indicates tendencies for higher centralization among nodes with higher scores on the attribute. We use gender as an example binary attribute, where males are represented by 1s, and seniority as an example of a continuous attribute for nodes in the node set *A*, which represents individuals. A positive significant *male-SA2* effect indicates that there is higher dispersion in the degree distribution for males, so that there are some males who are highly active and some who are not; hence, network ties are more centralized on a few higher-degree nodes for males than for females. Similarly, a positive significant *SEN-SA2* effect suggests that network activity is more centralized for actors with higher seniority.

With binary attributes for the ending nodes of 2-paths, we can define effects that test the tendency for nodes with certain attributes sharing partners with other nodes in the same set. This approach permits a bipartite version of homophily within node sets, whereby (for instance) individuals who share attributes tend to connect to the same organization (where *A* nodes are individuals and *P* nodes are organizations). Using gender as an example again, the *male-A-SP2* effect tests whether males tend to connect to more popular organizations, and *male-male-A-SP2* tests whether

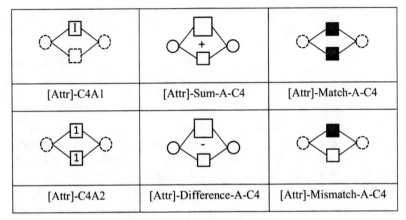

| [Attr]-C4A1 | [Attr]-Sum-A-C4 | [Attr]-Match-A-C4 |
| [Attr]-C4A2 | [Attr]-Difference-A-C4 | [Attr]-Mismatch-A-C4 |

Figure 10.14. Four-cycle attribute effects.

males tend to connect to the same organizations. Note that the bipartite version or homophily involves three nodes as compared to the unipartite network where homophily is specified on the dyad level.

For continuous attributes on the ending nodes of a 2-path, sum (*[Attr]-Sum-A-SP2*) and absolute difference (*[Attr]-Difference-A-SP2*) effects are possible, just as the case for unipartite social selection models (see Table 8.1 in Chapter 8). For instance, for the seniority attribute, a positive significant estimate of a *SEN-Sum-A-SP2* parameter indicates that people with higher combined seniority tend to connect to the same organizations, and a negative significant estimate of a *SEN-Difference-A-SP2* parameter suggests that nodes with similar seniority tend to connect to the same organizations.

For categorical attributes, the effects, *[Attr]-Match-SP2* and *[Attr]-Mismatch-SP2*, permit examination of bipartite homophily, whereby dyads from the same or different categories tend to connect to the same organizations.

At the 4-cycle level, we can define similar effects based on attributes of the pair of nodes from the same set (Figure 10.14).

The binary attribute effect *[Attr]-C4A1* is a measure of how likely a node of type *A* will be involved in a closure. *[Attr]-C4A2* indicates tendencies for closure to occur among nodes that share the attribute. For example, this may be used to express that men tend to share corporate board memberships to a greater extent than women (Koskinen & Edling, 2012).

For 4-cycle structures with continuous attributes, the *[Attr]-Sum-A-C4* effect identifies whether dyads with higher joint attribute values tend to exhibit closure, whereas the *[Attr]-Difference-A-C4* effect tests whether closure is more likely to occur involving dyads with similar attribute

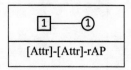

Figure 10.15. Dyadic between-set configurations.

values. For instance, using seniority as the continuous attribute, a positive *SEN-Difference-A-C4* suggests that closure is more likely to occur among individuals with different seniority. For categorical attributes, the *[Attr]-Match-A-C4* and *[Attr]-Mismatch-A-C4* parameters examine tendencies for closure to involve nodes of the same or different categories.

Between-Set Configurations. Between-set configurations are based on attributes from both sets. We can use model parameter specifications analogous to those of Chapter 8 for unipartite networks. If we had the same attribute defined for both sets of node (taking gender as an example if both sets of nodes were people), then we could use activity and homophily parameters analogous to those of Chapter 8 (see Table 8.1). However, because we are dealing with two types of nodes in bipartite networks, there are cases where the same attribute cannot be defined across both sets. Then the between-set configurations represent how the combined effects of the two types of attributes affect the structure of the network. As an example, the dyadic binary attribute configuration *[Attr]-[Attr]-rAP* is presented in Figure 10.15. Suppose the *A* nodes are individuals and the *P* nodes are sports clubs, with attributes as dummy variables for male and boxing clubs, respectively. Then the parameter permits inferences of whether males are more likely to be members of boxing clubs.

It is possible to extend the selection model specifications by applying realization dependence assumptions and combining node attributes with various forms of higher-order statistics. For the most part, however, a selection of the parameters referred to previously will suffice for empirical investigations. Chapter 20 illustrates applications and interpretations of ERGMs for bipartite networks using an empirical data set.

10.2.3   Additional Issues for Bipartite Networks

It is worth emphasizing some principal differences between two- and one-mode networks. The fact that we have two different types of nodes means that we have two distinct degree distributions, and if we are interested in modeling the degrees of nodes, we have to assume an ERGM that goes beyond the Bernoulli assumption in terms of dependence. Furthermore, it is important to keep in mind that the nodes are actually of different types when interpreting a model. Sometimes one type of node is truly constituent, one mode being constituted by a collection of the other type of node. Are dependencies between, say, corporate boards or a property of the boards, or because the boards are made up of the same directors? On occasion, we may use the *A-P* ties as proxies of underlying *A-A* or *P-P* ties. This is not to say that projecting *A-P* ties into their one-mode *A-A* or *P-P* projection is preferable. If anything, it can be shown that these projections give rise to spurious clustering and dependencies in the one-mode projections that are mere artefacts of the projection (Wang, Sharpe, Robins & Pattison, 2009). Current research into multilevel networks (Lazega et al., 2008) attempts to parse out the unique contribution of different types of ties between different types of nodes to the overall network structure.

In many research contexts, there is one type of node that per definition must have ties present. It may, for example, not make sense to consider a club without any constituent members (Niekamp et al., 2011). Such restrictions imposed on the structure by the nature of the network may make it difficult to fully capture the respective degree distributions. This may be solved by combining a variety of degree-based effects or by conditioning the inference on the condition that there are no isolates (e.g., as can be done in BPNet).

Although the boundary definition may be a difficult issue in bipartite networks and not have an optimal solution, it goes a long way to be aware of its consequences on the inference (Koskinen & Edling, 2010). Was the network sampled on one type of node, and how large of a fraction of each type of node was collected? Each consideration has a bearing on the degree of overlap between the neighborhoods (clustering) and the extent to which degree distributions are restricted. ERGM for bipartite networks does not have as long a history of research as ERGM for unipartite networks, and issues of model specification and inference are the target of much current research.

11

Longitudinal Models

Tom Snijders and Johan Koskinen

11.1 Network Dynamics

Like all things in the world, networks are subject to change. Sometimes researchers observe networks at one point in time – this is often called a "cross-sectional observation of a network." At other times, researchers make repeated observations of a network where the node set remains the same but ties may change – this can be called "longitudinal or dynamic network data." Although the data collection requires more effort, there can be an important payoff because dynamics often tell us more about what governs social behavior than a cross-sectional view. This chapter presents a natural extension of exponential random graph models (ERGMs) to the longitudinal case.

11.2 Data Structure

A finite number of observations on a network of the same relation on the same node set (e.g., collaboration among the employees in a firm) is called a "network panel data set." Such a data set may be denoted by $X(t_0)$, $X(t_1), \ldots, X(t_{M-1})$, where $X(t_m)$ is the adjacency matrix representing the network at observation moment t_m, and $M \geq 2$ is the number of observation moments. On all observation moments, we have the same set of n actors, but the ties between them may be different. The question treated in this chapter is not how to explain, or model, each network $X(t_m)$ by itself, but how to model the changes from $X(t_m)$ to $X(t_{m+1})$, for $m = 0, \ldots, M$.

Throughout, we take the initial network as given, and we only intend to model the subsequent changes to the network. The basic premise is that we observe a network at different points in time, and for every new

130

observation, there is change that we want to explain. It is also assumed that the changes in the network from one observation to the next have arisen gradually.

11.3 Model

11.3.1 Continuous-Time Markov Chain

We define the model in terms of a continuous-time Markov chain, which follows naturally if you first consider a change to only one tie-variable. At time point t_0, say, there is no tie between Bob and Fredric; however, at time point t_1, there is a tie between Bob and Fredric. We know that the tie was created between t_0 and t_1 but not when or if it was created, dissolved, and then re-created. Continuous time is important here because we consider modeling all changes to all tie-variables, and conceptually, it makes a difference whether another tie, say, between Bob and Erica, was formed before or after the tie between Bob and Fredric. After all, we are interested in modeling the dynamics, that is, how one change of the network reshapes the conditions for other potential changes to the network.

The assumption that the network changes gradually between observations is translated mathematically in the specification that we consider a time-dependent network $X(t)$, where the time parameter t takes all real values from the first to the last observation moment: the time domain is the interval $[t_0, t_{M-1}]$. One could say that in any split second, some tie might change. These individual tie changes are not observed – only the total network at the observation moments t_0 through t_{M-1} is observed. Between t_0 and t_{M-1}, there will be a finite number of times when the network changes, and at all other times, the network stays constant. Thus, we have a continuous-time parameter t, as well as both observations and changes at discrete moments – usually many more moments of change than moments of observation.

A convenient second assumption was proposed by Holland and Leinhardt (1977): at any moment, when the network changes, only one tie-variable can change. Thus, ties do not appear or disappear together but rather one by one. This assumption not only decomposes the change process into its smallest constituents but also rules out coordination, swapping partners, instantaneous group formation, and the like.

The third assumption is that the change probabilities of the network depend on the current state of the network but not on previous states – there is no memory, as it were. Mathematically, this assumption is expressed by saying that the stochastic process $X(t)$ is a continuous-time Markov process (this is further defined in textbooks such as Norris (1997)) on the set of all graphs on n nodes.

11.3.2   Tie-Oriented Dynamics

These three assumptions imply that the dynamic network process can be defined by specifying the probabilities for creating or terminating a given tie, conditional on the rest of the network. This process can still be specified in many ways. In this book, we treat a specification that is closely aligned with the ERGM. To introduce this specification, recall that in Chapter 6 we saw that the general form of the ERGM is given by

$$P_\theta(x) = \frac{1}{\kappa(\theta)} \exp\left\{\theta^T z(x)\right\} = \frac{1}{\kappa(\theta)} \exp\{\theta_1 z_1(x) + \theta_2 z_2(x) + \cdots + \theta_p z_p(x)\}. \quad (11.1)$$

The function $\theta_1 z_1(x) + \theta_2 z_2(x) + \cdots + \theta_p z_p(x)$ is sometimes called the "potential function." As described in Chapter 7, an interesting mathematical property of the ERGM is that it can be characterized completely by the conditional distribution of the tie-variables X_{ij} given the rest of the network.

We use notation first presented in Chapter 6. For any given network x, we denote x_{-ij} as the incomplete network from which the information about the value of the tie-variable x_{ij} is deleted. Furthermore, denote by $\Delta_{ij}^+ x$ the network in which the tie-variable x_{ij} is replaced by a 1, and denote by $\Delta_{ij}^- x$ the network in which the tie-variable x_{ij} is replaced by a 0. Thus, the tie (i,j) is forced to be present in $\Delta_{ij}^+ x$ and forced to be absent in $\Delta_{ij}^- x$; however, for the rest, these networks are just the same as the original x. Then the conditional distribution of the tie-variable X_{ij} given the rest of the network is defined by the probability

$$\Pr(X_{ij} = 1 | X_{-ij} = x_{-ij}) = \frac{\Pr\left(X = \Delta_{ij}^+ x\right)}{\Pr\left(X = \Delta_{ij}^+ x\right) + \Pr\left(X = \Delta_{ij}^- x\right)}.$$

For the probability distribution of the ERGM as in Equation (11.1), after some calculation this can be seen to be given by

$$\text{logit}\{\Pr(X_{ij} = 1 | X_{-ij} = x_{-ij})\} = \theta_1 \delta_{ij}^+ z_1(x) + \theta_2 \delta_{ij}^+ z_2(x) + \cdots + \theta_p \delta_{ij}^+ z_p(x) \quad (11.2)$$

where the logit function is defined by

$$\text{logit}(p) = \log\left(\frac{p}{1-p}\right),$$

and $\delta_{ij}^+ z_k(x)$ is defined as $\delta_{ij}^+ z_k(x) = z_k(\Delta_{ij}^+ x) - z_k(\Delta_{ij}^- x)$, often called the "change statistic" associated with the statistic $z_k(x)$. Equation (11.2) was first presented as Equation (6.1) in Chapter 6.

11.3.3 Definition of Dynamic Process

We now can define a dynamic process for the changing network $X(t)$. It depends not only on the parameters θ_k in Equations (11.1) and (11.2) but also on the rate of change, denoted here by the parameter ρ. The process is defined by specifying the next change, given that the process is currently at a time t and at a network $X(t) = x$. This is given in the following specification, which can be used to set up a simulation of the dynamic network process. It is formulated for directed networks, but exactly the same procedure can be followed for undirected networks.

Update Step for Dynamic Model

- Let the time increment be dt, a random variable with the exponential distribution with parameter ρ. This probability distribution is defined by the cumulative distribution function

$$\Pr\{dt \leq S\} = 1 - e^{-\rho S}$$

for $S \geq 0$.
- Change the time parameter to the new value $t + dt$.
- Choose a random directed pair (i, j) with $i \neq j$.
- Choose a new value for the tie-variable X_{ij} with probability distribution defined by Equation (11.2).

These four steps yield new values for the time parameter and the network; they can be repeated over and over, and thus define a stochastic process for the network. The steps do not always lead to a change in the network because in step 4 the new value for X_{ij} can be the same as the current value. The model is called a tie-oriented model because it is based on changes in tie-variables given the rest of the network, without considering a further structure.

The number of times that steps 1 to 4 are taken within a given time interval of duration $(t_b - t_a)$ has a Poisson distribution with expected value $\rho(t_b - t_a)$, but the number of changes will normally be smaller. The parameter ρ is a so-called nuisance parameter that must be present in the model, but its value is not of primary interest. There is a trade-off between this parameter and the duration of the time periods – measuring time in different units can be simply accounted for by a corresponding change in ρ, keeping the product $\rho(t_b - t_a)$ constant. Often the duration of intervals between successive observations is artificially set at $(t_{m+1} - t_m) = 1$ for all m, and separate rate parameters ρ_m are postulated for the separate time periods from t_m to t_{m+1}.

An alternative, mathematically equivalent, way to define this dynamic process is as follows. Consider an arbitrary time point t, a short time increment $dt > 0$, and an arbitrary graph x that is the value of $X(t)$. Recall that only a single tie can change at any moment. Therefore, the process is defined completely by specifying the probabilities of creation and termination of any single tie. If $x_{ij} = 0$ (i.e., at time t, there is no tie from i to j), then the probability that the tie (i,j) is created in this short time period can be approximated as follows:

$$\lim_{dt \to 0} \frac{\Pr\{X(t + dt) = \Delta_{ij}^+ x \mid X(t) = x\}}{dt} = \frac{\rho}{n(n-1)} \frac{e^{\theta^T z(\Delta_{ij}^+ x)}}{e^{\theta^T z(\Delta_{ij}^+ x)} + e^{\theta^T z(\Delta_{ij}^- x)}};$$

and if $x_{ij} = 1$ so that the tie from i to j does exist at time t, then the probability that the tie terminated in this short time period can be approximated by means of

$$\lim_{dt \to 0} \frac{\Pr\{X(t + dt) = \Delta_{ij}^- x \mid X(t) = x\}}{dt} = \frac{\rho}{n(n-1)} \frac{e^{\theta^T z(\Delta_{ij}^- x)}}{e^{\theta^T z(\Delta_{ij}^+ x)} + e^{\theta^T z(\Delta_{ij}^- x)}}.$$

This defines the so-called intensity matrix, or Q-matrix, of the Markov chain (see Norris (1997)).

11.3.4   Stationary Distribution

The preceding model was defined in terms of probabilities of change. This does not specify by itself the distribution of $X(t)$ for any given time point t. This distribution is called the "marginal distribution of $X(t)$," whereas the previously defined probabilities for change are called the "transition distribution." In this section, we treat some properties that follow directly from general properties of Markov processes, which are discussed in textbooks such as Norris (1997).

The marginal distribution of $X(t)$ is determined by the initial distribution $X(t_0)$ together with the transition distribution. The transition distribution corresponds to the ERGM in the sense that in step 4 the conditional probability according to the ERGM is used. This implies mathematically that the ERGM as defined by Equation (11.1), with parameter θ, is the stationary distribution in the sense that if $X(t_0)$ is a random network with this ERGM distribution, then each $X(t)$ for later time points t will have the same distribution. Also, if $X(t_0)$ is a random network with any other distribution – including a deterministic network and an empty network – then for very large time points t the marginal distribution of $X(t)$ will approximate this ERGM distribution. This is expressed by saying that the ERGM is also the asymptotic distribution of $X(t)$. The consequence is that this process can be used to generate random networks that may be considered, in excellent approximation, to be random draws from the ERGM distribution. In Markov chain Monte Carlo (MCMC) terminology, this process can be called a "Metropolis Hastings algorithm," with "proposal distribution" defined as the full conditional distribution for a randomly chosen tie-variable.

11.3.5 Estimation Based on Changes

It should be noted that although the process we model is the same as that which is used to produce graphs from the ERGM, because we terminated the simulation previously, the implied model for what we observe is not, strictly speaking, an ERGM (the model is usually not even an exponential family of distributions). This has some consequences for the way the model is estimated, which is slightly different from the ERGM, and for a subtly different interpretation of the model as compared to the ERGM – the focus is now on explaining change, conditional of previous states, and because we do not rely on stationarity assumptions, the model does not have to be interpreted as a process in equilibrium. The latter also means that we may allow for the model to be "explosive" and unstable; for a model to be realistic, we do not require that the process produces realistic graphs in the future.

The preceding discussion implies the dissociation between the distribution of the initially observed network $X(t_0)$ – which could be anything – and the transition distribution, which is defined by the probabilities in Equation (11.2) and the rate of change ρ. This dissociation is indeed pursued in this chapter, and we are interested solely in the transition distribution. In empirical research, this has the advantage that we do not have to be concerned with the processes that led to the initially observed network but can instead focus exclusively on the "social rules" represented by the transition probabilities governing the process of network change. The estimation of the parameters θ and ρ will be conditional on $X(t_0)$ (i.e., the first observed value of the network is taken for granted and influences the parameter estimates only by its role as a starting point for the changes observed in later observations).

Because, in contrast with the ERGM as used in other chapters in this book, the model here does not define an exponential family of distributions as presented in the statistical literature, the equivalence of the likelihood principle and the moment equation, given in Chapter 12, do not hold for this dynamic model. In this case, these two principles lead to different estimators.

11.3.6   Configurations for Networks

The statistics used to define the longitudinal model, denoted by $z_k(x)$ in Equation (11.1), can be chosen along exactly the same lines as the statistics in the cross-sectional ERGM, discussed in the other chapters (see for example chapter 3, 5, 6, 8 or any of the applications chapters). Thus, they will usually be counts of configurations, often combined with nodal or dyadic covariates. One thing is simpler, however. The difficulties connected to near-degeneracy (see the discussion around Figures 6.5 and 6.6 in Chapter 6) do not play a role here apart from some exceptional cases. Therefore, the Markov specifications, where transitivity is represented by triads or triplets, can be employed without problems for most longitudinal data sets.

The reason for this difference is that in the ERGM, dependence between ties operates simultaneously from all tie-variables to all tie-variables, whereas in the longitudinal model, dependence follows the arrow of time, and changes in tie-variables depend on current values of tie-variables. Starting from any probability distribution for $X(t_0)$, the transition process defined previously indicates a probability distribution for $X(t)$ for later time points $t > t_0$. The near-degeneracy will play a role only for far away time points that are – in all situations that we encountered – far removed from the time horizon of data collection. For parameters and time points in ranges that correspond well to observed network dynamics, the distributions of $X(t)$ are usually well behaved.[1]

The same kind of data structures that may be modeled with ERGMs, for which models have been presented in previous chapters, may be analyzed over time with the tie-based longitudinal model. We may have directed and undirected univariate or multivariate networks or hybrids thereof. The investigation over time of these structures gives a higher resolution and allows us to be more specific in our assertions about mechanisms that drive the network. We are furthermore able to interpret effects directly.

---

[1] For SAOMs, see Section 11.4.2. The Jaccard index is typically used to assess the amount of change between observations. As a rule of thumb, an index smaller than 0.3 indicates that there is too much change for the SAOM to be applicable (Snijders, van de Bunt, & Steglich, 2010b). For the models presented here, a Jaccard index smaller than 0.3 may suggest that more complicated statistics (e.g., alternating triangles) are required to achieve convergence.

For example, assume that we are interested in whether there is transitive closure in a univariate undirected network. Conditioning on the first observation, the 2-paths that were closed in-between observations will appear as triangles at the second observation point. Naturally, even triangles that consist of more than one new tie will provide information on the strength of the effect of closure, discounting for number of new 2-paths and edges. When interpreting the transitive closure effect, we can do this directly in terms of creating or deleting a tie that would close a 2-path.

Similarly, for multivariate networks (see Chapter 10), although cross-sectionally we may only hypothesize the direction of change (e.g., whether advice follows friendship), this may be directly observed for longitudinal data. Likewise for multiplex closure, when, say, an advice tie from one actor i to an actor j, who is a friend's friend of i, we can in principle infer whether the advice tie bridges the friendship 2-path, or whether k nominated by i as a friend is likely to nominate as a friend j who already receives advice from i. At present, these path dependencies are not fully explored in the tie-based models, mainly because of the large number of extra statistics needed and the relative bluntness of the method of moments estimator.

11.4 Relations to Other Models

11.4.1 Reciprocity Model as Precursor

The reciprocity model developed by Wasserman (1979, 1980), and studied by Leenders (1995) and Snijders (1999), is a precursor of this model. It assumes that the dyads $(X_{ij}(t), X_{ji}(t))$ are independent, but allows that reciprocation can play a role such that changes in $X_{ij}(t)$ may depend on the current state of $X_{ji}(t)$. This situation can be obtained in our model by defining the two statistics:

$$z_1(x) = \sum_{i,j} x_{ij},$$

$$z_2(x) = \sum_{i,j} x_{ij} x_{ji}.$$

Although Wasserman's model is slightly more general because it allows for a fourth parameter, our version of the reciprocity model has three parameters: ρ, θ_1, and θ_2. Leenders (1995) extended this model to allow covariates, while still postulating independence between dyads. For a model for network dynamics, this is a very unattractive assumption. It excludes triadic and higher-order dependencies, which are essential for social networks, and only has the technical advantage that, retaining independence between dyads, it allows the application of more traditional statistical approaches.

11.4.2   Stochastic Actor-Oriented Models as Alternatives

The previously defined model is called "tie-oriented" because primary elements of the model are the ties embedded in the network and the probabilities of tie changes. An alternative is the stochastic actor-oriented model (SAOM) proposed by Snijders and van Duijn (1997) and Snijders (2001). In the actor-oriented model, the primacy resides in the actors. The actors are assumed to control their outgoing ties and to make changes in these ties according to short-term goals and restrictions. Researchers using network analysis have to deal with units of different kinds and accordingly combine different levels of analysis: the tie, the dyad, the actor, and the network. How to navigate these various levels depends on the research at hand and the role played by the network. An actor-oriented approach may combine better with some social science theories than a tie-based approach whenever it is natural to consider social actors, embedded in a network with other actors, as a theoretical starting point (cf. Emirbayer & Goodwin, 1994). For yet other perspectives, the assumptions guiding the behavior of the actors may seem too strong, and the underlying assumption of the tie-based process whereby ties evolve out of other ties is sufficient. Instances might include an undirected relationship in which it does not seem plausible that the actor controls the ties (for a discussion of actor-oriented formulations for undirected ties, see Snijders (2006, 2010b)).

The basic function defining probabilities of change in the tie-based model is the potential function in Equation (11.1), $\theta_1 z_1(x) + \theta_2 z_2(x) + \cdots + \theta_p z_p(x)$. This function, defined for the whole network, indicates the likelihood of creation and disappearance of ties: the higher the increase of the potential function by a change of a particular tie-variable, the more likely is this change. The analogous position in the actor-oriented model is occupied by the so-called evaluation function, which is a function defined for each actor within the network that depends on the personal network, as well as the further network embeddedness, of the actor. The name is chosen because this function expresses the evaluation by the actor of a particular network structure. Here, also, for each actor, the more this actor's evaluation function increases by changing a particular outgoing tie-variable, the more likely is this change. Typically, the actor-oriented models have assumed directed networks. However, Snijders (2006, 2010b) described an actor-oriented model for undirected networks – where the evaluation is done by either node in the pair making up the tie or both – and provided examples of ways in which the previously mentioned tie-based processes may be formulated in terms of actor-oriented models. An introduction to actor-oriented models for network dynamics and their further ramifications is given in Snijders, van de Bunt, and Steglich (2010).

The choice between tie- and actor-oriented models is mainly a matter of theoretical preference. The former may be preferred when there is too much change for the actor-oriented model to deal with. It would also be interesting to compare these models based on goodness of fit to empirical data sets, but this depends on likelihood comparisons that have not been carried out in practice. It is to be expected that qualitative results of these two models will be roughly similar, but this has not been studied systematically. A comparison for one data set is presented in Snijders (2006).

11.5   Conclusion

We describe how all forms of ERGMs may be conceived in terms of longitudinal models and how this contributes more information about the dynamics, which in turn make the longitudinal models more stable to the point of allowing Markov configurations. Naturally, the longitudinal analysis requires extra data collection and analysis to be conditioned on the first observation.

Future directions include allowing for the process to have a memory through incorporating varying forms of path dependencies. For example, it is plausible to assume that once a tie between two actors has been severed, this is likely to affect the probability of it reforming. Related to this is that it may occasionally be useful to model the rate of change, as is frequently done in the actor-oriented models.

A fundamental assumption of the tie-based models (and, indeed, all ERGMs) is that the ties represent "states" of interaction rather than "events." Events such as e-mails, telephone calls, and economic transactions are likely to follow different processes from, for example, friendships. An important property of a state is that it has duration, something that creates overlaps between different states and thus makes it meaningful to define temporal dependencies such as those described previously. For events, a variety of dependencies are thinkable, and the tie-based models presented here may be elaborated in the direction of relational event history models such as those of Butts (2008) and Brandes, Lerner, and Snijders (2009). Note that the extension to time-stamped relational data is trivial as long as the relational data still represent states.

Models yet to be elaborated are tie-based models for bipartite networks, changing network auto-correlated attributes, and hybrids being combinations of different data structures. The first two have been described in a stochastic actor-oriented framework in Koskinen and Edling (2010) and

Steglich, Snijders, and Pearson (2010), respectively, but the extension to a tie-based (ERGM-like) model formulation is straightforward. A particularly fruitful direction from a theoretical perspective would be to model the evolution of multilevel networks in the sense of Brass et al. (2004) and Lazega et al. (2008). This would allow us to parse out how the different processes of interorganizational ties and actor-to-actor ties may interact with and be contingent on organization-to-actor ties.

12

Simulation, Estimation, and Goodness of Fit

Johan Koskinen and Tom Snijders

12.1 Exploring and Relating Model to Data in Practice

Previous chapters concentrated on the formulation and specification of exponential random graph models (ERGMs) for different types of relational data. In Chapter 6, we saw that effects represented by configurations and corresponding parameters define a distribution of graphs where the probability of getting any particular graph depends on the configurations in the graph. Chapter 7 showed that configurations are sufficient information in the sense that the probability of a graph is completely determined by statistics that are the counts of relevant configurations.

If we increase the strength of a parameter for a given configuration, graphs with more of that configuration become more likely in the resulting distribution. This simple fact is used in the three methods presented in this chapter:

Simulation: For a given model by fixing parameter values, it is possible to examine the features of graphs in the distribution through simulation to gain insight into the outcomes of the model.

Estimation: Empirically, for a given model and a given dataset, it is possible to estimate the parameter values that are most likely to have generated the observed graph, the "maximum likelihood estimates (MLEs)." Furthermore, it can be shown that the observed graph is central in the distribution of graphs determined by these estimates–but as we will see, because of the dependencies in the data, MLE requires simulation procedures.

Heuristic goodness of fit (GOF): For a fitted model (i.e., with parameters estimated from data), it is then possible to simulate the distribution of graphs to see whether other features of the data (i.e., nonfitted effects) are central or extreme in

141

the distribution. If a graph feature is not extreme, there is no evidence to suggest that it may not have arisen from processes implicit in this model, and hence we can say that the model can explain that particular feature of the data – in other words, that such a feature is well fitted by the model.

To illustrate the basic principle of estimation and how this relies on simulation, consider an example. Suppose we want to estimate parameters for a model with edges and alternating triangle (as defined in Equation (6.8) and Figure 6.9a; $\lambda = 2$) parameters for Kapferer's (1972) tailor shop data. The observed number of edges is 223, and the alternating triangle statistic is 406.4. In Figure 12.1, we try a few values for the edge and alternating triangle parameters. In the top left-hand chart, we have simulated graphs when both parameters are 0, and so have distributions from those graphs of the statistics for edges and alternating triangles. We see that the observed configurations are far from the distribution, so it would be unlikely to observe the data if these values were true. In the top right-hand chart, a decrease in the edge parameter (to -0.84) centers the distribution of edges over the observed number of edges but does not produce enough alternating triangles. If we then increase the alternating triangle parameter (to 0.029), we get closer to the observed number of alternating triangles but do not reproduce the number of edges (bottom left hand chart). For the parameters in the right-hand bottom chart (the edge and alternating triangle parameters equal to -4.413 and 1.45, respectively), however, the distribution of edges and alternating triangles are centered over the observed values. These parameter values determine a model that adequately represents data, at least on these two statistics.

12.2   Simulation: Obtaining Distribution of Graphs for a Given ERGM

The charts in Figure 12.1 plot edges against alternating triangles for samples of graphs from different distributions. Because of the vast number of possible graphs, we cannot plot the exact distribution, nor can we calculate properties of these distributions analytically. We have to rely on a sample of graphs. Sampling graphs is very central to ERGM inference.

12.2.1   Sampling Graphs Using Markov Chain Monte Carlo

To sample a graph x, we rely on the well-known procedure Markov chain Monte Carlo (MCMC), which here consists of generating a sequence of M graphs where graphs are successively updated through small changes. For large M, the last graph in the sequence is a draw from the target

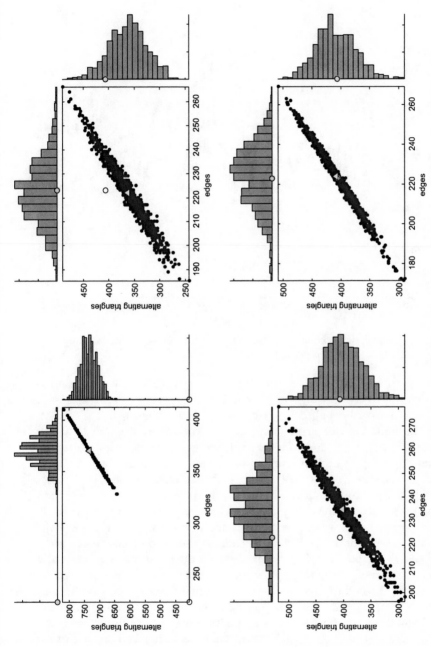

Figure 12.1. Distribution of edges and alternating triangles (mean represented by triangle) for different values of parameters compared to observed number of edges and alternating triangles (circle) for Kapferer's (1972) data.

143

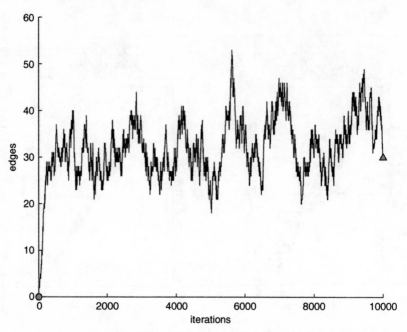

Figure 12.2. Number of edges in sequence of graphs in Markov chain starting with empty graph.

distribution – in our case, the ERGM. In particular, we may use the Metropolis-Hastings algorithm (Chib & Greenberg, 1995; Hastings, 1970; Metropolis et al., 1953; Tierney, 1994) to sample from the ERGM.

The updating rule in moving from the current (old) graph to a new graph in the simulation consists of choosing a pair of nodes at random and removing or adding a tie between them according to whether they are already tied. If the new graph with one changed tie has a higher probability than the old graph, the new graph is taken as the next graph in the sequence. If the new graph has a lower probability and is less likely than the old one, we only sometimes accept the proposed change to the graph, with a probability that depends on the ratio of how much more likely the old graph is than the new one. In the event that the new graph is not accepted, the next graph in the sequence remains the old graph.

Figure 12.2 illustrates the case of sampling from a model with edges and alternating triangles, with edge and alternating triangle parameters −2 and 0.3 respectively, on twenty nodes. Starting with the empty graph (with zero edges and zero alternating triangles), after 100 updates of the Markov chain, we have reached a graph with roughly ten edges. After around 500 iterations, graphs of between twenty and forty edges are being proposed. Between 1,000 and 10,000 iterations, the chain appears to have settled into a pattern, generating graphs with an average of about

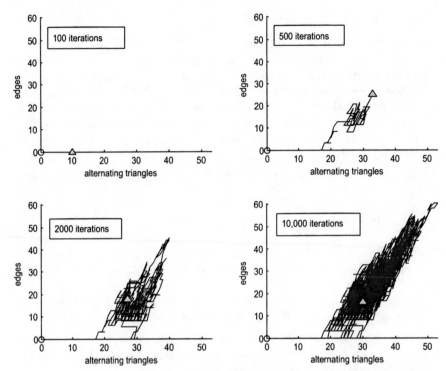

Figure 12.3. Number of edges against alternating triangles for sequence of graphs in Markov chain starting in empty graph. Model with edge and alternating triangle parameters equal to −2 and 0.3 respectively, $n = 20$.

thirty edges. We may tentatively conclude that the chain has "converged" into drawing graphs from a stationary distribution, and we may take the last graph in the sequence as our sample point. For the two statistics in Figure 12.3, we see clearly how the chain settles and starts filling in the area it is exploring.

The rationale behind the MCMC sampler is that if the current state is a draw from the target distribution, so will be the next state. That is, once we have started producing graphs from the ERGM, we will continue to do so. Determining how many iterations are necessary before the simulation has settled into the target distribution has to be decided on a case-by-case basis. The number of such iterations is commonly referred to as the "burn-in." From Figure 12.2, as far as edges are concerned, the simulation quickly burns in within a few hundred iterations. The burn-in is needed for the Markov chain to "forget" the state in which it started. In principle, as long as the burn-in is long enough, the choice of starting graph (empty, complete, or any arbitrary graph) does not matter.

12.2.2   Metropolis Algorithm

Many problems with simulation, estimation, and GOF are due to the simulation performing badly – the sampler does not move freely between graphs. In this section, we present a brief but more detailed description of the Metropolis sampler. A sequence $x^{(0)}, x^{(1)}, \ldots, x^{(M-1)}, x^{(M)}$ of graphs is generated as follows: in each iteration m, with the current state $x^{(m-1)}$, a pair of nodes i and j is chosen at random with a proposal to update the corresponding tie-variable such that the proposal graph x^* is equal to $x^{(m-1)}$, except that $x_{ij}^{(m-1)}$ is set to $1 - x_{ij}^{(m-1)}$ – we call this a "toggle." If the target distribution is $P_\theta(x)$, we accept the proposed move with probability

$$\min\left\{1, \frac{P_\theta(x^*)}{P_\theta(x^{(m-1)})}\right\},$$

where the ratio in the acceptance probability is called the "Hastings ratio." If the move is accepted, we set $x^{(m)} = x^*$; otherwise, we set $x^{(m)} = x^{(m-1)}$.

Note that the ratio of probabilities in the Hastings ratio may be expressed as a ratio of the conditional probability of $X_{ij} = 1 - x_{ij}^{(m-1)}$ to the conditional probability of $X_{ij} = x_{ij}^{(m-1)}$ given the rest $x_{-ij}^{(m-1)}$. Recall that this ratio is available in closed form and that the logarithm of this is the logit (or reciprocal of the logit):

$$\log\left\{\frac{P_\theta(x^*)}{P_\theta(x^{(m-1)})}\right\} = \log\left\{\Pr(X_{ij} = 1 - x_{ij}^{(m-1)} \mid X_{-ij} = x_{-ij}^{(m-1)}\right\}$$

$$= \theta_1(z_1(x^*) - z_1(x^{(m-1)})) + \theta_2(z_2(x^*)$$
$$- z_2(x^{(m-1)})) + \cdots + \theta_p(z_p(x^*) - z_p(x^{(m-1)})).$$

Furthermore, this Hastings ratio does not involve the normalizing constant, and we only need to calculate the differences in statistics that result in changing $x_{ij}^{(m-1)}$ to $1 - x_{ij}^{(m-1)}$. These differences are commonly called the "change statistics." (see Eq. 6.1)

Alternatives to proposing a move through a simple toggle are given in Snijders (2002) and generally involve proposing bigger moves or updating null ties and ties with unequal weights as in, for example, the tie–no tie sampler (Morris, Handcock, & Hunter, 2008). These alternative algorithms are generally more efficient because they reduce the required burn-in between graphs. From Figure 12.3, we note that when the chain has settled in, most graphs are sampled from the right area. Thus, there is no need to restart the chain if we want several graphs from the same distribution. Instead, we let the chain burn in for a shorter period of time between sample points. The number of iterations discarded in-between sample points is called "thinning." It is important to keep in mind that these sampled graphs will constitute a dependent sample, and for this reason, an important diagnostic when simulating graphs is to make sure the autocorrelation for the statistics is not too big (ideally, zero, but a maximum of 0.4 in absolute value is tolerated – see Section 12.4.2 on the multiplication factor).

12.3 Estimation

As mentioned previously, the inferential goal is to center the distribution of statistics over those of the observed network, thus fitting a model that we say gives maximal support to the data. We define the distribution as centered on the observed values when the values of the statistics from the distribution are the same as those observed on average. Formally, we want the expected value of the statistics $E_\theta(z(X))$ to be equal to the observed statistics (i.e., $E_\theta(z(X)) = z(x_{obs})$), where x_{obs} is the observed graph. Equivalently, $E_\theta(z(X)) - z(x_{obs}) = 0$, is known as the moment equation. Solving the moment equation for θ is to find the parameter values that provide maximal support to the data. For most models, we cannot solve the moment equation analytically, so we have to rely on simulation.

12.3.1 Maximum Likelihood Principle

The MLE of a parameter for a given model and observed data is the value of θ that makes observing data most likely – we want to find the vector θ that makes the probability $P_\theta(x_{obs})$ as large as possible. It can be shown that this value of θ is the same as the solution of the moment equation,[1] so that centering the distribution is equivalent to finding the MLE of θ. (This holds for all exponential family distributions, cf. Lehmann, 1983; for further details of statistical inference for ERGMs, see Corander, Dahmström, and Dahmström (1998, 2002); Crouch, Wasserman, and Trachtenberg (1998); Dahmström and Dahmström (1993); Handcock (2003); Hunter and Handcock (2006); Snijders (2002); Strauss and Ikeda (1990).)

12.3.2 Curved ERGMs

For the alternating statistics, as noted previously, we often fix the smoothing constant λ, but we can choose to consider it a free parameter to be estimated. The resulting model then belongs to the curved exponential

---

[1] Differentiating the logarithm of $P_\theta(x_{obs})$ with respect to θ, $\frac{\partial}{\partial \theta} \log P_\theta(x_{obs}) = z(x_{obs}) - \frac{\partial}{\partial \theta} \log \left\{ \sum_{x \in X} e^{\theta_1 z_1(x) + \cdots + \theta_p z_p(x)} \right\}$, reduces this to $z(x_{obs}) - \sum_{x \in X} z(x) P_\theta(x)$, which is exactly the moment equation.

family of distributions with more parameters than sufficient statistics – in the maximum likelihood equation, there are more unknowns, θ, than knowns. The moment equation is no longer equivalent to the maximum likelihood equation, but a similar equation may be constructed by a transformation, increasing the number of statistics and parameters so that they are equal (Hunter & Handcock, 2006).

12.3.3   Bayesian Inference

In the Bayesian paradigm, the uncertainty regarding what is unknown should be modeled by probabilities and probability distributions (see, e.g., Bernardo & Smith, 1994; Box & Tiao, 1973; Lindley, 1965). Because the values of the parameters are unknown, we model our uncertainty regarding the parameters using a prior distribution. When we have observed data, our model for data may be used to assess the likelihood of different values of the parameters, given the probability of observing data for these values. Hence, we may use the data model to update our uncertainty about the parameters into a posterior distribution.

The posterior distribution is not available in closed form, so a sampling procedure has to be performed in which we draw values from the posterior distribution. This may be done using MCMC, where we update the current parameter vector by proposing new values for the parameters and accept these with a probability that depends on how probable the proposed values are in relation to the current values, according to the posterior (an alternative is proposed by Atchade, Lartillot, and Robert (2008)). This does not rely on the moment equation and applies equally well to curved ERGMs. To evaluate the ratios of posterior distributions in the MCMC updating steps, we also need to draw some sample graphs from the model defined by that parameter value (Koskinen, 2008; Koskinen, Robins, & Pattison, 2010). A Bayesian estimation procedure is proposed by Koskinen (2008) and Koskinen et al. (2010), and it is argued that a Bayesian procedure offers advantages over the maximum likelihood approach. The estimation procedure returns a distribution of likely parameters and offers the possibility of using prior specification of uncertainty about the parameters (specified subjectively or through conjugacy – Diaconis & Ylvisaker, 1979). Caimo and Friel (2011) proposed a related but superior approach that uses the exchange algorithm of Murray, Ghahramani, and MacKay (2006), which makes Bayesian estimation more computationally efficient (and less complicated than maximum likelihood estimation). These algorithms produce an output $\theta^{(r)}, \theta^{(r+1)}, \theta^{(r+2)}, \ldots, \theta^{(T)}$, which is a draw from the posterior distribution of $\theta \mid x_{obs}$, where r is a suitably chosen burn-in. The relevant information about the parameters given our observation is contained in this output, and a point estimate is obtained as the mean

$\hat{\theta} = \frac{1}{T-r}(\theta^{(r)} + \theta^{(r+1)} + \cdots + \theta^{(T)})$, with uncertainty measured by the standard deviation $SD(\theta_k)$.

The algorithm of Caimo and Friel (2011) is surprisingly simple: in each iteration, a move is proposed to θ^*, drawn from a normal distribution centered on the current value $\theta^{(t)}$. Given this proposal, one graph is generated $x^* \sim ERGM(\theta^*)$. We draw a uniform random variate, $u \sim \text{Unif}(0, 1)$, and based on θ^* and the generated graph x^*, we accept θ^* and set $\theta^{(t+1)} = \theta^*$ if $\log(u) < (\theta^{(t)} - \theta^*)^T(z(x^*) - z(x_{obs}))$; otherwise, set $\theta^{(t+1)} = \theta^{(t)}$. Heuristically, this means that we accept parameters that generate graphs similar to what we have observed.

12.4 Solving the Likelihood Equation

The principle for solving the moment equation is to choose a value θ, simulating graphs $x^{(1)}, x^{(2)}, \ldots, x^{(M)}$, calculating the sample equivalent $\bar{z}_\theta = \frac{1}{M}(z(x^{(1)}) + z(x^{(2)}) + \cdots + z(x^{(M)}))$ of $E_\theta(z(X))$ over this sample, and then checking whether $\bar{z}_\theta$ is equal to $z(x_{obs})$. If the difference $\bar{z}_\theta - z(x_{obs})$ is not 0, we choose another value θ and repeat the process. This is done until we find a value θ for which $\bar{z}_\theta - z(x_{obs}) = 0$, the MLE. In other words, we gradually change the parameter values to adjust the distributions of statistics. There will always be a sampling variability in $\bar{z}_\theta$, the size of which depends on M.

A "brute force" procedure of trying different values of θ and determining whether $\bar{z}_\theta - z(x_{obs}) = 0$ is not very effective. Two main approaches for solving $\bar{z}_\theta - z(x_{obs}) = 0$ have been proposed in the literature – importance sampling and stochastic approximation. The first is the default of statnet, and the second is used in PNet and SIENA, and is available in statnet.

12.4.1 Importance Sampling: Geyer-Thompson Approach

The Geyer-Thompson (1992) algorithm takes one large sample of graphs for a provisional value of the parameter vector and then treats this sample as representing all possible graphs. Thus, even when we change the parameter vector, we use the same sample to calculate the sample average to determine whether $\bar{z}_\theta - z(x_{obs}) = 0$. Intuitively, this is much like the brute force approach, but we only need to use a small number of large samples, and there are effective minimization algorithms. A Geyer-Thompson algorithm is the main ingredient of the default method in the statnet program (Handcock, 2003; Handcock, et al., 2003; Hunter, Handcock, Butts, Goodreau, & Morris, 2008; Hunter & Handcock, 2006). To take into account that the sample of graphs is only a sample, and not the entire space of graphs, we need to take a weighted average of the statistics when we calculate $\bar{z}_\theta$. More specifically, if the sample is generated from the model $P_{\tilde{\theta}}(x)$, the sample average $\bar{f}_\theta = w^{(1)} f(x^{(1)}) + w^{(2)} f(x^{(2)}) + \cdots + w^{(M)} f(x^{(M)})$, of a function $f(x)$, with weights

$$w^{(m)} = \frac{e^{(\theta_1 - \tilde{\theta}_1)z_1(x^{(m)}) + \cdots + (\theta_p - \tilde{\theta}p)z_p(x^{(m)})}}{\sum_{k=1}^{M} e^{(\theta_1 - \tilde{\theta}_1)z_1(x^{(k)}) + \cdots + (\theta_p - \tilde{\theta}p)z_p(x^{(k)})}},$$

is a good approximation to the true expected value $E_\theta(f(X))$ when M gets large and θ is reasonably close to $\tilde{\theta}$. The closer θ is to $\tilde{\theta}$, the closer the weights are to $\frac{1}{M}$, and if, for example, $\tilde{\theta} = \theta$ and $f(x) = z(x)$, then $\bar{f}_\theta(x) = \bar{z}_\theta(x)$. If θ is not close to $\tilde{\theta}$, there will be a high dispersion between the weights $w^{(m)}$, and the estimate, although still centered, will have a large standard deviation.

Typically, the chain generating $x^{(1)}, x^{(2)}, \ldots, x^{(M)}$ is not allowed to burn in between successive sampling points. Instead, a smaller number of steps, k (the thinning), are discarded between sample points, thus giving a sample that is weakly correlated. This is generally acceptable as long as the autocorrelation of the chain is not too large, in which case the algorithm may perform badly. In statnet, the number of steps k is set by the argument "interval" to "ergm" (as described in Goodreau et al. (2008); the user may consider setting k according to the heuristic shown below in Section 12.4.2, which depends on the multiplication factor).

To solve the likelihood equation, a sequence of parameters $\theta^{(0)} = \tilde{\theta}, \theta^{(1)}, \theta^{(2)}, \ldots, \theta^{(G)}$ is generated using a version of Newton-Raphson (or Fisher scoring). An updating step of $\theta^{(g)}$ in the minimization algorithm is done through

$$\theta^{(g)} = \theta^{(g-1)} - D(\theta^{(g-1)})^{-1} \left\{ \sum_{m=1}^{M} w^{(m)} z(x^{(m)}) - z(x_{obs}) \right\}.$$

Because $\sum_{m=1}^{M} w^{(m)} z(x^{(m)})$ is an approximation of $E_\theta(z(X))$, if $\theta^{(g-1)}$ is truly the MLE, then $E_\theta(z(X)) - z(x_{obs}) = 0$, and the updating step will simply set $\theta^{(g)}$ equal to $\theta^{(g-1)}$.

The scaling matrix $D(\theta)$ in the algorithm scales the difference between the observed values and the expected values of the statistics. This is needed because statistics can differ in their sensitivity to changes in corresponding parameters, and the parameters will affect not only their "own" but also other statistics. The matrix $D(\theta)$ is set to the weighted sample covariance $\sum_m w^{(m)} z(x^{(m)}) z(x^{(m)})^T - \left[\sum_m w^{(m)} z(x^{(m)}) \right] \left[\sum_m w^{(m)} z(x^{(m)}) \right]^T$.

Typically, this algorithm has to be restarted several times, taking $\theta^{(G)}$ as the provisional MLE $\tilde{\theta}$, and then restarting the algorithm with $\tilde{\theta} = \theta^{(G)}$, (the number of restarts is set by the argument "maxit" to "ergm"). Of great importance is that $\tilde{\theta}$ is not too far from the true MLE, and in particular, the sample of statistics $z(x^{(1)}), z(x^{(2)}), \ldots, z(x^{(M)})$ must "cover" the observed statistics $z(x_{obs})$.[2] Hence, finding a good starting point for this algorithm may be difficult.

12.4.2   Stochastic Approximation: Robbins-Monro Algorithm

Snijders (2002) proposed stochastic approximation (a version of the Robbins-Monro (1951) algorithm) to obtain the MLE for the ERGM. Like the importance sampling scheme, it relies on incremental updating of parameters according to a Newton-Raphson–type equation, but without the need to draw large samples of graphs and calculating expected values. Although it may not appear efficient, it is a robust procedure that produces reliable estimates and does not require particularly good starting values.

The algorithm of Snijders (2002) consists of three main phases. These are presented here in some detail with a view to explaining the function of some algorithm settings to assist in situations where default settings may not be adequate. All phases use the Metropolis algorithm to generate draws from the model. It is important that there be sufficient burn-in. In PNet, burn-in is set to γ density $(x_{obs})[1 - \text{density}(x_{obs})]n^2$, where γ is called the "multiplication factor." If the multiplication factor is set too low, we might be generating the wrong kind of graphs, so increasing the multiplication factor improves the estimation procedure. The default is $\gamma = 10$ ($\gamma = 30$ for directed univariate networks), giving a burn-in of roughly 1,300 for a graph with $n = 30$ and 75 edges.[3] The default value can be too low and may be increased. If researchers are having difficulty obtaining converged parameter estimates, one trick is to increase the multiplication factor. A sample autocorrelation that is larger than 0.4 (in absolute value) generally indicates that the multiplication factor is too low.

Another simulation tuning constant is the gain factor, a. The "gain factor" controls how large the updating steps are when we update θ. If a is too large, the updating steps will be too large, and although the iterations may reach the general vicinity of the MLE quickly, they may constantly overshoot it. If a is too small, the iterations will move in very small and precise steps but take very long to reach the MLE. The default for a is 0.1, which can be too high if the initial parameters are close to the MLE.

---

[2]   Technically, we say that $z(x_{obs})$ is in the relative interior of the convex hull on $z(x^{(1)}), \ldots, z(x^{(M)})$ (Handcock, 2003).

[3]   The format of the algorithm here adheres to the settings in PNet. Some further modifications are found in Snijders (2002). In statnet, the thinning and the burn-in are set using "interval" and "burn-in", respectively. Other Robbins-Monro estimation settings are set using the "control" argument to ergm.

Phase 1: Initialization. In phase 1, a small number of iterations are performed to determine the scaling matrix D_0 and initial values for the parameters. The scaling matrix serves a similar purpose as in the importance sampling algorithm and is used to scale the updates of the different elements of the parameter vector. A sample $x^{(1)}, x^{(2)}, \ldots, x^{(M_1)}$ of size $M_1 = 7 + 3p$, where p is the number of parameters, is generated for initial parameter $\tilde{\theta}$. A rough estimate of the expected vector of statistics is given as

$$\tilde{z}_\theta = \frac{1}{M_1}(z(x^{(1)}) + z(x^{(2)}) + \cdots + z(x^{((M_1)})),$$

and the covariance matrix is given as

$$D = \frac{1}{M_1} \sum_m z(x^{(m)})z(x^{(m)})^{\mathrm{T}} - \tilde{z}_\theta \tilde{z}_\theta^{\mathrm{T}}.$$

The initial parameter vector for phase 2 is then set to $\theta^{(0)} = \tilde{\theta} - a D^{-1}(\tilde{z}_\theta - z_{obs})$, where z_{obs} henceforth denotes $z(x_{obs})$. The scaling matrix used throughout phase 2 is set to $D_0 = \mathrm{diag}(D)$.

Phase 2: Optimization. Phase 2 implements a Newton-Raphson minimization scheme to find the solution to $\tilde{z}_\theta - z_{obs} = 0$. It consists of several subphases, in which the steps taken in the updating are made progressively smaller under the assumption that the algorithm is getting closer to the MLE. In each subphase r and in each iteration m, the current parameter vector $\theta^{(m)}$ is updated to the new value $\theta^{(m+1)}$ through

$$\theta^{(m+1)} = \theta^{(m)} - a_r D_0^{-1}(z(x^{(m)}) - z_{obs}),$$

where $x^{(m)}$ is one graph generated from the model defined by the current parameter $\theta^{(m)}$. Because $z(x^{(m)})$ is based only on one graph, $x^{(m)}$, the difference $z(x^{(m)}) - z_{obs}$ is unlikely to equal 0; however, if $\theta^{(m)}$ is the MLE, the difference will be 0 on average. The gain factor in subphase r is set to $a_r = a_{r-1}/2$, and thus the changes to consecutive $\theta^{(m)}$ are progressively smaller for each subphase. The changes will thus get smaller and smaller as $z(x^{(m)})$ gets closer to z_{obs} and a_r gets closer to 0.

The subphase r is run until the number of iterations it takes for the trajectory of the generated statistics to cross the observed ones (i.e., $z_k(x^{(m-1)}) > z_k(x_{obs})$ and $z_k(x^{(m)}) < z_k(x_{obs})$, but at least $(7 + p)2^{4r/3}$ and at most $(7 + p)2^{4r/3} + 200$ iterations). The initial value of the parameters in a subphase is set to the average parameter values of the previous subphase. The average parameter values from the last subphase are taken as the MLE.

Figure 12.4 illustrates the Robbins-Monro algorithm for a network on 20 actors with 32 edges and 31.5 alternating triangles. In the left-hand panels, the five subphases (indicated by dotted lines) are visible as the shift

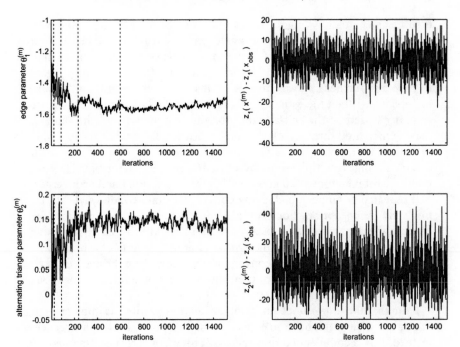

Figure 12.4. Robbins-Monro algorithm for network on n= 20 actors.

in the parameter values results from the starting value being the average from the previous subphase. The right-hand panels show the differences $z(x^{(m)}) - z_{obs}$ for edges and alternating triangles, and how this difference fluctuates around zero.

Phase 3: Convergence Check and Calculation of Measures of Uncertainty. If the parameter value $\hat{\theta}$ returned by phase 2 is truly the MLE, we know that the expected value $E_{\hat{\theta}}(z(X))$ should equal the observed $z(x_{obs})$ and for a sufficiently large sample $\bar{z}_\theta - z_{obs} \approx 0$. This is assessed in phase 3. If the expected values equal the observed ones, then we say that the estimation procedure has converged. Because the estimation procedure is numerical, we do not expect the equality to hold true exactly – we want the solution to be sufficiently close to the true MLE. We compare the difference between $\bar{z}_\theta$ and z_{obs} in relation to the overall variation in the distribution of statistics. If the difference is small in comparison to the variation, we deem $\hat{\theta}$ to be sufficiently close to the MLE. More specifically, we say the estimation has converged to the MLE when the convergence statistic

$$\frac{\bar{z}_\theta - z_{obs}}{SD_\theta(\{z_k(x^{(m)})\}_{m=1,\ldots,M_3})},$$

is sufficiently small, where the denominator is the sample standard deviation. We use the criterion that the convergence statistic should be between -0.1 and 0.1 for convergence.[4] If the convergence statistic is smaller than -0.1 or larger than 0.1, $\hat{\theta}$ is too far from the MLE for it to be appropriate to base any further analysis on this estimate, and the estimation should be repeated. When the estimation is repeated, the last obtained estimate should be used as the initial value for the parameter, and the burn-in may be increased through a larger multiplication factor. For the example of Figure 12.1, convergence was not achieved at the first attempt with default settings (multiplication factor of 10 and gain factor of 0.1). With multiplication factors of 20 and then 50, the estimation finally converges.

If repeated attempts at achieving convergence fail, conditional estimation may be an option. For example, the density of the graphs may be fixed to the density for the observation. This is akin to treating the edge parameter as a nuisance parameter that is of no interest for estimation.[5] Other conditions to facilitate convergence include fixing the degree distributions (in- and out-degrees) or treating some ties or actors as exogenous to the model.

Note that the importance sampling estimation routine, as implemented in `statnet`, does not have an equivalent of phase 3 to check convergence. Instead, it is recommended that the user check convergence "manually" using "`mcmc.diagnostics()`" and "`gof()`", as described in Goodreau et al. (2008, sections 6 and 8).

The second goal of phase 3 is to obtain approximate standard errors of the estimates. (Recall that the standard error is the standard deviation of an estimator in the sampling distribution.) For generalized linear models it is common to derive the approximate standard errors from the Fisher information matrix or the Hessian (for exponential family models, they are the same but different signs). It is straightforward to show that the information matrix is equal to the covariance matrix of the statistics (i.e., $E_{\hat{\theta}}(z(X)z(X)^T) - E_{\hat{\theta}}(z(X))^T$). A sample equivalent is easily obtainable from the sample generated in the third phase.

12.4.3   Modifications for Longitudinal Model

These estimation procedures are somewhat different for the longitudinal model described in Chapter 11. The method of moments, which may also be called the "method of estimating equations," can be applied here,

---

[4] This criterion has proved useful, but the choice of 0.1 is obviously somewhat arbitrary. More generally, the important issue is whether the deviation is due to simulation error or whether it reflects the fact that the identity cannot be satisfied. The choice of 0.1 appears to strike a good balance.

[5] Note that the conditioning has to be taken into consideration in the interpretation of results because the fitted model applies to graphs with a density equal to the observed density.

albeit with some additional complications compared to the previously described procedures. The moment equations are

$$\sum_{m=1}^{M-1} E_{\hat{\theta},\hat{\rho}}\{z(X(t_{m+1}))|X(t_m) = x(t_m)\} = \sum_{m=1}^{M-1} z(x(t_{m+1})), \qquad (12.1a)$$

$$\sum_{m=1}^{M-1} E_{\hat{\theta},\hat{\rho}}\{H(X(t_{m+1}), X(t_m))|X(t_m) = x(t_m)\}$$

$$= \sum_{m=1}^{M-1} H(x(t_{m+1}), x(t_m)), \qquad (12.1b)$$

where $H(x, x')$ is the Hamming distance between the adjacency matrices x and x', defined by

$$H(x, x') = \sum_{i,j=1}^{n} |x_{ij} - x'_{ij}|.$$

Equation (12.1a) is important for estimating θ, whereas Equation (12.1b) is important for estimating ρ, but both equations must be satisfied simultaneously. Parameter estimates that approximately solve these equations, as well as their standard errors, can be obtained following the algorithm proposed in Snijders (2001) for the actor-oriented model for network dynamics. These estimators are based entirely on the simulation model that simulates the networks given the starting network observed at t_1, and therefore, the same algorithm can be applied as in Snijders (2001), the only difference being that the update step given previously is followed to define the dynamics of the model. Increased computational efficiency, following the procedure in Schweinberger and Snijders (2007), can also be obtained here if appropriate adaptations are made. Similarly, a maximum likelihood estimator may be developed along the lines of Snijders, Koskinen, and Schweinberger (2010) or Bayesian procedures according to Koskinen and Snijders (2007).

The three phases of estimation for solving the moment equations are fundamentally the same for the longitudinal model with two main differences. First, when simulating $z(x^{(m)})$, we do not use a burn-in period because we are only simulating the changes between observation points (consecutive observations in the algorithm are independent realizations). The estimation of the parameters θ and ρ will be conditional on $x_{obs}(t_0)$ (i.e., the first observed value of the network is taken for granted and influences the parameter estimates only by its role as a starting point for the changes observed in later observations). The process, thus, is started in $x_{obs}(t_0)$, simulated forward according to the defined process, and stopped when a stopping criterion is met. If ρ is not estimated, the stopping criteria is either that $z(x^{(m)})$ should differ from $x_{obs}(t_0)$ for as many elements as $x_{obs}(t_1)$ differs from $x_{obs}(t_0)$ or a prescribed number of updates. If ρ is to be estimated through Equation (12.1b), the stopping criterion should be based on time, as simulated in the longitudinal model. Note that an update is done using a Gibbs updating step rather than a Metropolis updating step. That is, given the current state $x^{(r-1)}$ and for a pair $(i_r j_r)$ chosen uniformly at random, the next state is set to $\Delta_{i_r j_r} x^{(r-1)}$ with probability

$$\Pr(X^{(r)} = \Delta_{i_r j_r} x^{(r-1)} | (i_r, j_r))$$

$$= \frac{\exp(\theta^T z(\Delta_{i_r j_r} x^{(r-1)}))}{\exp(\theta^T z(\Delta_{i_r j_r} x^{(r-1)})) + \exp(\theta^T z(x^{(r-1)}))}.$$

If we let the change statistic $\delta^{(r)} = z(\Delta_{i_r j_r}^+ x^{(r-1)}) - z(\Delta_{i_r j_r}^- x^{(r-1)})$ denote the difference in statistics between setting the element $i_r j_r$ equal to 1 against setting it to 0, leaving all other elements of $x^{(r-1)}$ unchanged, we may write the probability of an updating step as $\Pr(X_{i_r j_r} = x_{i_r j_r}^{(r)} | X_{-i_r j_r} = x_{-i_r j_r}^{(r)}) = (1 + \exp\{(1 - 2x_{i_r j_r}^{(r)})\theta^T \delta^{(r)}\})^{-1}$. The second main difference in estimation between the longitudinal model and the cross-sectional model is that while $Cov_\theta\{\hat{\theta}\} = Cov_\theta\{z(X)\}^T$ for the latter, $Cov_\theta(\hat{\theta}) \approx D_I(\theta)^{-1} Cov_\theta\{z(X^{(M)}) | x_{obs}(t_0)\}[D_I(\theta)^{-1}]^T$ for the former, where $Cov_\theta\{z(X^{(M)}) | x_{obs}(t_0)\}$ is the covariance of statistics and $D_I(\theta)$ is the Jacobian $D_I(\theta) = (\partial/\partial\theta) E_\theta\{z(X^{(M)}) | x_{obs}(t_0)\}$. Schweinberger and Snijders (2007) showed that an efficient estimator of $D_I(\theta)$ is

$$D_I = -\frac{1}{G}\sum_{g=1}^{G} \left(z(x^{(M,g)}) - z(x_{obs})\right) S(\hat{\theta}; x^{(1,g)}, \ldots, x^{(M,g)})^T,$$

where

$$S(\theta, x^{(1)}, \ldots, x^{(M)})$$

$$= -\sum_{m=1}^{M} \frac{1}{1 + \exp\{-1 - 2x_{ij}^{(m)}\}\theta^T \delta^{(m)}\}}(1 - 2x_{ij}^{(m)})\delta^{(m)}$$

is the score calculated for a sample path from $x_{obs}(t_0)$ to $x^{(M)}$.

12.5   Testing Effects

So far, we have been concerned with fitting a model under the assumption that this model is the true model. A model can be seen as a collection of effects, and now we proceed to describe a procedure for assessing what effects are necessary to describe our data. If an effect of a fitted model turns out not to be important, a simpler model without this effect may suffice.

To determine the effects evidenced by data, we test the coefficients of the fitted model. If a parameter (e.g., the alternating triangle parameter) is different from zero, there is an effect of transitive closure in the process that generates data. That is, over and above the other effects, a tie is more likely to form or exist if it closes a (multiple) 2-path. As described in previous chapters, a nonzero parameter means that there are dependencies among ties of the kind prescribed by the corresponding configuration, and we see more of that configuration in the observed data than would be expected given the other effects in the model. For example, in the top right-hand panel of Figure 12.1, we see that a model with only an edge parameter (alternating triangle parameter is set to zero) still generates graphs with a nonzero alternating triangle statistic in the vicinity of the observed data. In what follows, we present procedures for testing whether the distance between the observed (circle) and predicted (triangle) is substantial.

12.5.1   Approximate Wald Test

For a given model, the approximate Wald test of whether a parameter is significantly different from zero is to take the parameter estimate and divide it by the (approximate) standard error of the estimator. If this ratio is smaller than -2 or larger than 2, we say that the parameter is significantly different from zero (and we can therefore say that we have, loosely speaking, a significant effect). In Figure 12.1, for the final model with edge parameter $\hat{\theta}_1 = -4.413$ and alternating triangle parameter $\hat{\theta}_2 = 1.445$, the latter has a standard error of 0.243 so that a test gives a ratio of $1.445/.243 = 5.95$, which is greater than 2. An equivalent way of stating this test is that we check whether the estimate is within two standard error units of 0:

$$\left| \frac{\hat{\theta}_k - \theta_{k,0}}{\mathrm{se}(\hat{\theta}_k)} \right| = \left| \frac{\hat{\theta}_k}{\mathrm{se}(\hat{\theta}_k)} \right| > 2.$$

The interpretation of this test is that if the parameter were zero, then the estimator would have a distribution that is centered on zero with a standard deviation equal to the standard error. On average, if we were to observe many data sets and obtain the MLE, we would on average get an MLE of zero. Occasionally, we would get much larger or much smaller estimates by chance, but it would be unlikely (about 5%) that we got an estimate much larger than two times the standard error away from zero. If the hypothesis that a parameter is equal to zero is rejected, we use the convention of saying that the parameter is "significantly different from zero."

Although there is some limited evidence from simulations to suggest that the sampling distribution of the MLE is not badly approximated by a normal distribution, too little is known to compare the Wald's test statistic to normal quartiles and report the corresponding levels of confidence (which would induce a false precision). As discussed in Hunter and Handcock (2006), there is little to suggest that asymptotic normality of estimators holds, and available results on limiting properties of ERGMs (Strauss, 1986) are reason for caution. A critical point of 2 is a suitably conservative choice that is fairly robust to distributional assumptions for the sampling distributions of the estimators, and in lieu of reporting a level of confidence, it seems sensible to merely use the convention of saying "significant."

In summary, if the estimation has converged (and only then), and if the estimate is more than two standard errors away from zero, we say that the corresponding parameter is significantly different from zero and that there is evidence for an effect of the corresponding dependency (or configuration).

12.5.2   Alternative Tests

Score Test. The interpretation of the Wald test, setting the parameter of interest to zero assuming everything else is equal, is confounded by the interdependence of effects.[6] Although the intention of setting a parameter to zero is to test whether the corresponding effect is evidenced in data, we not only test whether this parameter is needed for reproducing the observed number of configurations of the corresponding kind, but we also test whether all the other statistics are reproduced. Without fitting the model with the parameter of interest set to zero, we cannot know whether the restricted model is sensible.

For example, if we are interested in determining whether the alternating triangle effect is needed to capture the observed number of alternating triangles, it seems intuitive to fit the model without the alternating triangle parameter to determine whether the discrepancy between the observed number and predicted number of alternating triangles is (extremely) large. The Score test does just this. If the model we fit has MLE $\hat{\theta} = (\hat{\theta}_1, \ldots, \hat{\theta}_p)^T$, and we are interested in testing $\theta_p = 0$, we refit the model without including the pth effect, giving new MLEs $\tilde{\theta} = (\tilde{\theta}_1, \ldots, \tilde{\theta}_{p-1}, 0)^T$. The test of $\theta_p = 0$ is done by calculating (through simulation) the expected values $\bar{z}_{\tilde{\theta}} = (\bar{z}_{\tilde{\theta},1}, \ldots, \bar{z}_{\tilde{\theta},p-1}, \bar{z}_{\tilde{\theta},p})^T$ and covariance $Cov_{\tilde{\theta}}(z(X))$ under the

---

[6] The extent to which statistics are nested is described in Chapters 6 and 7, as well in Section 3.1.5. This is also evidenced in the changes in Figure 12.1

parameter $\tilde{\theta}$. We say that θ_p is significantly different from zero if the test statistic is as follows[7]:

$$\frac{(\bar{z}_{\tilde{\theta},p} - z_{obs,p})^2}{Var_{\tilde{\theta}}(z_p(X))} > c.$$

The critical level $c = 4$ may be used, which is again a rough guideline and corresponds to the 0.95 critical value for a chi-square–distributed random variable with 1 degree of freedom (as a matter of fact, this would be the critical value when the critical value for the underlying normal variate is 2). Similar caveats as in the case of Wald's test apply here.

For the example of Figure 12.1, in the upper right hand panel $\tilde{\theta} = (-.84450)^T$, $\bar{z}_{\tilde{\theta}} = (223.04, 365.47)^T$, and $Cov_{\tilde{\theta}}(z(X)) = \left(\begin{smallmatrix} 168 & 487 \\ 487 & 1.465 \end{smallmatrix}\right)$, so (after some arithmetic) the score test yields a test statistic of 29.36, which is far greater than 4. We may conclude that the alternating triangle parameter is significantly different from zero and that we need to include an effect of alternating triangles in order to capture the observed number of alternating triangles.

Information Criteria and Likelihood-Ratio Test. A popular approach for assessing the combination of parameters that best describes data is through the model specification that lends most support to data, subject to penalties on the model complexity. In the information theoretic context, support is measured by the probability of observing what we have observed as measured by $P_{\hat{\theta}}(x_{obs})$, or the log-likelihood $\ell(\theta;x) = \log P_\theta(z(x))$ (recall that in the case of ERGMs, the likelihood is uniquely determined by the sufficient statistics). As we cannot typically evaluate this function because of the normalizing constant, we have to rely on numerical approximations for evaluating this. Once we have listed the probabilities (conditional on the MLEs), they are typically penalized according to the number of parameters – a parsimonious model is preferred. Although the list of penalized likelihoods provides a ranking of best fitting models, it is notoriously difficult to account for the differences in model complexity adequately and to judge the differences in fit between the models. Hunter, Goodreau, and Handcock (2008) suggested using Akaike information criterion (AIC; Akaike, 1973), which for a model with the $p \times 1$ MLE $\hat{\theta}$ is defined as $-2\ell(\hat{\theta};x) + 2p$. The AIC thus penalizes models with more parameters. The Bayesian information criterion (BIC) also penalizes for the number of observations, substituting $2p$ for p multiplied by the log number of observations (for ergm AIC and BIC are reported in the output given by summary()). Yet, the sample

[7] If more than one parameter is tested, the general test statistic $(\bar{z}_{\hat{\theta}} - z_{obs})^T Cov_{\tilde{\theta}}(z(X))^{-1}(\bar{z}_{\hat{\theta}} - z_{obs})$ may be used.

size is not unambiguously defined for ERGMs as discussed in Hunter, Goodreau, and Handcock (2008), and using Bayes factors, it may be seen that model selection is sensitive to the penalty on model complexity (Koskinen, 2004).

Hunter and Handcock (2006) also proposed to use a likelihood-ratio test for testing the differences in fit. A test statistic equal to twice the difference in maximized likelihoods for two models, one of which is nested in the other, may then be compared to the critical value of a chi-square distribution with degrees of freedom equal to the difference in the number of parameters. The appropriateness of this chi-square approximation is unknown, and caution has to be exercised in interpreting the confidence level of the test.

12.5.3   Evaluating Log-Likelihood

We are prevented from evaluating the log-likelihood, $\ell(\theta, x) = \theta^T z(x) - \psi(\theta)$, directly by the intractability of the normalizing constant $\psi(\theta) = \log\left\{\sum_{x \in X} e^{\theta_1 z_1(x) + \cdots + \theta_p z_p(x)}\right\}$. However, there are computationally efficient algorithms for numerically approximating this relative to some reference parameter vector ϕ. In particular, Hunter and Handcock (2006) suggested using path sampling to approximate $\lambda(\theta, \phi) = \psi(\theta) - \psi(\phi)$. This relies on what may be loosely described as integrating both sides of the equality $\frac{\partial}{\partial \theta} \psi(\theta) = E_\theta(z(X))$ from θ to ϕ, resulting in an equality in terms of expected values that, in standard Monte Carlo fashion, may be approximated by their sample equivalents. More specifically, generate graphs $x^{(0)}, x^{(1)}, \ldots, x^{(M)}$, where $x^{(t)}$ is from a model defined by parameter $\theta^{(t)} = (t/M)\theta + [(1-t)/M]\phi$, and approximate

$$\lambda(\theta, \phi) \approx \hat{\lambda}(\theta, \phi) = \frac{1}{M} \sum_{m=0}^{M} (\theta - \phi)^T z(x^{(m)}).$$

Consequently, if ϕ defines a simple model for which $\ell(\phi; x)$ is easy to evaluate (e.g., a Bernoulli model), then we may approximate the log-likelihood for θ as

$$\hat{\ell}_\phi(\theta; x) = (\theta - \phi)^T z(x) - \hat{\lambda}(\theta, \phi) + \ell(\phi; x).$$

When comparing nested models such as the deviance (likelihood-ratio) tests, we only ever need to calculate differences in log-likelihoods, in which case $\ell(\phi; x)$ in the preceding expression is not needed.

12.6   Degeneracy and Near-Degeneracy

There are instances when a particular model cannot be fitted to a particular data set (Handcock, 2003; Snijders, 2002). This may be a

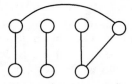

Figure 12.5. Graph on seven vertices with five edges.

computational consequence when the parameter estimates have a bimodal induced distribution of statistics. An example is the Markov model in Figure 6.6 of Chapter 6. Because the expected number of edges and triangles is located between the two modes (the two humps of Figure 6.6), the best model places almost no probability on the observed graph. Naturally, such a model is not a good description of data, and if repeated attempts at fitting the model fail as a result of this, it is advisable to fit another model specification.

In extreme cases, one may have what may be termed "perfect degeneracy"– an observed statistic does not provide any information on the corresponding effect. As an example, one cannot fit a model with edges and alternating triangle statistics if the observed alternating triangle count is zero. This is similar to the fact that one cannot say anything about the difference in income between male and female physicians if the sample does not contain any female physicians (Handcock (2003) identified complete separation as an analogous case in generalized linear models). A model may also be problematic if it gives degenerate graphs a high probability of occurring, degenerate in the sense of graphs for which the MLE does not exist. If the fitted model assigns a lot of probability to such degenerate graphs – graphs that are typically the empty graph and the complete graph and combinations thereof – the model is not a realistic one. Furthermore, although we may be able to obtain estimates in some instances, we cannot have much confidence in the results because the sampling distribution includes many nonexistent MLEs. These difficulties may occur if the observed graph is close to an extreme, or degenerate, graph in the space induced by the statistics.

As an example of a degenerate graph that is not the empty or full graph, consider the graph on seven vertices with five edges depicted in Figure 12.5. There are three 2-stars, but no 3- and higher-order stars. This graph has the minimum number of 2-stars given five edges on seven nodes. A model with star parameters of order 2 or greater cannot be estimated.

There has been extensive discussion of degeneracy, near-degeneracy, and related issues in the recent literature (Burda, Jurkiewicz, & Krzywicki, 2004; Häggström & Jonasson, 1999; Handcock, 2002, 2003; Jonasson, 1999; Park& Newman, 2004; Robins, Pattison, & Woolcock, 2005; Robins et al., 2007; Snijders, 2002; Snijders et al., 2006). Much of this has focused on Markov random graph models, which are very prone to near-degeneracy, making them generally problematic fits for real social network data. Social circuit models, particularly with the alternating parameterizations, are much more robust but may still be liable to degeneracy. It needs to be emphasized that if model estimation does not converge readily, especially, for instance, with generous multiplication factors, then the model could possibly be degenerate. Even apparently convergent models may suffer from near-degeneracy. A relatively long post-estimation simulation can give reassurance that the parameter estimates do indeed produce sensible model outcomes.

12.7   Missing or Partially Observed Data

As discussed in Koskinen et al. (2010), ignoring missing data may be particularly detrimental in social network analysis. Specifically, if we assume the type of dependencies discussed in Chapter 7, the state of missing tie-variables may potentially alter our interpretation of what we have observed. The central problem may be understood from a synthetic example: assume that several people know each other on account of a person who then leaves the room, whereupon a researcher arriving late will be at loss to explain how these strangers came to be together.

If ties are elicited from self-reports, the most likely form of missing data is usually nonresponses, which result in what Huisman (2009) terms "unit" missing. To use as much data as possible while allowing for the nonrespondents to differ from respondents, one may treat nonresponse as a covariate that interacts with configurations of interest as in Robins, Pattison, and Woolcock (2004). More recently, Handcock and Gile (2007, 2010) proposed a likelihood-based approach to treating missing data in ERGMs. Making the assumption that data are missing at random, missing data are simulated in the course of estimation so that the vector of observed statistics is substituted for the expected statistics conditional on the part that has been observed. Procedures for fitting ERGMs to data with missing values are available in statnet and PNet.

If there are missing data, an adapted maximum likelihood estimator can be used. This is the case only if the missingness is ignorable, which roughly means that the probability distribution of what is missing depends on the observed data only and not on nonobserved data, and parameters of the ERGM are distinct from parameters determining the missingness mechanism. For example, snowball sampling designs lead to ignorable missingness (Handcock & Gile, 2010; Thompson & Frank, 2000). Let $x = (x_{obs}, x_{mis})$, where x_{obs} denotes the array of observed tie-variables, and x_{mis} the array of nonobserved tie-variables. With ignorable missingness, the missing information principle of Orchard and Woodbury (1972) implies that the maximum likelihood equation may be written as

$$E_\theta\{z(X)\} = E_\theta\{z(X_{obs}, X_{mis}) \mid X_{obs} = x_{obs}\}.$$

Compare this to the maximum likelihood equation for complete data,

$$E_\theta \{z(X)\} = z(x_{obs}),$$

where x_{obs} is simply the total observed graph. The left-hand sides of both equations are the same and require calculating the expected value of the sufficient statistic for the ERGM. The right-hand side of the equation that is valid for incomplete data,

$$E_\theta \{z(X_{obs}, X_{mis}) \mid X_{obs} = x_{obs}\},$$

requires that we make simulated draws from the missing data, conditional on the observed data. The condition means that only the missing tie-variables are changed, not the observed tie-variables in the course of the Metropolis algorithm.

Koskinen et al. (2010) presented a Bayesian approach for dealing with missing data. Similarly to Handcock and Gile (2007, 2010), missing data are simulated in the course of estimation of the parameters. Although the Bayesian procedure was not designed for link prediction, it appears to do a reasonable job of predicting missing tie-variables.

Dealing with partially missing covariate values is complicated by the fact that we typically do not have a model for the covariates immediately available and that the missing covariates themselves would inherit some of the dependencies of the ERGM itself. Although this may be dealt with in a Bayesian framework, a convenient solution is to bootstrap missing covariates, to impute using sample means, or impute using some suitably chosen model.

For further conceptual issues and background on missing data in social network analysis, see, for example, Kossinets (2006).

12.8 Conditional Estimation from Snowball Samples

Link tracing designs have been proposed for sampling from populations for which it is difficult to use conventional sampling techniques (Frank, 1979; Frank & Snijders, 1994; Thompson & Frank, 2000). Link tracing does not rely on the availability of a sampling frame from which sampling units may be drawn. Instead, units are traced out from an initial small sample of units. For a given relation, say, friendship, new population units are obtained as the alters of units already in the sample.

More specifically, the initial sample is called the "seed set," and the people named by the units in the seed set constitute the first wave. The people nominated by people in the first wave make up the second wave and so on. From the perspective of a node a in the seed set, the nodes in the different waves may be classified according to their distance from a, as in Figure 12.6. Thus, a node in zone 3, $Z_3(a)$, is at a distance 3 from a. This and related types of sampling have been used for estimating the

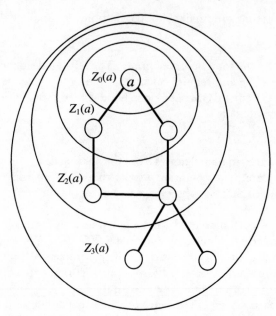

Figure 12.6. Zones of order 0 through 3 for seed node *a*.

size of difficult-to-sample populations (Frank & Snijders, 1994), or the prevalence of particular attributes in difficult-to-sample populations (Gile & Handcock, 2010). Typically, some simplifying assumptions regarding the population graph permits estimates of the size of the graph.

As noted in Handcock and Gile (2007), from a model-based perspective, ERGM estimation for graphs obtained from snowball sampling is conceptually equivalent to the common missing-at-random data framework. A snowball sample provides partial information on a population graph. Under fairly general conditions, the nonsampled part of the graph may be considered as missing data, and the previously mentioned approaches for fitting ERGMs to graphs with missing data applies. This approach requires that the size of the population graph is not too big and that the number of nodes n is known.

Pattison et al. (2012) proposed an approximate, conditional inference procedure that makes even large graphs amenable to estimation of ERGMs, even without knowledge of n. The idea is to condition on observed ties within and between a selection of zones so that the remainder of the observations is (conditionally) independent of what we have not observed. In Figure 12.6, if we model only ties between nodes in zone 1 (i.e., $Z_1(a)$) while treating as fixed, ties between nodes in other zones, as well as ties between nodes in other zones and nodes in $Z_1(a)$, then according to the Markov assumptions, ties between nodes in $Z_3(a)$ are conditionally independent of the tie-variables we are modeling. By conditioning on ties from zone 1 nodes to nodes in zones 0 and 2, we have also conditioned on the fact that there are no ties between nodes in zone 1 to nodes in zones 3, 4, 5, and higher.

The preceding conditioning also applies to models assuming the social circuit dependence assumption. For a homogeneous ERGM, it is plausible to assume that patterns of interaction in a local neighborhood may reflect the population graph process. A caveat is that the larger the population graph, the less likely it is to be homogeneous.

PNet offers a variety of different options for fixing zones in the analysis. All conditioning must include nodes in the last wave in order to "isolate" the rest of the sample. Some caution has to be exercised in selecting the seed set, especially in the data collection phase. If the seed nodes have neighborhoods that are too heavily overlapping or if the seeds have a large number of isolates, this may complicate the inference procedure (see Daraganova (2009) for a thorough treatment of snowball sampling for the purpose of ERGM estimation). The conditioning of the snowball sample may also be applied to the case of actor attribute autologistic models described in Chapter 9.

12.9 Goodness of Fit

Although we may test individual parameters and collections of parameters using Wald tests, score tests, and likelihood-ratio tests, these tests require a specific alternative model. Consequently, these tests only assess the fit of the model relative to another model, so our results are sensitive to the choice of model and the availability of models. Robins, Pattison, and Woolcock (2005) proposed to simulate from the model to investigate a range of graph features, and Hunter, Goodreau, and Handcock (2008) suggested that this procedure may be used for assessing goodness of fit (GOF). The basic idea is to assess how well the model manages to capture features of data that were *not explicitly modeled*. Are, for example, an edge parameter and an alternating triangle enough to explain the observed average path length or the observed degree distribution?

The GOF procedure is carried out as follows. Given that we have a model for which the estimation algorithm has converged, we simulate from the model to generate a distribution of graphs. If the fitted model is sufficient to explain a feature of the data, then we expect that the summary for the corresponding feature in data is not extreme in the distribution of graphs. To assess whether a summary measure $s_k(x_{obs})$ for the observed graph is far from what we would predict under the fitted model, the standardized difference $[S_k(x_{obs}) - \bar{S}_k]/SD(S_k(x))$ is calculated, where $\bar{S}_k$ and $SD(S_k(x))$ are the mean and standard deviation, respectively, calculated over the generated sample of graphs. If this ratio is large in absolute value, then the observed measure is far from what is expected under the model. The critical value for judging whether the absolute value of the ratio is large is typically 2, but it is prudent not to be strict about the exact figure. The PNet output for GOF may be complemented by graphical approaches, especially for degree distributions and the distribution of geodesic distances. The "gof()" function in statnet offers fit measures for arbitrarily chosen functions and also gives graphical summaries (as described in Goodreau et al., 2008).

The GOF procedure is conditioned on a converged model and, like the Wald test and score test, should only be carried out once the convergence statistics indicate that the likelihood equation is solved.

12.9.1 Approximate Bayesian GOF

A drawback of assessing model fit conditional on the MLE is that this ignores the uncertainty in estimates. That is to say, we know that the parameters are estimated with some uncertainty, so we cannot be certain the true parameter values are identical to our estimates. We believe that the parameters are within a close range of the estimates, and we are willing to allow for possible small changes to the parameter values – the model is equally well described by $\hat{\theta}_{MLE}$ and $\hat{\theta}_{MLE} + \varepsilon$, for changes ε. A Bayesian approach allows us to choose these deviations ε in a principled manner, and then by weighting parameter values according to the posterior distribution, to obtain a distribution of statistics that depend only on the model and not on the parameters. If draws from the posterior are available, a graph is simulated from $P_{\theta(m)}(X)$ for each $\theta^{(m)}$ in the posterior. A convenient approximation to this procedure is to approximate the posterior by draws from a multivariate normal distribution, $N(\hat{\theta}_{MLE} I(\hat{\theta}_{MLE})^{-1})$, where $I(\hat{\theta}_{MLE})$ is the information matrix (Koskinen, 2008).

13

Illustrations: Simulation, Estimation, and Goodness of Fit

Garry Robins and Dean Lusher

Chapter 12 introduces simulation of exponential random graph models (ERGMs) and shows how simulation could be used as a heuristic method of goodness of fit (GOF) to see whether a model can fit many features of an empirical network. In this chapter, we provide some specific examples, including some short simulation studies and a GOF analysis for models for The Corporation communication network first introduced in Chapter 5. The goals of this chapter are straightforward:

- Through simulation, we illustrate the effects of different parameters and show how they can work together. This can assist with model interpretation.
- We make some practical suggestions about model specification based on our own experience of fitting models.
- With a simplified GOF example, we show how GOF may guide model selection, so that effects may be added to a simpler model in order to improve fit.
- These illustrations can be replicated by interested readers who want to gain direct exposure in these procedures and experience in handling ERGMs using PNet.

13.1 Simulation

We begin with a series of simple simulations to make some points about parameters and their interpretations. We typically demonstrate the simulations by visualizing an individual graph from the distribution; however, once a simulation has burnt in, it is possible to take a sample of graphs and examine their general properties, including means and standard deviations (SDs) of relevant graph statistics. Throughout, we choose networks with thirty nodes and simulate according to the procedure in

167

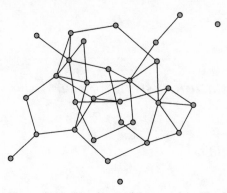

Figure 13.1. Simple random graph with thirty nodes and forty-three edges.

Section 12.2.2 with a burn-in of 100,000 iterations. After the burn-in, we simulate for 1 million iterations. When we extract a sample, we will take 1,000 graphs (i.e., every 1,000th graph of 1 million iterations). A visualization will be the last graph in the simulation. Readers who want to reproduce these simulations need to realize, of course, that because we only have a sample of graphs from the distribution, their results may differ slightly from those reported here. Nevertheless, they should be broadly consistent within the natural variation described by SDs.

For the purposes of visualization, it is often convenient to compare graphs with the same density because it can be difficult to visually distinguish important structural differences when graphs have different densities. Accordingly, unless we describe otherwise, the simulations here are all based on a fixed density of 0.10 (forty-three ties). We also restrict these examples to undirected networks.

When there are no effects in the model (apart from the density of 0.10), we produce the simple random graph distribution, more specifically, the graph distribution U|L = 43 (see Chapter 4). An illustrative graph from this distribution is presented in Figure 13.1. This distribution is a useful baseline comparison for the ensuing examples.

13.1.1   Triangulation

Our first examples illustrate the effect of triangulation parameters on network closure. In Figure 13.2, the left column of graphs comes from simulations with only a Markov triangle parameter with different values. The right column is from simulations with an alternating triangle parameter with a damping constant $\lambda = 2$ (see definition in Equation (6.8) and Figure 6.9a).

With the Markov triangle parameter at the lower values of 0.5 and 1.0, we do not see much obvious difference from the random graph

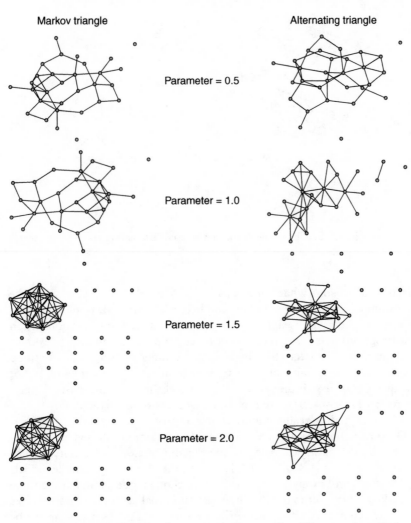

Figure 13.2. Graphs from simulations with different triangulation parameters.

in Figure 13.1. However, between parameter values of 1.0 and 1.5, there is a sudden jump in triangulation to a cliquelike structure (for a fixed number of edges, a clique is the most efficient means to create a maximum number of triangles). We are familiar with this jump for Markov graphs from Figure 6.5 in Chapter 6.

This "phase transition" is one reason why Markov graph models are not good models for much real network data. For a sample of graphs from the simple random graph distribution, the mean number of triangles is 3.6, with a SD of 1.8. A weak Markov triangle parameter increases the

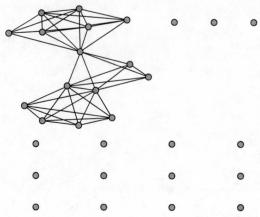

Figure 13.3. Example graph for massive alternating triangle parameter ($\lambda = 2$).

triangulation somewhat but not by a lot. When the parameter is 1.0, the mean number of triangles in the sample is 12.1 with a SD of 6.0 (a simple *t*-test will show this as significantly greater than the simple random graph distribution). However, there is not much scope for the model to produce a larger, but not overwhelmingly large, number of triangles. The jump with a parameter value of 1.5 is to a mean number of triangles of 102.5, with a SD of 3.9. Either there is a relatively small number of triangles (around 12 or so), or there is a clique with maximal triangulation.

The alternating triangle models, in contrast, can cope with triangulation that is midway between the simple random graph and the clique. With the alternating triangle parameter value of 2.0, the mean number of triangles is 44.8 with a SD of 6.1. In fact, the alternating triangle models with $\lambda = 2$ will rarely produce the single clique models familiar from the Markov effects, although they may produce smaller clique-like structures that are connected. If we force the alternating triangle parameter to be massively large (100), then the mean number of triangles only increases to 57.4 (SD = 1.8). An example graph is presented in Figure 13.3, where we see a number of denser connected regions in the network, smaller than the single clique.

The lambda value in effect controls the size of the denser regions of the networks. In Figure 13.4, we present example graphs for the simulation with the modest alternating triangle parameter value of 0.5 (see Figure 13.2). As we increase the value of λ, the denser regions become concentrated on larger subsets of nodes. With $\lambda = 4$, the example graph has no clique bigger than a triangle, whereas for $\lambda = 6$, there is an approximate clique involving six nodes; for $\lambda = 10$, we see overlapping clique-like structures of six or seven nodes; and, finally, for $\lambda = 14$, we have a single

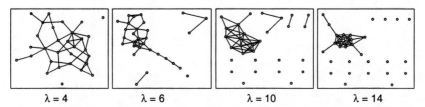

Figure 13.4. Example graphs for alternating triangle parameters with different λs.

clique of nine nodes. This has implications for model fitting if one is not going to estimate λ. If the model fit does not explain the higher-order clique structure well with a fixed λ = 2 (which is a good starting value), then it may be desirable to fix a larger value for λ.

13.1.2   Degrees

The alternating star statistic models the degree distribution of the network. Figure 13.5 presents example graphs from simulations of models where the only parameter is an alternating star statistic with fixed λ = 2 (as defined in Equation (6.5)), with parameter value of −1 in the top left-hand graph and +1 in the top right-hand graph.

The bottom row of Figure 13.5 presents the degree distributions across the samples of 1,000 graphs from each simulation. The horizontal axis indicates nodes of degree j, and the vertical axis the number of such nodes in each graph. The box plot for each node of degree j presents the range of degree j nodes across the 1,000 graphs, the "box" representing the range from the first to the third quartile, and the lines representing the rest of the data (outliers have been removed for a simpler visualization). The charts show that there is much greater dispersion of degrees for the positive star parameter, with some nodes having up to degree 8, whereas this is most unusual for the negative parameter, where the degrees are limited to a range of 1 to 6. This is evident from the two example graphs, where the graph from the distribution with the positive parameter shows higher-degree nodes and hence greater centralization.

Sometimes it is helpful to include both an alternating star parameter and a Markov star parameter, usually a 2-star parameter. This is particularly useful for modeling highly centralized graphs with a handful of very high-degree nodes. When fitting models to such data, we often find that the alternating star parameter is negative and the 2-star parameter is positive: the negative alternating star parameter handles a relatively equal distribution of degrees among low-degree nodes, whereas the Markov parameter caters for the high-degree nodes.

Negative alt.-star   Positive alt.-star

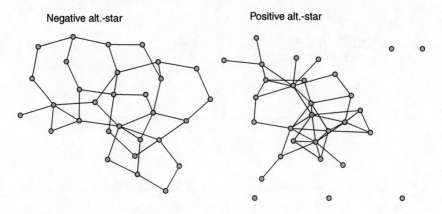

Degree distribution across 1000 graphs

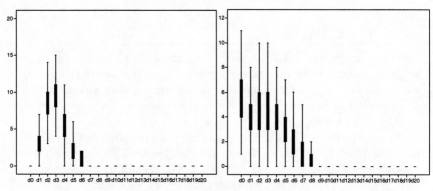

Figure 13.5. Simulation results for alternating star parameter (NB: in bottom row charts, "d-*j*" indicates "number of nodes of degree *j*").

Figure 13.6 presents graphs from two simulations, both with an alternating star parameter of −1, with the left-hand graph including a Markov 2-star parameter of +0.3 and the right-hand graph a Markov 3-star parameter of +0.3. In both cases, the Markov star creates strong centralization, with the 2-star parameter creating one hub and the 3-star parameter two hubs. These are in sharp contrast to the negative alternating star parameter alone as in the left-hand side of Figure 13.5.

13.1.3   Stars and Triangles Together

Finally, in Figure 13.7, we present an example graph from a simulation with an alternating triangle parameter of 2 and an alternating star parameter of −1, so that it compares with both the left-hand graph in Figure 13.5 and the bottom right-hand graph in Figure 13.2. In this case,

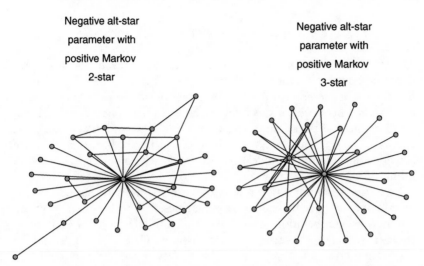

Negative alt-star parameter with positive Markov 2-star

Negative alt-star parameter with positive Markov 3-star

Figure 13.6. Example graphs from simulations with both alternating and Markov star parameters.

we see that the strong triangulation of Figure 13.2, consistent with the positive triangle parameter, is retained, but now it is distributed across a number of smaller, denser regions of the network, sometimes connected and sometimes in separate network components. Here, the effect of the negative star parameter is to break down the single clique of Figure 13.2 into smaller, clique-like regions because it attempts to limit the number of high-degree nodes. When fitting a model to data, the combination of a negative star and positive triangle parameter is not unusual. It indicates the presence of network closure processes but these processes are distributed across a number of smaller denser regions of the network, rather than in one central region. There is little network centralization, and few or no high-degree nodes, outside the triangulated areas of the graph.

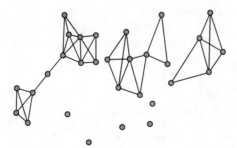

Figure 13.7. Example graph from simulation with positive triangle and negative star parameters.

13.2   Estimation and Model Specification

The choice of network configurations to include in an exponential random graph model is a theoretical statement about which combinations of parameters are important in describing the formation of network ties in an observed network. In specifying a model, one implicitly makes theoretical choices of the social processes by which the network came about, and as such, it is not always a straightforward task. In this section, we provide a short guide to model specification based on our experience with fitting ERGMs.

Two things are important to consider when specifying a model. First, social contexts have their own particularities, and so the ways in which the complex combination of parameters manifests itself in a specific local context is likely to have some unique aspects. Of course, there may be some common characteristics of a set of models for similar social contexts, a point demonstrated by Lubbers and Snijders (2007) with a multilevel examination of friendship relations in a number of different schools (they compare 102 different networks; the same technique is used in Koskinen and Stenberg (2012) to compare 587 school class networks). Nevertheless, a one-size-fits-all model specification will not always work.

A secondary source of variation is the relational content of a tie. For example, in Chapter 14, two contexts are explored with regard to the effect of perceived attitudes of others on network tie formation. Beyond the variability of one context to another (a school and a football team), there is also the fact that the network tie under observation differs (positive affect relations in the former, and aggression relations in the latter context). Without question, we theorize different processes for these relational contents. In summary, the selection of the parameters for a model may depend on the content of the relational tie.

We suggest that a good starting point for models for undirected networks is to include edge, alternating star, alternating triangle, and alternating 2-path parameters. For directed models, a model might include arc, reciprocity, popularity spread (alternating in-star), activity spread (alternating out-star), some form of alternating triangle and cyclic parameters, and perhaps connectivity (alternating 2-path and /or simple 2-path) parameters. In short, models should include at least a density parameter (edge or arc), as well as some control over the degree distribution (star parameters) and closure (triangle parameters.) Attribute effects are included as described in Chapter 8.

For directed positive affect networks (e.g., friendship), the pattern of results is often, but by no means always, as in Table 13.1.

Transitive closure – AT-T or general transitivity AT-TDU – may be a good compromise if researchers do not want to include all four separate

Table 13.1. *Suggested starting set of parameters for ERGM for positive affect networks*

parameter	PNet name	statnet name	interpretation
Arc	Arc	edges	This is a baseline propensity for tie formation.
Reciprocity	Reciprocity	mutual	This is often positive, suggesting that reciprocated ties are very likely to be observed for positive affect networks.
Simple connectivity	Mix2star	twopath	This measures the extent to which actors who send ties also receive them. It controls for the correlation between the in- and the out-degree. It is often negative.
Popularity spread	A-in-S	gwidegree	A negative popularity spread parameter indicates that most actors have similar levels of popularity (the network is not centralized on in-degree) (see Equation (6.7) in Chapter 6).
Activity spread	A-out-S	gwodegree	A negative activity spread parameter indicates that most actors have similar levels of activity (the network is not centralized on out-degrees) (see Equation (6.6) in Chapter 6).
Triangulation	One or more T, D, or U alternating *k*-triangle effects	gwesp (AT-T only)	A positive effect here indicates there is a high degree of closure, or multiple clusters of triangles, in the data (see Figures 6.10 and 6.11 in Chapter 6).
Cyclic closure	AT-C	ctriple (Markov only)	A negative effect indicates tendencies against cyclic triads (sometimes this is interpreted as a tendency against generalized exchange or generalized reciprocity).
Multiple connectivity	One or more alternating 2-path effects	gwdsp (A2P-T only)	This parameter relates to the 2-paths in the network. A negative estimate in conjunction with positive triangulation estimates indicates that 2-paths tend to be closed (i.e., triangles are formed) (see Figure 6.12 in Chapter 6).

triadic social circuit effects. Inclusion of additional Markov parameters (e.g., 2-in-star, 2-out-star, 2-paths) sometimes helps with convergence or with GOF for degree distributions.

For networks of negative relations (e.g., aggression), it may be helpful to start with this same set of parameters, as in Table 13.1. However, in our experience, these parameters may not prove important in models for negative relations. For instance, a substantial triangulation for negative ties may or may not be an important effect (e.g., an enemy of an enemy may not be an enemy, yet bullying relationships may prove to be transitive). Furthermore, it may be that reciprocity is not present in a negative tie network (e.g., for bullying ties, which indicate an imbalance of power, we might not expect symmetry). Remember, it is fine to include a parameter in a model if it is not significant, but if the value of the statistic is zero in the data (i.e., there are no mutual ties), then you cannot include this parameter in a model (roughly, as in regression, when you cannot include a variable such as gender if you only have females and no males; for more information, see Section 12.6 on degeneracy and near-degeneracy). As such, for negative tie networks, start with the same set of parameters as mentioned previously; however, if your model is degenerate, then you may want to determine whether there are mutual ties, or indeed, triangles in your data (which you do by examining the count statistics in GOF – see Section 13.3).

13.2.1   Some Example Model Specifications

In Table 13.2, we present selected model estimates for three differently specified models for the communication network within The Corporation from Chapter 5:

1. Model A includes the arc parameter (which is our baseline propensity for tie formation), the actor-relation effects, and a covariate advice network.
2. Model B includes the parameters from model A and some Markov structural effects.
3. Model C includes the parameters from model A, plus social circuit structural parameters.

We note that the results of model C in Table 13.2 are the same as those in Table 5.1 in Chapter 5. In Table 13.2, the first column is for the parameter name (e.g., Arc, Reciprocity). Then there are three additional columns referring to the (parameter) estimate, the standard error (SE) of the estimate, and the convergence statistic (as prescribed in Section 12.4.2, we want our convergence statistics to be less than 0.1 in absolute value to indicate properly converged parameter estimates).

Model A is a Bernoulli model that includes the baseline propensity to form ties (i.e., arc parameter), as well as attribute effects and a covariate for the advice network. We can see from our convergence statistics that this model is a stable model (i.e., the model has converged). However, we know from previous chapters that Bernoulli models are problematic because they do not capture network structures such as reciprocity or transitive closure. Thus, the model is good because it has converged, but

Table 13.2. *Three models for The Corporation communication network*

parameter [PNet name]	estimate	standard error (SE)	convergence statistic
Model A			
Arc	−1.17*	0.19	−0.02
Sender (seniority)	−1.21*	0.33	0.01
Sender (projects)	0.03	0.02	0.03
Receiver (seniority)	−0.54	0.28	0.02
Receiver (projects)	−0.01	0.02	−0.02
Homophily (seniority) [Interaction][a]	1.93*	0.42	0.05
Heterophily (projects) [Difference]	−0.18*	0.03	−0.01
Homophily (office) [Matching]	−0.05	0.19	0.04
Entrainment (advice) [Covariate arc]	1.90*	0.30	−0.09
Model B			
Arc	–	–	0.97
Reciprocity	–	–	0.85
2-path [2-path]	–	–	1.70
2-in-star [In-2-star]	–	–	1.70
2-out-star [Out-2-star]	–	–	1.62
Transitive triad [030T]	–	–	3.78
Cyclic triad [030C]	–	–	3.23
Sender (seniority)	–	–	0.38
Sender (projects)	–	–	0.51
Receiver (seniority)	–	–	0.49
Receiver (projects)	–	–	0.46
Homophily (seniority) [Interaction]	–	–	0.37
Heterophily (projects) [Difference]	–	–	0.15
Homophily – office [Matching]	–	–	0.46
Entrainment (advice) [Covariate arc]	–	–	0.02
			(*continued*)

* Significant effect (i.e., parameter estimate is greater than two times the standard error in absolute value, see Section 12.5.1 for details).

[a] As noted in Section 8.2.2, homophily (heterophily) is measured differently for the actor relation effects depending on whether they are binary, continuous, or categorical. "Seniority" is a binary variable, and homophily in this instance reflects the selection of actors with the attribute (i.e., actors with "1" as opposed to "0") selecting other actors with the attribute. In PNet, we use the "interaction" effect for binary variables to measure homophily, and a positive effect indicates homophily. "Projects" is a continuous variable, and heterophily is measured by the absolute difference in scores using the "difference" effect. For continuous variables, a positive difference effect indicates that they are heterophilous, whereas a negative score indicates a relative lack of difference (i.e., homophily). Finally, "office" is a categorical variable, which in PNet is measured using the "matching" effect, and (like binary variables) a positive effect is indicative of homophily.

as we see in the next section, when we do a GOF of this model, we find that this simple Bernoulli does not capture many of the network features that interest us.

The estimation in model B using Markov parameters failed to converge. We tried restarting the model using a larger multiplication factor,

Table 13.2 *(continued)*

parameter [PNet name]	estimate	standard error (SE)	convergence statistic
Model C			
Arc	−1.96*	0.73	−0.02
Reciprocity	2.88*	0.46	0.02
2-path [2-path]	−0.06	0.08	−0.02
Popularity spread [AinS]	−0.27	0.32	−0.03
Activity spread [AoutS]	−0.34	0.34	−0.02
Path closure [AT-T]	1.22*	0.19	−0.02
Cyclic closure [AT-C]	−0.37*	0.17	−0.02
Multiple 2-paths [A2P-T]	−0.06	0.09	−0.01
Sender (seniority)	−0.56	0.29	−0.01
Sender (projects)	0.01	0.02	−0.05
Receiver (seniority)	0.08	0.23	0.03
Receiver (projects)	−0.02	0.02	−0.06
Homophily (seniority) [Interaction]	0.64*	0.26	0.02
Heterophily (projects) [Difference]	−0.08*	0.02	0.02
Homophily (office) [Matching]^b	−0.01	0.17	0.02
Entrainment (advice) [Covariate arc]	1.76*	0.30	−0.07

^{b} "Office" is a categorical variable, and there are no sender and receiver effects for such variables in PNet, only homophily effects (there are more options in statnet, using, for example, "nodemix"). If you have categories that you want to analyze with regard to sender and receiver effects, you need to create dummy binary variables for each category. However, you must always have $n − 1$ binary variables, where n is the number of categories, so that there is a reference category to which all other attributes can be compared.

Model A is a Bernoulli model, model B is a Markov model, and model C is a social circuit model.

increased the maximum number of estimation runs, and used different gaining factors (*a*-values). However, for this set of Markov parameters, the model did not come close to convergence, and as such, we suggest that it is degenerate.[1] In Table 13.2, we insert "−" for all estimates and their SEs for model B to indicate that these figures are not appropriate because we have large convergence statistics for these estimates, which makes them meaningless. Importantly, all models will produce numerical output (i.e., you will *always* get some numbers from your estimation), but the numbers for the estimates are meaningless unless all parameters have converged. For instance, although not reported in Table 13.2, the PNet output for the transitive triangle 030T parameter is 0.46 and the SE is 0.13, but the convergence statistic is 3.78, which is very far from being

---

[1]   There are two things to note here. First, it is possible but perhaps unlikely that another model with Markov parameters does fit the data, so you would need to drop some parameters out of the model and/or include others to see if this improves model convergence (although experience tells us that Markov models often do not converge). Second, our experience suggests that where convergence statistics are consistently greater than, say, 0.3 across several updated estimation runs, it is unlikely that the model will converge especially for small networks and that other parameters will need to be included in the model and/or some removed from the model.

<0.1. As such, and we cannot stress this point enough, because this estimate has not converged, it is meaningless. We note that even if another parameter in the model did converge (e.g., the convergence statistic for the advice covariate parameter was <0.1), this is still meaningless because *all parameters in the model must converge.* Accordingly, this Markov model should not be used and should be treated as completely inadequate.

You can download the data and the PNet software (Wang, Robins, & Pattison, 2009) from the MelNet Web site (www.sna.unimelb.edu.au) to analyze this network yourself.[2]

13.3 GOF

13.3.1 How Do You Know Whether You Have a Good Model?

To say a model fits our data is to argue that the combination of such network structures specified in the model is a good representation of how this particular network could have been formed. GOF therefore allows us to know whether the specified model for our observed data represents particular network structures or graph features well. The GOF procedure gives us an indication of whether our model is able to represent important graph features.

To illustrate the utility of GOF in ERGM, let us examine the results of two GOFs (models A and C) for the communication network for The Corporation. These GOFs are presented in Table 13.3. What we see is that model A does not capture many of the structural network features because it does not include parameters for network self-organization (e.g., reciprocity, transitivity). However, when we included Markov parameters (model B), we were unable to obtain convergence for the model. This lack of convergence of model B, as shown in Table 13.2, demonstrates that the model cannot find a stable solution to the data, and as such, it is pointless to conduct a GOF. Finally, model C, which includes actor-relation and higher-order structural effects, successfully converges, and we see that GOF is considerably improved. Taken together, we argue that model C is the best of the three models for this communication network.

Specifically looking at Table 13.3, there are four columns that refer to the GOF. These are the count (or statistic), which is simply the relevant statistic for our data (often, simply the count of the relevant

---

[2] The corresponding effect names in statnet, when calling ergm, are edges, mutual, twopath, gwodegree, gwidegree, gwesp, ctriple (not identical to the AT-C), and gwdsp. The actor attribute effects are nodeicov, nodeocov, edgecov, absdiff, and nodematch. For this model and data, it is difficult to achieve convergence with the default method and setting style – choosing "Robbins-Monro" in control is helpful.

Table 13.3. *Selected goodness-of-fit (GOF) details for communication network (n = 38) for models A and C*

		GOF		
parameter [PNet name]	count	mean	standard deviation (SD)	GOF *t*-ratio
Model A				
Arc	146	146.14	10.54	−0.01
Reciprocity	44	12.60	3.48	9.01
2-path	559	541.68	83.38	0.21
2-in-star	313	280.92	43.49	0.74
2-out-star	283	276.30	42.44	0.16
Transitive triad [030T]	212	77.11	19.11	7.06
Popularity spread [AinS]	167.51	162.61	18.30	0.27
Activity spread [AoutS]	166.39	162.22	18.20	0.23
Path closure [AT-T]	153.97	67.72	15.23	5.67
Cyclic closure [AT-C]	120.97	63.85	17.19	3.32
Multiple 2-paths [A2P-T]	452.47	485.67	67.43	−0.49
Sender (seniority)	73	73.30	7.68	−0.04
Sender (projects)	993	994.63	96.12	−0.02
Receiver (seniority)	84	84.21	7.94	−0.03
Receiver (projects)	1005	1007.57	96.66	−0.03
Homophily (seniority) [interaction]	60	60.30	6.90	−0.04
Heterophily (projects) [difference]	584	585.91	62.66	−0.03
Homophily (office) [matching]	51	50.99	6.16	0.00
Advice entrainment [covariate arc]	24	24.17	3.57	−0.05
SD in-degree distribution	2.39	1.95	0.23	1.89
Skew in-degree distribution	0.37	0.40	0.34	−0.08
SD out-degree distribution	2.02	1.89	0.21	0.61
Skew out-degree distribution	−0.17	0.29	0.34	−1.38
Model C				
Arc	146	146.60	14.80	−0.04
Reciprocity	44	44.07	6.79	−0.01
2-path	559	566.36	116.35	−0.06
2-in-star	313	310.17	66.83	0.04
2-out-star	283	301.34	62.80	−0.29
Transitive triad [030T]	212	212.42	54.18	−0.01
Popularity spread [AinS[	167.51	168.56	25.91	−0.04
Activity spread [AoutS]	166.39	167.26	25.61	−0.03
Path closure [AT-T]	153.97	154.85	31.16	−0.03
Cyclic closure [AT-C]	120.97	121.92	29.30	−0.03
Multiple 2-paths (A2P-T)	452.47	457.20	79.75	−0.06
Sender (seniority)	73	73.83	11.06	−0.08
Sender (projects)	993	994.47	142.35	−0.01
Receiver (seniority)	84	84.59	12.18	−0.05
Receiver (projects)	1005	1008.53	141.21	−0.03
Homophily (seniority) [interaction]	60	61.11	11.33	−0.10
Heterophily (projects) [difference]	584	584.80	88.84	−0.01
Homophily (office) [matching]	51	51.20	7.92	−0.03
Advice entrainment [covariate arc]	24	23.86	4.06	0.03
SD in-degree distribution	2.39	2.28	0.31	0.35
Skew in-degree distribution	0.37	0.40	0.35	−0.08
SD out-degree distribution	2.02	2.18	0.28	−0.56
Skew out-degree distribution	−0.17	0.35	0.34	−1.56

configuration). The mean is the estimated statistic produced by our model, and the next column is the associated SDs. For a model to represent a particular graph feature well, we want the observed data to be plausible (i.e., not too far away from the mean). For example, in the first row of Table 13.3 for the arc effect, we observed 146 ties, whereas the sample mean from the model was 146.14. The final column is the *t*-ratio of the GOF, which is a measure of fit of the model.

Recall (see also Section 12.9) that GOF is carried out on the premise that the estimation has converged; in other words, the difference between simulated statistics and observed statistics for "fitted effects," as measured by the convergence statistic, is smaller than 0.1 in absolute value (e.g., in phase 3 of the Robbins-Monro procedure in PNet). Because the GOF also compares simulated average statistics under the fitted model with the observed statistics, the GOF *t*-ratios for the fitted statistics should be smaller than 0.1 (in absolute value). Of course, the estimation is a stochastic procedure, so we do not expect to obtain the exact same values for GOF and estimation for these *t*-ratios for fitted statistics. Thus, if the GOF statistics are a little over 0.1, there should be no need for concern. However, sometimes the GOF statistics can be substantially over 0.1. The first step is to run a much longer GOF simulation to determine whether the problem is resolved. If not, you may not have a fully converged model, and there may be a need to reestimate the model.

In detail, when the GOF statistic for a fitted effect is substantially over 0.1, the precision of either the samples in phase 3 of the Method of Moments estimation or the GOF is insufficient. Of these two, the sample with most iterations and lowest autocorrelation should be most trusted. If the number of iterations is the same, a discrepancy means that either the "number of iterations in each step" (given in the PNet output) for phase 3 is too small or the ratio of the number of iterations in the GOF to the "number of samples to be picked up" is too low (this is comparing the thinning; see Section 12.2.2). In case of the former, you will probably find that some of the autocorrelations are too big (in which case the basic premise of converged estimates is likely to be violated and the model needs refitting, with a larger multiplication factor; see Section 12.4.2). In the second case, we need to increase the number of iterations relative to the number of samples picked up for the GOF sample.

The "gof()" routine in statnet works both as an independent convergence check (like phase 3) and GOF (but note that the SEs are calculated in the basic fitting routine "ergm()"). The properties of the GOF sample may likewise have to be improved by increasing the burn-in, thinning, or sample length. If there is a need to do this, it is assessed using a combination of numerical criteria and graphic inspections of the sample. In general, it is a good idea to graph the sequences of statistics produced by ergm and PNet (see Section 12.2 on simulation).

For statistics not specifically included in our model, however, we are interested to see if their values are extreme. A graph statistic with a *t*-ratio greater than 2.0 can be regarded as extreme, in which case we infer that it is not plausible that a statistic of that value could have arisen from the model (the extreme value 2.0 is chosen with reference to the approximate critical value of a standard normal variate; for more on this, see Section 12.9). In other words, the model does not represent that graph feature well. In model A, we have a *t*-ratio of 0.74 for the number of 2-in-stars, which is clearly less than 2.0. Thus, the model reasonably captures the number of 2-in-stars in our observed network, even without including a parameter for it in the model. However, the number of reciprocated ties and the number of transitive triads are not well represented by the model. Because these are rather fundamental features of a directed social network, we conclude that model A is not a very good model for the data.

Table 13.3 lists only a small number of possible graph features that can be examined in a GOF as illustrations. For directed networks, Robins, Pattison, and Wang (2009) suggested examining GOF on the following graph features:

- *Graph counts and associated statistics:*
  - Dyadic statistics: numbers of arcs, reciprocated arcs
  - Markov graph configuration counts: numbers of 2-in-stars, 2-out-stars, 3-in-stars, 3-out-stars, mixed 2-stars (2-paths), cyclic triads, and transitive triads
  - Statistics for social circuit parameters: A-in-S, A-out-S, AT-T, AT-U, AT-D, AT-C, A2P-T, A2P-D, A2P-U
- *Degree distributions:*
  - SDs and skewness of both in- and out-degree distributions
  - Correlation between in- and out-degrees across nodes
- *Closure:*
  - For single triangle closure, global clustering coefficients, that is, 3 × (no. of triangles)/(no. of 2-stars). For directed graphs, there are four ways to complete a single triangle: from a 2-path to complete a 3-cycle (clustering-C); from a 2-path to complete a transitive triad (clustering-T); from a 2-in-star to complete a transitive triad (clustering-U); and from a 2-out-star to complete a transitive triad (clustering-D).
  - Clustering coefficients based on social circuit parameters: the ratio of the alternating *k*-triangle statistic to the analogous alternating *k*-2-path statistic (i.e., this coefficient is a measure of the proportion of alternating *k*-2-paths that have a base present to complete an alternating *k*-triangle). This gives an

additional four higher-order clustering coefficients, AC-T, AC-D, AC-U, and AC-C, where "AC" stands for "alternating *k*-cluster."

- *Geodesic distributions*:
  - Quartiles of the geodesic distribution (labeled G25, G50, G75, and G100, respectively – G50 as the median can be taken as a measure of average geodesic length for the graph). Because some geodesics may be infinite, rather than use means and SDs, and hence *t*-ratios, Robins, Pattison, and Wang (2009) proposed to examine the percentile of these statistics for the observed graph in the distribution of statistics from the simulated distribution.
- *Triad census*:
  - Counts of the sixteen triad types defined by Holland and Leinhardt (1970)

These features, along with some others, are included in GOF in PNet and most of them in statnet.

Let's now look more specifically at the GOF for models A and C in Table 13.3. Model A does not reproduce many of the features of the data. For example, there are 44 reciprocated ties in the data, yet the model suggests a mean of 12.60. The GOF *t*-ratio for this reciprocity count is 9.01, much higher than 2. Model A substantially underestimates reciprocated ties for our observed network, and the same occurs for transitive triads. However, the count of Markov 2-out-stars is 283, and our model produces a mean of 276.30. The associated GOF *t*-ratio of 0.16, which is much less than 2, suggested that our model is able to capture the presence of 2-out-stars sufficiently even without specifically including a 2-out-star parameter.

For model C, reciprocity is modeled explicitly as a parameter in the model, and we also see that model C represents the number of transitive triads well (not surprising, given that there is an alternating triangle parameter in the model).

The inclusion of effects for network self-organization (i.e., purely structural effects) alters some of the actor-relation estimates (Table 13.2). For example, the negative sender effect for seniority that was significant for model A is no longer significant in model C. However, the inclusion of the purely structural effects does not "wash away" the actor-relation effects entirely. Although estimates differ slightly, there are still homophily effects for seniority and number of projects in model C as there were in model A. The attributes of the actors and network self-organization tendencies both have a role in explaining the presence of ties in this communication network.

GOF may be helpful in choosing which network configurations to include for model specification. If a feature is not well fitted by a model, a judicious choice of an additional parameter in a new model may help. However, we stress that GOF should not in any way be seen as a replacement to theoretical motivation.

13.3.2   What If Your Model Does Not Fit a Graph Feature?

If a graph feature is extreme for a model, then it may be possible to include an additional parameter in the model to see if it assists model fit. Of course, you may have several extreme features, and it may be that the inclusion of one new parameter will improve fit on a number of these. For example, it may be that the 2-in-star and 3-in-star statistics are not well fitted. In this case, inclusion of a social circuit alternating-in-star effect in the model may improve fit of both statistics. As another example, many of the alternating triangle statistics (T, D, U) may not be well fitted, and a parameter for one of these effects may be sufficient to fit all three well.

The simulations presented previously in the chapter are also informative. Note that to cater for high-degree nodes, including a Markov star parameter in addition to social circuit alternating star parameters, might be useful. Degree distributions can often be hard to model. The inclusion of both alternating star and Markov star effects may be necessary because this can assist with bimodal degree distributions. In addition, where models show deficiencies in capturing 2-in-stars then alternating downward 2-paths (A2p-D) may be a useful inclusion, and for 2-out-stars, the inclusion of alternating upward 2-paths (A2p-U) may be useful for improving model fit. If there are a few very high-degree nodes, it may be necessary to treat them as exogenous – that is, the ties to those nodes are treated as predictors of other network ties. This approach then models the rest of the network conditional on these high-degree hubs. The underlying justification is that the hubs are so different from the rest of the network that they can be treated as special, influencing other network ties but not themselves much affected by the rest of the structure. In some cases, it will be that primary interest does not lie in degree-related effects, and differential popularity or activity is simply regarded as a nuisance. It then makes sense to condition on the density of the network or on one or both of the (in- and out-) degree distributions (Snijders & Van Duijn, 2002).

As indicated previously, each network is unique, so trial and error may be needed to decide which parameters to include.

13.3.3   Should a Model Explain Everything?

We conclude by stressing that a model of observed data is just that – a model. We do not and should not expect an exponential random graph model to fit all features of a network, just as we do not expect a regression to explain 100% of the variance. Thus, the purpose of GOF depends in part on the research question. If the research question is primarily concerned with degree, then you might want to fit the degree distribution well. However, if the research question has to do with other network features, then perhaps controlling for the degree distribution, but not fitting it perfectly well, is adequate.

Section III

Applications

14

Personal Attitudes, Perceived Attitudes, and Social Structures: A Social Selection Model

Dean Lusher and Garry Robins

14.1 Perceptions of Others and Social Behavior

An important insight of social network analysis is that social action may arise due to actor characteristics (Emirbayer & Goodwin, 1994; Kilduff & Krackhardt, 2008). The process of social selection specifies an interaction between social relations and actor-level attributes. Examples include gender homophily (McPherson et al., 2001), network closure and psychological predispositions (Kalish & Robins, 2006), and delinquency behaviors (Snijders & Baerveldt, 2003). Furthermore, interdependency between social relationships and identity was argued by White (1992) and implied by social identity theorists (Tajfel & Turner, 1979; Turner et al., 1987).

Apart from the personal characteristics of network actors, social action may also be motivated by the cues people take from others around them in the social setting. Previous work on perceptions and social networks focused on the perception of social ties (e.g., "cognitive social structures"; Krackhardt, 1987). Also, both social position in the network and individual personality differences were shown to be important for the accurate perception of the network (Casciaro, 1998). In this chapter, however, we discuss the effects of individual perceptions of the attributes of others in the network rather than the perception of ties. The attributes under consideration are perceived attitudes. To delineate terminology clearly, we note a fundamental difference between personally held attitudes ("personal attitudes") and an individual's perception of the attitudes of others ("perceived attitudes"). In the study described in this chapter, perceived attitudes are based on individual perceptions of the attitudes "generally held" in the group.

The importance of perceived attitudes on the behavior of the individual is well supported by a number of social psychological theories. For instance, "groupthink" (Janis, 1971) refers to conforming to or conferring

189

with group beliefs. This group consensus may override realistic situation appraisals and/or the individuality of group members, resulting in suboptimal decisions and outcomes for the group and its individual members. "Social comparison theory" (Festinger, 1954) suggests that in ambiguous situations or where objective criteria are lacking, people assess the veracity of their own views through comparison with the attitudes of others around them. Social comparison theory highlights how perceptions of the attitudes of others may guide personal attitudes, and therefore behavior, in part because they can resolve uncertainty. "Pluralistic ignorance" (Katz & Allport, 1931) – where most of a group's members do not endorse a particular norm but incorrectly assume that it is accepted by most others – is also relevant. In essence, pluralistic ignorance is about "systematic errors in norm estimation" (Prentice & Miller, 1993, 244), although the "illusion of support is validated when it motivates widespread public compliance" (Centola, Willer, & Macy, 2005, 1010). Perceptions of the attitudes of others have regulatory effects on people's behaviors, in part because people fear social sanctions (Centola et al., 2005).

The preceding social psychological theories indicate the importance of considering both personal and perceived attitudes with regard to social action. It is plausible, then, that personal and perceived attitudes may jointly affect social tie formation, and a notable limitation of the social psychological theories discussed previously is that they tend not to consider social relationships, either theoretically or empirically.

A theoretical perspective through which social relationships, personal attitudes, and perceived attitudes may be integrated is provided by "social identity theory" (Tajfel & Turner, 1979) and the theoretically related "self-categorization theory" (Turner et al., 1987), jointly referred to as SIT. SIT is a social psychological theory of group processes, intergroup relations, and norms. Social groups are cognitively represented in terms of prototypes, a subjective representation of the beliefs, attitudes, and behaviors definitive of a social category (Hogg, Terry, & White, 1995). Prototypes emphasize the similarities within and the differences between groups. Group identification occurs because "self-enhancement is best achieved through strategies that achieve a sense of in-group superiority relative to an out-group" (Hornsey & Hogg, 2002, 203). Those within the group who best exemplify the prototype are the most admired. It is important to note that the prototype is not the "average" in the group but is more extreme, a standard or norm to which group members may aspire. SIT suggests that the norm may reflect the attitudes of the powerful, the "more extreme individuals" and "their individual attitudes or characteristics." SIT therefore proposes that conceptualizing group attitudes as the average of all individual attitudes is not sensible because power is not evenly spread throughout a group. Instead, SIT indicates that social norms more likely reflect the personal attitudes of powerful people in the group who have "a common interest in creating categories and stereotypes which are favorable to their power position and their social identity" (Lindenberg, 1997, 304).

From a social network perspective, the idea that some individuals in a social network may be more prominent than others is well accepted (e.g., "centrality" implies the importance of prominent actors within a network – see Freeman, 1979). Our research goal is to combine the theoretical insights of centrality and SIT to examine how perceptions of the attitudes of others relate to social network ties. Our argument is that group norms are related to the individual attitudes of popular individuals in the group. In line with SIT, we propose that individuals exemplify the group identity by holding certain extreme prototypical attitudes. Other actors, who themselves may not hold such extreme personal attitudes, perceive the prototypical attitudes as generally held among the group and acknowledge the prominence of those individuals who exemplify them. As an outcome, social ties tend to be directed toward these leading individuals, who thereby become more central in the network. To examine this proposition empirically, we analyze actor-relation effects for both personal and perceived attitudes. We do this while controlling for purely structural self-organizing effects in our networks (e.g., reciprocity, transitivity).

14.2 Data and Measures

14.2.1 Social Network Questions

The data comprise two different networks: a network of seventy-two year 10 secondary school boys from a private, religious, all-male secondary college (mean age = 15.5, standard deviation (SD) = 0.5), and a network of thirty-eight professional footballers (mean age = 22.7, SD = 4.0) from an all-male professional football team (Lusher, 2008). These two studies provide an illustration of how perceived attitudes can be important in different contexts and with different networks.

The schoolboys' network involved "positive affect" relations, derived from three name generator questions: (1) friends, and/or (2) who you admire, and/or (3) who you would like to be seen with. Nominating any student on any of these relations led to the presence of a tie in the network, the result being a binary, composite tie network. The densities of the three networks were *friend* = 0.0497, *admire* = 0.0067, and *seen with* = 0.0262. Pearson correlations of networks using the Quadratic Assignment Procedure (QAP) were as follows: *friend-seen with* = 0.594**; *friend-admire* = 0.236**; and *admire-seen with* = 0.182**.

For the football team, we examined "aggression" relations because this sport requires an element of controlled aggression professionally. Participants were asked about their involvement in specific habitual behaviors comprising physical (e.g., "unnecessarily aggressive toward you during training activities"), verbal (e.g. "tease, puts you down"), or social (e.g., "exclude, not socialize with") aggression. Ties are represented as self-nominations of victimization. For ease of interpretation, we transformed the network such that "aggressors are senders" of aggression ties, whereas "victims are receivers" of ties. Again, a binary and composite aggression network was produced.

14.2.2   Attribute Measures

Attitudes toward masculinity have been theorized as contributing to social hierarchy formation among males (Connell, 1995). Personal and perceived attitudes toward masculinity were measured through the Masculine Attitudes Index (MAI; Lusher, 2008). This inventory has both adolescent and adult versions, with major subscales including antifemininity, gay male homophobia, and violence. For adolescents, an antiacademic subscale is also included, and for adults, a subscale measuring masculinity as playboy attitudes (i.e., manliness pertaining to sexual success with women). Scale scores are averaged across all items of the four subscales (minimum = 1, maximum = 7). Higher scores more strongly endorse antifeminine, homophobic, and violence attitudes (as well as antiacademic and playboy attitudes), which we refer to as indicative of a more "dominative masculinity." That is, high scores on the MAI imply that males hold antifeminine, homophobic, and violent attitudes, whereas low scores on the scale imply that they do not. The MAI is derived from psychological characteristics deemed pertinent to masculinity, empirical research, and theoretical work by Connell (1995), assessing some core components of masculinity in Western English-speaking countries. The inclusion of the "violence as manly" subscale is especially pertinent for the football team context (Lusher, 2008).

To measure both personal and perceived attitudes, participants were asked to answer the MAI items twice: first, with respect to their personal attitudes, and second, with regard to their perceptions of the attitudes of others around them (i.e., their "reference group"). Prentice and Miller (1993) found that paired-sample t-tests showed significant differences between personal and perceived attitudes measured in this way, with the perceived attitudes always more extreme. For school students, the reference group comprised the students' close friends,[1] indicative of a peer group that has been shown to be important to young people (e.g., Poteat, Espelage, & Green, 2007). For the football team, the reference group was the team itself, given the strong identification players (are

---

[1]   As measured by the network question, "Who is in your close group of friends?"

encouraged to) develop for the team in which they play. We refer to an individual's endorsement as "personal MAI" and to the individual's perceived attitudes of their reference group as "perceived MAI." For the schoolboys, personal MAI had a mean of 3.77 (SD = 0.92) and perceived MAI a mean of 4.15 (SD = 0.89); for the footballers, personal MAI had a mean of 2.88 (SD = 0.63), and perceived MAI a mean of 3.15 (SD = 0.69).

Other individual-level measures acted as control variables and were introduced as other actor-relation effects in our model. For schools, these were ethnocultural background and socioeconomic status (SES). Ethnocultural background was a binary variable. Dominant culture students were those who identified as Australian or Anglo-Australian, or of British or Irish heritage, and spoke only English at home. All other students were considered to be of nondominant cultural status. SES was calculated using the Socio-Economic Index For Areas (SEIFA) Index of Relative Socio-Economic Advantage/Disadvantage (ABS, 2001), derived from household postal codes, with higher scores indicative of greater socioeconomic advantage.

For the footballers, control variables were playing ability, experience, and relationship status. A measure of playing ability was included as an exogenous covariate network, which constituted binary responses to "Who are the best players in the club?" Experience was measured by the number of games played. A binary variable indicating whether players were in an ongoing romantic relationship was also included.

14.2.3   Analyses

The analyses use the social selection models of Chapter 8. These models assume that attributes are fixed and that social ties may vary (i.e., given the actor attributes, where do we expect the ties to be?).

ERGM estimation was done using the PNet program (Wang, Robins, & Pattison, 2009). The estimation procedure successfully converged (see Chapter 12) for all parameters presented for all models in this chapter. (The practice of only presenting results for converging estimations is followed in all subsequent chapters.)

14.2.4   Goodness of Fit

Goodness of fit (GOF) statistics were calculated for the second (final) model for both schoolboys and footballers networks. The GOF statistics (see Chapter 12) were less than 2.0 (in absolute value) for features that were not explicitly modeled, suggesting that the models manage to reproduce and fit the data. However, the t-statistic for the skewness of the out-degree distribution (for the schoolboys) was larger (2.71). Such a result is not unusual and indicates that there was some difficulty in capturing the out-degree distribution in that there are some highly active actors who are not completely represented by the model. Attempts to improve the skew on the out-degree distribution by including additional parameters were unsuccessful; however, in all other respects, we may consider the fit of the models excellent.

14.3   Model Specification

14.3.1   Purely Structural Effects

The purely structural effects refer to those network configurations that do not depend on the characteristics of the network nodes (e.g., reciprocity, clustering). For the social contexts of schoolboys and footballers, we used a similar set of parameters, with six of these parameters identical for both networks.[2] The parameter names as they appear in PNet are written in square brackets (e.g., [PNet parameter]) and are presented Tables 14.1 and 14.2. The purely structural parameters used for the footballers were the same for the schoolboys, except for the measures of multiple connectivity. For the football team, multiple 2-paths [A2P-T] were employed, whereas, in the school, the multiple connectivity parameter was a combination of multiple 2-paths and shared popularity [A2P-TD].

14.3.2   Actor-Relation Effects

Effects that include the characteristics of the actors in the network are known as "actor-relation effects." We use three basic effect types: sender, receiver, and homophily/heterophily (see Table 8.2 in Chapter 8). The sender and receiver parameters can be seen as main effects of attributes because they take into consideration only the attributes of one actor in the dyad with regard to a social tie. The homophily effect (used for binary and categorical attributes) is an interaction-type effect because the attributes of both actors in the dyad are modeled. The heterophily effect is for continuous attributes and is the converse of homophily (looking for difference rather than similarity).

14.3.3   Covariate Network Effects

Finally, one extra parameter included in the football network was a covariate network [Covariate Arc], which measures nominations of the best players in the team. Covariate networks are treated as exogenous in the model (see Chapter 8, Section 8.3).

---

[2]   See Chapter 13, Section 13.2, for a discussion of possible parameters to include in a model. See Table 13.1 for a suggested set of parameters for positive networks.

Table 14.1. *Two models for positive affect relations among schoolboys*

parameter	estimates (SEs)	
	model A	model B
Purely structural effects (endogenous)		
Arc	−2.67 (1.30)*	−2.91 (1.36)*
Reciprocity	2.19 (0.29)*	2.30 (0.28)*
Simple 2-path	−0.13 (0.05)*	−0.11 (0.04)*
Popularity spread [AinS]^a	−0.68 (0.29)*	−0.78 (0.29)*
Activity spread [AoutS]	−0.71 (0.30)*	−0.76 (0.29)*
Path closure [AT-T]	1.57 (0.13)*	1.54 (0.12)*
Multiple 2-paths [A2P-TD]	0.08 (0.08)	0.06 (0.07)
Actor-relation effects (exogenous)		
Heterophily^b – personal attitudes	−0.15 (0.06)*	−0.25 (0.08)*
Heterophily – perceived attitudes		0.16 (0.09)
Sender – personal attitudes	0.01 (0.08)	−0.26 (0.12)*
Sender – perceived attitudes		0.35 (0.12)*
Receiver – personal attitudes	0.03 (0.08)	0.33 (0.15)*
Receiver – perceived attitudes		−0.37 (0.15)*
Homophily – ethnoculture	0.48 (0.14)*	0.46 (0.12)*
Sender – ethnoculture	−0.06 (0.15)	−0.04 (0.15)
Receiver – ethnoculture	−0.32 (0.16)	−0.35 (0.17)*
Heterophily – socioeconomic status (SES)	−0.16 (0.10)	−0.17 (0.10)
Sender – SES	−0.29 (0.13)*	−0.27 (0.13)*
Receiver – SES	0.36 (0.14)*	0.37 (0.15)*

* Significant effect (i.e., parameter estimate is greater than two times the standard error in absolute value, see Section 12.5.1 for details)

^{a} Even if the popularity spread [A-in-S] and activity spread [A-out-S] parameters are not significant, it is still useful to include them in the model because they control for popularity and activity. If these parameters are included and there are still substantial sender and receiver effects, then this is stronger support for the impact of individual-level attributes as explaining ties that are sent or received.

^{b} Remember that the homophily parameters presented in Chapter 8 have different valence for binary and continuous variables (also noted in the example in Chapter 13). For the binary variable, we examine pairs of nodes to determine whether they both have the presence of "1" as their attribute, so homophily is represented by a significant positive parameter, and we refer to this here as homophily. For continuous variables, we examine the absolute difference between the continuous attributes for the dyad, and this difference effect is called "heterophily" – that is, a significantly positive parameter indicates that actors are different in an attribute, whereas a significant negative parameter estimate indicates that actors are similar people and have less of a difference in the attribute.

14.4   Results

To begin, we analyze personal attitudes and perceived attitudes with standard statistical approaches. There were significant associations between personal MAI and perceived MAI (schoolboys, $r = 0.80$, $p < .001$; footballers, $r = 0.54$, $p < .001$). Paired sample t-tests showed that the perceived MAI was significantly higher than personal MAI (schoolboys, $t(71) = 5.70$, $p < .001$; footballers, $t(37) = 2.58$, $p < .05$). Thus, the students and the footballers perceived that masculine attitudes were more

Table 14.2. *Two models for aggression relations among the footballers*

parameter	model	
	A	B
	structural (higher-order) and personal attitudes	structural (higher-order), personal attitudes, and perceived attitudes
Purely structural effects (endogenous)		
Arc	−5.49 (0.81)*	−6.45 (0.91)*
Reciprocity	0.25 (0.72)	0.17 (0.67)
Simple connectivity [Mix2star]	−0.09 (0.34)	−0.08 (0.36)
Popularity spread [AinS]	0.65 (0.25)*	0.62 (0.29)*
Activity spread [AoutS]	1.05 (0.25)*	1.02 (0.26)*
Path closure [AT-T]	−0.18 (0.29)	−0.21 (0.29)
Multiple 2-paths [A2P-T]	0.12 (0.39)	0.10 (0.41)
Actor-relation effects (exogenous)		
Heterophily − personal attitudes	0.19 (0.19)	0.15 (0.21)
Heterophily − perceived attitudes		−0.10 (0.18)
Sender − personal attitudes	0.03 (0.14)	−0.17 (0.17)
Sender − perceived attitudes		0.36 (0.18)*
Receiver − personal attitudes	−0.02 (0.16)	−0.29 (0.21)
Receiver − perceived attitudes		0.44 (0.21)*
Sender − relationship	0.02 (0.31)	−0.01 (0.34)
Receiver − relationship[a]	−1.32 (0.52)*	−1.68 (0.62)*
Heterophily − experience	0.003 (0.002)	0.005 (0.002)*
Sender − experience	0.000 (0.002)	−0.002 (0.002)
Receiver − experience	0.004 (0.003)	0.004 (0.003)
Covariate network effects (exogenous)		
Covariate arc ("best player" network)	−0.21 (0.40)	−0.45 (0.40)

* Significant effect

[a] There is no homophily effect for "relationship" because there are no such ties in the network. Trying to fit a model with an observed value of zero will result in a degenerate model (see Section 13.2).

dominative than the actual average score of personal attitudes. The pattern of these findings suggests evidence for pluralistic ignorance. We now present exponential random graph model (ERGM) results for our two networks separately.

14.4.1 Example 1: Schoolboys

Results from two different ERGMs for positive affect relations for schoolboys are presented in Table 14.1. The models differ in the following ways. Model A examines purely structural factors and actor-relation effects without perceived MAI effects. Model B includes all parameters from model A, plus perceived MAI effects. Model B is our main interest because it simultaneously examines the interdependent effects of personal attitudes, perceived attitudes, and social structures. We present two models with different parameters for the same social network to demonstrate how effects are interdependent and parameter interpretations change with the inclusion of additional effects.

Table 14.1 contains parameter estimates with standard errors in brackets. In line with Chapter 12 (see Section 12.5.1), a significant effect is denoted by an asterisk when the parameter estimate is greater than two times the standard error in absolute value.

Results: Purely Structural Effects. A significant parameter estimate indicates the associated configuration is observed more than expected (had the parameter been 0), given the other effects in the model. We note that we do not usually interpret the arc parameter because it is analogous to the intercept in a linear regression.

For model A, the interpretation is as follows: positive affect ties are more likely to occur if they are reciprocated (positive significant reciprocity parameter estimate). There is not a lot of variation in the students' activity unless[3] it occurs in regions of high triangulation (see later in this chapter) (negative significant activity spread or A-out-S parameter). Similarly, there is little variation in the spread of popularity, unless it occurs within areas of high transitive closure (negative significant popularity spread or A-in-S parameter). Finally, students' positive affect relations tend to occur in regions of transitive closure (positive significant AT-T parameter), thus joining a friend of a friend to a friend, but multiple 2-paths do not occur more than expected (positive but not significant A2P-TD parameter). In conclusion, one might say that most people tend to be economical in their positive affect nominations, which usually occur as reciprocated or in transitive closure. Levels of popularity and activity tend to be homogeneous, so there are no strong effects for degree centralization. These results are not surprising, but by controlling for these types of structures through these parameters, it is possible to make principled inferences about the actor-relation effects in the model.

Results: Actor-Relation Effects. First, there were some effects for the control variables. In model B, there is a homophily effect for ethnocultural background and a negative receiver effect for ethnoculture, indicating that students from nondominant ethnocultural backgrounds are more likely to receive positive affect nominations. Further for model B, the negative and significant sender effect for SES indicates that students with lower SES are more likely to make nominations of positive affect or send more ties. There is also a substantial and positive receiver effect for SES, indicating

---

[3] We say "unless" here to highlight that there could still be high-degree nodes in the triangulated regions – arising from triangulation, not from star effects.

that students with higher SES are more likely to receive nominations of positive affect or be more popular.

Our primary interest is on the impact of perceived attitudes on social tie formation. There is an important change in parameter values from model A to model B for sender and receiver effects for personal MAI when perceived MAI is also included. Without perceived MAI in the model, personal MAI is not as important to social tie formation. In model A, there is a substantial and negative heterophily effect for personal MAI, indicating that students have positive affect for others with similar personal attitudes toward masculinity. Yet, the introduction of perceived MAI in model B is associated with two new significant network effects for personal MAI: a negative sender effect and a positive receiver effect. This is striking evidence for interdependency between the parameters for personal attitudes and perceived attitudes, suggesting that both are necessary to understand the processes underpinning this network. Now we may infer that, given perceived attitudes, boys with higher personal MAI will send out fewer ties but receive more ties. In other words, those boys who have less dominative personal attitudes tend to be more active, and those boys who have more dominative personal attitudes tend to be more popular.

Of particular interest is the negative and substantial receiver effect for perceived MAI, given a positive receiver effect for personal MAI. This suggests that students who personally hold dominative masculine attitudes are of high status (popular), and students who perceive that others hold nondominative masculine attitudes are also popular. That is, popular students tend to be those who have high dominative attitudes and/or believe that others hold nondominative beliefs. So, although personal and perceived MAI are correlated in this data set, those students who themselves have dominative masculine attitudes and/or see their fellows as not holding such an extreme position are substantially more popular. Moreover, individuals who believe a dominative masculinity is generally held by others within the network are substantially more active (i.e., sender effect for perceived MAI). These effects occur above and beyond the substantial homophily effects for personal MAI.

The two receiver effects are main effects, not an interaction effect. As such, we use the term "and/or" because people may be popular due to high personal MAI or due to low perceived MAI, or both. Of course, we know from the correlation between personal and perceived MAI that the same people tend to score highly on both. Furthermore, the sender effects are also separate main effects in our model. One interpretation is to construe the co-occurrence of these two independent effects as evidence for the emergence of social hierarchy as students seek to exemplify a social prototype based on dominative masculinity. If an actor's perceived attitude is much higher than his personal attitude, he will tend to send out more ties. In other words, schoolboys who perceive the school as a context where dominative masculinity prevails will seek more social connections, especially if they themselves do not have dominative masculine attitudes. However, popularity is associated with the opposite effect: popular actors hold personal masculine attitudes that are much more dominative than those they think are held by their school friends.

14.4.2 Example 2: Football Team

We examine two models for aggression relations within an all-male football team. Remember, in this network, the sender of a tie is the aggressor, and the receiver of the tie is the victim. Results are presented in Table 14.2.

Results: Purely Structural Effects. In contrast to the schoolboys, the parameter estimates for reciprocity and closure are not significant for the football team. This is not surprising for a network based on negative ties (i.e., aggression). Instead there is both a significant and positive effect for activity and popularity spread, indicating that some players are overly "active" as aggressors, and some are overly "active" as victims of aggression.

Results: Actor-Relation Effects. The control variables offer some insights for the footballers. In model B, a negative and significant receiver effect for relationship indicates that single men were substantially more likely to be the recipient of aggression. Furthermore, aggression relations were much more likely between players of differing levels of experience, as noted by the significant positive heterophily effect for experience. Interestingly, it is the inclusion of perceived attitudes that brings out the heterophily effect for experience (compare models A and B).

For this football team, we see an effect of perceived attitudes that is independent of personal attitudes. Again, the focus is on the difference made by including perceived attitudes. Unlike the schoolboys' network, for the footballers there are no significant effects for personal MAI for either model. Furthermore, although the parameter values of personal MAI change when including perceived MAI attitudes, the personal attitudes have no substantial impact on social tie formation. However, perceived MAI attitudes *are* significantly related to both sending and receiving ties. Therefore, footballers with high perceived MAI are significantly more likely to be aggressive toward others. Players with high perceived MAI are significantly more likely to be victims of aggression. Interestingly, there is no homophily effect for perceived MAI. Here, we have the extreme situation where perceptions about the collective determine behaviors independently of personal motivations.

Results: Covariate Network Effects. Finally, there is no effect of best player covariate network on the aggression network.

14.5   Discussion

The analysis of personal attitudes and perceived attitudes with social network relations demonstrates some interesting results in these two local contexts. In the school, students who do not personally hold high dominative masculine attitudes send many social ties. In addition, students who perceive that others do hold high dominative masculine attitudes also send many ties. Furthermore, students who hold high personal masculine attitudes receive the most social ties (i.e., are popular individuals). We suggest that some form of social hierarchy may explain these results. SIT assumes that the norm (or prototype) is more extreme than the average attitude (Hogg et al., 1995) and representative of the qualities of the leaders of the group (Lindenberg, 1997). In combination, these effects suggest that those who perceive high dominative masculine attitudes send many ties to others in the network potentially because the personal attitudes of those who are popular (and thus the leaders) are also high. Social norms (measured here as perceived attitudes) are dictated by the attitudes of prestigious people of a social setting, affecting the formation of social ties.

However, in the football team, we have a different story in that perceived attitudes have an independent explanatory capacity regarding social tie formation. We note that masculine attitudes include a component about violence, and that we might anticipate those most demonstrating aggression to be high in personal MAI attitudes. Yet, aggression toward others within this team is not associated with personal attitudes to masculinity; rather, perceived attitudes are significantly associated with aggressive behaviors. Specifically, those who were aggressive to others were high in perceived MAI, as were those who were the victims of aggression. Thus, it is principally the perception by individuals of the attitudes of those around them that may push players to engage in aggression relations. The notion that "culture is a 'tool kit' for constructing 'strategies of action'" (Swidler, 1998, 176) may well explain why players without a strong personal endorsement of violence, but with perceived attitudes that aggression is valued, are more likely to be aggressive toward others. The results for the team, based on a negative affect social tie, are therefore different than the results for the boys based on a positive affect network. However, the results of the footballers suggest that the "misperception" of social norms implied by the notion of pluralistic ignorance is also a feasible explanation.

These effects for perceived attitudes raise a fundamental question of whether social behavior, including tie formation, is related to personal attitudes, perceived attitudes, or some interaction of the two. Frosh et al. (2001) stated that boys in schools present different behaviors, depending on whether they are engaging with boys, girls, or adults. The presentation of contradictory masculine identities in these different scenarios is hardly likely to result from changing personal attitudes of the boys from one context to the next. Instead, the embodiment of different masculine behaviors is likely to be related to an individual's differing perceptions of the attitudes of others in the context – that is, something we conceive of as an individual's idea of the social norm. These perceived attitudes certainly interact with the personal attitudes of the individual and the specific social relations he has with others. We address these issues in terms of a social selection model, which makes theoretical sense from SIT. However, it is also possible that the personal attitudes of prominent (i.e., central) individuals may *influence* the perceived attitudes of peripheral network members. An alternative analysis using a social influence–type model such as autologistic actor attribute model (ALAAM: Chapter 9) could be used, but of course the direction of effect cannot be fully resolved without the use of longitudinal data.

Finally, the findings for the footballers suggest that certain contexts may invoke behaviors and relations (i.e., aggression) through expectations or norms, and personal attitudes may not be directly related to social behavior. Further theorizing about specific ways in which perceived attitudes may operate in relation to personal attitudes and local social structures may provide an enriched understanding of the processes that people engage in within their social worlds.

15

How To Close a Hole: Exploring Alternative Closure Mechanisms in Interorganizational Networks

Alessandro Lomi and Francesca Pallotti

15.1 Mechanisms of Network Closure

One way to think about social networks is as social structures built from the bottom up through combinations of simpler components defined in terms of local configurations of ties, or "motifs" (Milo et al., 2002; Pattison & Robins, 2002). Local configurations of network ties may be interpreted as observable outcomes of specific social mechanisms such as reciprocity. Because organizations display a strong tendency toward forming ties with their partner's partners, processes of tie maintenance and formation based on closure mechanisms have been of particular interest to scholars of interorganizational networks (Gulati & Gargiulo, 1999; Hallen, 2008; Laumann & Marsden, 1982; Lomi & Pattison, 2006). Closure has been found to shape the formation and maintenance of network ties between organizations operating in a variety of empirical settings ranging from manufacturing relations in the automotive industry (Lomi & Pattison, 2006), to strategic alliances in various industrial sectors (Gulati & Gargiulo, 1999), to equity relations between organizations belonging to the same "keiretsu" (Lincoln, Gerlach, & Ahmadjian, 1996). The accumulation of empirical experiences in the study of interorganizational relations has given shape to the general expectation that partners of partners are (more likely to be) partners. What social mechanisms may be underlying such expectations?

In theoretical terms, the tendency toward transitive closure in interorganizational networks has been framed and interpreted as the direct

We gratefully acknowledge the financial support provided by the *Schweizerische Nationalfonds* (Swiss National Science Foundation Grant No. 124537). We thank the participants to the Quantitative Methods in the Social Sciences 2 (QMSS2) seminar "Networks, Markets and Organizations," August 27–29, 2009, University of Groningen, for comments and discussion.

consequence of the costs and risks inherent in the formation and maintenance of network ties with partners whose quality, capability, and trust-
worthiness are only imperfectly observable (Baum et al., 2005; Sorenson & Stuart, 2008). To manage these different sources of uncertainty
and reduce the exposure to opportunistic behavior of potential partners,
organizations tend to form new ties with their partners' partners based on
referrals and shared information (Baker, 1990; Uzzi, 1996). Ties to common third parties also promote adherence to norms by promoting trust
and by facilitating social monitoring and sanctioning of opportunistic
behavior (Burt & Knez, 1995; Rousseau et al., 1998). In fact, fundamental third-party effects such as reputation and status affect the formation
of network ties precisely because direct information about the quality
of potential partners is not easily available (Gulati & Gargiulo, 1999;
Podolny, 2001). As Coleman succinctly put it: "reputation cannot arise
in an open structure" (1988, S107).

In analytical terms, the tendency toward network closure may be interpreted as the "outcome" of path-shortening behavior whereby indirect
connectivity between organizations in the form of (possibly multiple)
2-paths leads to a direct tie. This particular type of path closure is represented graphically in Figure 15.1a, and discussed in greater detail in
Snijders et al. (2006) and Robins et al. (2009). The configurations in
Figure 15.1 are presented in Chapter 6.

The configuration of local network ties in Figure 15.1a embodies the
expectation that "partners of my partner are my partners." This specific
closure mechanism, perhaps the most commonly encountered mechanism
in studies of interorganizational networks, is described by Uzzi as resulting from the fact that "[e]xpectations of trust and reciprocity between
two economic actors could be 'rolled over' to a new third party, thereby
establishing trust and reciprocal obligations between two parties that
lacked a prior history of exchange" (1996, 490).

Mechanisms of "expectations rollover" are perfectly capable of producing direct ties between indirectly connected partners, but other possible mechanisms exist that may be responsible for closure in interorganizational networks. Although sketched by Laumann and Marsden (1982),
to the best of our knowledge, these mechanisms have not been examined
systematically in contemporary studies of interorganizational networks.

Two organizations may come to form a tie because they are both
related in the same way to the same other. This may be viewed as a kind
of structural homophily, whereby similarity in choice leads to the formation or maintenance of network ties (DiMaggio, 1986). As noted in
Chapter 6, this mechanism is called "activity closure" and is represented
in Figure 15.1b. Activity closure can be interpreted as structural equivalence in outgoing ties, or the outcome of joint dependence on common
resources, information, and knowledge, or, possibly, of shared capacity

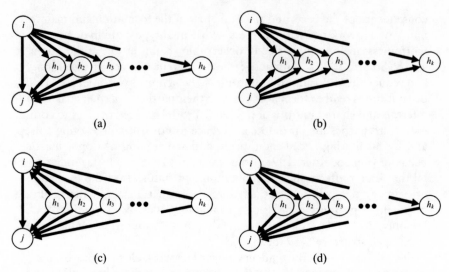

Figure 15.1. Local configurations of network ties representing different closure mechanisms: (a) path closure, (b) activity closure, (c) popularity closure, and (d) cyclic closure.

constraints. A clear example in which this interpretation is appropriate is offered by the study of technological innovation in interorganizational communities within which "common dependence on technological antecedents indicates substitutability and thus a competitive relation between two organizations" (Podolny, Stuart, & Hannan, 1996, 667). Of course, the extent to which common dependence on technological (or any other) resources generates competition rather than relational coordination remains an open empirical issue (Bothner, 2003). Depending on the specific relational context, a positive estimate of activity closure may indicate a general tendency toward cooperation among potential competitors.

Organizations may form a tie not only because they choose the same others as partners, or because they depend on resources controlled by the same others, but also because they are chosen as exchange partners by the same others. This situation is depicted in Figure 15.1c, and the corresponding mechanism is called "popularity closure." To the extent that the unreciprocated flow of activity (or relations) received may be interpreted as a signal of deference, this particular closure mechanism is relevant to studies of status homophily because "status (direct ties) provides strong signals of quality" (Podolny et al., 1996, 669). This interpretation seems to be particularly apposite when the qualities of potential partners are difficult to ascertain – a situation in which status is typically interpreted as a signal of quality (Podolny, 1994). A positive estimate of the popularity closure parameter would provide some evidence that status homophily is an important uncertainty reduction mechanism underlying the selection of network partners.

A fourth distinct closure mechanism is based on generalized exchange, a triadic pattern of network ties that does not involve immediate needs for reciprocation (Bearman, 1997). Generalized exchange defines a situation in which "the recipient of benefit does not return benefit directly to the giver, but to another actor in the social circle. The giver eventually receives some benefit in return, *but from a different actor*" (Molm, Collet, & Schaefer, 2007, 207–208). In other words, in a system of generalized exchange, participants have to be "givers" before they may become "receivers." Generalized exchange is associated with the cyclic closure configuration of network ties depicted in Figure 15.1d. It plays an important coordination role in interorganizational networks because "any particular exchange or transfer of resources occurs in a context of other exchanges and transfers, and regularities in patterns of exchange involving more than two members provide one possible means by which particular exchanges are integrated into a wider collaborative effort" (Lazega & Pattison, 1999, 68). A positive estimate of the cyclic closure parameter would be consistent with the presence of diffuse cooperation or, perhaps, "organic" solidarity among members of an interorganizational community (Ekeh, 1974).

In summary, triadic closure may result as an "outcome" of alternative mechanisms, but each mechanism implies that network ties arise for different reasons, and that they have different implications and interpretations. As explained in Chapter 6, exponential random graph models for directed social networks permit specification and empirical identification of these alternative closure mechanisms.

15.2   Data and Measures

15.2.1   Setting and Data

The empirical opportunity to examine different mechanisms of network closure is provided by data that we collected on relations of patient transfer among members of a community of ninety-one hospital organizations located in Lazio, a large geographic region in central Italy with roughly 5.3 million inhabitants. In our analysis, we concentrate specifically on the transfer of in-patients. In-patients are individuals who have already acquired the status of "admitted patient" and, therefore, who have consented to follow the clinical and therapeutic paths proposed by professional medical staff who are clinically responsible and legally liable for their conditions. This is an important qualification because individual network ties induced by in-patient transfers are the outcome of

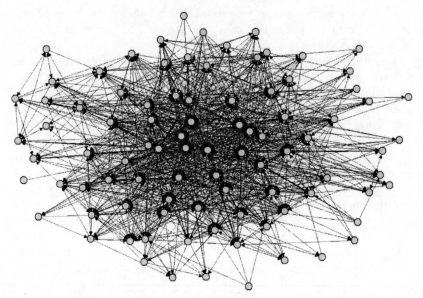

Figure 15.2. Network structure of interhospital patient mobility.

organizational decisions over which patients have conceded control at admission. Of course, patients retain the right to refuse transfer in the same way as they retain the right to refuse treatment. However, they cannot choose where they will be transferred – a decision that remains a prerogative of the doctor in charge of the patient. Hence, the network structure of in-patient (henceforth, simply "patient") transfer between hospitals in our sample can be legitimately seen – and modeled – as the outcome of a complex system of interrelated organizational decisions.

Using public data on transferred patients during the year 2003, we constructed a matrix of size 91 × 91. The matrix contains in each row/column, the hospital sending/receiving patients, and in the intersection cells, the number of patients transferred from the row to the column hospital (with zeroes down the diagonal). The overall number of patients transferred between hospitals is 13,178. The volume of transferred patients within dyads ranges from 0 to 525 patients, with an average of 1.6. The matrix of patient transfer relations is asymmetric because, for any hospital in the sample, the number of patients sent typically differs from the number of patients received; in other words, this is a directed network. We dichotomized the matrix by using the overall mean number of transferred patients as a cut-off value. Figure 15.2 illustrates the dichotomized version of the network induced by patient transfer relations between the hospitals in the sample. More detailed information on the sample and the institutional setting of the study is found in Lomi and Pallotti (2012).

15.3 Model Specification

The main analytical objective of this chapter is to examine and interpret alternative closure mechanisms implied by different local configurations of interorganizational network ties. However general, triadic closure is not the only mechanism responsible for the formation of local structure. The tendency of organizations to construct network ties may also be affected by a variety of other endogenous relational mechanisms (or purely structural effects) and by a number of attributional cofactors (frequently referred to as "actor-relation" effects).

The effects specified in our model are as follows, with PNet parameter in brackets. First, we include effects for path closure [AT-T], cyclic closure [AT-C], activity closure [AT-U], and popularity closure [AT-D]. We control for the tendency of organizations to establish network ties [Arc] and engage in reciprocated relations [Reciprocity], and for the tendency of *in-* and *out*-degrees to be correlated [Mixed-2-star]. We also control for higher-order, starlike configurations that have the function of spreading the in- and out-degree distributions ("popularity spread," or "alternating-in-star" [A-in-S], and "activity spread," or "alternating-out-star" [A-out-S], respectively). Finally, we control for the presence of "localized multiple connectivity," or multiple (open) 2-paths [A2p-TDU]. Through multiple connectivity effects, we allow for the possibility that tendencies toward closure and brokerage coexist in our network (Burt, 2001). Localized multiple connectivity configurations may be defined in reference to the corresponding triangular path closure configurations depicted in Figure 15.1. Different types of brokerage in the form of multiple (open) 2-paths are derived from the corresponding closure configurations simply by removing the base (multiple 2-paths, shared activity, and shared popularity corresponding to path closure, activity closure, and popularity closure, respectively). For parsimony, in the models estimated, we include only the general version of multiple connectivity, which combines all three distinct multiple 2-path substructures. Positive estimates of closure in models accounting for the presence of (open) multiple 2-paths may be interpreted as evidence that closure in the network occurs because of the completion of the base of the multiple triangles (Robins et al., 2009).

In our analysis of closure mechanisms, we also control for a number of organization-specific covariates that may account for differences in the propensity of single organizations to enter into collaborative ties. We control for hospital *size* as measured in terms of total number of employees (clinicians, nurses, and other health care professionals, as well as administrative staff). This continuous variable (range: 11–2,924) enters our model specifications as sender, receiver, and heterophily effects because interorganizational differences in resource endowments may affect the propensity of individual hospitals to transfer patients in a number of ways. To control for the effect of potential resource complementarities, we use the degree of specialization in the health care services provided to patients by every hospital in the sample as measured by the "level of care." This binary dummy variable takes the value of 1 if a hospital provides specialized tertiary care services, and 0 otherwise. Approximately 12% of the hospitals in our sample provide tertiary care. "Level of care" enters our model specifications as a homophily effect because we expect hospitals offering complementary services to be more likely to collaborate.

Extant literature suggests that the likelihood of observing cooperative relationships among organizations is strongly influenced by the geographic proximity of potential partners (Whittington, Powell, & Owen-Smith, 2009). To control for proximity and for the possible effect of transportation costs, we include a dyadic covariate measuring the distance (in kilometers) of each pair of hospitals within the region ("geographic distance"). The distance between hospitals in our sample ranges from 0 to 222.6 kilometers.

15.4   Results

The first column in Table 15.1 reports the estimates of the baseline dyad independence model (M1) containing only the arc and reciprocity parameters. Considered together, the estimates suggest that hospitals in our sample consider establishing network ties costly and tend to shy away from engaging in nonreciprocated patient transfers.

The second column reports the estimates of a model (M2) containing the full specification of endogenous network effects. The negative estimates of parameters associated with popularity spread and activity spread suggest that there is a clear upper bound to the number of other partners that a given hospital may consider as both receivers and senders of patients. The estimates also reveal the presence of two significant but distinct tendencies toward closure in the interhospital patient transfer network. One mechanism is activity closure: hospitals that are structurally equivalent (in outgoing ties) tend to be directly connected, suggesting that, in our sample, structural equivalence (in choices of patient transfers) facilitates interorganizational collaboration. The significantly positive effect of activity closure suggests that structural equivalence tends to induce cooperative rather than competitive behavior: hospitals sending patients to the same third parties tend to establish direct ties of collaboration rather than competing for scarce resources such as hospital beds or surgery rooms controlled by their shared partners. This effect of activity closure should be interpreted net of the effect of path closure, which

Table 15.1. *ERGM estimates of structural and actor-relation effects on the presence of patient transfers between hospitals*

parameter	estimates (SEs)		
purely structural effects	M1	M2	M3M
Arc	−2.39 (0.05)*	−1.62 (0.58)*	−0.80 (0.57)
Reciprocity	1.97 (0.11)*	1.16 (0.14)*	1.00 (0.14)*
Simple 2-path[2-path]		−0.002 (0.004)	−0.04 (0.01)*
Popularity spread [AinS]		−0.82 (0.19)*	−0.72 (0.20)
Activity spread [AoutS]		−1.28 (0.27)*	−1.28 (0.27)*
Path closure [AT-T]		1.32 (0.13)*	1.20 (0.13)*
Cyclic closure [AT-C]		−0.26 (0.06)*	−0.21 (0.06)*
Popularity closure [AT-D]		0.06 (0.07)	0.07 (0.08)
Activity closure [AT-U]		0.72 (0.10)*	0.61 (0.11)*
Multiple connectivity [A2P-TDU]		−0.06 (0.01)*	−0.07 (0.01)*
Actor-relations effects			
Sender (size)			0.0012 (0.0002)*
Receiver (size)			0.0009 (0.0001)*
Heterophily (size) [difference]			−0.0006 (0.0001)*
Homophily (level of care) [Interaction]			−1.55 (0.28)*
Geographic distance [Covariate Arc]			−0.01 (0.001)*

* Significant effect

was also found to be significantly positive. Following Uzzi (1996), the system of path-closing transfers could indicate that expectations of trust between hospitals can be "rolled over" to new third parties. However, we find no evidence for popularity closure. We also found a significantly negative tendency against cyclic closure: the formation of network ties between hospitals in our sample does not seem to respond to a logic of generalized exchange. Finally, the significantly negative estimate of the parameter for generalized multiconnectivity suggests that open 2-paths are unlikely in our sample. This result strengthens our conclusions about closure.

In our discussion so far, we concentrate exclusively on the effect of purely structural mechanisms related to characteristics of the degree distribution and triadic closure on observed network ties. However, research indicates that organizations are more or less attractive network partners depending also on a variety of individual characteristics. For example, organizations may be preferentially attracted to specific partners with complementary resources and capabilities (Gulati & Gargiulo, 1999), or partners that are similar along specific dimensions (Powell et al., 2005), or those that are geographically more proximate (Whittington et al., 2009). We find that resource complementarities significantly affect the likelihood of observing the presence of network ties: as expected, patient transfer is more likely between hospitals offering different typologies of assistance. The presence of a patient transfer relation between hospitals offering a different level of care (secondary vs. tertiary) is significantly more likely (because this is a binary variable, the negative parameter indicates ties are associated with difference in care – see Chapter 8). In terms of size, larger hospitals are more likely to send and receive more patients. The negative difference effect (for a continuous variable – see Chapter 8) indicates that hospitals of similar size tend to share patients. The combination of these effects implies that ties occur most frequently for larger hospitals. Finally, the estimates confirm the intuition that distant hospitals are unlikely to exchange patients. Incorporating these attribute-based mechanisms leaves virtually unaltered the conclusions we have reached about the endogenous network mechanisms that we have postulated and documented.

The parameter estimates in the full model M3 seem to capture salient features of the overall network with reasonable accuracy. For example, the observed number of network ties is 999, whereas the number of network ties predicted by the model is 1,000.93, with standard deviation = 32.29. Yet, in terms of goodness of fit (Chapter 12), the model tends to underestimate the standard deviation of the in-degree (observed standard deviation of in-degree distribution = 11.909, estimated = 10.158, standard deviation = 0.398) and out-degree (observed standard deviation of out-degree distribution = 7.1529, estimated = 6.498, standard deviation = 0.3197), and the skewness of the in-degree distribution (observed skewness of the in-degree distribution = 1.6183, predicted = 0.9671, standard deviation = 0.1609). These are not uncommon findings with respect to model fit. However, the model implied by the estimates reproduces with acceptable accuracy all other important structural features of the observed network.

15.5   Discussion

Observed tendencies toward closure in interorganizational networks may be interpreted as the outcome of attempts at controlling uncertainty and reducing the risks inherent in collaborating with complementary partners who may be different along multiple unobservable dimensions. Network closure, therefore, represents a particularly transparent mechanism through which control attempts generate network ties (White, 1992). In the interorganizational community of hospitals that we examine here, decisions to transfer patients would have disastrous consequences without a considerable degree of coordination and collaboration between hospitals, and indeed between doctors working in different hospitals. Because relational coordination requires the allocation of considerable resources, the selection of network partners represents a decision that is both risky and consequential. We show that partner selection decisions are significantly affected by a tendency toward network closure: hospitals tend to select as partners their partners' partners. The tendency toward multiple interorganizational triangles that share the same base suggests an overall network structure organized around denser closed regions with triads appearing in clusters. Figure 15.2 suggests that there is one such region, giving the network a core-periphery nature. The negative signs of the parameters associated with multiple starlike configurations suggest that the core-periphery structure is not generated by individual differences in activity or popularity (i.e., in sending or receiving network ties). Our analysis also sustains more specific conclusions. We document a significant tendency against generalized exchange – a result that emphasizes the hierarchical nature of interhospital patient transfer activities. We find this result particularly interesting in our empirical context because, according to Laumann and Marsden, generalized exchange "will be avoided in systems of organizations operating under competitive conditions... due to the emphasis in that context on the maintenance of the autonomy of the units and the minimization of dependence on other units" (1982, 341). We found no evidence of popularity closure: patient transfer relations are unlikely between hospitals that are structurally equivalent in incoming ties. However, we do have evidence that the formation and maintenance of network ties among the hospitals in our sample is based on mechanisms of activity closure: hospitals that are structurally equivalent in outgoing ties are significantly more likely to cooperate. Our results suggest that relations between hospitals in our sample tend to be affected by uncertainty coming from shared capacity constraints rather than by potential competition for patients that other hospitals have decided to transfer. Considered together, these results are consistent with the view that "competing organizations are often defined by their... structural equivalence in resource dependence, but the very structure that defines competitors can also identify cooperators" (Ingram & Yue, 2008, 275). Local processes of structural equivalence of the kind we document here not only affect the likelihood of direct collaboration, but may also drive the adoption/diffusion of innovation (Bothner, 2003) and, ultimately, the tendency toward isomorphism frequently observed in studies of organizational communities and fields (DiMaggio, 1986). Particularly deserving of notice is the fact that the inclusion of actor-relation effects leaves the closure effects virtually unaltered. We interpret this result as evidence of the robustness of structural network effects with respect to attributional elements that might affect relations.

In this chapter, we restrict the scope of our discussion and interpretation of the various local patterns of interorganizational relations to acts of collaboration. However, interpretation of the various path-shortening strategies is obviously not independent from relational contents – an argument also suggested by Robins et al. (2009) in the context of intraorganizational relations. For example, if relations between organizations are reconstructed in terms of acts of aggression, or observable signals of enmity or rivalry, then the various network "motifs" could be interpreted in terms of dominance hierarchies analyzed by Ivan Chase (1980), with activity-based closure playing the role of the "double receive" sequence, popularity closure interpretable as "double attack," and cyclic closure similar to the "pass on" (or perhaps "attack the attacker") aggression sequence. This conjecture suggests that the approach to the analysis of interorganizational networks that we have only sketched in this chapter may be applicable well beyond the study of cooperation and competition, and extended to cover important areas in contemporary interorganizational research on the emergence of status hierarchies and on the diffusion of innovation, competitive strategies, and managerial practices within organizational communities. Much more research is obviously needed to derive the possible implications of this conjecture.

16

Interdependencies between Working Relations: Multivariate ERGMs for Advice and Satisfaction

Yu Zhao and Olaf Rank

16.1 Multirelational Networks in Organizations

A relationship between two people may occur for several reasons: working on the same project, physical proximity to one another, shared interests, or disagreements over a task. Yet, it is not just that different processes can lead to creation of one type of social tie – indeed, the connections of individuals comprise multiple types of ties simultaneously. Clearly, people negotiate many types of relationships in their everyday lives. Different relationships entail different meanings – for instance, friendship and advice are unlikely to be regarded as synonymous. Moreover, a social connection between two people may involve many different facets, each of which can be usefully analyzed as a separate type of relational tie. For instance, a relationship between two individuals may involve both working collaboration and social support. These different types of relational ties may tend to be aligned in a relationship – a person may seek advice from a friend – or even exchanged – one person might deliver a service while the other provides a payment.

Focusing on only one type of relational tie may disregard important information about the complexity of social life, and doing so may also yield an incomplete representation of individuals' embeddedness in social settings (e.g., those provided by the structure of an organization). As Nohria suggested, "From a network perspective, [...] the structure of any organization must be understood and analyzed in terms of multiple networks of relationships in the organization (both prescribed and emergent) and how they are patterned, singly and in various combinations" (1992, 5). Similarly, Kenis and Knoke argued that "No single type of relationship constitutes 'the' network of an organizational field. Multiple types of ties may be relevant in constructing an explanation of structure and action. Which types of networks an analyst should take into account and which ones he or she can safely ignore ultimately depend on the substantive issues driving a specific empirical inquiry" (2002, 276). The different relational ties in which an actor is embedded are typically not independent of each other. Instead, it is more realistic to assume that ties are characterized by manifold interdependencies (Lazega & Pattison, 1999; Rank, Robins, & Pattison, 2010). Relational ties may either co-occur between two individuals or one type of tie may be regarded as an antecedent to another type of tie. In an organizational context, for example, it is plausible that two members who have collaborated for some time may also develop a friendship tie. Alternatively, two friends may be more likely to establish collaboration on an informal basis.

In addition to considering multiple relations, the inclusion of actor attributes into the analysis of organizational networks is important. The characteristics of individuals are likely to shape their embeddedness in multirelational networks. For example, people may be inclined to collaborate with others because of their expertise or experience within the organization. Similarly, people may seek friendships with those who have positive personal characteristics.

In this chapter, we illustrate how to simultaneously investigate multiple networks within organizations. Analyzing network data from two bank branches, we consider two types of relational ties to model interdependencies between different aspects of collaboration. Ibarra (1992) classified emergent relational ties in organizations into two distinct categories – instrumental and expressive – with instrumental ties used primarily for particular purposes or goals, and expressive ties carrying emotional content. In our example, the first network we examine is the "advice-giving network." Advice, construed as an "instrumental" network, comprises giving assistance and help to those colleagues who want to discuss work-related issues. The second relation, an "expressive" network, is "satisfaction," which in our context captures work interactions that yield a level of satisfaction to employees.

Our motivation for studying these two networks simultaneously is to investigate whether advice-giving relationships align with satisfying work interactions within organizations. In particular, we seek to examine whether advice and satisfaction may be entrained, so that individuals who provide advice also find that relationship satisfying. It is possible that providing advice increases satisfaction; or, alternatively, that actors are more inclined to provide advice to those network partners with whom they are most satisfied.[1]

---

[1] With the cross-sectional data available, it is impossible to determine the direction of the effect (i.e., whether advice giving leads to satisfaction or vice versa), and it would not be surprising if both processes were present. However, it is possible to use a multivariate ERGM to examine whether entrainment of advice and satisfaction tends to occur.

Another research question of interest is that advice and satisfaction may be exchanged, in which case those who *receive* advice tend to be satisfied with the advice giver. Both entrainment and exchange are the two important bivariate dyadic effects for directed networks (as described in Chapter 10). Whatever the focus of a given study, a model for directed bivariate networks should include at least these two effects. (Additional possible effects are set out in Chapter 10, and we include some here.) We also investigate whether individual-level characteristics of the organizations' members (e.g., seniority) have an effect on the entrainment or exchange of network ties.

An exponential random graph model (ERGM) approach allows us to investigate entrainment and exchange at the same time as we take into account any relevant within-network dependencies that are present. That is, advice-giving and satisfaction relationships will have their own internal organizing principles. We could assess whether advice-giving and satisfaction ties align simply by counting the number of multiplex ties, or perhaps by correlating the two networks using Quadratic Assignment Procedure (QAP; Krackhardt, 1987). QAP correlation is a well-established test for inferring association between two networks at the dyadic level. However, we want not only to assess whether there is such an alignment between the two networks, but also to investigate whether both entrainment and exchange occur after taking into account the internal logics of each network, as well as the attributes of the actors in the network. Zhao (2007) provided an empirical example where the simple correlation between two networks was low and insignificant according to a QAP test, but where there were in fact important cross-network dependencies. The low correlation occurs because a number of dependencies operate in competing ways. Through a model-based approach that controls for within-network effects such as ERGM, we can be more confident in our inferences about cross-network associations.

16.2   Data, Measures, and Analyses

The empirical investigation comprised all employees of two branches of a major Australian retail bank. The data were part of a larger study of multiple bank branches, but these two branches were chosen as case studies for this chapter because of the similarity in overall performance based on retail data provided by the bank. Although the two branches employed a similar number of individuals, they differed substantially in the densities of their advice-giving and satisfaction networks. For this reason, we refer to one as a high advice satisfaction (or High-AS) bank and the other as a low advice satisfaction (or Low-AS) bank. This enables us to compare our assumptions of exchange and entrainment across two different contexts, one where advice giving and satisfaction is highly prevalent, and one where it is not.

To measure the advice-giving and satisfaction networks, identical rosters were used for each network that included all employee names in each respective branch. Ties in the advice-giving network were obtained using the following name generator: "Suppose an issue arises in other people's work. Who do you find comes to you from time to time to discuss such issues?" This question is different from the standard advice-seeking network of "To whom do you go to for advice?" and as such, ties go from the advice giver to the person seeking advice. Ties in the satisfaction network were collected by asking respondents, "With whom do you feel that your work interactions are particularly satisfying to you personally?" Subsequently, we label the advice-giving network "A" and the satisfaction network "S".

We measured seniority as a binary variable, distinguishing between senior (=1) and junior (=0) positions. Both bank branches had two recognized senior positions (a manager and a deputy manager) and a number of more junior categories of staff. We include employees' seniority as an actor attribute because we expect seniority to influence an individual's embeddedness in the advice-giving and satisfaction networks.

We proceed in two steps in the analysis. First, we compare the two organizations and their relational characteristics on a descriptive level. Second, we turn to the simultaneous analysis of the multirelational network structure using the XPNet program, a multirelational version of the PNet program (Wang, Robins, & Pattison, 2009), which implements the bivariate network model presented in Chapter 10.

16.3   Descriptive Results

Visualizations of the networks for the two bank branches are presented here. Figure 16.1 presents the advice-giving and satisfaction networks among all fifteen employees in the Low-AS bank branch, whereas Figure 16.2 presents the two networks among all twelve employees in the High-AS bank branch. The coordinates of the nodes in Figures 16.1 and 16.2 have been fixed within branches across the advice-giving and satisfaction visualizations, so that for both types of network the nodes are in the same spatial positions. The black nodes represent people with senior positions.

Table 16.1 presents descriptive statistics for the two bank branches. For the Low-AS bank, the advice-giving and satisfaction networks are relatively sparse with densities of 0.22 and 0.23, respectively. In the High-AS bank, the networks are substantially denser with network densities of 0.41 for the advice-giving network and 0.40 for the satisfaction network.

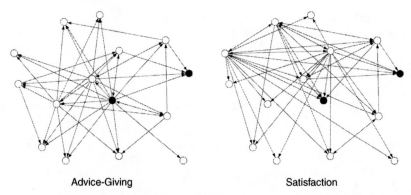

Advice-Giving   Satisfaction

Figure 16.1. Advice-giving and satisfaction network in Low-AS bank branch.

That the densities across networks are consistently low for the Low-AS bank and high for High-AS bank is a first indication that the two network relations are interdependent. (It is worth noting that even though the number of nodes differs slightly, the average degree is actually higher in both networks for the smaller branch; thus, the difference in density does not merely reflect more opportunities for relationships in the larger branch.)

The networks can also be characterized by looking at the level of reciprocation. Although Table 16.1 reveals that a relatively low proportion of all relational ties are reciprocated within the networks, two specific aspects warrant closer inspection. First, reciprocation is lower for the advice-giving network than for the satisfaction network in both branches. Obviously, actors within an advice-giving network may be characterized by different advice roles. On the one hand, there may be actors who serve primarily as sources of advice but who do not seek a lot of advice from

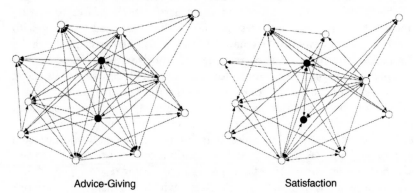

Advice-Giving   Satisfaction

Figure 16.2. Advice-giving and satisfaction network in High-AS bank branch.

Table 16.1. *Descriptive statistics of two bank branches*

	Low-AS bank		High-AS bank	
No. of people	15		12	
No. of senior positions	2		2	
No. of junior positions	13		10	
univariate network	advice giving	satisfaction	advice giving	satisfaction
No. of arcs	46	49	54	53
No. of reciprocated pairs	3	8	6	16
bivariate network	advice giving and satisfaction		advice giving and satisfaction	
No. of entrained arcs	9		38	
No. of exchanged arcs	15		22	
QAP correlation Jaccard coefficients	0.106		0.551*	

* Indicates that for 2,500 permutations, less than 1% had stronger associations between advice-giving and satisfaction networks.

others. On the other hand, there may be actors who tend to have mutual advice relations with several others. In these two bank branches, the number of reciprocated advice-giving ties seems relatively low, thereby suggesting a rather hierarchical advice structure. In contrast, there seems to be higher levels of mutual agreement with respect to satisfying work relations. Second, the level of reciprocation is higher for both types of networks in the High-AS bank. If we were to derive and consider an undirected network only from mutual ties, then we would see that the density for the High-AS bank is more than twice that of the Low-AS bank.

Further insights can be gained by examining the co-occurrence of relational ties in the two networks. Specifically, two measures of association of the advice-giving and satisfaction relational ties are very informative. First, the number of "entrained" ties is substantially higher in the High-AS bank. An entrained tie occurs when actor i gives advice to actor j and at the same time indicates that he or she is satisfied working with j. Second, the number of "exchanged" ties is also higher in the High-AS bank. Exchanged ties can be regarded as multivariate reciprocation in which advice giving is exchanged for satisfaction. Of course, at this stage, a discussion of the number of exchanged ties does not permit us to make inferences about whether exchange is more likely in one network than the other because the difference in densities may simply mean more exchange by chance. To make that inference, we need a statistical approach. Table 16.1 provides the associations between advice-giving and satisfaction networks using QAP Jaccard coefficient results. The advice-giving network is significantly correlated with the satisfaction network for the High-AS branch, but not so for the Low-AS branch.

16.4   Multivariate ERGM Results

Albeit insightful, the descriptive analyses are not a sufficient means to fully understand the various types of tie interdependencies existing in these networks. To analyze the networks of the two branches more thoroughly, we apply multivariate ERGMs to the network structures of both High- and Low-AS branches. In addition to considering advice-giving and satisfaction ties, we include employees' seniority as an actor attribute. The final models for the two branches are presented in Tables 16.2 and 16.3. We present each model in a separate table as follows: structural effects for both network relations separately (within-network effects); structural effects comprising both network relations simultaneously (across-network, multivariate, or joint network effects); and, finally, actor-relation effects.

One could argue that a comparison across networks and across branches requires models with the same network parameters; however, we also know that the internal structural logics (i.e., the network configurations) that explain one network may not necessarily be appropriate for another network. This is the case with the networks in this study. Although we initially set up identical models for each bank branch, in reaching converged and well-fitting final models, the data demanded that different parameters be specified for different branches (i.e., different network configurations be included). In some cases, the inclusion of specific effects resulted in model degeneracy (i.e., the estimation did not converge). Sometimes network effects had to be included to obtain model convergence even if these effects were not significant themselves. These models are also a case where experimenting with the inclusion of various Markov star parameters improved convergence and/or goodness of fit. As a result, the models of the two banks differ with respect to some of the effects included, indicating that the structures of the networks in the two contexts differed.

16.4.1   Low-AS Bank

The results for the final model of the Low-AS bank are given in Table 16.2. The advice-giving network is first characterized by a significant and positive path closure effect, suggesting transitive closure of advice-giving ties. Advice that gets passed on through third parties also tends to be given directly. In contrast, no significant result was obtained for reciprocity. Employees do not tend to exchange advice directly, an insight that is obvious from Table 16.1, in which there are only three recipro-cated ties for advice. Transitive closure and the absence of reciprocation

Table 16.2. *Model estimates for Low-AS bank advice-giving and satisfaction network*

parameter	figure	estimates (SEs)
Purely structural effects		
Advice-giving network (A)		
Arc		0.11 (2.52)
Reciprocity		−1.82 (1.28)
Popularity spread [AinS]		−1.86 (1.40)
Activity spread [AoutS]		0.87 (0.57)
Path closure [AT-T]		1.34 (0.63)*
Popularity closure [AT-D]		−1.88 (0.43)*
Multiple 2-paths [A2P-T]		0.02 (0.16)
Shared popularity [A2P-D]		1.04 (0.28)*
Satisfaction network (S)		
Arc		−4.98 (1.15)*
Reciprocity		3.63 (1.31)*
In-3-star		−0.09 (0.17)
Out-3-star		0.06 (0.01)*
2-Path		−0.20 (0.14)
Activity spread [AoutS]		2.02 (0.57)*
Shared popularity/multiple 2-paths [A2P-TD]		−0.05 (0.23)
Joint (multivariate) effects		
Entrainment AS [Arc AS]		−0.41 (0.35)
Exchange AS [Reciprocity AS]		1.47 (0.72)*
2-path-SA		−0.05 (0.09)
Actor-relation effects		
Receiver seniorA		−0.73 (1.06)
Receiver seniorS		1.93 (1.44)
Receiver entrainment AS		2.65 (1.24)*

* Significant effect (i.e., parameter estimate is greater than two times the standard error in absolute value, see Section 12.5.1 for details)

  Table notes: $\lambda = 2$ for all alternating parameters.

  Networks: Advice-giving ⟶; satisfaction ⟶

  Attributes: Senior position ●; senior/junior position ○

lead us to suggest that clusters of employees giving advice form into denser regions of the network so that advice giving in the Low-AS bank is hierarchical and not mutual. In addition, the advice-giving network is characterized by a strong and negative popularity closure effect, suggesting that there is less closure for people who are jointly nominated as receiving advice. (Recall that a popular actor in the advice-giving network is someone nominated by many others as being the recipient of advice.) In other words, two actors nominated as receiving advice from many of the same others are unlikely to nominate each other as advice partners.

In contrast to the advice-giving network, the satisfaction network is characterized by a strong positive effect for reciprocity: employees tend to be mutually satisfied with each other. In addition, the satisfaction network is characterized by tendencies of out-degree centralization, which can be seen from the positive out-3-star parameter and the positive activity spread parameter. In other words, there are a number of employees who are satisfied with many of their colleagues. Overall, the satisfaction network of the Low-AS branch is not overly complex because the final model does not contain any higher-order triangulation effects, so that satisfaction here is not characterized by network closure. Instead, satisfaction mostly occurs at the dyadic level, except for the tendency for higher expansiveness by some actors.

Remember that from Table 16.1, the QAP results indicated no strong association between the advice-giving and satisfaction networks. Consistent with the result, the multivariate network effects reveal that advice giving and satisfaction is not entrained, which is demonstrated by a nonsignificant parameter estimate. However, the two relations are exchanged, which can be seen from the positive and significant exchange effect. This result can be interpreted as indicating that those who receive advice tend to nominate the advice giver as a satisfying work partner.[2]

With respect to the attribute-related effects, the separate receiver effects for advice giving and satisfaction are both insignificant, but they help considerably with model convergence. In contrast, the inclusion of other actor-relation effects leads to nonconvergence of the model. The only exception is a joint network effect that also takes seniority into account.

---

[2] It is, of course, possible to transpose the advice-giving network, and then correlate it with the satisfaction network using QAP. We ran this correlation (although it is not shown in Table 16.1), and it indicated a strong association that is consistent with the strong and significant Exchange AS effect. However, we do note that with multivariate ERGM, we can examine entrainment and exchange simultaneously, something not possible with QAP. Furthermore, we can see how the networks are also aligned with respect to the attributes of network actors – again, a technique not possible with QAP.

The positive effect for receiver entrainment AS indicates that advice-giving and satisfaction ties are likely to be entrained if they are directed toward senior staff. In other words, giving advice to a senior person in the network is associated with satisfaction for the advice giver.

In summary, the results show that for the Low-AS branch, the advice-giving and satisfaction networks are interdependent and co-occur beyond chance levels in two specific ways. The formal organization role (i.e., junior or senior position) has an impact on the structural configurations. For example, while advice giving and satisfaction were not entrained on a purely structural level, such entrainment is substantial when also taking seniority into account. In other words, advice and satisfaction ties are likely to be entrained if the receiver holds a senior position. In contrast, advice giving and satisfaction are exchanged at the dyadic level, irrespective of the seniority of the dyadic partners. The ERGM results are consistent with QAP results; however, applying ERGM allows us to obtain additional information on, and control for, other structural effects that explain the emergence of social ties in these networks.

16.4.2   High-AS Bank

The results for the High-AS bank are displayed in Table 16.3. In this branch, the only significant effect for the advice-giving network is a strong positive out-2-star parameter. This effect suggests that some actors are sources of advice to several of their colleagues. Unlike the advice-giving network in the Low-AS bank, no significant results were obtained for closure, suggesting that there is no tendency to close paths of advice-giving ties.

Similar to the advice-giving network, the satisfaction network is characterized by a strong positive effect for out-2-stars. In addition, a negative estimate can be seen for the activity spread effect. The two results can be explained by the highly skewed degree distribution of the network, with many people nominating only a few satisfying partners (catered for by the negative activity spread) but a few nominating many others as satisfying (the positive 2-stars). This pattern of effects and its interpretation are discussed in Chapter 13 (see Section 13.1). The positive estimate for general transitivity suggests that all three different processes of closure (i.e., path closure, popularity closure, activity closure) are present within the satisfaction network with similar strengths (see Chapter 6). It can be argued that the core of the satisfaction network in the High-AS bank arises from these different processes of transitive (but not cyclic) closure, emphasizing the hierarchical nature of satisfaction ties in this branch.

Table 16.3. *Model estimates for High-AS bank advice-giving and satisfaction network*

parameter	figure	estimates (SEs)
Purely structural effects		
Advice-giving network (A)		
Arc		0.12 (1.60)
Reciprocity		−0.35 (1.07)
Out-2-star		0.49 (0.23)*
Popularity spread		−1.34 (0.87)
Activity spread		0.88 (0.89)
Path closure		−0.65 (0.34)
Satisfaction network (S)		
Arc		−0.75 (2.19)
Reciprocity		1.77 (1.09)
Out-2-star		0.63 (0.17)*
Popularity spread		−1.74 (1.42)
Activity spread		−2.94 (1.17)*
Generalized transitivity (AT-TDU)		1.89 (0.86)*
Joint (multivariate) effects		
Entrainment AS [Arc AS]		2.71 (0.75)*
Exchange AS [Reciprocity AS]		−0.31 (0.91)
T-ASS		−0.21 (0.17)
Actor-relation effects		
Sender seniorA		0.97 (1.26)
Receiver seniorA		−4.16 (1.54)*
Sender seniorS		−0.74 (0.46)
Receiver seniorS		0.75 (0.82)

* Significant effect (i.e., parameter estimate is greater than two times the standard error in absolute value, see Section 12.5.1 for details)

  Table notes:
  λ = 2 for all alternating parameters.
  Networks: Advice-giving →; satisfaction --→
  Attributes: Senior position ●; senior/junior position ○

With respect to the association of advice-giving and satisfaction ties, the positive effect for entrainment indicates that advice giving and satisfaction tend to be aligned.[3] People give advice to those with whom they are satisfied, or, equally, they are satisfied with those to whom they give advice. With respect to attribute-related effects, a significant positive estimate is obtained for the receiver-advice parameter, suggesting that senior employees are less likely to receive advice as compared to more junior employees.

In summary, the ERGM results show that for the High-AS branch the advice-giving and satisfaction networks are entrained. The ERGM results are consistent with QAP results, which indicated a strong association between the advice-giving and satisfaction networks. Moreover, ERGM provides information on other structural effects that explain the emergence of social ties in these networks.

16.5   Discussion

In this chapter, we examine network associations within two bank branches. Initial QAP results for the two bank branches provide measures of entrainment processes, but not of exchange processes or other network effects that can take actor attributes into consideration. In contrast, multivariate ERGMs were conducted for each bank branch separately, including actor attributes, entrainment, and exchange effects, as well as a range of other network processes. The relational networks of the High- and Low-AS branches differed in several ways with respect to both within- and cross-network effects. Interestingly, in the low-density branch, there is evidence for some closure processes among advice-giving ties, but not among satisfaction ties; however, the reverse is found in the high-density branch. Furthermore, there is significant reciprocity for satisfaction in the Low- but not the High-AS branch. Both branches display tendencies for out-degree centralization. Multivariately, employees in the Low-AS bank exchange advice giving and satisfaction, whereas the High-AS bank is characterized by a strong and significant entrainment of advice giving and satisfaction. In other words, receiving advice is associated with satisfaction at the Low-AS branch, whereas giving advice is satisfying in the High-AS bank. In the Low-AS bank, giving advice only seems to be associated with satisfaction to employees if it is directed toward senior staff.

We began this study by asking whether there is evidence for the alignment of advice-giving and satisfaction ties in our two cases, representing

---

[3]   The negative T-ASS parameter effect is not significant but helps considerably with the model convergence.

high- and low-density networks. Although we see entrainment in both bank branches, it differs slightly between them. In the low-density branch, entrainment occurs when the multiplex tie is directed toward the senior staff. In this branch, being asked for advice by management is associated with satisfaction. The low density suggests that individual actors are more discriminating in this branch in how they assess satisfaction and to whom they disburse advice. In these circumstances, ties to managers may take on increased importance. Nevertheless, in these circumstances of more selective advice, advice givers are viewed as satisfying associates. In the higher-density network, advice is given more freely, and working relationships tend to be more satisfying. Here, however, giving advice is satisfying for the advice giver, but not necessarily for the receiver, so the abundance of advice may not necessarily mean that it always hits its mark. In this branch, managers tend not to be recipients of advice, so the impression is of a network in which much of the advice action occurs at more junior levels.

The results illustrate how different contexts can lead to different arrangements of social ties. It is reasonable to assume that the network effects that adequately represent one context may not necessarily capture the social networks of different contexts. Unfortunately, we have limited information on these two bank branches to shed more light on why these differences are apparent, and the information we do have suggests many similarities between them, including in branch performance as measured by the bank. Although this limits the generalizability of this particular case study, it does emphasize the need for researchers to be sensitive to possible differences in context, and to seek observations and measures that might help explain differences in results. It seems that in our study we may be dealing with two different organizational subcultures. In one, advice and satisfaction are freely given and received; in the other, there is more selectivity and discrimination about advice and satisfaction. In terms of informal organizational structures, these different subcultures seem to play out in subtle ways that affect how satisfaction and advice are intertwined. They also implicate rather different roles for senior branch management in that process.

17

Brain, Brawn, or Optimism? Structure and Correlates of Emergent Military Leadership

Yuval Kalish and Gil Luria

17.1 Emergent Leadership in Military Context

Traditional approaches to leadership tend to focus on the characteristics and behaviors of formal, appointed leaders (see Yukl, 2010, for a review of theories). Little is known, however, about the distribution of leadership potential within a group or how informal leadership emerges. With the shift to flattened, self-managed teams, researchers have now begun to explore the emergence of informal leadership (Neubert & Taggar, 2004). Emergent leadership is defined as "the process by which informal leaders emerge in a team, typically in leaderless groups." Emergent leaders are often "internal champions," people who exert significant influence over other members of their group although no formal authority has been vested in them (Goktepe & Schneier, 1989).

The study of emergent leadership originates in small group research (e.g., Bales, 1953), where it was often found that in leaderless group discussions, one or two informal leaders emerge. Since then, most of the research on emergent leadership has focused on two main issues. The first is the examination of the antecedents of leadership emergence, in an attempt to predict which individual will eventually emerge as a leader. The second focus is on the structure of emergent leadership. We briefly describe each of these.

17.1.1 Antecedents to Emergent Leadership

Emergent leadership is often explained by referring to implicit leadership theory (ILT). According to ILT, individuals rely on schemas or prototypes, defined as "abstractions of the most widely shared features or attributes of category members" (Lord, 1985, 93) to simplify information-processing tasks. ILT suggests that individuals have a shared prototype of "the leader," which comprises a set of attributes and

226

behaviors associated with leadership. When followers perceive that an individual possesses the traits that match the followers' leadership prototype, the followers infer that the individual is a leader irrespective of whether they hold a formal position (Lord & Maher, 1991). In other words, as Rubin, Bartels, and Bommer noted, "Individuals seem to share a common understanding about the traits that leaders possess and these traits are used as benchmarks for deciding on emergent leadership" (2002, 106). Although individuals can explicate their leadership prototype (e.g., Eden & Leviatan, 1975), the process of leadership emergence operates automatically, producing effects that are outside perceiver's conscious awareness (Lord, 2005). Social Identity Theory's approach to leadership (e.g., Hogg & van Knippenberg, 2003) makes similar assumptions, suggesting that in some situations a leadership prototype becomes salient, and that leaders emerge to the extent that others judge them as fitting the prototype.

Research suggests that the prototype of leaders, and therefore the benchmark by which potential leaders are evaluated, is similar across individuals within a given culture and context (Rubin, et al., 2002). The prototype generally includes aspects of intellectual ability (Lord, Devader, & Alliger, 1986), context-specific knowledge (e.g., industry knowledge; Kirkpatrick & Locke, 1991), extraversion, emotional stability and optimism (Judge et al., 2002).

In this chapter, we examine emergent leadership within the selection process to an elite unit in the Israeli Defense Force (IDF). Although the context for our analyses is the military, we argue that the IDF is just one particular instantiation of an organization, and that our results could generalize to other organizations as well. In fact, our data are on civilians who have not yet entered the IDF and thus have not yet socialized into the military context.

In Israel, military psychologists from the IDF conducted research that aimed to identify the prototype of "the leader." They performed in-depth interviews with effective leaders, soldiers, and leadership experts, and supplemented the results with job analyses to reach an agreed list of traits and behaviors that are required for, and expected of, military leaders in the IDF. This list has been formulated in a paper publicly known as "the officers' attributes paper" (IDF, 2004). The list includes attributes that constitute the formal definition of the leadership prototype endorsed by the IDF, and is consistent with the research on leadership prototypes in nonmilitary organizational settings (e.g., Judge et al., 2002; Kirkpatrick & Locke, 1991; Lord et al., 1986). In this study, we test if recruits with these prescribed attributes will tend to emerge as leaders. We focus on three attributes of the IDF's (2004) formal definition of the leadership prototype that have been consistently found to relate to leadership effectiveness: cognitive ability, physical ability, and optimism. We briefly provide the IDF's definition for each, and present research findings that support the link between these attributes and emergent leadership.

"Cognitive ability" is defined in "the officers' attributes paper" as "... the officers' ability to use their inductive and deductive reasoning" (IDF, 2004). In non-military settings, research found that general intelligence (e.g., Lord, Foti, & Devader, 1984) and industry-relevant knowledge (e.g., Kirkpatrick & Locke, 1991) was a recurring characteristic attribute of a leader. Thus, we expect that people with higher general but also with industry-specific cognitive ability should emerge as leaders.

Physical strength: The officers' attributes paper suggests that an officer should "enhance their physical fitness... to enhance their health, alertness... and ability to perform under challenging physical and mental conditions" (IDF, 2004). Being physically strong is part of the leadership prototype expected of Israeli officers. The link between physical strength and hierarchy is also supported by Connell's (1995) theory of hegemonic masculinity (see also Chapter 14). We expect that people with higher physical ability will more often be chosen as leaders.

Self-control and optimism: "[T]he officer will perform under stress while exhibiting calmness, self-restraint, self control... and optimism" (IDF, 2004). Leaders are expected to be optimistic and not stressed, a finding corroborated by the literature on leadership traits (Judge et al., 2002). We propose that emergent leaders will be less stressed and display high levels of optimism.

To summarize, ILT suggests that leadership emerges because followers perceive individuals to be more concordant with followers' schemas of "the leader." We examine how four of these – general cognitive ability, context-specific cognitive ability, physical strength, and optimism – are related to leadership emergence. Because emergent leadership is a relational phenomenon (Carson, Tesluk, & Marrone, 2007), using a social selection model is appropriate because such models predict the presence of social ties based on the characteristics of actors in the network. Our first research question is which of these characteristics in the individual enhances the likelihood of their being selected by others as a leader.

17.1.2   Structure of Emergent Leadership

The second strand of research on emergent leadership examined the structure of leadership. Leaderless group discussion studies in the 1950s generally found that leadership behaviors were performed by more than one individual (Mehra et al., 2006). Recently, Misiolek and Heckman (2005) examined the distribution of emergent leadership in virtual teams and found between one and three leaders emerged within each team of five or six individuals. Other studies (e.g., Guastello, 2007) found that the number of leaders to emerge in teams of seven to nine players in an online decision-making game had a "power-law" distribution, so that a few individuals received a disproportionate amount of leadership choices, whereas many others received none or very few leadership choices. Finally, Carson et al. (2007) examined "shared leadership" in teams and found that there was some variability in the structure of teams' leadership networks. However, these studies used small teams with low-frequency contact and did not examine network structure, focusing only on in-degree distributions or densities. This study models the structure of larger, high-contact teams using an exponential random graph model (ERGM), to examine the structure of emergent leadership in real life groups.

17.1.3   Setting and Participants

The study was conducted in a candidate selection process for an elite military unit in Israel. The participants were eighty-seven male civilians, age 18, who voluntarily participated in a two-day selection for an all-male military unit (see Luria and Berson (2008) and Luria and Torjman (2008) for a more detailed description of the selection procedure). All participants were assigned to one of six teams (three of size fourteen, three of size fifteen) and were given identification numbers. All were physically fit and had completed their high school studies. During the selection process, recruits underwent intense physical and emotional challenges, and were free to withdraw at any time.

Social Network Question. During the second day of the selection process, participants were approached by a member of the research team, who assured them of confidentiality and that participation (or lack thereof) would not have an impact on the selection process in any way. They were further assured that personal data obtained from the study would not be provided to the military. They were then asked to list the identification numbers of other recruits in their team who they viewed as leaders. Selection officers were not present while recruits completed the questionnaires. We note that within the ERGM framework that self-nominations are not permissible, and so we have no measurement of recruits nominating themselves as leaders.

Individual Attributes. Each participant was rated on the following:

> *Performance on tasks*: Throughout the selection process, respondents completed nine different tasks, ranging from the highly physical (e.g., stretcher hike) to the cognitively complex (e.g., navigation). Independent assessors rated the success of each respondent on a 5-point Likert scale.

Positive and Negative Affect Scale (PANAS; Watson, Clark, & Tellegen, 1988): measures the independent positive and negative dimensions of affect. Participants self-rate the extent to which they experienced twenty emotions over the previous few hours on a 5-point scale ranging from 1 – "Never" to 5 – "Very often". Internal consistency for the positive affectivity subscale was 0.84 and for the negative affectivity subscale was 0.83, consistent with previous research (Watson et al., 1988).

Perceived Stress Scale (PSS; Cohen, Kamarck, & Mermelstein, 1983) measures stress. The original, ten-item questionnaire was reworded to reflect frequency of events during the previous few hours (as opposed to month). Some questions were determined inappropriate to military experiences, and were thus eliminated. Responses were given on a 5-point scale, ranging from 1 – "Never" to 5 – "Very often". Internal consistency for the seven-item scale was 0.81, similar to that obtained from the full scale in other studies (e.g., Cohen et al., 1983).

Data reduction into composite scores: A principal component analysis of the tasks and questionnaires suggested three underlying components, explaining 73.2% of the variance. The first component reflected performance on nonphysical, military-specific, cognitively complex tasks (e.g., navigation and paper-and-pencil tests). It therefore relates to industry-specific (military) knowledge. The second component reflected performance on physical tasks such as stretcher hike and field performance. It is therefore an aggregated, objective score of the level of "physical ability" attribute as described by "the officers' attributes paper." The third component reflected the respondents' (negative) emotional state, with negative affectivity and stress loaded positively on the component, and positive affectivity loaded negatively on it. It is therefore a self-report quantitative measure of the "optimism and self-control" attribute.

Component scores were saved for each individual and used in further analyses. These are referred to as nonphysical (military-specific cognitive ability), physical, and optimism scores, respectively.

"General cognitive ability" was obtained through a basic paper-and-pencil cognitive abilities test, which is given to all new recruits prior to being drafted to the IDF. The test battery includes verbal and shape analogy tests, mathematical ability tests, Raven matrices, and a test that examines the understanding of instruction and their accurate performance. Test scores are standardized across recruits with a mean of 50 and a range of 10 (low) to 90 (high) cognitive abilities.

17.2   Model Specification

17.2.1   Modeling Issues

The data pose two major modeling challenges. The first is that we have no previous knowledge of the structure of leadership networks, and thus do not know which parameters to include in the model. We therefore started with the customary social circuit parameters (see Table 13.1 in Section 13.2), and by examination of goodness of fit (GOF) statistics (see Section 13.3), added new parameters.

The second problem is that our data is restricted by the presence of distinct and nonoverlapping groups: Recruits are embedded within teams. Moreover, the selection process is structured so that interaction between teams is not possible: recruits only interact with (and can therefore select) others from their own team. Estimating the model needs to account for this complexity. We take this into account by using structural zeros, thus specifying only specific actors (allocated into the same team) with whom interaction is possible. In essence, this approach takes all six teams and examines them in a single ERGM. By fixing "structural zeroes" in the ties between groups, nominations between groups are specifically disavowed.[1] The model estimates apply to all six groups. This means that we make the implicit assumption that the same endogenous processes apply in all teams. As great care is taken during selection to standardize the groups, this assumption with respect to endogenous factors is not unreasonable. We show later that this approach is warranted empirically because no differences were found between teams. An alternative would have been to allow the parameters to be different for the different groups, and afterward combining the estimates using the approach of Lubbers and Snijders (2007).

17.2.2   Purely Structural Effects

Initially, we fitted a model that included six structural effects: arc, reciprocity, popularity spread and activity spread, path closure, and multiple connectivity. Although the model converged, GOF statistics suggested that our model failed to capture the skewness of the in- and out-degree distributions: it did not account for the fact that some actors were very central in the leadership network (had high in-degrees), and that some actors did not choose any other actors as leaders, whereas others chose many (high variance in the out-degree).

---

[1] We note that the "structural zero" is the fixing of ties, where in PNet "0" means a tie cannot vary, and "1" means it can. We have fixed ties here using this process so that they can never be present, but it is also possible to fix network ties using the same process so that they are always present.

Following Robins, Pattison, and Wang (2009), we fitted a second model, which included the above six parameters together with sink, source, and isolates effects. The model converged, and GOF statistics suggested that the inclusion of these three parameters successfully controlled for the skewed degree distributions.

17.2.3   Actor-Relation Effects

We use three basic attribute effect types: sender, receiver, and heterophily (Chapter 8). These three effects were fit for each of the four continuous attributes that we collected: general cognitive ability, performance on physical tasks, nonphysical performance (military-related, specific cognitive abilities), and optimism. The full model therefore includes twenty-one parameters: nine parameters for purely structural effects, and twelve parameters for actor-relation effects. We are especially interested in the receiver effects because they represent emergent leadership.

17.3   Results

We suggested that in order to use the structural zero approach, we must first ascertain that no exogenous team-level effects influence our data. Analyses of variance suggested recruits in the six teams experienced the same levels of psychological stress ($F_{(5,75)} = 1.17$, $p = .33$), negative emotions ($F_{(5,76)} = 1.26$, $p = .292$), and positive ($F_{(5,75)} = 1.43$, $p = .22$) emotions. All teams received similar scores on physical ($F_{(5,76)} = 0.085$, $p = .99$) and nonphysical ($F_{(5,76)} = 2.14$, $p = .07$) tasks. There were no differences among teams in the number of leadership nominations ($F_{(5,76)} = 1.5$, $p = .20$). Taking these results together, there is no evidence that the exogenous attribute variables are subject to team-based effects; thus, we proceed with the structural zero approach under the assumption that the teams are relatively similar. We note, however, that this analysis does not take into account the association of leadership nominations with any of these attributes, which may be different across the groups.

Parameter estimates of two models are presented in Table 17.1. Model A is inappropriate because, as the GOF analysis showed, it did not reproduce the degree distribution well. We present model A as a comparison to the final model B to show how the exclusion of certain structural parameters may lead to different conclusions regarding the formation of network ties.

17.3.1   Results for Purely Structural Effects

The interpretation of the structural part of the model is interesting, particularly because the literature on the structure of leadership emergence

Table 17.1. *Parameter estimates for two models examining emergent leadership among recruits in military training*

parameter	estimates (SEs) model A	model B
Purely structural effects		
Arc	−5.42 (2.68)*	−3.06 (3.19)
Reciprocity	1.14 (0.39)*	1.27 (0.43)*
Sink		5.60 (1.44)*
Source		−0.45 (1.00)
Isolates		4.10 (1.71)*
Popularity spread [AinS]	0.38 (0.27)	0.77 (0.56)
Activity spread [AoutS]	0.47 (0.24)	−1.97 (0.69)*
Path closure [AT-T]	0.30 (0.18)	0.33 (0.19)
Multiple connectivity [A2P-T]	−0.11 (0.09)	−0.06 (0.10)
Actor-relation effects		
Sender (general cognitive ability)	−0.22 (0.13)	−0.20 (0.14)
Sender (physical tasks)	0.17 (0.10)	0.18 (0.11)
Sender (optimism)	−0.05 (0.12)	−0.05 (0.12)
Sender (nonphysical tasks)	−0.11 (0.11)	−0.11 (0.12)
Receiver (general cognitive ability)	0.28 (0.14)*	0.28 (0.14)*
Receiver (physical tasks)	0.20 (0.11)	0.17 (0.10)
Receiver (optimism)	−0.15 (0.12)	−0.13 (0.11)
Receiver (nonphysical tasks)	0.30 (0.12)*	0.29 (0.11)*
Heterophily (general cognitive ability) [difference]	−0.21 (0.14)	−0.22 (0.15)
Heterophily (physical tasks) [difference]	−0.20 (0.11)	−0.21 (0.11)
Heterophily (optimism) [difference]	0.09 (0.12)	0.08 (0.11)
Heterophily (nonphysical tasks) [difference]	0.02 (0.13)	0.00 (0.13)

* Significant effect

has been inconclusive. We note that leadership choices tend to be reciprocated in both models. Comparing model A with the better fitting model, model B, reveals that the addition of the three parameters altered parameter estimates – and our interpretation. First, some individuals who are part of the selection do not nominate leaders nor are they nominated by others as leaders (the strong, positive, significant isolates parameter). Once accounting for these individuals (and possibly due to the inclusion of the source parameter), the activity spread parameter becomes strongly negative. (In model A, the activity spread parameter was positive, but not significant.) The interpretation is that once we account for the isolates, there is less variance than we expect in leadership choices: some individuals are "out of the leadership loop" altogether, and those that are "playing the leadership game" tend to restrict the range of others they select as leaders. The positive reciprocity parameter suggests that overall recruits tend to select each other as leaders. Furthermore, the positive sink parameter indicates that above and beyond this reciprocity effect, there are some individuals who are selected as leaders by many others, but these individuals do not select anyone else as a leader. Because self-nomination is forbidden, this may suggest that these individuals are aware of their status as leader. Interestingly, and contrary to most other social networks, no evidence was found for path closure.

Taken together, these results suggest that the structure of emergent leadership is hub-like, although within each team some members are leadership isolates. Others, the hub, are chosen by many others, but these small numbers of people do not choose anyone else as leader. Finally, there is reciprocation of leadership choices across the network, but the lack of triangulation suggests that transitive closure is not a process involved in leadership nominations.

17.3.2   Results for Actor-Relation Effects

"Traditional" analyses of emergent leadership (e.g., Neubert & Taggar, 2004) use correlation to find significant relationships between the number of leadership nominations and the other variables. Correlation analysis of our data suggests that the number of leadership nominations was positively associated with physical ($r = 0.366$, $p < .05$) and nonphysical ($r = 0.430$, $p < .01$) capabilities, as well as with general cognitive ability ($r = 0.299$, $p < .05$). Leadership nominations were not significantly correlated with optimism ($r = 0.210$, ns).

We now interpret the ERGM results for the actor-relation effects. We discovered evidence that the higher the individuals' general cognitive ability, the more leadership nominations they receive (the significant and positive receiver effect). We also found a significant and positive receiver effect for the nonphysical tasks, tasks that involve military-related cognitive skills. Somewhat surprisingly, although we found a nearly significant negative heterophily effect for physical performance, no receiver effect was found for performance on actual physical tasks (e.g., stretcher hike). This suggests that although recruits tend to choose others with similar levels of physical performance as themselves as leaders, higher levels of physical performance are not associated with emergent leadership. Finally, no effect was found for optimism. Being optimistic (and not stressed) was not significantly related to leadership nominations.

To summarize, our data suggest that both general and context-specific cognitive ability is related to leadership emergence. Contrary to expectations, being physically successful or being optimistic was not related to emergent leadership; that is, emergent leadership is more related to brain than brawn or optimism. Our data also suggest that leadership potential is distributed in a hub like structure that includes isolated individuals, whereby the core comprises emergent leaders, the periphery comprises followers who select the leaders, and the isolates comprise individuals who do not select and are not selected as leaders.

17.4   Discussion

This chapter addresses two research questions: (1) which individual characteristics are associated with being selected by others as a leader? and (2) what is the structure of emergent leadership? Our results are consistent with findings by Lord and colleagues (1984): general intelligence and context-specific cognitive ability are associated with emerging leaders. Future studies may find even stronger relationships between intelligence and leadership by asking respondents questions on the perceived intelligence of others.

Contrary to previous studies, we did not find that physical strength was related to leadership, or that optimism and reduced stress were related to emergence as a leader. These two findings contradict some of the propositions raised by theories of charismatic leadership (for a review, see Yukl, 2010), which propose that the charismatic leader has to convey optimism and faith in the future and in the ability to transcend difficulties. We note that in the correlation analysis, leadership nominations were positively associated with physical strength, and there was a trend toward a significant positive association between leadership nominations and optimism. The correlations we found between physical capabilities, optimism, and leadership nominations are artifactual results that arise because the structure of leadership nominations is not well controlled. This could be an issue for previous empirical work on emergent leadership.

The structure of the leadership network was interesting because it was different than other structures typically found in social networks. The leadership networks exhibit a core-periphery-isolate structure. Previous research has been inconclusive on whether leadership networks exhibit one or more leaders, and whether leadership networks exhibit a "power-law" distribution or a core-periphery structure. Our findings suggest that the discrepant results may have been due to the fact that these researchers did not model the structure of the leadership network, focusing instead on simple descriptive statistics (in-degree distributions and average density). The only study that examined the structure of leadership networks provides some support to our findings. Mehra et al. (2006) visually examined the structure of teams and found that most teams had more than one leader, and these leaders reciprocated each other's leadership choices. In our data, we found a hierarchy of leaders, such that overall there was reciprocity in leadership nominations, but above and beyond that effect, there was a tendency for leadership to be selected by others, and not to choose anyone else as a leader. These results suggest that it may be the case that emergent leaders are aware of their leadership status, and as a result, do not select others (given that self-nominations are impossible in the ERGM framework), leading to the significant sink effect we found.

We found that the leadership network was dissimilar to many other social networks: it did not exhibit transitivity and had a significant number of isolates and sinks. To our knowledge, the only network with similar characteristics to the one we have examined is the negative relationship network described by Robins, Pattison, and Wang (2009). It may be the case that when relationships are uncommon (e.g., leadership or negative relationships), they create different network structures than when relationships are more mundane (friendship, advice, and trust). We encourage researchers to turn their attention to these important, although infrequent, relationships.

Our results can be explained by leader-member exchange (LMX) theory. First proposed by Dansereau, Graen, and Cashman (1973), LMX focuses on the relationship between the leader and each team member. The level of analysis for LMX is the dyadic relationship, making it especially suitable for network analysis (see Sparrowe & Liden, 2005). Findings of LMX studies concur with our results. In LMX studies, some followers (the "in-group") reported "high-quality exchanges" with their leader. Their relationship is characterized by a high degree of mutual obligation. We propose that these individuals form the hubs in our leadership network, nominated as leaders by others with high-quality LMX. At the other extreme, some employees (the "out-group") reported "low-quality exchanges" and low obligation (Zalensky & Graen, 1987). These may form the isolates of our network. A possible future research direction could be superimposing the structure of the in- and out-groups as measured by LMX with the emergent leadership network by examining, for example, the level of trust between emergent leaders and those who nominate them.

Although our results were consistent overall with previous research, future studies should replicate our findings with larger samples, using a wider population with mixed gender, larger age range, and a variety of organizations. Furthermore, a longitudinal study of leadership network, perhaps by using Snijders, Steglich, and Schweinberger (2007) model for the coevolution of networks and attributes, may deepen our understanding of the process of leadership emergence.

18

Autologistic Actor Attribute Model Analysis of Unemployment: Dual Importance of Who You Know and Where You Live

Galina Daraganova and Pip Pattison

18.1   Unemployment: Location and Connections

Persistent regional unemployment disparities have been characterized as a major cause of regional decay and impose significant costs on communities (Bill, 2005; Mitchell & Bill, 2004). Macroeconomic explanations for the persistence of unemployment often revolve around economic factors, including spatial changes in the skill requirements of jobs, migration of jobs to the suburbs, persistent demand constraints, wage differentials, low labor mobility and related structural impediments, and variations in the distribution of industries across space (see reviews, for example, in Ihlanfeldt and Sjoquist (1998) and Ramakrishnan and Cerisola (2004)). Outside traditional macroeconomic explanations of unemployment at the local area level (e.g., suburb), explanations draw on theories of residential segregation (Cheshire, Monastiriotis, & Sheppard, 2003; Hunter, 1996), which suggest that similar educational background and socioeconomic status along with housing market factors play a substantial role in determining how people are distributed across geographic space. Over time, these differences may become more pronounced as people sort further along lines of race and income (Bill, 2005). Cheshire et al. argued that where people live does not drive inequality but rather determines geographic location of inequality:

> Where people live and the incidence of segregation and ultimately of exclusion, mainly reflects the increasing inequality of incomes. So if either the incidence of unemployment rises and/or if the distribution of earning becomes more unequal then social segregation intensifies . . . the poor are not poor, isolated and excluded for the reason which makes them poor. They are not poor because of where they live; rather they live where they do because they are poor. (2003, 83–84)

237

Although the importance of economic reasons and residential sorting of the population cannot be denied, the argument that there is no independent or additional effect of where you live and who you know on the likelihood of being unemployed may be overstated. A number of economists have emphasized that neighborhoods are not static units but comprise people who constantly interact with each other in particular times and places (Akerlof, 1997; Bill, 2005; Calvó-Armengol, 2006; Durlauf, 2004; Topa, 2001) – a point also echoed more generally by Abbott (1997). At the same time, these people are influenced by the choices of those others (Durlauf & Young, 2001), and the employment-related choices and outcomes of any one individual may well be dependent on the employment-related choices and outcomes of other individuals. These dependencies might be driven by either spatial or network proximity, so that the behavior of proximal others affects the information received by any one individual arising from the knowledge or behavior of others. As a result, decisions by different individuals about labor market activity may interact to influence the distribution of employment outcomes across individuals and neighborhoods leading, potentially, to suboptimal outcomes that persist in equilibrium (Durlauf, 2004; Wilson, 1987). That network proximity might have significant implications on a global scale was clearly illustrated in a study by Granovetter (1973) on job finding. He showed that less than 20% of male professional, technical, and managerial workers in Newton and Boston, Massachusetts, suburbs had obtained their jobs by formal means, such as simply replying to an advertisement or working through an employment agency.

Although the role of neighbors (defined by some suitable spatial or network proximity metric) in the persistence of unemployment has been documented in a number of empirical studies (e.g., Beaman, 2008; Conley & Topa, 2006; Hedström, Kolm, & Aberg, 2003; Topa, 2001; Wahba & Zenou, 2005), none of these studies has conducted an analysis at the level of data on individuals and networks, nor has the interdependence of network structure and spatial locations been studied.

Hence, the principal goal for the current empirical study was to assess the associations between employment status, social network ties and spatial proximity between individuals. The main hypotheses were (1) a person would be more likely to be unemployed if she/he was not socially active (i.e., not connected to many others); (2) employment status of individuals would be positively related to their partners' employment status and the employment status of their partners' partners; and (3) a person would more likely be unemployed if he or she resided in a region of unemployed individuals. To examine these three hypotheses empirically, we simultaneously analyze the individual impact of social network processes and geographic proximity effects on the distribution of employment outcomes using the detailed survey data on individuals and their network members.

18.2   Data, Analysis, and Estimation

18.2.1   Data

A comprehensive social survey was conducted in the selected region of Melbourne, Australia. The region was chosen based on evidence of persistent spatial clustering of high unemployment (11.5%: the second highest unemployment rate in urban areas of the Australian state of Victoria) from an analysis of 2001 Australian Census Data of unemployment rates at the Collection District[1] (CD) level using spatial statistics known as Local Indicators of Spatial Association (LISA) by Bill and Mitchell (personal communication, July 21, 2006). There were 177 CDs in the study area with the population size of approximately 113,561 individuals.

The respondents were recruited via a two-wave snowball sampling procedure (e.g., Frank, 2005; Frank & Snijders, 1994; Goodman, 1961). A random sample of individuals was drawn from the relevant geographic area and comprised the "initial sample" (also called wave 0). Individuals in the initial sample were asked to name their network partners and were also asked to recruit their network partners to the study. Recruited network partners comprised the "first wave" unless they were already part of the initial sample. Then first-wave respondents were asked about their network partners and were also asked to recruit the latter. Recruited network partners of wave one respondents comprised the "second wave" unless they were already part of the initial sample or wave one. Second-wave individuals were asked about their network partners, but the latter were not recruited. Ideally, the snowball sampling design assumes that a respondent nominates his or her network partners and a researcher follows these nominees, and therefore, there are no network ties between individuals who are two waves away from each other (i.e., there are no ties between wave 0 and wave 2 respondents, and wave 1 and nominees of wave two respondents). In real world data collection, however, neither respondent nor researcher can provide or follow all network partners, respectively. Therefore, to preserve the snowball sampling design, only recruited individuals were part of the snowball sample, even though respondents were not limited to a particular number of nominations.

---

[1] The Australian Bureau of Statistics (ABS) defines a census collection district (CD) as the smallest geographic unit of collection. It is defined as an area that one census collector can cover while delivering and collecting census forms over a specified period. On average, there are about 150 to 250 dwellings per CD; however, it can vary across urban and rural areas (ABS, 2001).

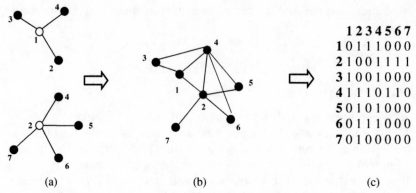

Figure 18.1. Process of constructing augmented network: (a) represents respondents' networks, where white and black nodes correspond to respondents and nominees, respectively; (b) network, which is based on two respondents' networks; and (c) adjacency matrix, constructed from two ego networks.

That is, if a respondent nominated ten network partners but recruited only three network partners, then only these three recruited individuals were included in the sample and the other seven were omitted. On average, we were able to follow up to four nominees. (Further details on snowball sampling designs are in Section 12.8.)

Given that the reference geographic area was approximately 14 km in length and 6 km wide, it was possible that different respondents could nominate the same people. To identify common identities of individuals across respondents' ego networks, a rules-based record linkage technique was employed based on first name, initial of surname, residential street, suburb, gender, and age. When unique individuals were identified, all ego networks were augmented to construct a social network for all respondents (further details can be found in Daraganova (2008, 167)). The process of aggregation of respondents' networks is schematically presented in Figure 18.1.

As a result, a network of 551 individuals, comprising 306 respondents and 245 noninterviewed participants, was constructed (we refer to this network as the "augmented network"). It is worth noting that the 245 noninterviewed participants were network partners of second-wave respondents who were not followed.

The following key variables were measured for all individuals in the sample: employment status and residential location. Employment status was a binary measure with the following categories: (1) "employed individuals" were those individuals who worked full or part time, and students who worked part time; and (2) "unemployed individuals" were those individuals who did not work at the time of the interview.

Table 18.1. *Descriptive statistics*

	continuous variables		
	min	max	mean
Age (years)	19	67	36.87 (12.97)
Number of years lived in area (NYA)	0.01	40	12.27 (9.36)
	categorical variables		
	categories	count	%
Place of birth	Australia = 0	240	78.4
	Not Australia = 1	66	21.6
Gender	Male = 0	160	52.3
	Female = 1	146	47.7
Unemployment history	Have not been unemployed = 0	245	80.07
	Have been unemployed at least once = 1	61	19.93
Highest education	University degree	70	22.9
	Certificate/diploma	61	19.9
	School education	175	57.2

Residential location was recorded using street name, street type, and suburb. In this study, it was impossible to collect information on street numbers because of privacy issues. To overcome this problem, possible address points for the street were constructed, and one was sampled at random and assigned to the sample address. This method takes account of the fact that street numbers are not necessarily consecutive and that the same number can refer to different households (apartments/units/townhouses). For example, for address point "Albatross Court, Southside," all possible street numbers are 1, 2, 3, 4, 5, 6, 7, 8, 9, 10, 12, 14, 14, and one item from this list is sampled at random. This approach recognizes that 11 is missing and 14 appears twice. This method assigns a unique identifier to each address point and affords the approximate calculation of geographic distance between residential locations of individuals, taking into account that distance equals zero for people who live in the same household.

Residential locations were geocoded, and using latitude and longitude coordinates, the Euclidean distance was calculated from one address point to another, ignoring roads and natural barriers for all address points in the sample data. To deal with very large distances, a logarithmic transformation of distance was applied.

A number of control variables were measured for respondents: network ties, age, gender, education, place of birth, unemployment history, and number of years lived in the area (NYA). Table 18.1 represents descriptive statistics of control variables.

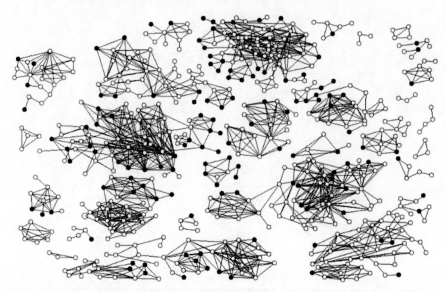

Figure 18.2. Employment status and social connections ($n = 551$, white – employed, black – unemployed).

The network ties were derived as a binary network from two name generator questions: (1) who are you closest to – name people whom you see or talk to regularly and with whom you share your personal thoughts and feelings?, and/or (2) whom do you discuss employment matters with – name people who may have helped you look for or get a job, or to whom you have talked about job opportunities, where to look for a job, or how to apply for a job? Nominating any individual on any or both of these relations led to the presence of a tie in the network, the result being an undirected binary, composite tie network. Figure 18.2 depicts the network of 551 individuals with nodes colored according to employment status disregarding geospatial location of the nodes. There were 132 unemployed (black nodes) and 419 employed (white nodes) individuals in the network.

Figure 18.3 presents the spatial layout of the part of the network data that comprises 527 individuals within a maximum distance of 25 kilometers of each other. Twenty-four nonrespondents who resided at very large distances away were excluded from Figure 18.3 for illustrative purposes but were included in the modeling.

18.2.2   Analysis

The analyses use the autologistic actor attribute model (ALAAM) presented in Chapter 9. As a reminder, the ALAAM assumes that network ties

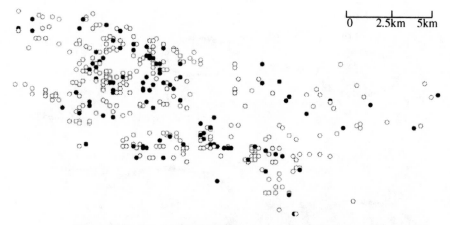

Figure 18.3. Geographic distribution of employed and unemployed individuals ($n = 527$, white – employed, black – unemployed). Spatial layout is drawn in NetDraw using standardized values for spatial coordinates, that is, latitude and longitude coordinates obtained from the geocoding process.

are fixed and that an individual's attribute of interest may vary depending on the number of ties the individual has or on the corresponding attribute of others to whom the individual is connected, controlling for different dyadic and individual covariates. In particular, these models allow us to estimate the conditional probability of being unemployed as a function of the number of network partners, the employment status of network partners, and the geographic distance to other individuals, while also controlling for basic demographic characteristics of all individuals such as age and gender.

18.2.3 Estimation

Given that the data were collected via a snowball sampling approach, and nominees of wave 2 respondents were not followed, the conditional maximum likelihood estimation (MLE) procedure described in Section 12.8 was employed. As a reminder, the conditional estimation procedure can be used when the data on a complete set of observations are not available. In particular, in k-wave snowball sampling design, the parameters can be estimated from the observed data conditioning on attributes in zones k and $k + 1$ and ties between individuals (i.e., $(Z_0, Z_1 \mid Z_2, Z_3)$). Technically, the estimation proceeds as for the MLE for the model on complete network; however, in the Markov chain Monte Carlo (MCMC), MLE values in the two outer zones $(k, k + 1)$ are considered to be fixed, and only attribute variables in zones $0, 1, \ldots, (k - 1)$ are allowed to be

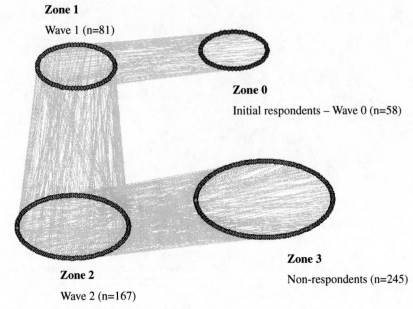

Zone 1

Wave 1 (n=81)

Zone 0

Initial respondents – Wave 0 (n=58)

Zone 3

Non-respondents (n=245)

Zone 2

Wave 2 (n=167)

Figure 18.4. Number of participants by wave.

changed in the MCMC. Theoretically, the conditioning on two outer zones allows researchers to evaluate indirect social influence processes (i.e., whether social position and social milieu of partners is associated with presence or absence of the attribute). This approach can be simplified to the conditional estimation using attribute data in zones $0, 1, \ldots, k$, conditioning on attribute data in zone $k+1$ and all ties (i.e., $(Z_0, Z_1, Z_2 \mid Z_3)$). Technically, the latter condition is associated with improved statistical power. Theoretically, the simplified condition constrains researchers to the estimation of the influence effects involving only immediate network partners for individuals up to zone k. Figure 18.4 presents the correspondence between waves in the survey and zones in the analysis.

The following models were estimated using the simplified condition (i.e., $(Z_0, Z_1, Z_2 \mid Z_3)$). The conditioning on two outer zones was associated with less data and led to lower statistical power, and so is not presented here.

18.3   Results

To address the hypotheses, we fitted a model that included two network-attribute effects and a geospatial covariate effect while controlling for a

Table 18.2. *ALAAM estimates (and SEs) for predicting unemployment using network, geospatial, and actor attribute effects (*n = 551*)*

parameters		estimates (SEs)
Network-attribute effects		
Attribute-density	●	− 2.47 (0.24)*
Actor activity	●———○	− 0.10 (0.09)
Partner attribute [contagion]	●———●	0.51 (0.20)*
Geospatial covariate effects (log of distance)		
Attribute proximity [geographic homophily]	●--------●	− 0.01 (0.002)*
Attribute only effects		
Gender		0.48 (0.35)
Place of birth		− 0.26 (0.45)
Unemployment history		1.13 (0.39)*
University degree[a]		− 1.43 (0.67)*
Certificate/diploma[b]		− 0.45 (0.48)
Age		− 0.03 (0.07)
Number of years lived in area (NYA)		0.04 (0.07)

* Significant effect.
[a] University degree relative to school qualification.
[b] Certificate/diploma relative to school qualification.

number of basic predictors of unemployment. Recall that the attribute-density parameter relates to the baseline probability of the attribute being present, that is, the intercept or attribute frequency; the actor activity effect relates to the social position of an individual in the network on the probability of being unemployed; the partner attribute effect addresses contagion process via network ties; and attribute proximity effect (represented as dyadic covariate of logarithm of distance) examines whether being geographically close to unemployed individuals affects the probability of being unemployed. Parameter estimates converged and goodness-of-fit (GOF) *t*-ratios were less than 1 for all unfitted effects and less than 0.1 for fitted effects. The model was fitted using the iPnet software, a social influence-type version of the PNet program (Wang, Robins, & Pattison, 2009), available at http://www.sna.unimelb.edu.au/. Parameter estimates and approximate standard errors are presented in Table 18.2, with significant parameters marked with an asterisk.

The interpretation is relatively straightforward. The positive estimate for the partner attribute (i.e., contagion) effect suggests that the probability of being unemployed is greater if network partners are unemployed, everything else being equal. Given that the geospatial covariate is represented as a logarithm of distance, the negative estimate for the attribute proximity parameter provides evidence that the probability of being unemployed is higher for people who live geographically close to other unemployed people, regardless of whether these people are friends.

The actor activity effect is not significant, suggesting that there is no empirical evidence that the number of network ties might affect the probability of being unemployed. Gender, non-Australian origin, age, and number of years lived in the area are not important factors in determining the probability of being unemployed. Although there is no difference in the probability of being unemployed for those with only school qualifications compared with those who have certificate or diploma, the latter is more likely to be unemployed compared with individuals who possess a university degree. Previous experience of unemployment is also associated with higher probability of being unemployed.

18.4   Discussion

In this chapter, an ALAAM is used to assess the potential role of microlevel spatial and network-based influence processes on employment outcomes in a particular region in Melbourne, Australia. The main advantage of applying this statistical approach is its ability to simultaneously use four types of information: (1) attribute variables that are assumed to be autologistic in nature (i.e., the employment status of individuals), (2) a network of interpersonal relations, (3) geographic arrangements of individuals, and (4) explanatory attribute variables. It should be noted that these analyses are based on the assumption that an employment outcome is purely a function of the social influence processes and the basic sociodemographic characteristics included (i.e., age, gender, ethnicity, education, unemployment history). Of course, the individual determinants of employment outcomes are likely to be more numerous than just these measures; nevertheless, it is evident that the economic analysis of the labor market cannot ignore the social and geographic embeddedness of individuals without sacrificing explanatory power.

The results from the ALAAM suggest that social networks may be important in understanding the distribution of unemployment outcomes in a suburban population. Both network processes and spatial dependence among individuals contribute considerably to the explanation of employment outcomes, and the geographically embedded nature of networks reinforces the spatial clustering of unemployment. In particular, people are more likely to be unemployed if they have unemployed friends and when they live in close proximity to unemployed people. The analyses provide support for these hypotheses while taking account of exogenous factors such as age, gender, ethnicity, and education, suggesting that there are additional and independent effects of who you know *and* where you live on your employment status. Therefore, these models provide evidence that social networks and geographic proximity are associated with spillover between individuals across nearby social locations, influencing employment outcomes independently of other simply measured characteristics. This is an important observation because most research has either examined network and geographic effects separately or simply ignored the possible geospatial and network dependence. Although these results are tentative given the cross-sectional design, they nonetheless emphasize the potential importance of social and spatial embeddedness of individuals, particularly in understanding disparities in labor market outcomes. Indeed, it is likely that they can be generalized to assist in understanding the distribution of a diverse range of social phenomena, including crime, education choices, smoking, and drinking behavior.

Possible implications of the results can be addressed in policy development. The fact that the employment status of a particular individual shapes the employment perspectives for the individual's network partners (contagion effect) reinforces the importance of highly localized interventions, suggesting that interventions such as education subsidies and labor market regulations may be targeted toward particular individuals rather than being implemented across the community. Given that people are not isolated entities, individually targeted interventions will amplify the initial effect of the policy because more individuals will be affected by the subsidies and programs through network ties. For this reason, targeting may be more efficient than spreading resources more broadly, and the more localized the interventions, the better the outcomes at the community level.

19

Longitudinal Changes in Face-to-Face and Text Message–Mediated Friendship Networks

Tasuku Igarashi

19.1 Evolution of Friendship Networks, Communication Media, and Psychological Dispositions

Social relationships change over time. Within a social gathering, people form and maintain interpersonal relationships in several ways, whereas some relationships decline and others lapse after a certain period of time. The underlying processes of such relationship formation, maintenance, and dissolution can be differentiated in terms of purely structural network effects (see Chapter 3) and actor-relation effects (i.e., "social selection," see Chapter 8; also see de Klepper et al., 2010; Robins, Elliott, & Pattison, 2001). To test how purely structural and social selection processes promote network formation respectively, this chapter examines the development of friendship networks expressed through face-to-face communication and mobile phone text messages among first-year undergraduates through an academic year.

Making friends at a university is one of the central concerns of first-year undergraduates. Friendship plays an important role in adaptation to novel social environments, especially during a major life transition such as university enrollment. Previous research has investigated the relationship between friendship network development among first-year undergraduates and its impact on adaptation to university (Hays & Oxley, 1986; Newcomb, 1961; van Duijn et al., 2003). However, the impact of different types of communication media on network formation and maintenance has not been fully studied. This chapter introduces patterns of longitudinal changes in interpersonal relationships and characteristics of communication media, especially text messages, in relation to strength

I greatly acknowledge Toshikazu Yoshida for his helpful support in this longitudinal survey.

of friendship ties. The effects of individual factors such as gender and social identity on the evolution of friendship network structure are also elaborated.

Interpersonal relationships are naturally managed in multiple ways (White, 2008). This chapter broadly classifies friendship networks into two types based on low and high intimate relationships (Altman & Taylor, 1973). A "superficial network" is composed of low intimate and weak ties that are stable but changeable. Although greetings have a function to show intimacy, people tend to consider sending greeting messages (e.g., via greeting cards) as useful in the maintenance of a greater number of low intimate relationships that are established partly on surface politeness (Dindia et al., 2004). It is therefore reasonable to assume that greetings in general play a significant role to maintain superficial relationships. In contrast, a "self-disclosing network" includes high intimate and strong ties that are likely to be exclusive and mutual. People usually disclose themselves to a small number of intimate others by verbally revealing personal information and by nonverbal involvement in conversation (Cozby, 1973). The dyadic setting often encourages reciprocal self-disclosure (Jourard, 1964). In a context of social capital, superficial and self-disclosing networks might be related to Putnam's (2000) typology of "bridging" and "bonding" social networks, respectively. Also, strong tie relations (i.e., in the self-disclosing networks) are more likely to be transitive than weak tie relations (i.e., in the superficial networks) (Granovetter, 1973). In line with these notions, people would receive and share novel information through sparsely knitted superficial ties connecting different social clusters (Burt, 1992), whereas they would feel secure and bonded with a small number of others in tightly knitted self-disclosing friendship ties. Consequently, different types of functions give rise to different structural signatures: a superficial friendship network may be less reciprocal and transitive, as well as more expansive than a self-disclosing friendship network over time.

Emotional bonding and information exchange are partly matched to particular types of media of communication. People are connected to others they feel close to via multiple channels of communication (i.e., the so-called media multiplexity; see Haythornthwaite, 2005). Recently, among young people, there has been a rise in text messages (SMS and e-mails via mobile phones) to communicate with friends (Ito, Okabe, & Matsuda, 2005; Ling, 2004). In contrast to face-to-face conversation, text messaging communication is predominantly verbal (text)-based (i.e., there are few if any nonverbal clues), indirect, asynchronous (but reciprocal), personal, and portable, and more likely to be used among close friends than e-mail and other electronic communication tools (Boase et al., 2006; Igarashi, Takai, & Yoshida, 2005; Johnsen, 2006).

In other words, text messages are used to supplement face-to-face comm-unication by sharing their experience whenever and wherever they want. A social network where communication occurs through such media is beneficial not only for maintaining weak ties for information resources (Wellman et al., 1996) but also for fostering self-disclosure (Joinson, 2001).

In the process of social selection, visible and invisible individual fac-tors are important determinants of network formation (de Klepper et al., 2010). Gender is one of the important visible attributes affecting friend-ship network structure. Compared to males, females are more likely to form intimate social networks, encourage self-disclosure to intimate oth-ers, and avoid isolation (Boneva, Kraut, & Frohlich, 2001), whereas pre-vious research has confirmed a strong tendency of gender homophily in a friendship network (Ibarra, 1992; McPherson, Smith-Lovin, & Cook, 2001). van Duijn et al. (2003) revealed that the friendship selection based on gender similarity in face-to-face networks among first-year under-graduates emerges only at an initial stage of relationships. Regarding text message usage, Igarashi et al. (2005) showed that undergraduates tend to form same-gender friendship ties, and in particular, females tend to expand their social networks via text messages more than males. This study sought to investigate the social selection process based on gen-der similarity in face-to-face and text message–mediated friendship net-works over time, while controlling for the structural effects of social networks.

With regard to invisible interpersonal attitudes, social identity is also an influential factor in friendship formation and maintenance (Turner et al., 1987). Previous research revealed that members of a sorority embedded in a central position showed a stronger sense of belongingness than those in a peripheral position (Paxton & Moody, 2003). To sustain self-esteem and adapt to a novel environment, first-year undergraduates may invest in the university to increase their sense of belongingness and thus come to regard themselves as a typical member of the university. This iden-tification may lead to more active participation in university social life. Thus, strong identification with the university and its members at an ini-tial period may lead to more active nomination of other classmates over time.

In sum, this chapter investigates the evolution of superficial and self-disclosing friendship networks among first-year undergraduates formed and maintained via face-to-face and text messages in relation to gender and social identity throughout the academic year. Purely structural and social selection processes among different types of friendship networks are explored and compared over time. Purely structural effects and actor-relation effects are analyzed simultaneously to examine the impacts of each effect on friendship network evolution.

19.2   Data and Measures

The data were composed of seventy first-year undergraduates (twelve males and fifty-eight females; mean age = 18.4 years) of the same educational department at a university in central Japan. All participants had their own mobile phone.

19.2.1   Social Network Questions

In this study, four types of friendship networks were classified according to intimacy (superficial, self-disclosing) and communication media (face-to-face, text messages). Participants were asked about their communication patterns over the past 2 weeks. They were asked to choose up to five of their classmates with whom they had (1) greeted face-to-face ("face-to-face superficial networks"), (2) disclosed personal matters face-to-face ("face-to-face self-disclosing networks"), (3) casually greeted via mobile phone text messages ("text message–mediated superficial networks"), and (4) disclosed personal matters via mobile phone text messages ("text message–mediated self-disclosing networks"). In this chapter, we examine the questionnaire data from the third (the beginning of the first semester) and forty-first (the end of the second semester) weeks of their academic year after matriculation to study the changes in social network structure across the academic year. The response rate of this longitudinal survey was 100% in both periods.

19.2.2   Actor-Relation Measures

Participants were asked about their gender (i.e., a visible attribute) and responded to items measuring social identity (i.e., an invisible disposition) at the beginning of the first semester. With regard to gender, male is coded as 0 and female as 1. The group identification scale (Karasawa, 1991) measured the strength of participants' identification with the education department. This scale contains two subscales: the identification with member (ID_{MEMBER}), including the feelings of closeness toward classmates (five items), and the identification with group (ID_{GROUP}), including attachments with the department (seven items), all of which were rated on 7-point scales. The averaged score across all items was separately calculated for each subscale. Higher scores of ID_{MEMBER} or ID_{GROUP} indicate stronger identification with other classmates or the department, respectively. The attribute variables for these longitudinal models were measured at the first time period of the study.[1]

---

[1]   Gender is (to a large extent) immutable; thus, it does not matter whether attributes are examined from the initial or final measurement point. However, social identity may

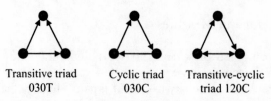

Transitive triad   Cyclic triad   Transitive-cyclic
030T   030C   triad 120C

Figure 19.1. Triadic configurations used in models. Labeling of configurations comes from standard triad census for directed graphs.

19.2.3   Analyses

The longitudinal exponential random graph model (ERGM; Chapter 11)
was used to analyze the data. Purely structural and actor-relation effects
were included simultaneously in the model. The four types of friendship
networks were each modeled separately and longitudinally, using the
network at the first period (matriculation) as an initial state for the last
period (end of the academic year). LPNet, a version of the PNet software
(Wang, Robins & Pattison, 2009) for longitudinal data, was used for the
parameter estimation.

19.3   Model Specification

In each type of friendship network, eight Markov parameters of directed
networks were included as purely structural effects: "arc," "reciprocity,"
"in-2-star," "out-2-star," "2-path," "transitive triad" (030T), "cyclic
triad" (030C), and "transitive-cyclic triad" (120C) (see Figure 19.1). In
a friendship network, the transitive triad parameter reflects the degree
of transitive clustering (path closure), and the cyclic triad parameter is
interpreted as a measure of the generalized exchange (cyclic closure) cycle
(Lazega & Pattison, 1999). The transitive-cyclic parameter (120C) is not
often used in ERGMs but here examines the extent to which path and
cyclic closure is associated with reciprocity.

A total of seven actor-relation effects were included in the model.
Parameters included homophily, sender and receiver effects for gender,
and sender and receiver effects for ID_{MEMBER} and ID_{GROUP}, respectively.

19.4   Results

A longitudinal ERGM with eight structural effects and seven actor-
relation effects was fitted separately for four types of networks. Overall,
all models successfully converged and fitted the data well. Results of

(perhaps is likely to) vary over time, but under the assumption that these changes may be
considered exogenous and that social selection is the predominant process, the researcher
may choose to use only one measurement.

Table 19.1. *Parameter estimates and standard errors in face-to-face friendship networks*

	estimates (SEs)			
parameters	face-to-face superficial networks		face-to-face self-disclosing networks	
Purely structural effects				
Arc	− 4.99	(1.04)*	− 6.72	(1.53)*
Reciprocity	4.05	(0.45)*	5.42	(0.52)*
2-In-star	− 0.25	(0.11)*	− 0.20	(0.20)
2-Out-star	0.08	(0.08)	0.18	(0.11)
2-path	− 0.57	(0.10)*	− 0.37	(0.12)*
Transitive triad	1.12	(0.13)*	1.33	(0.29)*
Cyclic triad	1.77	(0.45)*	2.82	(1.02)*
Transitive-cyclic triad	− 1.11	(0.18)*	− 1.88	(0.50)*
Actor-relation effects				
Homophily – gender	− 0.30	(0.75)	− 0.51	(1.14)
Sender – gender	0.58	(0.59)	0.59	(1.20)
Receiver – gender	− 0.10	(0.63)	0.78	(1.04)
Sender – ID$_{MEMBER}$	0.04	(0.04)	− 0.07	(0.05)
Sender – ID$_{GROUP}$	0.02	(0.03)	0.11	(0.04)*
Receiver – ID$_{MEMBER}$	0.03	(0.04)	0.01	(0.05)
Receiver – ID$_{GROUP}$	0.03	(0.03)	0.003	(0.04)

* Significant effect

the parameter estimation in the face-to-face and text message–mediated friendship networks are presented in Tables 19.1 and 19.2, respectively.

In all types of networks, the positive and significant effects of reciprocity indicated the strong tendency of mutual and direct exchange. Regardless of communication media and intimacy, positive and significant effects of transitive triads and negative and significant 2-path effects were consistently found, suggesting that indirect links between two people rarely occurred when controlling for other structural effects, especially given transitive path closure. These results indicated the strength of the purely structural processes in network evolution when controlling for the effect of gender homophily.

Except for text message–mediated self-disclosing networks, the positive effects of cyclic triads and the negative effects of transitive-cyclic triad were significant. These results suggested the emergence of cyclic closure through network evolution in face-to-face superficial/self-disclosing and text message–mediated superficial networks.

19.4.1   Results for Face-to-Face Superficial Networks

In the face-to-face superficial network, all but the 2-out-star structural parameters were significant. The negative and significant 2-in-star parameter revealed a relatively even distribution of in-degrees (i.e., an absence

Table 19.2 *Parameter estimates and standard errors in text message–mediated friendship networks*

parameters	estimates (SEs)			
	text message–mediated superficial networks		text message–mediated self-disclosing networks	
Purely structural effects				
Arc	− 3.79	(1.20)*	− 2.11	(1.29)
Reciprocity	4.19	(0.39)*	4.66	(0.56)*
2-In-star	− 0.12	(0.10)	− 0.04	(0.18)
2-Out-star	0.10	(0.09)	0.23	(0.09)*
2-path	− 0.39	(0.09)*	− 0.34	(0.15)*
Transitive triad	1.01	(0.19)*	1.28	(0.25)*
Cyclic triad	1.38	(0.53)*	0.58	(1.83)
Transitive-cyclic triad	− 0.87	(0.22)*	− 0.87	(0.77)
Actor-relation effects				
Homophily – gender	0.74	(0.65)	1.79	(0.78)*
Sender – gender	− 0.86	(0.57)	− 2.12	(0.63)*
Receiver – gender	− 1.16	(0.56)*	− 2.04	(0.615)*
Sender – ID_{MEMBER}	− 0.04	(0.04)	− 0.07	(0.05)
Sender – ID_{GROUP}	0.06	(0.03)*	0.07	(0.04)
Receiver – ID_{MEMBER}	− 0.02	(0.04)	− 0.01	(0.05)
Receiver – ID_{GROUP}	0.05	(0.03)	− 0.02	(0.04)

* Significant effect

of particularly popular people in the class). In combination with other parameters, this finding suggested the tendencies of local clustering and direct and generalized exchange of greetings among first-year undergraduates. In terms of actor-relation effects, no significant effects of gender and social identity were obtained.

19.4.2   Results for Face-to-Face Self-Disclosing Networks

The value of the reciprocity parameter in face-to-face self-disclosing networks was positive and significant. As such, the structure of self-disclosing friendship networks was in part composed of mutual nominations based on the norm of reciprocity. Meanwhile, nonsignificant effects of the 2-in-star and 2-out-star parameters suggested a lack of particular hubs of face-to-face self-disclosing ties in the class. The significant and positive effects of transitive triads and cyclic triads suggested transitive clustering and indirect reciprocity of face-to-face self-disclosing networks.

What is interesting is that no significant gender differences were found for homophily, sender effects, or receiver effects. Males and females were likely to nominate, as well as be nominated by, other classmates for self-disclosure to the same extent. The significant and positive effect of

ID$_{\text{GROUP}}$ showed that high initial identification with the department promoted the formation of self-disclosing ties with other classmates. There were no significant receiver effects for social identity.

19.4.3   Results for Text Message–Mediated Superficial Networks

Structural effects in text message–mediated superficial networks were similar to those in face-to-face self-disclosing networks. The reciprocity parameter was significantly positive, reflecting a reciprocity norm via casual text messages. The significant and positive effects of transitive triad and cyclic triad suggested the evolution of transitive clustering and indirect reciprocity of text messaging networks. No significant effects of the 2-in-star and 2-out-star parameters suggested relatively even in-degree and out-degree distributions, respectively.

Unlike the face-to-face friendship networks, the negative and significant receiver effect of gender was observed, suggesting that males were more likely to receive casual text messages than females. In other words, friendship nomination was partly based on social selection, resulting in the popularity of males over females in text message–mediated superficial networks. The sender effect of ID$_{\text{GROUP}}$ was significantly positive, implying that identification with the department at the start of the academic year encouraged friendship nomination via casual text messages throughout the academic year.

19.4.4   Results for Text Message–Mediated Self-Disclosing Networks

Some of the structural effects of text message–mediated self-disclosing networks differed from those of the other three friendship networks, whereas some were consistent. The positive and significant effect of reciprocity revealed the strong norm of direct reciprocity in disclosing personal matters via text messages. The significant contribution of the 2-out-star effect is also notable because the maximum number of friendship nominations in the questionnaire was restricted up to five.[2] In addition, whereas the effects of cyclic triad and transitive-cyclic triad were not significant, the effect of transitive triad was positive and significant. This pattern of parameter values suggested the evolution of transitive clustering without strong tendencies of cyclic-based generalized exchange

---

[2] The limitation of the out-degree requires that in estimation and simulation procedures, no node can have more than five network partners. The parameter estimation was thus conditional on a maximum out-degree of five.

in friendship networks. Meanwhile, the positive and significant 2-out-star parameter showed that some active people (i.e., hubs) disclosed themselves more via text messages to other classmates. It may be that some self-disclosing ties via text messages might develop as bridges over local and dense clusters.

In terms of actor-relation effects, the evolution of self-disclosing networks via text messages was strongly based on the social selection process. The homophily effect of gender was positive and significant, whereas the sender and receiver effects of gender were negative and significant. These results suggest the dominance of the same-gender relationships (male–male, female–female). In sum, people tended to disclose private matters via text messages within same-gender relationships, and males were more active and popular than females.

All transitive-cyclic triadic parameters had negative estimates, and all were significant except for the text-mediated self-disclosing network. The use of this parameter in the models is unusual, but it does permit interpretation about triadic closure processes involving reciprocated ties. The negative effect suggests that reciprocated ties are involved in fewer triadic configurations than would otherwise be expected, given the other effects in the model. It is possible that a stronger reciprocated tie does not need to have as much grouplike scaffolding through triadic effects compared to weaker nonreciprocated ties.

19.5   Discussion

In longitudinal ERGM, several purely structural effects were found that were common to all four types of friendship networks. Overall, the signs of all parameters were identical for the structural effects across the four types of networks. The reciprocity effect was consistently observed. In a similar vein to previous findings (Hachen et al., 2009), the structure of friendship networks might be rooted in a dyadic and mutual exchange of activity as a basic social function in both face-to-face and text message–mediated communication. Also, the combination of the positive transitive triad and negative 2-path parameters was found regardless of network type.

The differences in parameter significance across the networks also suggest that the purely structural processes played out in different ways in each type of friendship network. The obtained patterns for triad parameters were similar in face-to-face superficial networks, face-to-face self-disclosing networks, and text message–mediated superficial networks, suggesting that friendship networks evolve through transitive clustering and cyclic-based generalized exchange. This finding is contrary to the

Granovetter's (1973) notion that weak ties show less transitivity than strong ties. In terms of the social network measure used in this study, it might be possible that the characteristics of superficial (i.e., greeting) and self-disclosing networks that were determined a priori by the researcher did not perfectly reflect the nature of nonintimate and intimate relationships. Thus, first-year undergraduates might include both nonintimate and intimate relationships when answering their greeting networks. Future research should consider using alternative social network questions that can clearly differentiate nonintimate from intimate relationships.

However, text message–mediated self-disclosing networks indicated a unique process of network evolution: first-year undergraduates developed self-disclosing networks via text messages through the formation of transitive clusters but not cyclic clusters. As shown in the reciprocity effect, people tend to disclose themselves to intimate friends at a dyadic level and in a triadic hierarchical manner.

Concerning actor-relation effects of a visible attribute, no systematic effect of gender on the social selection process was observed in face-to-face friendship networks. In other words, the evolution of face-to-face friendship selection was *not* particularly gender specific. In previous research, gender-based friendship selection emerged only in the initial stage of relationship processes (van Duijn et al., 2003). As suggested in Newcomb's (1961) seminal work on friendship selection processes, people tend to form connections with accessible others in their immediate environment. In face-to-face settings, male or female activity might be a trigger to make their relationships more proximate, but from a year-long perspective, the purely structural processes and other invisible individual dispositions play a more important role on friendship formation.

In contrast, significant gender effects were observed in text message–mediated friendship networks. In text message–mediated superficial networks, males tended to be more popular than females, suggesting that text messages might promote gender intermixing in terms of the formation of casual and unidirectional relationships from females to males. In self-disclosing friendship networks, the homophily effect of gender was exhibited in the process of network evolution. Also, compared to females, males were more likely to send and receive self-disclosing text messages to and from others. In summary, both males and females prefer empathic bonds with the same gender via text messages, but at the same time, males took positive actions to nominate, and were also nominated by females, through text-based intimate communication. These findings might be explained by the evidence that males are more likely to disclose themselves to strangers and acquaintances, whereas females are more likely to disclose to intimate friends (Stokes, Fuehrer, & Childs,

1980). Although these results are contrary to the findings by Igarashi et al. (2005), this inconsistency can be interpreted according to the significant differences between the current research and Igarashi et al. (2005) with regard to the sample (first-year undergraduates only vs. undergraduates of several grades) and the study period (1 year vs. one semester). In addition, Igarashi et al. used a dyad independent method without containing other structural parameters, a method that may underestimate (or even ignore) regularity in self-organizing features of friendship networks. Moreover, longitudinal ERGM allows us to test social selection processes of gender homophily (male–male, female–female) and heterophily (male–female) in tie formation and dissolution over time when controlling for purely structural effects. In sum, the current findings revealed that forming and maintaining intimate relationships linked via text messages are explained by the social selection process based on gender.

In terms of actor-relation effects of invisible individual dispositions, ID_{GROUP} had a significant impact on relationship formation in the process of network evolution. As suggested in the previous literature (Lawler & Yoon, 1996; Paxton & Moody, 2003), social identity is rooted in self-esteem and emotional bonding with others, and would serve as an adaptive motive to form friendship networks in a novice setting. First-year undergraduates identifying with their university immediately after matriculation might behave actively toward others, resulting in the nomination of a greater number of ties through the evolution of friendship networks. However, it is not clear why the significant sender effect of ID_{GROUP} was observed only in face-to-face self-disclosing networks and text message–mediated superficial networks, each located at the opposite end of friendship intimacy. This nonsystematic pattern of findings may be partly due to a lack of salient cues regarding the social identity of others. Although there is evidence that invisible attributes have significant impacts on friendship network development (van Duijn et al., 2003), the application of salient cues for social identity each first-year undergraduate manifests, such as the ownership of university merchandise (e.g., T-shirts, mugs), may provide a more consistent effect of social identity on friendship selection across the four types of networks.

In conclusion, the current longitudinal research provides fruitful evidence of the social selection and purely structural processes through the evolution of friendship networks, in that both structural and individual factors have a great impact on people's friendship choices in novel social environments. Future research should focus more on event-related effects on friendship network formation and maintenance over time. Also, the examination of other types of micro–macro dynamics, such as group norms and individual knowledge of groups, would expand the validity of the findings reported here. To further understand the dynamics of network evolution with individual factors, it is also intriguing to consider analyzing actual text message records and modeling the multiplex coevolution of different types of friendship networks. For these purposes, stochastic actor-oriented models implemented in SIENA software (Snijders, van de Bunt, & Steglich, 2010; Steglich, Snijders, & West, 2006; van Duijn et al., 2003) would also draw insightful findings.

Chapter 20

Differential Impact of Directors' Social and Financial Capital on Corporate Interlock Formation

Nicholas Harrigan and Matthew Bond

20.1 Bipartite Society: The Individual and the Group

The interdependence of the individual and the organization is an enduring theme in sociological thought. Cooley wrote that "man may be regarded as the point of intersection of an indefinite number of circles representing social groups, having as many arcs passing through him as there are groups" (1902/1964, 148). Simmel (1955) captured the tension between the individual and the organization when he defined two types of group affiliation: "organic membership," where the organization is not chosen by the individual as an expression of his or her traits (e.g., as in the case of the family), and "rational membership," where the organization is chosen as a conscious expression of the individual's traits. For Simmel, the most important outcome of an individual's affiliation to an organization was the constraint and socialization of the individual; an individual, he laments, "is determined sociologically in the sense that groups 'intersect' in his person by virtue of his affiliations with them" (150).

Social network analysis has developed a distinctive and highly systematic set of methods for representation, measurement, and (more recently) modeling of this interdependence called, variously, "membership networks," "affiliation networks," "bipartite networks," and "two-mode networks" (Breiger, 1974; Robins & Alexander, 2004; Wang, Sharpe, Robins, & Pattison, 2009). The advantage of bipartite networks is that they preserve the dualistic structure of organization–individual relations, representing the network as ties between a set of individuals and a set of organizations. They avoid simplifying the relationships into the one-mode form of either a network of individuals or a network of organizations (see Chapter 10, Section 10.2, for more on bipartite networks).

We are deeply indebted to Eleina Ailmchandani, Christine Chen, and Isaac Chin for their heroic and patient research support for this chapter.

Corporate interlocks have been one of the most studied affiliation networks in sociology (Domhoff, 1967, 1970, 1978, 1998, 2009; Domhoff & Dye, 1987; Dooley, 1969; Emerson, 1962; Fitch & Oppenheimer, 1970; Koenig, Gogel, & Sonquist, 1979; Levine, 1972; Mace, 1971; Mills, 1956; Mintz & Schwartz, 1985; Mizruchi, 1982; Ornstein, 1984; Pfeffer & Salancik, 1978; Scott, 1997; Scott & Griff, 1984; Stearns & Mizruchi, 1986; Sweezy, 1953; Useem, 1984; Zeitlin, 1974; Zweigenhaft & Domhoff, 2006). Corporate interlocks are formed by the affiliation of directors of corporations to corporate boards of governance. The popularity of the study of corporate interlock networks stems from the data's public nature and therefore its relative accessibility, and the importance of these networks of the governing boards of the largest economic actors in the private economy.

20.1.1   Director Capital and Interlock Formation

This chapter models an Australian corporate interlock data set with a bipartite exponential random graph model (ERGM) (see Chapter 10) using the BPNet software, a version of the PNet software (Wang, Robins, & Pattison, 2009) for bipartite data. By using bipartite modeling, we are able to directly examine the interdependence long talked about in the sociological literature. That is, we are able to study social tie formation (corporate interlocks) as a function of (1) the individuals' attributes (directors), (2) the groups' attributes (corporations), (3) the interaction of individual and group attributes, and (4) purely structural network effects (social ties that form without reference to actor attributes).

Our primary substantive objective is to study the effects of director characteristics on the pattern of corporate interlock formation. In particular, we are interested in the effects of three types of corporate director power on the formation of corporate interlocks: (1) physical or financial capital (i.e., wealth), (2) membership of exclusive businessmen's clubs, and (3) attendance at elite private schools.

Traditional elite and corporate interlock studies have tended to emphasize the unifying role of director social capital and the convergence of the many dimensions of director, corporate, social, and economic power at the apex of the corporate community. We argue that there is considerable differentiation in the purpose and effects of the many different forms of social and economic power within the corporate community. In particular, we argue that the alienability of the benefits of physical capital (Coleman, 1990/1994) leads owners to place relatively low emphasis on their own social capital (e.g., interlocks). We also argue that businessmen's clubs and elite private schools, traditionally viewed as markers of upper-class membership and facilitators of corporate unity, play different roles within the Australian corporate community: we hypothesize that businessmen's clubs are bonding social capital (Putnam, 2000, 22–24) closer to in-group social capital, binding those corporations with common interests and identities, whereas private schools act as bridging social capital, providing between-group social capital, drawing together the disparate parts of the corporate community, with little differentiation on the basis of interests and identities of corporate groups united by private school ties.

In addition, we make three methodological contributions. First, we demonstrate that there are purely structural network effects that operate on corporate interlocks, independent of the economic, political, and sociological attributes of directors and corporations. In this, we are looking for effects similar to the one-mode effects we call "path closure" (Robins, Pattison, & Wang, 2009) or "transitivity" (Granovetter, 1973; Holland & Leinhardt, 1976; Watts & Strogatz, 1998), and other effects such as "popularity" (Barabasi & Albert, 1999; Frank & Strauss, 1986; Wasserman & Pattison, 1996), in which ties form purely in response to the pattern of ties that comprise the local neighborhood. In the case of bipartite networks, we expect to find effects such as a tendency for 3-paths (L3) to close and become 4-cycles (C4), and a tendency for popular directors to become more popular (modeled with star configurations of various sizes). Second, we demonstrate the added benefits, both in terms of model fit and sociological explanatory power, of introducing director and corporation attributes into bipartite modeling. We model the effects of corporate attributes such as political donations, public listing, foreign ownership, regulated industries, and turnover. We model the effect of director attributes such as individual wealth, members of businessmen's clubs, and education at elite private schools. Finally, we explore the benefit of the inclusion of interaction effects for the increased or decreased likelihood of directorship formation between particular types of directors and corporations.

20.2   Data and Measures

20.2.1   Social Network Data

The data comprise a network of directors and corporations collected by Harrigan (2008). It is the network of the largest 248 corporations (as measured by revenue) in Australia in February 2006. It includes publicly listed and private corporations, as well as Australian and foreign-owned corporations. There are 1,251 directors, who hold a total of 1,464 directorships. Data on corporations and directors were obtained from IBISWorld (2006), the company that compiles the yearly *Business Review Weekly*'s "Top 2000 Enterprises."[1]

---

[1] The authors want to express their gratitude to IBISWorld and Crown Content for their provision, respectively, of the "Top 2000 Enterprises" and the "Who's Who" databases.

20.2.2   Actor-Relation Measures

Corporations have six binary attributes. Company size is a binary variable that divides the corporations into two equal groups: the largest 124 corporations and the smallest 124 corporations, as measured by revenue. Revenue data were also provided by IBISWorld. Corporations have two (mutually exclusive) binary donation variables: "donate to both major parties" (an indicator of moderate political activity) and "donate to conservatives only" (indicating donations to either the National Party or the Liberal Party – the two major conservative parties that are typically in coalition). Political donation data were downloaded from the Australian Electoral Commission (AEC; 2006) Web site. Companies that were publicly listed corporations were coded by the variable "public" ("1" indicates that the company was listed on the stock exchange). Australian ownership (=1) or foreign ownership (=0) was coded by the variable "Australian." As an indicator of interest in and interaction with the political process of the state, firms were classified as to whether they were located in "highly regulated industries." The regulated industries were coded using Burris's (1987) classification and matched against the two-digit Standard Industry Codes in the IBISWorld data set. "Regulated industries" can be thought of as comprising four categories: transport (road, rail, and air), communication, utilities (water, gas, and electricity), and banking and insurance.[2]

Individual directors have three binary attributes: director wealth (or, more accurately, "superwealth" = 1), attendance at an exclusive private school (=1), and membership of an exclusive establishment gentlemen's club (=1). Previous studies suggest that wealth, especially old wealth, may lead to political conservatism (Bond, 2003, 2004; Bond, Glouharova, & Harrigan, 2010; Burris, 2000). Directors are classified as "superwealthy" (=1) if they were listed in the *Business Review Weekly*'s (2005) "Rich 200" list. In Australia, data were obtained from the social directories "Who's Who in Australia" and "Who's Who in Australian Business" (Crown Content, 2005a, 2005b). The majority (59.1%) of the Australian directors had an entry in "Who's Who." This sample compares favorably to previous studies, for example, 33.7% of Useem's (1984) UK sample and 30.3% of Bond's (2007) UK sample were found in directories.

"School" was defined as attendance at one of 17 exclusive private schools.[3] This list was obtained by comparing the 3,000 secondary

---

[2]   Industries classified as highly regulated were air and space transport, communication services, electricity and gas supply, finance, insurance, other transport, rail transport, road transport, services to finance and insurance, services to transport, water supply, sewerage and drainage services, and water transport.

[3]   These exclusive private schools include Anglican Church Grammar School (QLD), Brisbane Boys College (QLD), Brisbane Grammar School (QLD), Geelong Grammar School (VIC), Melbourne Grammar School (VIC), Scotch College (VIC), Wesley College (VIC),

schools in Australia on a range of socioeconomic and status measures, including the socioeconomic status of parents, school fees, listing in "Who's Who," and the percentage of ex-students who were members of the exclusive businessmen's clubs. In Australia, "clubs" were defined as a list of eleven prominent businessmen's clubs.[4] This list was identified through the use of secondary sources such as studies of upper-class clubs, reciprocal membership arrangements, and membership procedures.

Summary statistics for the attributes and derived attribute interaction effects are provided in Table 20.1. All variables are binary. We provide a count of corporations/directors/directorships with each attribute (column 1). To provide a baseline value (expected value) for interaction effects, we calculate the number of directorships that would occur if directorships arose from the random assortment of ties between corporations and directors. The second column (percentage of total corporations/directors/expected directorships) divides the first column by the total number of corporations (248), directors (1,251), or directorships (1,464), respectively. Column 3 is a count of the total observed directorships for this attribute–attribute interaction. Column 4 is column 3 divided by the total number of directorships (1,464). Column 5 "overrepresentation" is percent directorships (column 4) divided by column 2: a value greater than one indicates that directors/corporations/director–corporation interactions have more directorships than would be expected given a random assortment of directorships. Column 6 indicates whether the over- or underrepresentation is statistically significant (using a chi-square test on the 2×2 matrix of the expected and realized number of directorships).

20.2.3   Analyses

The analyses in this chapter begin with a brief discussion of the bivariate analysis presented in Table 20.1, attempting to show what can be achieved with cross-tabulation and establishing a baseline against which to judge the added utility of more complex modeling, in particular, the bipartite ERGM. The remainder of the chapter uses the bipartite social selection model presented in Chapter 10.

Xavier College (VIC), Knox Grammar School (NSW), St. Ignatius' College, Senior School (NSW), Sydney Church of England Grammar School (NSW), Sydney Grammar School (NSW), The King's School (NSW), Aquinas College (WA), Scotch College (WA), Hale School (WA), and Collegiate School of St Peter (SA).

[4]   These prominent businessmen's clubs include Athenaeum (VIC), Australian (VIC), Melbourne (VIC), Australian (NSW), Union (NSW), Brisbane (QLD), Weld (WA), Adelaide (SA), Tasmanian (TAS), Launceston (TAS), and Elanora (NSW).

Table 20.1. *Summary statistics for attributes and attribute interactions*

corporation attributes	(1) count corporations	(2) % corporations	(3) count directorships	(4) % directorships	(5) over-representation	(6) sign. (chi-square test)
Conservative	10	4.0	47	3.2	0.80	
Bipartisan	45	18.1	346	23.6	1.30	***
Australian	144	58.1	1070	73.1	1.26	***
Listed	115	46.4	958	65.4	1.41	***
Regulated	67	27.0	419	28.6	1.06	
Revenue	124	50.0	837	57.2	1.14	***

director attributes	count directors	% directors	count directorships	% directorships	over-representation	sign. (chi-square test)
Wealth	34	2.7	36	2.5	0.90	
Club	155	12.4	229	15.6	1.26	***
School	83	6.6	135	9.2	1.39	***

interaction effects	expected directorships	expected % directorships	count directorships	% directorships	over-representation	sign. (chi-square test)
Conservative& Wealth	2	0.1	3	0.2	1.87	
Bipartisan& Wealth	7	0.5	12	0.8	1.66	
Australian& Wealth	23	1.6	35	2.4	1.51	*
Listed& Wealth	18	1.3	27	1.8	1.46	
Regulated& Wealth	11	0.7	6	0.4	0.56	
Revenue&Wealth	20	1.4	16	1.1	0.80	
Conservative& Club	7	0.5	5	0.3	0.68	
Bipartisan&Club	33	2.2	76	5.2	2.31	***
Australian&Club	105	7.2	199	13.6	1.89	***
Listed&Club	84	5.7	191	13.0	2.27	***
Regulated&Club	49	3.3	89	6.1	1.82	***
Revenue&Club	91	6.2	159	10.9	1.75	***
Conservative& School	4	0.3	1	0.1	0.26	
Bipartisan& School	18	1.2	50	3.4	2.84	***
Australian& School	56	3.9	114	7.8	2.02	***
Listed&School	45	3.1	114	7.8	2.53	***
Regulated& School	26	1.8	50	3.4	1.91	***
Revenue&School	49	3.3	94	6.4	1.94	***

* p value < .05.
*** p value < .001.

20.3   Model Specification

20.3.1   Independent Bivariate Attribute Analysis

A considerable section of the interlocking directorates research does not go beyond descriptive statistics similar to those in Table 20.1. The purpose of these studies is to find over- or underrepresented groups by comparing directorships across groups and with a baseline random distribution.

20.3.2   Purely Structural Effects

In our bipartite ERGM, up to five structural effects are used in various combinations: the edge parameter [L], alternating k-stars for directors [K-Sp] and corporations [K-Sa], and alternating k-cycles for directors [K-Cp] and corporations [K-Ca]. The edge parameter [L] represents the baseline probability of forming a tie and is similar to the intercept in a classic regression model. The star effects can be thought of as a "popularity" effect or a "rich get richer" effect (also called the "Matthew effect"), whereby actors with ties have an increased likelihood of receiving further ties. In this chapter, we use the alternating k-star parameters described in Chapter 10 (see Figure 10.8; the rationale for the alternating version of these statistics is given in Chapter 6). The alternating k-cycles ([K-Cp] and [K-Ca]) parameters capture the propensity of directors (p) and corporations (a) to be part of 4-cycles (i.e., to engage in closed bipartite network structures) (see Chapter 10 and Figure 10.11).

20.3.3   Models with Attributes: Actor-Relation Effects

Three types of attribute parameters are used in our models: director attribute activity [rP], corporation attribute activity [rA] (see Figure 10.12), and corporation–director attribute interaction [rAP] (see Figure 10.15). rP and rA are simply the main effect for each director and corporation attribute. Thus, our models include nine of these effects (six corporation effects: [rA_Conservative], [rA_Bipartisan], [rA_Australian], [rA_Listed], [rA_Regulated], and [rA_Revenue], and three director effects: [rP_Wealth], [rP_Club], and [rP_School]). A significant positive parameter estimate for one of the attribute effects would mean that corporations (directors) with this attribute have a greater probability (than corporations (directors) who do not have this attribute) of holding directorships.

rAP parameters capture the increased (or decreased) likelihood of a tie forming between a corporation with a particular attribute (e.g., "Australian") and a director with a particular attribute (e.g., "school"). These were described as "between node set" parameters in Chapter 10. For our data set, there are eighteen possible interaction effects (6 corporation attributes × 3 director attributes). A range of higher-order attribute parameters are available in BPNet (see Chapter 10), but for reasons of parsimony, we restricted ourselves to the thirty-two parameters mentioned.

20.4 Results

20.4.1 Results for Independent Bivariate Analysis

Table 20.1 presents a classic bivariate overrepresentation analysis that is common to the interlock literature. There are three notable effects present. First, bipartisan donor corporations, Australian and publicly listed corporations, and directors with elite private schooling or membership of exclusive gentlemen's clubs have, on average, considerably more directorships. Second, the wealthy are significantly overrepresented in Australian-owned corporations. Third, directors from exclusive clubs and schools are significantly overrepresented in bipartisan, Australian, public-listed, regulated, and large corporations.

In addition, a number of characteristics seem to predispose directors and/or corporations to underrepresentation (e.g., conservative directors and the interaction of regulated corporations and wealthy directors). However, the "law of small numbers" means that it is difficult to be statistically confident that a "rare event" is even rarer than (un)expected. Thus, none of the underrepresentation findings in Table 20.1 are statistically significant.

These bivariate tables, however, involve no controls for either structural network effects or any of the other attribute effects. As is shown, the addition of these elements to our modeling considerably changes the interpretation of the underlying data.

20.4.2 Results for Purely Structural Effects

Table 20.2 presents two fitted models with purely structural effects. We found for this particular network that we cannot have both K-Cp and K-Ca in the same model due to convergence issues. In line with Wang, Sharpe, Robins, and Pattison (2009), we present two alternative models, one with each possible k-cycle parameter.

Both models perform significantly better than a random graph in capturing structural graph statistics (results of which are not shown but that were estimated with edge parameter [L] = −5.34). There is a negative value of the director popularity [K-Sp], indicating that there is little variation on the degree distribution and not many high-degree nodes. However, in line with Wang, Sharpe, Robins, and Pattison (2009), we had a poor fit on the classic 4-cycle parameter [C4], which suggests that improving these structural effects is a substantial area of future research.

Table 20.2. *Results of two bipartite ERGMs of directorships including only purely structural effects*

	estimates (SEs)	
parameter	model A	model B
Purely structural effects	with director 4-cycle effect	with corporation 4-cycle effect
Edge [L]	−3.47 (0.26)*	−2.38 (0.37)*
Director popularity [K-Sp]		−4.54 (0.21)*
Corporation popularity [K-Sa]	0.65 (0.10)*	0.15 (0.18)
Director 4-cycles [K-Cp]	−4.00 (0.19)*	
Corporation 4-cycles [K-Ca]		0.06 (0.01)*

* Significant effect

20.4.3   Results for Models Including Purely Structural and Actor-Relation Effects

Table 20.3 presents two fitted models: the first (model C) with structural and actor-relation effects; and the second (model D) with structural, actor-relation, and interaction effects for actor-relations.

For model D, several interaction effects had to be dropped because estimations showed that they were unstable, either because there were almost no ties (e.g., [rAP_Conservative&School] had one observation) or because they represented virtually all ties of the main effect (e.g., [rAP_Wealth&Australian] overlapped with thirty-five of the thirty-six directorships of the [rA_Wealth] statistic). All main effects for attributes were left in model D as controls for the interaction effects.

The purely structural effects from model B are robust and remain significant in both models C and D, despite the addition of up to sixteen attribute effects. The main effects of the actor-relation effects in model C suggest a slightly different interpretation to descriptive statistics in Table 20.1. In particular, bipartisan donor corporations, the second most over-represented type of corporation in Table 20.1, do not have significantly greater directorships in either model C or model D.

The addition of interaction effects to the bipartite ERGM draws out two further findings. Although in Table 20.1, club and school interaction effects follow almost identical patterns, model D shows that they operate according to very different principles. In model D, the effect of the clubs variable loads completely on the club interaction effects. The main effect for club becomes insignificant, and the high number of directorships of club members is explained by their high propensity to hold directorships on Australian, public listed, regulated, and large (revenue) corporations. In contrast, the main effect for schools remains highly significant, and only seems to be associated with positive interaction effects with public

Table 20.3. *Two bipartite ERGM of directorships, with structural,*
actor-relation, and actor-relation interaction effects

parameter	estimates (SEs)	
	model C	model D
	structural effects and director and corporation attribute effects	structural effects, attribute effects, and company-director attribute interactions
Purely structural effects		
Edge [L]	−2.14 (0.22)*	−1.98 (0.24)*
Director popularity [K-Sp]	−4.90 (0.23)*	−4.91 (0.23)*
Corporation popularity [K-Sa]		
Director 4-cycles [K-Cp]		
Corporation 4-cycles [K-Ca]	−0.05 (0.02)*	−0.05 (0.02)*
Actor-relation effects		
Corporation (a) attribute main effects		
rA_Conservative		−0.17 (0.18)
rA_Bipartisan		0.01 (0.08)
rA_Australian	0.28 (0.09)*	0.25 (0.10)*
rA_Listed	0.78 (0.11)*	0.67 (0.12)*
rA_Regulated		0.01 (0.07)
rA_Revenue	0.17 (0.06)*	0.13 (0.07)
Director (p) attribute main effects		
rP_Wealth	−0.87 (0.48)	−0.59 (0.52)
rP_Club	1.08 (0.19)*	−0.06 (0.29)
rP_School	1.37 (0.24)*	0.82 (0.34)*
Interaction effects		
rAP_Revenue&Wealth		−0.55 (0.37)
rAP_Australian&Club		0.34 (0.27)
rAP_Listed&Club		0.65 (0.27)*
rAP_Regulated&Club		0.54 (0.15)*
rAP_Revenue&Club		0.36 (0.17)*
rAP_Bipartisan&School		0.44 (0.20)*
rAP_Listed&School		0.53 (0.29)

* Significant effect

listed corporations and bipartisan donor corporations. As is discussed in
the next section, these patterns of interaction suggest very different social
and socializing roles for these two upper-class institutions.

In line with the bivariate analysis, there remains sharp contrast between
the high numbers of directorships held by directors belonging to elite clubs
or from elite schools and the low number of positions held by wealthy
directors. There is a negative but nonsignificant relationship between
wealthy directors and fewer directorships in model C. In model D, there is
a negative but nonsignificant interaction of wealth and revenue. Although

both effects are nonsignificant, they are both negative, and importantly, we would expect wealth to be positively related to directorships.

20.5 Discussion

Substantively, there are three major lessons about the nature of the "capital" that directors wield in the corporate boardroom and broader corporate community. In this Australian sample, different forms of "capital" lead to diametrically opposed director behavior. Directors with "financial" or "physical" capital (i.e., the owners and superwealthy) have fewer directorships than would be expected for their status. They have the same, or possibly fewer, directorships than the average director of a top 248 company. The reason for this is not entirely clear. One possible mechanism is provided by Coleman's (1990/1994, 315–316) observation that physical capital is alienable, and therefore the benefits of an investment may be captured by the owner. In contrast, the social capital contained in interlocks is inherently inalienable; that is, it belongs in the relationships between people. The observed effect may be driven by a mechanism that is as simple as follows: for an owner-director, the returns of focused attention on one company are much greater than they are for any other type of director. An owner not only gains the benefits of improvement to his or her own property, but he or she can also focus attention on what is potentially the greatest loss. In contrast, a non-owning director appropriates less of his or her own work in any particular company and has *less* to lose by serving on multiple boards, particularly if one of the companies fails.

Directors with upper-class social capital appear to fulfill very different functions depending on their specific social capital. Directors with membership of exclusive businessmen's clubs appear to have a form of social capital that is much like Putnam's (2000) "bonding social capital": it is specific to a particular group of Australian, regulated, large, and public listed corporations. Outside this circle, it provides little advantage (no main effect). However, within this grouping, it provides a substantial social bond, integrating a particularly important grouping of the Australian corporate elite. Undoubtedly, the specificity of this form of social capital arises partly because of its constant renewal. Clubs are not a place you graduate from at age 18. Rather you join them at 40 or 50 years of age, and they introduce you to a specific active social world that has a physical location, events, membership lists, and culture.

In contrast, elite private school attendance appears to provide a much more diffuse and generalized form of social capital, and one that is in many ways akin to Putnam's (2000) "bridging social capital." Private school attendance is much less specific to a particular corporate community. The main effect of school attendance on directorships is still highly significant once interactions are taken into account. The specific corporations that school attendance interacts with are very general categories of corporations: bipartisan corporations are not a community, but rather a set of more politically active corporations that potentially need directors with social capital. Thus, the relationship between bipartisan corporations and school graduates could simply reflect a form of mutually beneficial exchanges taking place between more "political" corporations and more "reputable" directors. Similarly, public listed companies have concerns with public and investor relations. Director social capital can add prestige to a public company that would be completely superfluous for a private corporation with two shareholders. The view of school attendance as "bridging social capital" is further supported by the lack of a significant relationship with other corporate attributes: they are equally likely to serve on foreign or Australian boards, small or large companies, and companies with high government regulation or those with little.

Methodologically, there are a number of important findings. We note that with this data set, we had trouble fully modeling the purely structural features of bipartite networks. Specifically, 4-cycles were an issue. Nonetheless, we found substantial purely structural network effects that could not be effectively accounted for by the incorporation of director and company attribute effects into an ERGM. There are tendencies toward dispersal of degree and the generation of 4-cycles, which require purely structural network effects to properly model director networks. The importance of this finding is that it provides evidence that directorships cannot simply be explained by the attributes of companies and directors. Methods that focus only on director and company attributes may overestimate the impact of these attributes and therefore underplay some of the purely structural social processes through which directorships emerge.

21

Comparing Networks: Structural Correspondence between Behavioral and Recall Networks

Eric Quintane

21.1 Relationship between Behavior and Recall

The question of whether we, as individuals, are reliable sources of information concerning our behavior has been debated for many decades in social network research. Because most research in this field uses individuals' recollection of their behavior as a source of data (Marsden, 2005), assessing the reliability of our informants is not a trivial issue. This study focuses on comparing individuals' actual behavior to their recall of that behavior. As such, I am not concerned with perception-based networks (e.g., friendship or trust) because they do not have to be related to the occurrence or frequency of a specific behavior. The reliability of individual recollection is, however, critical for research that relies on an accurate account of interactions between individuals. For example, the study of the diffusion of information relies on the account by informants of their actual communication behavior – was the message transmitted? – and not just on the interactions that they can recall.

Existing research comparing behavior and recall has mainly sought to understand how and why recall and behavior differ from each other at the individual or dyadic level. The BKS studies – a series of articles published by Bernard, Killworth, and Sailer (1979, 1981, 1982) – are the main body of work in this strand of research. They made an early attempt to assess the reliability of informants by observing the communication behavior of several groups of actors in different contexts and comparing it to the interactions that the actors reported during the same period of time. Their findings showed that respondents had a poor recollection of whom they communicated with and the frequency of these communications (Bernard et al., 1979), as well as questioned the reliability of social network data collected based on respondents' recall (Bernard & Killworth, 1977; Killworth & Bernard, 1976).

Further research suggests that specific factors may affect individuals' recall of their interactions. Freeman, Romney, and Freeman (1987) showed that the difference between individuals' behaviors and their recall in the BKS studies could be explained by biases in individuals' recollection patterns. They found that respondents had a tendency to remember their interactions based on stable and repetitive patterns. Hence, individuals will be more likely to remember others with whom they interact regularly, even though they might not have interacted during a specific observation period. A corollary conclusion is that individuals tend to forget infrequent communication episodes (Tversky & Kahneman, 1974). Although respondents are more likely to report interactions that are frequent and regular, other factors contribute to making certain interactions stand out in an individual's memory. In an organizational context, hierarchical status has been shown to affect individuals' recollection of their interactions. Webster (1995) reported that respondents with similar status tended to remember reciprocal interactions more than if they had different hierarchical status. This indicates that certain attributes of the relationship (e.g., frequency, regularity of behaviors) and of the individuals (e.g., seniority) can alter the patterns of recall of respondents.

My approach in this chapter is to explore whether networks based on the observation of a behavior and networks based on the recall of this behavior are structurally different. More specifically, I examine whether actors' recall relates to the behavioral networks, and if it does, whether any differences between recall and behavior are systematic.

21.2 Data and Measures

The data collected by Bernard and Killworth (1977) and Bernard et al. (1979) comprise two networks (behavioral and recall) of the communication frequency of four different groups of individuals. Table 21.1 provides a basic description of these networks. The Ham, Off, and Tech data sets were collected by Bernard and Killworth (1977), and the Frat data set was collected by Bernard et al. (1979). The original data files (i.e., before transformation) for these networks are part of the public data sets included in UCINET (Borgatti, Everett, & Freeman, 2006).

21.2.1 Description of Networks

Table 21.1 provides an overview of the four data sets. For each data set, the behavioral network captures the frequency of dyadic interactions, and the recall network presents actors' recall of these interactions. The recall information for the Off and Tech networks was obtained using a ranking procedure: each actor was given a deck of cards containing the names of

Table 21.1. *Overview of four different networks*

	FRAT	HAM	OFF	TECH
No. of actors	58	44	40	34
Context	College fraternity	Amateur radio operators	Social science research firm	Graduate program in technology
Communication mode	Face to face	Radio	Face to face	Face to face
Method of observation	Observer (15 min)	Continuous monitor	Observer (30 min)	Observer (15 min)
Ranked/scaled	Scaled (1–9)	Scaled (1–5)	Ranked	Ranked
Thresholds K (recall/behavioral)	5/5	9/7	8/8	8/8

the other employees and was asked to rank the cards according to "how often they talked to others in the office during a normal working day" (Bernard et al., 1979, 194). For the Frat and Ham networks, each actor was asked to give a rating of his or her interactions with the other participants on a scale from 1 to 5 for the Frat network and 1 to 9 for the Ham network. Additional information can be obtained from Bernard et al.

21.2.2   Data Transformations

For comparability purposes, I transformed the behavioral and recall networks into binary and symmetric matrices using the procedure explained by Bernard et al. (1979). I used the dichotomization thresholds (K) indicated in Bernard at al. (198, table 2) and reported in Table 21.1. For the recall networks, ranked data were dichotomized by allocating 1 to all dyads with a value inferior or equal to K and 0 to all others, and scaled data were dichotomized by allocating 1 to all dyads greater than or equal to K and 0 to all other values. For the behavioral networks, the frequency of interaction had to be ranked from the most frequent to the least frequent before it could be dichotomized. I obtained density results that are similar to those reported by Bernard et al.[1] After having dichotomized the networks, I symmetrized them such that if at least one tie is present in one dyad, then the edge is said to be present (Bernard et al.).

21.2.3   Model Specification

I begin by modeling each network individually because the univariate models serve as a baseline to understand the changes in significance levels

---

[1] There is a difference between Bernard et al.'s (1979) density of the behavioral network of the Off data set and my results. It can be explained by the fact that Bernard et al. made some undocumented judgment calls during the ranking procedure of the behavioral data.

in the next stages of modeling (models with dyadic covariate and multivariate models), as well as providing information about the structure of the networks. Then, I model the recall networks using the behavioral networks as a covariate, effectively asking the question of the extent to which recall deviates from a dyadic association to behavior. Finally, I model the recall and behavioral networks together (multivariate networks) to provide further insights into their patterns of association and into the structural differences between the two.

Because there are no actor attributes in the data, the exponential random graph models (ERGMs) presented here focus only on structural parameters for these nondirected networks. A similar set of parameters has been used for all networks in order to improve the comparability of the results. Most models include an *Edge* parameter, although for some networks the density was fixed to assist convergence (see the comments about conditional estimation in Section 12.4.2). For the sparser networks, the inclusion of an *Isolates* parameter in the model was needed. The alternating *Star* parameter [A-S] is included to control for the degree distribution in the networks; in some models, inclusion of a Markov 2-star parameter assisted convergence. The *Path Closure* parameter [AT-T] and the counterpart *Multiple Connectivity* parameter [A2P-T] were also used. For the covariate models, the behavioral network was included as a dyadic attribute (covariate edge) in each model (see Chapter 8). Finally, in the multivariate models (see Chapter 10), different configurations representing the association between networks have been included. Similar to the covariate models, the inclusion of the *Edge B-R* parameter captures the extent to which the two networks align at a dyadic level. Then, more complex forms of associations are explored. Alternating triangle *AT-BRB* (see Figure 10.4 in Chapter 10) represents the extent to which two individuals who communicate with the same alters tend to report communication with each other. In contrast, alternating triangle *AT-RBR* captures the extent to which individuals who recall communicating with the same alters tend to communicate together.

21.3   Results

21.3.1   Visualization

A visual examination of the networks in Figure 21.1 highlights differences not only between data sets (e.g., Frat, Ham) but also between networks in the same data set. For example, the Frat behavioral network has a very dense core, which does not seem to exist in the recall network. Similarly, the Tech recall network is almost separated into two distinct components, which is much less obvious when looking at the Tech behavioral network.

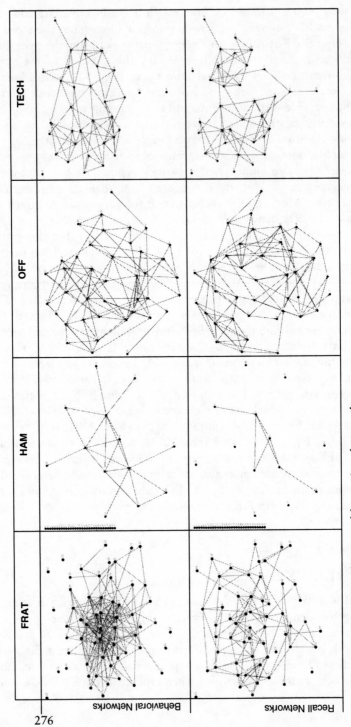

Figure 21.1. Visualization of four pairs of networks.

Table 21.2. *Descriptive statistics of four networks for behavior and recall*

	FRAT		HAM		OFF		TECH	
	behavior	recall	behavior	recall	behavior	recall	behavior	recall
Size	58		44		40		34	
Density	0.12	0.064	0.022	0.0074	0.13	0.13	0.13	0.12
Average degree	6.79	3.65	0.95	0.38	4.95	5.15	4.47	4.12
Clustering	0.61	0.35	0.68	0.58	0.25	0.38	0.46	0.43
Centralization	46	13	17	9	8	8	11	12
QAP correlations	0.29		0.46		0.32		0.34	

21.4 Preliminary Statistical Analysis

The key statistics presented in Table 21.2 provide little evidence of systematic differences between the behavioral and recall networks. For the Frat and Ham data sets, the recall network is much sparser than the behavioral network, whereas the densities are similar for the two networks in the Off and Tech data sets. QAP correlations confirm the moderate level of correspondence in the global structure of the networks that Bernard et al. (1979) found at the actor level.

21.5 Univariate Models

Table 21.3 presents eight univariate ERGMs. Each model gives an indication of the local processes occurring in each network, independently of the other networks. Goodness-of-fit (GOF) statistics for these models are generally very good: for the Frat behavior network, some clique counts had a GOF statistic higher than 2 (but less than 4), indicating that the model has difficulties reproducing the very dense region in the center of the network.

In the Ham data set, the low density of the recall network is reflected in the substantial *Isolates* parameter. Because of the low density, there were some difficulties in getting convergence, so the model here differs from the others (similarly, the connectivity parameter was not included for the Off behavior network to assist convergence). A consistent result across networks is the substantial *Closure* parameter (apart from the Ham networks, which can be explained by the difficulty for triangles to emerge in very sparse networks), linked to the nonsignificant or negative *Multiple Connectivity* parameter. This suggests that a key driving force behind the structure of these networks is a closure process. In other words, both behavioral and recall networks are based on the tendency for individuals to interact in denser grouplike structures, either as a behavior or as a recall

Table 21.3. *Univariate ERGM parameter estimates (SEs) for four data sets*

	FRAT		HAM		OFF		TECH	
	behavior	recall	behavior	recall	behavior	recall	behavior	recall
Edge	*Fixed density*	−2.68* (0.83)	*Fixed density*	*Fixed density*	1.51 (2.39)	−4.06* (1.42)	−4.50* (1.13)	−3.44* (1.19)
2−Stars	0.13* (0.02)			0.68 (0.64)		−0.27* (0.11)	−0.30* (0.14)	−0.15 (0.13)
Isolates			−2.94 (2.30)	3.93* (1.59)				
Star [A-S]	−0.69* (0.29)	−0.01 (0.42)	2.88* (1.34)		−1.15 (0.66)	−1.82* (0.67)	1.42* (0.63)	0.95 (0.62)
Path closure [AT-T]	1.07* (0.28)	0.87* (0.14)	0.98 (0.87)		0.48* (0.13)	0.54* (0.13)	0.88* (0.23)	0.78* (0.20)
Connectivity [A2P-T]	0.10* (0.02)	−0.16 (0.10)	0.24 (0.14)			−0.46* (0.07)	−0.20 (0.13)	−0.31* (0.12)

* Significant effect

of that behavior. However, because the behavioral and recall networks are modeled independently, we do not know whether the same dyads are implicated in the building of these groups in the recall and behavioral networks. The *Star* parameter is much less consistent across the networks. Here, the most important role of the parameter is to control for the degree distribution, and it is not surprising that degree-based effects may differ across the different networks. The multiple connectivity parameter ensures that the closure mechanisms can be properly interpreted.

The models indicate that recall and behavior incorporate a closure process reflecting actors' propensity to interact in groups and to recall their interactions based on group formation patterns. A key question for the rest of the analysis is to understand whether these closure processes operate independently, or whether the association between networks can explain the closure effects.

21.6 Models of Recall Networks with Behavioral Networks as Covariates

In the four models in Table 21.4, we model the recall networks using the behavioral networks as a covariate. In effect, we calculate the dyadic association between recall and behavioral networks, and examine the remaining structure in the recall networks. In other words, we ask the question, "Given the structure of behavioral interactions, how well do people remember these interactions?" If there are no substantial structural effects in the models given the behavioral network, apart from an

Table 21.4. *Parameter estimates (SEs) for four recall networks (with behavioral network included as covariate network)*

	FRAT	HAM	OFF	TECH
Edge	−1.54 (0.88)	Fixed density	−4.67 (1.33)*	−3.06 (0.90)*
Isolates		3.56 (1.71)*		
2-Stars			−0.25 (0.11)*	
Star [A-S]	−0.41 (0.36)	−0.83 (1.02)	1.84 (0.64)*	0.38 (0.37)
Closure [AT-T]	0.73 (0.14)*		0.50 (0.14)*	0.61 (0.19)*
Connectivity [A2P-T]	−0.19 (0.07)*		−0.45 (0.07)*	−0.30 (0.10)*
Covariate edge (behavioral)	2.20 (0.24)*	6.38 (2.88)*	2.06 (0.23)*	2.27 (0.25)*

* Significant effect

association with the covariate, then we infer that there is no particular bias in recall.

The *Covariate Edge (Behavioral)* parameter is an indication of the degree to which the behavioral and recall networks correspond. For all data sets, there is a substantial positive association between the behavioral and recall networks. Once the correspondence between the two networks is controlled by the covariate edge parameter, the remaining parameters indicate the remaining structure of the recall network not explained by the strong dyadic association with behavior.

The negative *Edge* parameters (Frat, Tech, Off) suggest a tendency against actors' reporting ties not observed in their behavior unless they are involved in more complex patterns of recall. The *Star* parameter is significant only for the Off network. Because the star parameter obtained in the univariate model of the recall network was negative, the fact that the parameter becomes positive (and significant) once the behavioral covariate is included indicates that there is substantial heterogeneity in the degree distribution of the recall network, beyond the dyadic association between behavior and recall. Taken together, the *Path Closure* and *Multiple Connectivity* parameters indicate the extent to which clustering exists in the recall networks, and is not explained by the dyadic association with behavior. Here, the results are very consistent. With the exception of the Ham network, all networks have a positive and substantial *Path Closure* parameter. This shows that there is clustering in the recall network that goes beyond the dyadic association between the recall and behavioral networks, even though this was not obvious from the use of global statistics (Table 21.2).

The covariate models show a substantial association between recall and behavior. They also suggest that when the networks do not align, it is because recall ties are embedded in complex patterns involving triangles and groups and not because actors forget isolated interactions. The corollary is that actors do report ties that go beyond those that exist in

Table 21.5. *Multivariate ERGM parameter estimates (SE) for four data sets*

	FRAT		HAM		OFF		TECH	
	behavior	recall	behavior	recall	behavior	recall	behavior	recall
Edge	*Fixed density*	*Fixed density*	*Fixed density*	*Fixed density*	1.48 (2.46)	1.14 (1.84)	−4.90* (1.22)	−3.33* (1.21)
2-Stars	0.15* (0.02)	0.01 (0.16)	0.38* (0.10)	0.51 (0.40)			−0.45* (0.17)	−0.08 (0.15)
Star [A-S]	−0.65* (0.28)	−0.22 (0.46)			−1.28 (0.68)	−1.46* (0.51)	1.30* (0.63)	0.55 (0.63)
Closure [AT-T]	0.99* (0.26)	0.81* (0.17)			0.34* (0.16)	0.95* (0.18)	0.75* (0.25)	0.32 (0.24)
Connectivity [A2P-T]	−0.09* (0.02)	−0.06 (0.17)					0.04 (0.15)	−0.29 (0.15)
Edge B-R	2.53* (0.31)		6.70 (3.39)		2.11* (0.29)		1.64* (0.37)	
Isolates B-R			1.44 (0.88)					
3-Star BRR	−0.02* (0.01)							
AT-BRB	0.01 (0.21)		3.26* (1.58)		0.25 (0.25)		−0.15 (0.38)	
AT-RBR	0.25 (0.17)		−0.71 (0.70)		−0.04 (0.28)		1.07* (0.37)	

* Significant effect

their behavior, and these ties occur within complex grouping patterns. Hence, there is evidence that actors' biases in recall suggest more closure than is actually observed in behavior.

21.7   Multivariate Models

In this final set of models (Table 21.5), I estimate behavior and recall simultaneously. The difference with the preceding models is twofold. First, the multivariate models enable the exploration of more complex patterns of association between the networks (e.g., AT-BRB, AT-RBR). Second, because recall and behavior are modeled at the same time, a direct comparison can be made of the structure of each network as it departs from the associations between the networks. As before, the differences in model specifications assisted with convergence. For the low-density Ham networks, isolates parameters were included, and some higher-order within-network effects were excluded, within-network Markov 2-stars assisted with modeling the degree distribution in some networks, and the Frat network model included a multivariate Markov 3-star effect.

The *Edge B-R (Behavioral-Recall)* parameter provides information about the extent to which behavior and recall networks align with each other. The results here are similar to those of the covariate edge parameter in Table 21.4; they show that there is a substantial alignment between the two types of networks. The parameter is strong and significant for the Tech, Off, and Frat networks, and it is almost significant for the Ham network. To the direct alignment between the networks, these models add other potential forms of alignment. For the Tech network, we see that the *AT-RBR* is significant. This indicates a strong propensity for actors who behaviorally interact to recall interactions with the same third alters. These tendencies exist beyond the alignment between the two networks represented by the *Edge B-R* parameter. For the Ham networks, it is the *AT-BRB* alternating triangle parameter that is significant. It suggests a tendency for two individuals who interacted with the same alters to recall an interaction between themselves. For the Frat networks, the *3-Star BRR* parameter is significant and negative, indicating that there is a tendency against individuals who are simultaneously central in both networks. Therefore, behavioral and recall networks have a substantial level of alignment not only as a direct dyadic association but also as part of more complex patterns of closure.

Beyond the measures of alignment, the remaining parameters enable us to examine the structural differences between the networks. For the Tech recall network, we see that the closure and connectivity parameters are now nonsignificant (they were significant in the single and covariate models). The closure and connectivity processes are explained by the *AT-RBR* (and the *Edge B-R*), which gives us more insight about the nature of the difference between recall and behavior than the covariate model. Specifically, the structure in actors' recall is explicable once their behavior is fully taken into account in terms of associations between behavior and recall (including the triadic association). The opposite is not true: the existence of significant parameters in the Tech behavioral network shows that there are processes within actors' behavior that are not well captured by their recall of that behavior. These processes include additional degree distribution (Star) and closure effects. In other words, behavior in this multivariate network seems to largely explain the structure of recall, but not vice versa, suggesting that behavior is an antecedent to recall.

The remaining models can be interpreted in similar ways but present slightly different conclusions. In the Off networks, the closure parameter is significant for both networks, indicating that there are closure effects in both behavioral and recall networks not captured by the alignment between the two networks. The model for the Frat networks is similar: closure is significant and positive in both networks. In the Ham network, only the existence of 2-stars in the behavioral network is not explained by the association between the two networks.

The multivariate models show a substantial level of dyadic alignment between the behavior and recall networks. Yet, there is also evidence for additional structure within behavioral and recall networks that is not explained by this dyadic association. We also find that in several cases, the two networks are intertwined in closure processes that involve both recall and behavior.

21.8   Discussion

This chapter uses several methods to explore the ways in which the structure of recall-based networks may systematically depart from the structure of behavioral networks. The aim is to understand whether different social processes can be identified as producing the structure of behavioral and recall networks. The results confirm the findings of the BKS studies to some extent. Consistent with the BKS studies, we find that the structures of behavioral and recall networks are different. Actors do not recall all their interactions, and they mention interactions that did not take place. The results also show that there is a substantial amount of similarity between the networks. Recall follows behavior strongly. This result is consistent with the BKS studies even though it was not emphasized in the original articles. The chapter nevertheless goes beyond the analysis in the BKS studies as it shows that discrepancies between behavior and recall networks occur when these are part of complex structural patterns. More specifically, it is mainly the closure process that follows different logics in both behavior and recall. Yet, in some networks, this closure process is also a source of alignment between the networks because actors' behavior and recall of that behavior relate to each other to form multivariate triangles.

As such, there is a systematic difference between behavior and recall, and it is mainly related to the closure process. I find that in most cases, the closure that exists in the recall networks is not completely explained by the closure found in the behavioral networks. Finally, I find that in two of the data sets, a closure process involving both networks also explains the patterns of associations between recall and behavior. Together, these results provide evidence that a purely dyadic explanation of the differences between behavioral and recall networks may be limited.

The current explanation of the lack of association between recall and behavioral network is proposed by Freeman et al. (1987), who posit that recall is based on stable patterns of relationships that may differ from day-to-day interactions. It is rooted in cognitive information processing theory and highlights the role of informant's mental schemas in their recall of events and interactions. However, interactions are considered as dyadic units of analysis, independent from each other. In other words,

Freeman et al. assume that respondents' recall is based on the frequency and stability of interactions between the respondent and his or her alters. It does not explicitly consider that an individual's recall of his or her interactions with an alter may depend on the interactions that these two individuals have with third parties. This calls for a more precise set of explanations that include social influence and group dynamics. The work on cognitive social structures (Kilduff et al., 2008; Kilduff & Krackhardt, 2008; Krackhardt, 1987) points in that direction by discussing cognitive biases at the triadic level in individuals' perceptions of social relations. In the same vein, Koehly and Pattison (2005) also found that individuals' recall may be subject to a structural bias at a triadic level (i.e., more closure).

As such, the results of this chapter add further evidence to the finding that actors perceive their social environment in a structured way. The recall of an interaction is linked to the existence of this interaction itself, but also to the extent to which an interaction is embedded within a group-like structure and provides closure to other interactions (which leads to an exaggeration of triads). In other words, it is not only stable relationships that actors recall, but also stable relationships that are embedded in closed social groupings. Further research following this line of investigation would provide additional insights in the relation between recall and behavior by analyzing directed data, which would enable distinctions to be made between different closure processes (transitivity, popularity, activity, cyclic), as described in Chapter 6.

Section IV

Future

22

Modeling Social Networks: Next Steps

Pip Pattison and Tom Snijders

In this final chapter, we review the progress made in modeling social networks using exponential random graph models (ERGMs) and identify some important questions that remain to be addressed, along with possible ways of approaching them. We also consider the development of ERGMs in the context of broader modeling developments for social networks.

22.1   Distinctive Features of ERGMs

As the preceding chapters demonstrate, ERGMs offer four features that are likely to be attractive to social scientists who are interested in deepening our understanding of social networks and the social processes associated with them.

First, and perhaps most important, ERGMs conceptualize social networks as the outcome of social processes that are dynamic, interactive, and local. They are therefore well aligned with many contemporary theoretical views about the evolution of social networks (e.g., Emirbayer, 1997), even though there are a variety of distinct views about the precise social mechanisms involved (e.g., Jackson, 2008; Pattison, Robins, & Kashima, 2008; Rivera, Soderstrom, & Uzzi, 2010; Snijders, 2006). ERGMs give expression to propositions about the outcomes of the dynamic, interactive, local processes that drive network formation and allow us to quantify and assess the observable regularities in social network structure implied by these propositions. Moreover, these assessments are set within a clear statistical framework. Even though there may not necessarily be a fine-grained match between hypothesized theoretical mechanisms and the form of an ERGM, or the means to explore model assumptions in detail (as we discuss later in the chapter), ERGMs nonetheless provide a valuable new capacity to demonstrate potential

287

links between hypothesized network processes and observable network regularities. In brief, they provide social scientists with access to a statistical approach for exploring regularities in social networks and describing these regularities with greater precision.

The second major feature of ERGMs relative to alternative approaches for modeling social networks is a new capacity for models to reproduce many important observed network characteristics, including global network features that are not parameterized as effects in the model. This advantage has now been demonstrated on a number of occasions and provides some confidence that the approach that ERGMs afford to the specification of local dependencies is an effective one (Hunter & Handcock, 2006; Robins et al., 2007; Robins, Pattison, & Wang, 2009; Snijders et al., 2006). This is a particularly noteworthy feature of this class of models, and it supports the assumption of endogeneity in tie formation processes. Indeed, it is often impressive that models can reproduce a variety of characteristics of observed features of a network with a relatively small number of explicitly parameterized network effects in the model; Goodreau (2007), for example, provides an excellent illustration. The nature and extent of local clustering among nodes, the general distribution of node-to-node connectivity, and variations in local connectivity of each network node, are among the aspects of network structure that can often be satisfactorily reproduced (Hunter, 2007; Hunter & Handcock, 2006; Snijders et al., 2006).

Third, ERGMs can be applied in flexible ways to many different types of network or relational data. They have been developed for directed and nondirected networks and for bipartite and multirelational networks (Robins, Pattison, & Wang, 2009; Wang, Sharpe, Robins, & Pattison, 2009; see also Chapters 6, 10, 16, 20, and 21). In each case, a flexible approach can be adopted to building plausible model specification that rely on natural underlying graph-theoretical local dependencies, as explained further later in this chapter. More generally, ERGMs can be developed for relational observations among multiple types of nodes and multiple types of ties. It is straightforward to add a variety of node-level and dyadic covariates, including spatial and other relational covariates (e.g., Daraganova et al., 2012; Robins, Elliott, & Pattison, 2001; see Chapter 8). Furthermore, the general framework used to construct models for relational data can also be used to construct models for node-level characteristics in mutual dependence with network ties (Robins, Pattison, & Elliott, 2001). Chapters 9 and 18 illustrate application of this general approach to these various types of relational data.

Fourth, because ERGMs can be understood as the outcome of dynamic, interactive, local processes that drive network formation, it is possible to assess these processes more directly when longitudinal observations are available. As Chapters 11 and 19 illustrate, these ERGM-like models provide a more direct approach to understanding tie formation processes and are a valuable complement to the less direct approach for cross-sectional data. This approach is the tie-oriented analogue of the actor-oriented models for longitudinal network data of Snijders (2001) and Snijders, van de Bunt, and Steglich (2010). Through the increased application of models to longitudinal observations, we stand to learn a great deal about the applicability and robustness of the stronger assumptions we make in cross-sectional applications.

Of course, it would be wrong to give the impression that we have reached the point where ERGM model fitting and model comparison are straightforward. Rather, it is not always easy to choose and fit an appropriate set of competing model specifications given some relevant data, nor can we necessarily make straightforward choices in selecting a preferred model. A number of important modeling challenges remain, and we consider several of these in this chapter. We first address the important topic of model specification, and then more general issues of model evaluation and comparison.

22.2   Model Specification

As the history of ERGM model development has revealed, the choice of a specific model form is particularly important (e.g., see Handcock, 2003; Snijders, 2002; Snijders et al., 2006). Radically misspecified models may not only fail to reproduce vital features of the observed network but may also be inestimable because the equations characterizing the maximum likelihood estimator (or other estimators) are satisfied only by random graph distributions that are effectively a mixture of complete/almost complete graphs (i.e., with density 1 or very close to 1) and very sparse graphs (Robins et al., 2007; Snijders, 2002). These distributions do not put high probability on graphs that are similar to the observed network, and although they formally solve the likelihood equation, they do not represent the data (as in the example of Figures 6.5 and 6.6 in Chapter 6). They are at the boundary of the part of the parameter space where the misspecified model is near-degenerate. By a *near-degenerate* distribution, we mean one that places high probability on a relatively small number of graphs in the model state space, and zero or close-to-zero probability on the rest (Handcock, 2003). We now know that when the Markov chain Monte Carlo (MCMC) algorithms (Chapter 12) for maximum likelihood (ML) or Bayesian estimation of an ERGM in a given specification fail to converge, this most likely is a sign not of algorithmic deficiencies but of the inability of the specified model to represent the observed network. As a result, model specification is vital. Indeed, it was only when new realization-dependent specifications (Pattison & Robins, 2002) were developed that genuine progress in developing plausible ERGMs was made (Hunter & Handcock, 2006; Snijders et al., 2006). These more recent developments have led to gradually improving model specifications that reproduce, with increasing accuracy, many important local and global features of human social networks. The inability of the more restrictive Markov specification (Chapter 6) to represent most observed networks in the social sciences permits the conclusion that the corresponding conditional independence assumption is not usually met in social reality.

Yet, it is important to recognize that the endogenous tie formation processes reflected in many ERGM specifications are not always easy to separate from one another, or from the effects of unobserved exogenous variables. For example, observed clustering could be explained in part by endogenous closure processes, in part by a degree assortativity process, and in part by homophily processes involving observed or unobserved node attributes. To tease these possible processes apart, it is important to use models that can reflect the various possible processes at work and make careful comparisons among them. As in all modeling contexts, it is also ideal to build models that have a strong basis in theory and, where possible, the understanding that has emerged from use in related empirical circumstances. It is likewise important to obtain data on important covariates and use them in model building.

A second consideration is the value of various approaches to limiting the number of network effects in the model specification, which is desirable in view of Occam's razor. One fundamental assumption has been to equate potential model parameters when they correspond to isomorphic network configurations, thereby obtaining homogeneous network models, such as those described by Frank and Strauss (1986). As explained in Chapter 7, the consequence of this assumption is that relevant network statistics are counts of these (isomorphic) configurations in the network, for example, the number of triangles, 4-cycles, or 5-stars. The importance of counts of general triadic configurations to express local dependencies in social networks was noted already by Holland and Leinhardt (1976). Of course, where interactions of these effects with observed node- or dyad-level covariates is anticipated, such interactions can be readily incorporated, as illustrated in Chapters 8, 14, and 17.

A further approach has been to assume specific relationships among related network effects, for example, to assume that the parameters for 2-stars, 3-stars, 4-stars, and so on, are related to one another in a particular way. This approach yields a reduced number of model effects, each of which describes some property of a family of homogeneous network effects. For example, the construction of so-called alternating statistics (Snijders et al., 2006), or, equivalently, geometrically weighted statistics (Hunter & Handcock, 2006), has led to models with a small number of network effects that have an impressive capacity to yield effective network model specifications. In the case of the star statistics, for example, we obtain a single effect reflecting the dispersion of the degree distribution rather than a family of effects that allow the degree distribution to be described in full. Although this latter strategy is effective, often at the cost of a large number of parameters, it is not always clear when it is a useful approach, or when and how more subtle characterizations of the associated families of statistics should be sought.

In the following sections, we describe some of the approaches being taken, first to separate and characterize different possible endogenous processes, and second, to explore endogenous processes in the presence of unobserved exogenous explanatory variables.

22.2.1 Dependence Hierarchy

Pattison et al. (2011a) described a systematic framework for characterizing the dependence assumptions that may underlie ERGM model specifications (see also Wang, Pattison, & Robins, in press, for a dependence hierarchy for bipartite networks). The framework provides an overarching conceptual structure within which assumptions about dependence structures can be located and hence compared. Because each dependence hypothesis is associated with a set of corresponding network statistics, the framework also yields a classification of network effects, as we describe further here.

In developing the framework, Pattison et al. (2011a) observed that the various dependence assumptions for a pair of tie-variables X_{ij} and X_{kl} that have been proposed to date may be differentiated in two distinct ways. These two distinctions serve to characterize the graph-theoretical proximity of the two node pairs $\{i, j\}$ and $\{j, l\}$ for which the tie-variables X_{ij} and X_{kl} are allowed to be conditionally[1] dependent.

The first distinction concerns the "form" of proximity among the two node pairs, and the second concerns the "distance" in terms of which proximity is judged. If we are judging the proximity between two single nodes, there is a straightforward choice for its characterization in terms of internode graph distance. In the case of judging the proximity of two *pairs* of nodes, though, the choice is less straightforward. For the two pairs to be judged as close, should each node in a pair have some minimum level of proximity to each node in the other pair, or should it suffice that at least one node in the first pair has some minimum level of proximity to at least one node in the second? These two possible characterizations and two intermediate forms constitute a set of the four possible proximity forms proposed by Pattison et al. (2011a):

---

[1] The word "conditionally" here refers to conditioning on all other tie-variables but these two.

- Each of the two nodes i and j is within proximity p of each of the two nodes k and l (and, hence, it is also the case that each of the two nodes k and l is within proximity p of each of the two nodes i and j).
- Each of the two nodes i and j is within proximity p of at least one of the two nodes k and l, *and*, symmetrically, each of the two nodes k and l is within proximity p of at least one of the two nodes i and j.
- Each of the two nodes i and j is within proximity p of at least one of the two nodes k and l, *or*, alternatively, each of the two nodes k and l is within proximity p of at least one of the two nodes i and j.
- At least one of the two nodes i and j is within proximity p of at least one of the two nodes k and l (and, hence, it is also the case that at least one of the two nodes k and l is within proximity p of at least one of the two nodes i and j).

Pattison et al. (2011a) referred to these four forms of proximity at the value p as strict inclusion (SI_p), inclusion (I_p), partial inclusion (PI_p), and distance (D_p), respectively. As they also demonstrated, these four forms are increasingly general in the sense that if any of the conditions in the preceding list holds, then so do all those conditions that follow it in the list. Moreover, for any specific form, increasing p also leads to an increasingly general model because if the condition holds for a given value of p, then it also holds for all higher values. These two distinctions therefore define a two-dimensional hierarchy of assumptions for the circumstances under which the ties X_{ij} and X_{kl} are presumed to be conditionally dependent. The hierarchy is represented in Figure 22.1.

It should be noted that the condition SI_0 is degenerate and therefore omitted from consideration because it can only hold if all four nodes are identical. In addition, the conditions I_0 and PI_0 are identical since each implies that the pair of nodes $\{i,j\}$ is identical to the pair $\{k,l\}$ and hence that tie-variables are conditionally independent unless they coincide. This latter requirement corresponds, when the homogeneity assumption is added, to the Bernoulli model.

The various dependence assumptions described in detail in Chapters 6 and 7 and elsewhere in the literature may be classified according to this hierarchy:

- Dyad independence is the condition I_0 or PI_0 as just noted (Erdös & Renyi, 1959; Holland & Leinhardt, 1981).
- Markov dependence is the condition D_0 (Frank & Strauss, 1986).
- Social circuit dependence is the condition SI_1 (Snijders, 2001).
- Three-path dependence is the condition D_1 (Pattison & Robins, 2002).

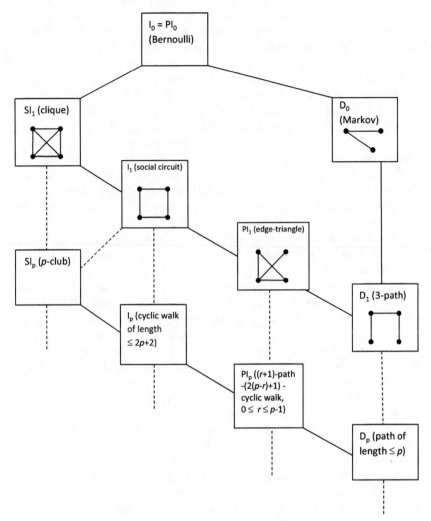

Figure 22.1. Hierarchy of dependence structures.

- The edge-triangle model is associated with the condition PI_1 (Robins, Pattison, Snijders, & Wang, 2009).
- The concept of "component independence," defined by Snijders (2010a), is equivalent to the condition D_{n-1} for a network on n nodes.

All but the first two of these forms of dependence give rise to realization-dependent models (Baddeley & Möller, 1989) in the sense that the conditional dependence of two tie-variables X_{ij} and X_{kl} depends on the presence or absence of other ties that are close to the node pairs, $\{i,j\}$ and $\{k,l\}$.

In these models, therefore, as a new tie is realized, so it potentially gives rise to new conditional dependencies within a neighborhood and hence, in turn, to altered probabilities of ties in the neighborhood.

The last two conditions were briefly described in Chapter 6 (see Figure 6.13) but deserve some further discussion here. The "edge-triangle" model arises from the PI_1 assumption that X_{ij} and X_{kl} are conditionally dependent when both k and l have a preexisting link to either i or j or both (or, conversely, when both i and j have a preexisting link to k or l or both). As for the social circuit model, the assumption is that X_{ij} and X_{kl} are conditionally dependent when one pair of nodes is already within distance 1 of the other pair, but it is a more general condition because it is not required that this hold for both pairs of nodes simultaneously. Robins, Pattison, Snijders, and Wang (2009) observed that the edge-triangle model is valuable where brokerage is of interest because it allows exploration of the dependence of "within-group" ties (e.g., the tie between nodes k and j, which have preexisting connections to another group member i) and the tie of the shared partner i to a fourth node (e.g., node l) outside the group of nodes i, k, and j. The type of social mechanism that can be reflected by this edge-triangle model includes the case where node i seeks ties outside the triple $\{i,j,k\}$ in the knowledge that nodes i, j, and k are fully connected, and therefore i might stand to gain from reaching out to a fourth node l, unconnected to j and k, that could possess social resources previously unavailable to i. A positive edge-triangle effect would suggest an association between degree and closure, and hence the potential presence of individuals whose network positions are characterized by both closure and brokerage (Burt, 2005). Of course, several alternating forms of the edge-triangle statistic may also be constructed (see Pattison et al., 2011a).

Snijders (2010a) introduced the very general "component" dependence assumption that X_{ij} and X_{kl} are conditionally dependent only if they belong to the same graph component and, thus, if there is some path connecting the pairs $\{i,j\}$ and $\{k,l\}$. In other words, dependence cannot occur across disconnected parts of the network. Snijders showed that, under this assumption, induced subgraphs on node sets disconnected from the other nodes in the network have distributions from an exponential random graph model. This is a useful result in contexts where the boundary of the network is difficult to specify clearly because it means we can reasonably confine our attention to connected components of a network.

Pattison et al. (2011a) also determined the network configurations implied by each of the preceding conditions. The network configurations in any model correspond to those subsets of tie-variables that satisfy the condition that each pair of variables is allowed to be conditionally dependent. Pattison et al. demonstrated that network configurations for the four proximity forms included various forms of cohesive subgraphs, cyclic subgraph structures, edge-triangle or edge-cycle subgraph structures, and connected subgraphs. These configurations are shown schematically in Figure 22.1 and illustrate distinct ways in which the Bernoulli model can be generalized by allowing p to increase, and/or choosing one of four increasingly more general forms of proximity.

The hierarchy provides a systematic framework for classifying potential network effects and has a number of interesting features. It suggests two natural generalizations of the Bernoulli model. One, unsurprisingly, is the class of Markov random graphs described by Frank and Strauss (1986). The other, more surprisingly perhaps, is the model SI_1, termed here the "clique" model. In this model, the sufficient statistics are cliques of any size, and the most general homogeneous version of the model has the "clique distribution" – that is the frequency distribution of cliques of various sizes – as its set of sufficient statistics. The only effects shared by the Markov and clique models are edges and triangles. The clique model is not likely to be a useful model on its own in many empirical contexts because the relatively high number of cliques often observed empirically in networks is likely to lead to degenerate clique model forms, a property shared with Markov graphs. However, clique effects may well be very important in generalizations of the clique model, such as the social circuit or edge-triangle models. Indeed, careful assessment suggests that the clique distribution for networks observed empirically is often not well characterized beyond the number of 3-cliques; therefore, paying extra attention to clique-related effects may markedly improve the fit of ERGMs in many practical situations.

The clique model also illustrates another important property of the dependence hierarchy: that it is distinct from the more customary model hierarchy for a system of discrete binary variables in which models with higher-order interactions among variables inevitably include all of the implied lower-order interactions. In contrast with the latter, clique models include lower-order interactions only when those lower-order interactions themselves correspond to cliques.

A second interesting feature of the hierarchy is that the social circuit model is a natural generalization of the clique model, and its network effects have, in conjunction with Markov effects, proved to yield a remarkably successful form of model specification (Snijders et al., 2006). The effectiveness of social circuit models suggests that there are many circumstances in which the specific forms of conditional dependence among network tie-variables characterized by SI_1 are reasonable ones. It remains to be seen in what contexts the additional effects associated with the edge-triangle model are also of value; however, as Robins, Pattison, Snijders, and Wang (2009) demonstrated, there are certainly some. It seems reasonable to speculate that edge-triangle effects are likely to be necessary in larger networks, where it will be necessary to capture the varying ways in which denser subregions of the network are themselves connected.

22.2.2   Building Model Specifications

Given the wealth of potential effects associated with the models represented in Figure 22.1, how can one reasonably approach the task of finding an effective model specification? As noted previously, theory and experience are excellent guides. It is inevitable that different types of ties may require different model forms: for example, a model for marriage ties is likely to be very different than a model for friendships in the same population. An important substantive project is to understand what systematic differences are likely to underlie forms of conditional dependence among tie-variables of the same and distinct types.

In general, the choice of model specification should be driven by a consideration of whether dependence is likely along short paths as exemplified by the Markov and social circuit specifications, or whether a different proximity condition is required. It has been rare to choose specifications entailed by stronger proximity conditions, but there may be circumstances in which dependence is only likely in the presence of all actors in some subset (e.g., in the creation of groups). As just noted, such models are likely to be degenerate or almost degenerate where highest-order clique effects are positive, but models with negative higher-order effects and positive lower-order effects may reproduce distinct grouping structures reasonably well. Of course, for most networks of interest, it is not likely that a grouping structure only is of interest, so these clique models will rarely suffice. The assumption of dependence along short paths also means the potential inclusion of effects that reflect the degree distribution.

Second, it may be useful to incorporate configurations implied by the social circuit model. This model has been remarkably successful in a number of empirical contexts, and therefore often provides a useful starting point. The inclusion of 4-cycle, 2-triangle, or alternating 2-path and triangle effects adds the capacity for dependence under a more general proximity condition and allows for more variation in the form of bicomponents[2] of the network.

Third, the edge-triangle (and, possibly, more general path-cycle) effects might be added as a means of allowing variation in the ways in which closed structures are loosely connected through bridging ties and paths.

Finally, although rarely, it may be helpful to consider 3-path effects as a means of allowing a very general diversity in the forms of connectivity within the graph, for example the capacity to capture degree-based

---

[2]   A "bicomponent" is a connected subgraph such that deleting one node still leaves the remainder connected.

assortativity or disassortativity effects. If present, 3-path effects are likely to be negative, reflecting the cost of creating ties freely in loosely connected structures.

Each basic structural form – cohesive substructures such as cliques, closed substructures such as bicomponents and cyclic walks, bridging structures such as edge-triangles and more general path-cycle structures, and weak connecting structures such as paths – may be used to create an aggregate statistic using an alternating construction, as in Snijders et al. (2006).

Experience suggests that the alternating forms of the statistics for stars (AS), 2-paths (A2P), and triangles (AT) often provide a valuable first step in modeling because the robust nature of the alternating effects means that convergence of the estimation algorithm is more likely, and hence diagnostics associated with model evaluation (see Chapters 12 and 13) are more likely to be useful. Nonetheless, although experience suggests that such statistics give rise to much more robust models than statistics based solely on small subgraph counts, there remains value in considering models based on effects corresponding to subgraph counts in addition to relevant node and edge covariates.

The model hierarchy also suggests some valuable ways of framing the evaluation of fit. For example, we might ask how well the following are characterized:

- Degree distribution
- Number of triangles
- m-Clique distribution across values of m
- m-Cycle distribution across values of m
- m-Triangle distribution across values of m
- Distribution of various edge-triangle statistics
- Geodesic path length distribution

Of course, some of these are computationally demanding and would not necessarily be of interest in the early stages of modeling, or in all circumstances. However, they nonetheless provide a useful framework for evaluating the fit of models in the manner proposed by Hunter, Goodreau, and Handcock (2008); see also Snijders et al. (2006) and described in Chapters 12 and 13.

22.2.3   Models with Latent Variables: Hybrid Forms

The various effects just described are endogenous ones, arising from dependencies among proximal tie-variables. In most cases, ties will also be dependent on covariates. Where these covariates are observed, they can be included in a straightforward way in the model, as described in Chapter 8. This is the case whether they are characteristics of the nodes or properties of dyads. Where covariates have not been observed, they may be represented as latent variables, and it is to these types of models that we now turn.

Latent variable models have been proposed to represent a variety of unobserved structural indicators in networks. For example, Nowicki and Snijders (2001) proposed a model in which ties are conditionally independent given the membership of each node in an unobserved class of a partition of the nodes, and a set of underlying propensities for nodes from one class to be tied to nodes in another. The resulting "stochastic blockmodel" assumes that the unobserved classification of nodes and their interclass probabilities of connection "explain" the network structure. Estimation of the model entails estimation of the probability of membership of each node in each of a specified number of classes, as well interclass tie probabilities. Airoldi et al. (2008) proposed a more general "mixed membership" stochastic blockmodel, in which each node can belong to multiple latent classes. Schweinberger and Snijders (2003) proposed an assignment of nodes to an unobserved ultrametric structure: in their model, ties are assumed to be conditionally independent given the matrix of ultrametric distances among nodes, equivalent to an underlying hierarchical classification of nodes. Hoff, Raftery, and Handcock (2002) proposed a similar model, but in this case assumed that ties are conditionally independent given the assignment of nodes to a location in a Euclidean space of some fixed dimension k and hence a matrix of internode distances. In a related "projection" model, variations in levels of node activity are accommodated.

In each case, where the form of the assumed latent structure is approximately correct, an elegant analysis of an observed network is obtained. Although not widely used, the same approach to model evaluation described in Chapters 12 and 13 could be used to assess the capacity of these latent variable models to explain unmodeled features of the network, such as the degree distribution, nature and extent of clustering, clique distribution, and distribution of geodesic distances. Each model yields a set of parameter estimates that defines an explicit probability model for the network. The conditional independence assumption underpinning each model means that samples of networks can be readily drawn from the model and used to construct distributions of graph statistics against which observed values of those statistics can be compared.

It is likely in many cases that endogenous effects are present in addition to the effects of unobserved exogenous variables. In such cases, the latent structure model will have a poor fit, although it still may have a very useful descriptive value. It will be of interest to specify and fit appropriate hybrid ERGM – latent space model forms. Schweinberger (2009) took some initial steps in this direction, combining a stochastic blockmodel with endogenous clustering effects constrained to occur within classes of the stochastic blockmodel. The rationale for his approach is that the classes of the blockmodel represent distinct settings within which endogenous network effects are most likely to be at play, but between which dependencies are much more limited. Koskinen (2009) also developed an approach to stochastic blockmodeling with ERGM network effects. Likewise, Handcock and colleagues developed the capacity to combine the latent space model with endogenous effects. Applications of these approaches have been rare, however, possibly because of an inherent difficulty in separating endogenous from unobserved exogenous effects. There is a likely need for better diagnostics for unmodeled endogeneity; in addition, explicit measurement of factors predictive of network ties will almost always yield more effective network models.

22.2.4   Assessing Homogeneity Assumptions

The assumption of homogeneity of network effects is a strong one, although as noted previously it is possible to include interactions among network effects and other characteristics. For example, the interaction between a dyadic characteristic and the reciprocity effect allows for variation in the size of the reciprocity effect as a function of that dyadic characteristic. Indeed, in some data sets, reciprocity is stronger outside than inside settings represented by dyadic variables, which might be interpreted as the greater relational effort, or intensity, required to maintain a tie outside a relevant social setting. Likewise, an interaction between a node characteristic and the alternating star effect provides for variation in degree dispersion across nodes that vary in the measured characteristic. In other words, this approach allows for the assessment of homogeneity of the network effect as a function of specified nodal or dyadic characteristics.

More generally, the assumption of homogeneity might be explored by a variety of means. For example, the conditional estimation strategy developed for snowball sampling designs by Pattison et al. (2011b – see also Chapter 12) or the general missing data approaches developed by Handcock and Gile (2010) or Koskinen, Robins, and Pattison (2010) could be used to obtain estimates for effects based on initial samples of nodes from different regions of the network. The variability of these estimates could then be used to assess the appropriateness of the homogeneity assumption.

22.3   General Issues for ERGMs

Five particular issues are in need of further development if ERGMs are to be more readily and effectively used in general network modeling situations. The first is that considerable art can be required to obtain a well-fitting ERGM. Part of the "art" lies in the choice of model specification, part in the choice of values driving the estimation algorithm. Although the advice set out in previous chapters describes the current state of the science of model fitting, there remains a gap between this science and model fitting in practice. In some respects, the problem is a general one for Markov chain Monte Carlo maximum likelihood estimation (MCMCMLE) – and indeed for other estimation approaches – and will be addressed by general improvements in our capacity to devise fast and effective MCMCMLE algorithms (see Chapter 12). In other respects, the problem is a consequence of specific features of ERGMs, including the often high correlations among network effects and the presence of degenerate regions of the parameter space, which are generally difficult to characterize in advance, although some progress has been made here by Schweinberger (2011).

The second is the need to know more about robustness of the results obtained by fitting ERGMs to incomplete specification of the model. Often a major focus of network studies is to test effects of covariates (e.g., actor-relation effects). To what extent are such tests compromised if some endogenous terms are omitted from the model specification, and as a consequence, the network dependencies are represented only incompletely? In particular, will we draw the wrong inference if network dependence is not taken into proper account? Very little is known about this question, and more knowledge about this will have important consequences for how careful researchers must be in model specification.

The third is that we are in need of more rigorous approaches to model comparison. Although tests of parameters as treated in Chapter 12 are basic tools for model construction and the heuristic approaches to model evaluation also described in Chapter 12 (also Hunter et al., 2008; Wang, Sharpe, Robins, & Pattison, 2009) are often helpfully diagnostic and can be used for qualitative comparisons between models, it would be valuable to be able to conduct formal model comparisons in ways that balance the goodness of fit provided by a model and the number of parameters required.

Fourth, ERGMs make many strong assumptions about the processes that give rise to observed networks, and it would also be of great value to develop approaches for diagnosing significant failure of such assumptions. For example, we assume that the network is the outcome of processes that are accurately captured by the network effects included in the model, and that the homogeneity assumptions underpinning the chosen network effects are reasonable ones. As noted previously, longitudinal observations on a network allow more direct analysis of these network processes and can therefore provide one important approach to their interrogation. Likewise, the exploration of homogeneity in network effects as described previously is a potential approach to diagnosing heterogeneity. Just as many approaches for diagnosing model adequacy have been developed for general linear models, so more general diagnostic approaches are needed for ERGMs and constitute an additional area for valuable future work.

Finally, the ERGMs described in the book are for binary random tie-variables. Although generalization to categorical tie-variables is straightforward in principle (Robins, Pattison, & Wasserman, 1999), the development of effective model parameterizations for the case of ordered or nonordered categorical tie-variables is less so and in need of careful consideration. The development of models for the case of tie-variables that are counts is also an important area for future work, given that network data often comprise counts and/or discrete volumes of transactions or interactions between pairs of nodes.

References

Abbott, A. (1997). Of time and space: The contemporary relevance of the Chicago School. *Social Forces*, 75(4), 1149–1182.

Agneessens, F., Roose, H., & Waege, H. (2004). Choices of theatre events: *p** model for affiliation networks with attributes. *Metodološki zvezki*, 1(2), 419–439.

Agneessens, F., &, Roose, H. (2008). Local structural patterns and attribute characteristics in 2-mode networks: *p** models to map choices of theater events. *Journal of Mathematical Sociology*, 32, 204–237.

Airoldi, E. M., Blei, D. M., Fienberg, S. E., & Xing, E. P. (2008). Mixed membership stochastic blockmodels. *Journal of Machine Learning Research*, 9, 1981–2014.

Akaike, H. (1973). *Information theory and an extension of the maximum likelihood principle*. Paper presented at the Second International Symposium on Information Theory, Budapest.

Akerlof, G. A. (1997). Social distance and social decisions. *Econometrica*, 65(5), 1005–1027.

Altman, I., & Taylor, D. A. (1973). *Social penetration: The development of interpersonal relationships*. New York: Holt, Rinehart, & Winston.

Anselin, L. (1982). A note on the small sample properties of estimators in a first order autoregressive model. *Environment and Planning A*, 14(8), 1023–1030.

Anselin, L. (1984). Specification tests on the structure of interaction in spatial econometric models. *Papers in Regional Science*, 54(1), 165–182.

Atchade, Y. F., Lartillot, N., & Robert, C. (2008). *Bayesian computation for statistical models with intractable normalizing constants*. Unpublished manuscript.

Australian Bureau of Statistics (ABS). (2001). 1216.0 – Australian Standard Geographical Classification (ASGC). Belconnen, Canberra, Australia: ABS.

Australian Electoral Commission (AEC). (2006). *Funding and discloser annual returns*. Kingston, ACT: Australia. http://www.aec.gov.au/Parties_and_Representatives/index.htm

Baddeley, A., & Möller, J. (1989). Nearest-neighbor Markov point processes and random sets. *International Statistical Review*, 57(2), 89–121.

Baker, W. E. (1990). Market networks and corporate behavior. *American Journal of Sociology*, 96(3), 589–625.

Bales, R. F. (1953). The equilibrium problem in small groups. In T. Parsons, R. F. Bales, & E. A. Shils (Eds.), *Working papers in the theory of action* (pp. 259–306). Glencoe, IL: Free Press.

Barabási, A. L., & Albert, R. (1999). Emergence of scaling in random networks. *Science*, 286(5439), 509–512.

Baum, J. A. C., Rowley, T. J., Shipilov, A. V., & Chuang, Y-T. (2005). Dancing with strangers: Aspiration performance and the search for underwriting syndicate partners. *Administrative Science Quarterly*, 50, 536–575.

Bavelas, A. (1950). Communication patterns in task-oriented groups. *Journal of the Acoustical Society of America*, 22(6), 723–730.

Beaman, L. A. (2012). Social Networks and the Dynamics of Labour Market Outcomes: Evidence from Refugees Resettled in the U.S. *Review of Economic Studies*, 79, 128–161.

Bearman, P. (1997). Generalized exchange. *American Journal of Sociology*, 102(5), 1383–1415.

Bernard, H. R., & Killworth, P. D. (1977). Informant accuracy in social network data II. *Human Communication Research*, 4(1), 3–18.

Bernard, H. R., Killworth, P. D., & Sailer, L. (1979). Informant accuracy in social network data IV: a comparison of clique-level structure in behavioral and cognitive network data. *Social Networks*, 2(3), 191.

Bernard, H. R., Killworth, P. D., & Sailer, L. (1981). Summary of research on informant accuracy in network data and the reverse small world problem. *Connections*, 4(2), 11–25.

Bernard, H. R., Killworth, P. D., & Sailer, L. (1982). Informant accuracy in social-network data V. An experimental attempt to predict actual communications from recall data. *Social Science Research*, 11(1), 30–66.

Bernardo, J. M., & Smith, A. F. M. (1994). *Bayesian theory*. New York: Wiley.

Besag, J.E. (1972). Nearest-neighbour systems and the auto-logistic model for binary data. *Journal of the Royal Statistical Society B*, 34 (1), 75–83.

Besag, J. (1974). Spatial interaction and the statistical analysis of lattice systems. *Journal of the Royal Statistical Society, Series B (Methodological)*, 36(2), 192–236.

Bian, Y. (1997). Bringing strong ties back in: Indirect ties, network bridges, and job searches in China. *American Sociological Review*, 62(3), 366–385.

Bill, A. (2005). *Neighbourhood inequality: Do small area interactions influence economic outcomes?* Working paper no. 05-11. Centre of Full Employment and Equity, The University of Newcastle, Australia.

Blau, P. M. (1964). *Exchange and power in social life*. New York: Wiley.

Boase, J., Horrigan, J. B., Wellman, B., & Rainie, L. (2006). *The strength of Internet ties*. Washington, DC: Pew Internet & American Life Project.

Bollobás, B. (1985). *Random graphs*. London: Academic Press.

Bond, M. (2003). *Social networks and corporate donations in Britain*. London: London School of Economics.

Bond, M. (2004). Social influences on corporate donations in Britain. *British Journal of Sociology*, 55(1), 55–77.

Bond, M. (2007). Elite social relations and corporate political donations in Britain. *Political Studies*, 55(1), 59–85.

Bond, M., Glouharova, S., & Harrigan, N. (2010). The political mobilisation of corporate directors: Socio-economic correlates of affiliation to European pressure groups. *British Journal of Sociology*, 61(1), 306–335.

Boneva, B., Kraut, R., & Frohlich, D. (2001). Using e-mail for personal relationships: The difference gender makes. *American Behavioral Scientist*, 45(3), 530–549.

Borgatti, S., Everett, M., & Freeman, L. (2006). *UCINET 6 for Windows: Software for social network analysis*. Cambridge, MA: Analytic Technologies.

Bothner, M. S. (2003). Competition and social influence: The diffusion of the sixth-generation processor in the global computer industry. *American Journal of Sociology*, 108(6), 1175–1210.

Box, G. P., & Tiao, G. C. (1973). *Bayesian inference in statistical analysis*. Reading, MA: Addison-Wesley.

Brandes, U., Lerner, J., & Snijders, T. A. B. (2009). *Networks evolving step by step: Statistical analysis of dyadic event data*. Paper presented at the International Conference on Advances in Social Network Analysis and Mining (ASONAM), Athens, Greece, July 20–22.

Brass, D. J., Galaskiewicz, J., Greve, H. R., & Tsai, W. (2004). Taking stock of networks and organizations: A multilevel perspective. *Academy of Management Journal*, 47(6), 795–817.

Breiger, R. L. (1974). The duality of persons and groups. *Social Forces*, 53(2, Special Issue), 181–190.

Brock, W. A., & Durlauf, S. N. (2002). A multinomial-choice model of neighborhood effects. *American Economic Review*, 92(2), 298–303.

Burda, Z., Jurkiewicz, J., & Krzywicki, A. (2004). Network transitivity and matrix models. *Physical Review E*, 69(026106).

Burris, V. (1987). The political partisanship of American business: A study of corporate political action committees. *American Sociological Review*, 52(6), 732–744.

Burris, V. (2000). The myth of old money liberalism: The politics of the Forbes 400 richest Americans. *Social Problems*, 47(3), 360–378.

Burt, R. S. (1987). Social contagion and innovation: Cohesion versus structural equivalence. *American Journal of Sociology*, 1287–1335.

Burt, R. S. (1992). *Structural holes: The social structure of competition*. Cambridge, MA: Harvard University Press.

Burt, R. S. (2001). Structural holes versus network closure as social capital. In N. Lin, C. Cook, & R. Burt (Eds.), *Social capital: Theory and research* (pp. 31–56). Berlin: Aldine de Gruyter.

Burt, R. S. (2005). *Brokerage and closure: An introduction to social capital*. Oxford: Oxford University Press.

Burt, R. S., & Doreian, P. (1982). Testing a structural model of perception: Conformity and deviance with respect to journal norms in elite sociological methodology. *Quality and Quantity*, 16(2), 109–150.

Burt, R. S., & Knez, M. (1995). Kinds of third-party effects on trust. *Rationality and Society*, 7(3), 255–292.

Business Review Weekly. (2005). *Business Review Weekly*. Melbourne: Fairfax Business Media. Volume 27, Issue 44.

Butts, C. T. (2002). Predictability of large-scale spatially embedded networks. In R. Breiger, K. M. Carley, & P. Pattison (Eds.), *Dynamic social network modelling and analysis: Workshop summary and papers* (pp. 313–323). Washington, DC: National Academies Press.

Butts, C. T. (2006). *Cycle census statistics for exponential random graph models*. Irvine: University of California.

Butts, C. T. (2008). Social network analysis: A methodological introduction. *Asian Journal of Social Psychology*, 11(1), 13–41.

Butts, C. T. (2012, expected). *Space and structure: Methods and models for large-scale interpersonal networks*. Springer.

Caimo, A., & Friel, N. (2011). Bayesian inference for exponential random graph models. *Social Networks*, 33(1), 41–55.

Calvó-Armengol, A. (2006). *Social networks and labour market outcomes*. Barcelona: Centre de Recerca en Economia Internacional (CREI).

Carson, J. B., Tesluk, P. E., & Marrone, J. A. (2007). Shared leadership in teams: An investigation of antecedent conditions and performance. *Academy of Management Journal*, 50(5), 1217–1234.

Cartwright, D., & Harary, F. (1956). Structural balance – A generalization of Heider's theory. *Psychological Review*, 63(5), 277–293.

Casciaro, T. (1998). Seeing things clearly: Social structure, personality, and accuracy in social network perception. *Social Networks*, 20(4), 331–351.

Centola, D., Willer, R., & Macy, M. (2005). The emperor's dilemma: A computational model of self-enforcing norms. *American Journal of Sociology*, 110(4), 1009–1040.

Chase, I. (1980). Process and hierarchy formation in small groups: A comparative perspective. *American Sociological Review*, 45, 905–924.

Cheshire, P., Monastiriotis, V., & Sheppard, S. (2003). Income inequality and residential segregation: Labour market sorting and the demand for positional goods. In R. Martin & P. Morrison (Eds.), *Geographies of labour market inequality* (pp. 83–109). London: Routledge.

Chib, S., & Greenberg, E. (1995). Understanding the metropolis algorithm. *American Statistician*, 49(4), 327–335.

Cliff, A. D., & Ord, J. K. (1973). *Spatial autocorrelation*. London: Pion.

Cliff, A. D., & Ord, J. K. (1981). *Spatial processes: Models and applications*. London: Pion.

Cohen, S., Kamarck, T., & Mermelstein, R. (1983). A global measure of perceived stress. *Journal of Health and Social Behavior*, 24(4), 385–396.

Coleman, J. S. (1988). Social capital in the creation of human capital. *American Journal of Sociology*, 94(s1), S95–S120.

Coleman, J. S. (1990/1994). *Foundations of social theory*. Cambridge, MA: Harvard University Press.

Conley, T., & Topa, G. (2006). Estimating dynamic local interactions models. *Journal of Econometrics*, 140(1), 282–303.

Connell, R. W. (1995). *Masculinities*. St. Leonards, New South Wales, Australia: Allen & Unwin.

Contractor, N. S., Wasserman, S., & Faust, K. (2006). Testing multi-theoretical multilevel hypotheses about organizational networks: An analytic framework and empirical example. *Academy of Management Review*, 31(3), 681–703.

Cooley, C. H. (1902/1964). *Human nature and the social order*. New York: Schocken Books.

Corander, J., Dahmström, K., & Dahmström, P. (1998). *Maximum likelihood estimation for Markov graphs*. Department of Statistics, University of Stockholm.

Corander, J., Dahmström, K., & Dahmström, P. (2002). Maximum likelihood estimation for exponential random graph model. In J. Hagberg (Ed.), *Contributions to social network analysis, information theory, and other topics in statistics: A festschrift in honour of Ove Frank* (pp. 1–17). Stockholm: Department of Statistics, University of Stockholm.

Cozby, P. C. (1973). Effects of density, activity, and personality on environmental preferences. *Journal of Research in Personality*, 7(1), 45–60.

Cressie, N.A.C. (1993). *Statistics for spatial data*. NY: Wiley

Crouch, B., Wasserman, S., & Trachtenberg, F. (1998). *Markov chain Monte Carlo maximum likelihood estimation for p* social network models*. Paper presented at the XVIII International Sunbelt Social Network Conference, Sitges, Spain.

Crown Content. (2005a). *Who's who in Australia 2005*. Melbourne: Crown Content.

Crown Content. (2005b). *Who's who in business in Australia 2005*. Melbourne, Victoria: Crown Content.

Dahmström, K., & Dahmström, P. (1993). *ML-estimation of the clustering parameter in a Markov graph model (Research report)*. Stockholm: Department of Statistics, University of Stockholm.

Dansereau, F., Graen, G., & Cashman, J. (1973). Instrumentality and equity theory as complementary approaches in predicting the relationship of leadership and turnover among managers. *Organizational Behavior and Human Performance*, 10(2), 184–200.

Daraganova, G. (2009). *Statistical models for social networks and network-mediated social influence processes: Theory and application*. Unpublished PhD thesis, University of Melbourne, Australia.

Daraganova, G., Pattison, P. E., Koskinen, J. H., Mitchell, B., Bill, A., Watts, M., et al. (2012). Networks and geography: modelling community network structures as the outcome of both spatial and network processes. *Social Networks*, 34(1), 6–17.

Davies, M., & Kandel, D. B. (1981). Parental and peer influences on adolescents' educational plans: Some future evidence. *American Journal of Sociology*, 87(2), 363–387.

Davis, J. A. (1970). Clustering and hierarchy in interpersonal relations: Testing two theoretical models in 742 sociograms. *American Sociological Review*, 35(5), 843–852.

Dawid, A. P. (1979). Conditional independence in statistical theory. *Journal of the Royal Statistical Society*, 41(1), 1–31.

Dawid, A. P. (1980). Conditional independence for statistical operations. *Annals of Statistics*, 8(3), 598–617.

de Klepper, M., Sleebos, E., van de Bunt, G., & Agneessens, F. (2010). Similarity in friendship networks: Selection or infiuence? The effect of constraining contexts and non-visible individual attributes. *Social Networks*, 32(1), 82–90.

de Nooy, W., Mrvar, A., & Batagelj, V. (2005). *Exploratory social network analysis with Pajek*. Cambridge: Cambridge University Press.

de Solla Price, D. (1976). A general theory of bibliometric and other advantage processes. *American Society for Information Science*, 27(5), 292–306.

DeGroot, M. H. (1974). Reaching a consensus. *Journal of the American Statistical Association*, 69(345), 118–121.

Dekker, D., Krackhardt, D., & Snijders, T. A. B. (2007). Sensitivity of MRQAP tests to collinearity and autocorrelation conditions. *Psychometrika*, 72(4), 563–581.

Denrell, J., & Mens, G. (2007). Interdependent sampling and social influence. *Psychological Review*, 114(2), 398–422.

Diaconis, P., & Ylvisaker, D. (1979). Conjugate priors for exponential families. *Annals of Statistics*, 7(2), 269–281.

DiMaggio, P. J. (1986). Structural analysis of organizational fields: A blockmodel approach. *Research in Organizational Behavior*, 8, 335–370.

Dindia, K., Timmerman, L., Langan, E., Sahlstein, E. M., & Quandt, J. (2004). The function of holiday greetings in maintaining relationships. *Journal of Social and Personal Relationships*, 21(5), 577–593.

Domhoff, G. W. (1967). *Who rules America?* Englewood Cliffs, NJ: Prentice Hall.

Domhoff, G. W. (1970). *The higher circles: The governing class in America*. New York: Random House.

Domhoff, G. W. (1978). *The powers that be: Processes of ruling-class domination in America*. New York: Random House.

Domhoff, G. W. (1998). *Who rules America? Power and politics in the year 2000* (3rd ed.). Mountain View, CA: Mayfield.

Domhoff, G. W. (2009). *Who rules America? Challenges to corporate and class dominance* (6th ed.). Boston: McGraw-Hill.

Domhoff, G. W., & Dye, T. R. (Eds.). (1987). *Power elites and organizations*. CA: Sage Publications.

Dooley, P. C. (1969). The interlocking directorate. *American Economic Review*, 59(3), 314–323.

Doreian, P. (1982). Maximum likelihood methods for linear models. *Sociological Methods and Research*, 10(3), 243–269.

Doreian, P. (1990). Network autocorrelation models: Problems and prospects. In D. A. Griffith (Ed.), *Spatial statistics: past, present, future* (Institute of Mathematical Geography, Monograph Series No. 12) (pp. 369–389). Ann Arbor, MI: Institute of Mathematical Geography.

Doreian, P. (1989). Models of network effects on social actors. In L. C. Freeman, D. R. White, & A. K. Romney (Eds.), *Research methods in social network analysis* (pp. 295–317). Fairfax, VA: George Mason University Press.

Doreian, P., Batagelj, V., & Ferligoj, A. (2004). Generalized blockmodeling of two-mode data. *Social Networks, 26,* 29–53.

Doreian, P., Teuter, K., & Wang, C. (1984). Network autocorrelation models. *Sociological Methods and Research,* 13(2), 155–200.

Durlauf, S. (2001). A framework for the study of individual behavior and social interactions. *Sociological Methodology,* 31(1), 47–87.

Durlauf, S. (2004). Neighborhood effects. In J. V. Henderson and J. -F. Thisse (Eds.), *Handbook of Regional and Urban Economics, vol 4.* Amsterdam: North Holland.

Durlauf, S., & Young, H. (2001). The new social economics. In S. Durlauf & H. Young (Eds.), *Social dynamics* (pp. 1–14). Washington, DC: Brookings Institution.

Eden, D., & Leviatan, U. (1975). Implicit leadership theory as a determinant of factor structure underlying supervisory behavior scales. *Journal of Applied Psychology,* 60(6), 736–741.

Ekeh, P. (1974). *Social exchange theories: Two traditions.* Cambridge, MA: Harvard University Press.

Emerson, R. (1962). Power-dependence relations. *American Sociological Review,* 27, 31–41.

Emirbayer, M. (1997). Manifesto for a relational sociology. *American Journal of Sociology,* 103(2), 281–317.

Emirbayer, M., & Goodwin, J. (1994). Network analysis, culture, and the problem of agency. *American Journal of Sociology,* 99(6), 1411–1454.

Epstein, J. L. (1983). The influence of friends on achievement and affective outcomes. In J. L. Epstein & N. Karweit (Eds.), *Friends in school: Patterns of selection and influence in secondary schools* (pp. 177–200). New York: Cambridge University Press.

Erbring, L., & Young, A. A. (1979). Individuals and social structure: Contextual effects as endogenous feedback. *Sociological Methods and Research,* 7(4), 396–430.

Erdös, P., & Rényi, A. (1959). On random graphs. *Publicationes Mathematicae (Debrecen),* 6, 290–297.

Faust, K. (2005). Using correspondence analysis for joint displays of affiliation networks. In P. J. Carrington, J. Scott, & S. Wasserman (Eds.), *Models and methods in social network analysis* (pp. 117–147). New York: Cambridge University Press.

Festinger, L. (1954). A theory of social comparison processes. *Human Relations,* 7(117–140).

Fienberg, S., & Wasserman, S. S. (1981). Categorical data analysis of single sociometric relations. In S. Leinhardt (Ed.), *Sociological methodology* (pp. 156–192). San Francisco: Jossey-Bass.

Fitch, R., & Oppenheimer, M. (1970). Who rules the corporations? *Socialist Reform,* 1(4), 73–108.

Frank, O. (1979). Estimation of population totals by use of snowball samples. In P. W. Holland & S. Leinhardt (Eds.), *Perspectives on social network research* (pp. 319–347). New York: Academic Press.

Frank, O. (1981). A survey of statistical methods for graph analysis. *Sociological Methodology,* 11, 110–155.

Frank, O. (2005). Network sampling and model fitting. In P. Carrington, J. Scott, & S. Wasserman (Eds.), *Models and methods in social network analysis* (pp. 31–56). Cambridge: Cambridge University Press.

Frank, O., & Harary, F. (1982). The line-distinguishing chromatic number of a graph. *Ars Combinatoria*, 14, 241–252.

Frank, O., & Snijders, T. A. B. (1994). Estimating the size of hidden populations using snowball sampling. *Journal of Official Statistics*, 10, 53–67.

Frank, O., & Strauss, D. (1986). Markov graphs. *Journal of the American Statistical Association*, 81(395), 832–842.

Freeman, L. C. (1977). Set of measures of centrality based on betweenness. *Sociometry*, 40(1), 35–41.

Freeman, L. C. (1979). Centrality in social networks: conceptual clarification. *Social Networks*, 1(3), 215–239.

Freeman, L. C., Romney, K. A., & Freeman, S. C. (1987). Cognitive structure and informant accuracy. *American Anthropologist*, 89(2), 310–325.

French, J. R. P. (1956). A formal theory of social power. *Psychological Review*, 63(3), 181–194.

Friedkin, N. E. (1998). *A structural theory of social influence*. Cambridge: Cambridge University Press.

Friedkin, N. E. (2003). Social influence network theory: Toward a science of strategic modification of interpersonal influence systems. In R. Breiger, K. M. Carley, & P. Pattison (Eds.), *Dynamic social network modeling and analysis* (pp. 89–100). Washington, DC: National Academy of Sciences/National Research Council Committee on Human Factors.

Friedkin, N. E., & Johnsen, E. C. (1997). Social positions in influence networks. *Social Networks*, 19(3), 209–222.

Frosh, S., Phoenix, A., & Pattman, R. (2001). *Young masculinities: Understanding boys in contemporary society*. Basingstoke: Palgrave.

Geyer, C. J., & Thompson, E. (1992). Constrained Monte Carlo maximum likelihood for dependent data. *Journal of the Royal Statistical Society*, 54(3), 657–699.

Gile, K., & Handcock, M. S. (2010). Respondent-driven sampling: An assessment of current methodology. *Sociological Methodology*, 40(1), 285–327.

Goktepe, J. R., & Schneier, C. E. (1989). Role of sex, gender roles, and attraction in predicting emergent leaders. *Journal of Applied Psychology*, 74(1), 165–167.

Goodman, L. A. (1961). Snowball sampling. *Annals of Mathematical Statistics*, 32(1), 148–170.

Goodreau, S. M. (2007). Advances in exponential random graph (p^*) models applied to a large social network. *Social Networks*, 29(2), 231–248.

Goodreau, S. M., Handcock, M. S., Hunter, D. R., Butts, C. T., & Morris, M. (2008). A statnet tutorial. *Journal of Statistical Software*, 24(9), 1–27.

Gould, R. V. (1991). Multiple networks and mobilization in the Paris Commune, 1871. *American Sociological Review*, 56(6), 716–729.

Granovetter, M. S. (1973). The strength of weak ties. *American Journal of Sociology*, 78(6), 1360–1380.

Guastello, S. J. (2007). Non-linear dynamics and leadership emergence. *Leadership Quarterly*, 18(4), 357–369.

Gulati, R., & Gargiulo, M. (1999). Where do inter-organizational networks come from? *American Journal of Sociology*, 104(5), 1439–1493.

Hachen, D., Lizardo, O., Wang, C., & Zhou, Z. (2009). *Correlates of reciprocity in a large-scale communication network: A weighted edge approach.* Paper presented at the International Sunbelt Social Network Conference, San Diego, March.

Hagberg, J. (2004). *On degree variance in random graphs.* Unpublished PhD thesis, Stockholm University, Stockholm.

Häggström, O., & Jonasson, J. (1999). Phase transition in the random triangle model. *Journal of Applied Probability*, 36(4), 1101–1115.

Hallen, B. L. (2008). The causes and consequences of the initial network positions of new organizations: From whom do entrepreneurs receive investments? *Administrative Science Quarterly*, 53(4), 685–718.

Handcock, M. S. (2002). Statistical models for social networks: Degeneracy and inference. In R. Breiger, K. M. Carley, & P. Pattison (Eds.), *Dynamic social network modeling and analysis* (pp. 229–240). Washington, DC: National Academies Press.

Handcock, M. S. (2003). *Assessing degeneracy in statistical models of social networks.* Working paper no. 39. Center for Statistics and the Social Sciences, University of Washington, Seattle.

Handcock, M. S., & Gile, K. (2007). *Modeling social networks with sampled or missing data.* Working paper no. 75. Center for Statistics and the Social Sciences, University of Washington, Seattle.

Handcock, M. S., & Gile, K. J. (2010). Modeling social networks from sampled data. *Annals of Applied Statistics*, 4(2), 5–25.

Handcock, M. S., Hunter, D. R., Butts, C., Goodreau, S., & Morris, M. (2003). statnet: An r package for the statistical modeling of social networks, http://www.csde.washington.edu/statnet.

Handcock, M. S., Hunter, D. R., Butts, C., Goodreau, S., & Morris, M. (2008). statnet: Software tools for the representation, visualization, analysis and simulation of network data. *Journal of Statistical Software*, 24(1), 1–11.

Handcock, M. S., Raftery, A. E., & Tantrum, J. M. (2007). Model-based clustering for social networks. *Journal of the Royal Statistical Society, Series A (Statistics in Society)*, 170(2), 301–354.

Hanneman, R. A., & Riddle, M. (2005). *Introduction to social network methods.* Riverside: University of California.

Harary, F. (1959). A criterion for unanimity in French's theory of social power. In D. Cartwright (Ed.), *Studies in social power* (pp. 168–182). Ann Arbor: University of Michigan.

Harrigan, N. (2008). *The social foundations of corporate political strategy.* Unpublished PhD thesis, Australian National University, Canberra.

Hastings, W. K. (1970). Monte Carlo sampling methods using Markov chains and their application. *Biometrika*, 57(1), 97–109.

Hays, R. B., & Oxley, D. (1986). Social network development and functioning during a life transition. *Journal of Personality and Social Psychology*, 50(2), 305–313.

Haythornthwaite, C. (2005). Social networks and Internet connectivity effects. *Information, Communication & Society*, 8(2), 125–147.

Hedström, P., Kolm, A-S., & Åberg, Y. (2003). *Social interactions and unemployment*. Working paper no. 2003:15. Uppsala, Sweden: Institute for Labour Market Policy Evaluation (IFAU).

Hedström, P., & Swedberg, R. (1998). *Social mechanisms: An analytical approach to social theory*. Cambridge: Cambridge University Press.

Heider, F. (1958). *The psychology of interpersonal relations*. New York: Wiley.

Hoff, P. D., Raftery, A. E., & Handcock, M. S. (2002). Latent space approaches to social network analysis. *Journal of the American Statistical Association*, 97(460), 1090–1098.

Hogg, M. A., & van Knippenberg, D. (2003). Social identity and leadership processes in groups. *Advances in Experimental Social Psychology*, 35(35), 1–52.

Hogg, M. A., Terry, D. J., & White, K. M. (1995). A tale of two theories: A critical comparison of identity theory with social identity theory. *Social Psychology Quarterly*, 58(4), 255–269.

Holland, P. W., & Leinhardt, S. (1970). A method for detecting structure in sociometric data. *American Journal of Sociology*, 76, 492–513.

Holland, P. W., & Leinhardt, S. (1971). Transitivity in structural models of small groups. *Comparative Group Studies*, 2(2), 107–124.

Holland, P. W., & Leinhardt, S. (1976). Local structure in social networks. *Sociological Methodology*, 7, 1–45.

Holland, P. W., & Leinhardt, S. (1977). A dynamic model for social networks. *Journal of Mathematical Sociology*, 5(1), 5–20.

Holland, P. W., & Leinhardt, S. (1981). An exponential family of probability-distributions for directed-graphs. *Journal of the American Statistical Association*, 76(373), 33–50.

Hornsey, M. J., & Hogg, M. A. (2002). The effects of status on subgroup relations. *British Journal of Social Psychology*, 41, 203–218.

Huisman, M. (2009). Imputation of missing network data: Some simple procedures. *Journal of Social Structure*, 10(1), 1–29.

Hunter, B. H. (1996). *Explaining changes in the social structure of employment: The importance of geography*. Discussion paper no. 67. Social Policy Research Centre (SPRC), University of New South Wales, Australia.

Hunter, D. R. (2007). Curved exponential family models for social networks. *Social Networks*, 29(2), 216–230.

Hunter, D. R., & Handcock, M. S. (2006). Inference in curved exponential family models for networks. *Journal of Computational and Graphical Statistics*, 15(3), 565–583.

Hunter, D. R., Goodreau, S. M., & Handcock, M. S. (2008). Goodness of fit of social network models. *Journal of the American Statistical Association*, 103(481), 248–258.

Hunter, D. R., Handcock, M. S., Butts, C. T., Goodreau, S. M., & Morris, M. (2008). ergm: A package to fit, simulate and diagnose exponential-family models for networks. *Journal of Statistical Software*, 24(3).

Ibarra, H. (1992). Homophily and differential returns: Sex differences in network structure and access in an advertising firm. *Administrative Science Quarterly*, 37(3), 422–447.

IBISWorld. (2006). *IBISWorld's top 2000 enterprises in Australia and New Zealand 2006*. Melbourne: IBISWorld.

Igarashi, T., Takai, J., & Yoshida, T. (2005). Gender differences in social network development via mobile phone text messages: A longitudinal study. *Journal of Social and Personal Relationships*, 22, 691–713.

Ihlanfeldt, K. R., & Sjoquist, D. L. (1998). The spatial mismatch hypothesis: A review of recent studies and their implications for welfare reform. *Housing Policy Debate*, 9(4), 849–892

Ingram, P., & Yue, L. Q. (2008). Structure, affect and identity as bases or organizational competition and cooperation. *The Academy of Management Annuals*, 2(1), 275–303.

Israeli Defense Forces (IDF). (2004). Officer's attribute paper. Available at: http://www.aka.idf.il/SIP_STORAGE/files/1/45741.pdf. Accessed December 27, 2009.

Ito, M., Okabe, D., & Matsuda, M. (2005). *Personal, portable, pedestrian: Mobile phones in Japanese life*. Cambridge, MA: The MIT Press.

Jackson, M. (2008). *Social and economic networks*. Princeton, NJ: Princeton University Press.

Janis, I. L. (1971). Groupthink. *Psychology Today*, 5(6), 43–46, 74–76.

Johnsen, T. E. (2006). The social context of the mobile phone use of Norwegian teens. In J. E. Katz (Ed.), *Machines that become us: The social context of personal communication technology* (pp. 161–169). New Brunswick, NJ: Transaction.

Joinson, A. N. (2001). Self-disclosure in computer-mediated communication: The role of self-awareness and visual anonymity. *European Journal of Social Psychology*, 31(2), 177–192.

Jonasson, J. (1999). The random triangle model. *Journal of Applied Probability*, 36(3), 852–867.

Jourard, S. M. (1964). *The transparent self: Self-disclosure and well-being*. New York: Van Nostrand Reinhold.

Judge, T. A., Bono, J. E., Ilies, R., & Gerhardt, M. W. (2002). Personality and leadership: A qualitative and quantitative review. *Journal of Applied Psychology*, 87(4), 765–780.

Kalish, Y., & Robins, G. (2006). Psychological predispositions and network structure: The relationship between individual predispositions, structural holes and network closure. *Social Networks*, 28(1), 56–84.

Kapferer, B. (1972). *Strategy and transaction in an African factory*. Manchester, UK: Manchester University Press.

Karasawa, M. (1991). Toward an assessment of social identity: The structure of group identication and its effects on in-group evaluations. *British Journal of Social Psychology*, 30, 293–307.

Karlberg, M. (1997). Testing transitivity in graphs. *Social Networks*, 19(4), 325–343.

Karlberg, M. (2002). Transitivity testing revisited: Power properties of a modified local density measure. In J. Hagberg (Ed.), *Contributions to social network analysis, information theory, and other topics in statistics: A Festschrift in honour of Ove Frank (2002)*. Stockholm: Department of Statistics, Stockholm University.

Karoński, M. (1982). A review of random graphs. *Journal of Graph Theory*, 6(4), 349–389.

Katz, D., & Allport, F. H. (1931). *Student attitudes*. Syracuse, NY: Craftsman.

Kenis, P., & Knoke, D. (2002). How organizational field networks shape inter-organizational tie-formation rates. *Academy of Management Review*, 27(2), 275–293.

Kilduff, M., & Krackhardt, D. (2008). *Interpersonal networks in organizations*. New York: Cambridge University Press.

Kilduff, M., Crossland, C., Tsai, W. P., & Krackhardt, D. (2008). Organizational network perceptions versus reality: A small world after all? *Organizational Behavior and Human Decision Processes*, 107(1), 15–28.

Killworth, P. D., & Bernard, H. R. (1976). Informant accuracy in social network data. *Human Organization*, 35(3), 269–286.

Kirkpatrick, S., & Locke, E. (1991). Leadership: Do traits matter? *Academy of Management Executive*, 5(2), 48–60.

Kleinberg, J. M. (2000). Navigation in a small world. *Nature*, 406, 845.

Knoke, D., & Yang, S. (2008). *Social network analysis* (2nd ed.). Thousand Oaks, CA: Sage Publications.

Koehly, L. M., & Pattison, P. (2005). Random graph models for social networks: Multiple relations or multiple raters. In P. J. Carrington, J. Scott, & S. Wasserman (Eds.), *Models and methods in social network analysis* (pp. 162–191). New York: Cambridge University Press.

Koenig, T., Gogel, R., & Sonquist, J. (1979). Models of the significance of inter-locking corporate directorates. *American Journal of Economics and Sociology* 38(2), 173–186.

Kolaczyk, E. D. (2009). *Statistical analysis of network data: Methods and models*. New York: Springer.

Koskinen, J. H. (2004). *Bayesian analysis of exponential random graphs – Estimation of parameters and model selection*: Research Report 2004:2, Department of Statistics, Stockholm University. (http://gauss.stat.su.se/site/pdfer/RR2004_2.pdf).

Koskinen, J. H. (2008). *The linked importance sampler auxiliary variable metropolis Hastings algorithm for distributions with intractable normalising constants*. Department of Psychology, School of Behavioural Science, University of Melbourne.

Koskinen, J. H. (2009). Using latent variables to account for heterogeneity in exponential family random graph models. In S. M. Ermakov, V. B. Melas, & A. N. Pepelyshev (Eds.), *Proceedings of the 6th St. Petersburg workshop on simulation* (Vol. ii, pp. 845–849). St. Petersburg: St. Petersburg State University.

Koskinen, J. H., & Edling, C. (2012). Modeling the evolution of a bipartite network – Peer referral in interlocking directorates. *Social Networks*, 34(3), 309–322.

Koskinen, J. H., & Snijders, T. A. B. (2007). Bayesian inference for dynamic social network data. *Journal of Statistical Planning and Inference*, 137(12), 3930–3938.

Koskinen, J. H., Robins, G. L., & Pattison, P. E. (2010). Analysing exponential random graph (*p*-star) models with missing data using Bayesian data augmentation. *Statistical Methodology*, 7(3), 366–384.

Koskinen, J. H., and Stenberg, S-Å, (2012). Bayesian Analysis of Multilevel Probit Models for Data with Friendship Dependencies. *Journal of Educational and Behavioural Statistics*, 37(2), 203–230.

Kossinets, G. (2006). Effects of missing data in social networks. *Social Networks*, 28(3), 247.

Krackardt, D. (1987). Cognitive social structures. *Social Networks*, 9(2), 109–134.

Krackhardt. (1987). QAP partialling as a test of spuriousness. *Social Networks*, 9, 171–186.

Latané, B. (1996). Dynamic social impact: The creation of culture by communication. *Journal of Communication*, 46(4), 13–25.

Laumann, P., & Marsden, P. V. (1982). Microstructural analysis of inter-organizational systems. *Social Networks*, 4(4), 329–348.

Lauritzen, S. L. (1996). *Graphical models*. Oxford: Oxford University Press.

Lawler, E. J., & Yoon, J. (1996). Commitment in exchange relations: Test of a theory of relational cohesion. *American Sociological Review*, 61(1), 89–108.

Lazega, E., & Pattison, P. E. (1999). Multiplexity, generalized exchange and cooperation in organizations: A case study. *Social Networks*, 21(1), 67–90.

Lazega, E., Jourda, M. T., Mounier, L., & Stofer, R. (2008). Catching up with big fish in the big pond? Multi-level network analysis through linked design. *Social Networks*, 30(2), 159–176.

Leenders, R. (2002). Modelling social influence through network autocorrelation: constructing the weight matrix. *Social Networks*, 24(1), 21–47.

Leenders, R. T. A. J. (1995). Models for network dynamics: A Markovian framework. *Journal of Mathematical Sociology*, 20(1), 1–21.

Lehmann, E. L. (1983). *Theory of point estimation*. New York: Wiley.

Levine, J. H. (1972). The sphere of influence. *American Sociological Review*, 37(1), 14–27.

Lincoln, J., Gerlach, M., & Ahmadjian, C. (1996). Keiretsu networks and corporate performance in Japan. *American Sociological Review*, 61(1), 67–68.

Lindenberg, S. (1997). Grounding groups in theory: Functional, cognitive, and structural interdependencies. *Advances in Group Process*, 14, 281–331.

Lindley, D. V. (1965). *Introduction to probability and statistics from a bayesian viewpoint* (Vols. 1 and 2). Cambridge: Cambridge University Press.

Ling, R. (2004). *The mobile connection: The cell phone's impact on society*. Waltham, MA: Morgan Kaufmann.

Lomi, A., & Pallotti, F. (2012). Relational collaboration among spatial multipoint competitors. *Social Networks*, 34(1), 101–111.

Lomi, A., & Pattison, P. (2006). Manufacturing relations: An empirical study of the organization of production across multiple networks. *Organization Science*, 17(3), 313–332.

Lord, R. G. (2005). Preface: Implicit leadership theory. In B. Schyns & J. R. Meindl (Eds.), *Implicit leadership theories: Essays and explorations* (pp. vii–xii). Greenwich, CT: Information Age Publishing (IAP).

Lord, R. G., & Maher, K. J. (1991). *Leadership and information processing: Linking perceptions and performance*. Boston: Unwin Hyman.

Lord, R. G., Devader, C. L., & Alliger, G. M. (1986). A metaanalysis of the relation between personality-traits and leadership perceptions – An application of validity generalization procedures. *Journal of Applied Psychology*, 71(3), 402–410.

Lord, R. G. (1985). An information processing approach to social perceptions, leadership and behavioral measurement in organizations. *Research in Organizational Behavior*, 7, 87–128.

Lord, R. G., Foti, R. J., & Devader, C. L. (1984). A test of leadership categorization theory – Internal structure, information processing, and leadership perceptions. *Organizational Behavior and Human Performance*, 34(3), 343–378.

Lubbers, M. J., & Snijders, T. A. B. (2007). A comparison of various approaches to the exponential random graph model: A reanalysis of 102 student networks in school classes. *Social Networks*, 29(4), 489–507.

Luria, G., & Berson, Y. (2008). *The motivation to lead: Effects on stress and performance*. Paper presented at the Annual Meeting of the Academy of Management, Anaheim, CA, August 8–13.

Luria, G., & Torjman, A. (2008). Resources and coping with stressful events. *Journal of Organizational Behavior*, 30(6), 685–707.

Lusher, D. (2008). *Masculinities in local contexts: Structural, individual and cultural interdependencies*. Saarbrücken, Germany: VDM Verlag.

Mace, M. L. (1971). *Directors: Myth and reality*. Boston: Harvard Business School.

Manski, C. F. (1993). Identification of endogenous social effects: The reflection problem. *Review of Economic Studies*, 60(3), 531–542.

Marsden, P. V. (2005). Recent developments in network measurement. In P. J. Carrington, J. Scott, & S. Wasserman (Eds.), *Models and methods in social network* (pp. 8–30). Cambridge: Cambridge University Press.

Marsden, P. V., & Friedkin, N. E. (1993). Network studies of social influence. *Sociological Methods and Research*, 22(1), 127–151.

Mason, W., Conrey, F., & Smith, E. (2007). Situating social influence processes: Dynamic, multidirectional flows of influence within social network. *Personality and Social Psychology Review*, 11(3), 279–300.

McPherson, M., Smith-Lovin, L., & Cook, J. M. (2001). Birds of a feather: Homophily in social networks. *Annual Review of Sociology*, 27, 415–444.

Mehra, A., Dixon, A. L., Brass, D. J., & Robertson, B. (2006). The social network ties of group leaders: Implications for group performance and leader reputation. *Organization Science*, 17(1), 64–79.

Merton, R. K. (1968). The Matthew effect in science. *Science*, 159(3810), 56–63.

Metropolis, N., Rosenbluth, A. W., Rosenbluth, M. N., Teller, A. H., & Teller, E. (1953). Equations of state calculations by fast computing machine. *Journal of Chemical Physics*, 21(6), 1087–1091.

Meyers, L. A. (2007). Contact network epidemiology: Bond percolation applied to infectious disease prediction and control. *Bulletin of the American Mathematical Society*, 44(1), 63–86.

Mills, C. W. (1956). *The power elite*. New York: Oxford University Press.

Milo, R., Shen-Orr, S., Itzkovitz, S., Kashtan, N., Chklovskii, D., & Alon, U. (2002). Network motifs: Simple building blocks of complex networks. *Science*, 298(5594), 824–827.

Mintz, B., & Schwartz, M. (1985). *The power structure of American business*. Chicago: The University Of Chicago Press.

Misiolek, N. I., & Heckman, R. (2005). *Patterns of emergent leadership in virtual teams*. Paper presented at the 38th Hawaii International Conference on System Science (HICSS 38), Big Island, January 3–6.

Mitchell, B., & Bill, A. (2004). *Spatial dependence in regional unemployment in Australia*. Working Paper No. 04–11. Centre of Full Employment and Equity, The University of Newcastle, Callaghan, New South Wales, Australia.

Mizruchi, M. S. (1982). *The American corporate network: 1904–1974*. Beverly Hills, CA: Sage.

Molm, L., Collet, J., & Schaefer, D. (2007). Building solidarity through generalized exchange: A theory of reciprocity. *American Journal of Sociology*, 113(1), 205–242.

Monge, P. R., & Contractor, N. S. (2003). *Theories of communication networks*. New York: Oxford University Press.

Moreno, J., & Jennings, H. (1938). Statistics of social configurations. *Sociometry*, 1(3/4), 342–374.

Morris, M., Handcock, M. S., & Hunter, D. R. (2008). Specification of exponential-family random graph models: terms and computational aspects. *Journal of Statistical Software*, 24(4), 1548–7660.

Murray, I., Ghahramani, Z., & MacKay, D. J. C. (2006). *MCMC for doubly intractable distributions*. Paper presented at the 22nd Annual Conference on Uncertainty in Artificial Intelligence (UAI), Cambridge, MA, July 13–16.

Nadel, S. F. (1952). *The theory of social structure*. Melbourne, Victoria, Australia: Melbourne University Press.

Neubert, M. J., & Taggar, S. (2004). Pathways to informal leadership: The moderating role of gender on the relationship of individual differences and team member network centrality to informal leadership emergence. *Leadership Quarterly*, 15(2), 175–194.

Newbold, P., Carlson, W. L., & Thorne, B. (2007). *Statistics for business and economics* (6th ed.). Upper Saddle River, NJ: Prentice Hall.

Newcomb, T. M. (1961). *The acquaintance process*. New York: Holt, Rinehart and Winston.

Newman, M. E. J., & Park, J. (2003). Why social networks are different from other types of networks? *Physical Review E*, 68(3), 036122.

Niekamp, A-M., Hoebe, C., Mercken, L., & Dukers-Muijrers, N. (2011). A sexual affiliation network of swingers, heterosexuals practicing risk behaviour related to sexually transmitted infections: A two-mode approach. Unpublished manuscript.

Nohria, N. (1992). Is a network perspective a useful way of studying organizations? In N. Nohria & R. G. Eccles (Eds.), *Networks and organizations: Structure, form and action* (pp. 1–22). Boston: Harvard University Press.

Norris, J. R. (1997). *Markov chains*. Cambridge: Cambridge University Press.

Nowicki, K., & Snijders, T. A. B. (2001). Estimation and prediction for stochastic blockstructures. *Journal of the American Statistical Association*, 96(455), 1077–1087.

Opsahl, T. (2009). Clustering in two-mode networks. *Proceedings of the Conference and Workshop on Two-Mode Social Analysis*, VU University Amsterdam, Amsterdam, The Netherlands.

Orchard, T., & Woodbury, M. A. (1972). A missing information principle: Theory and applications. *Proceedings of the 6th Berkeley Symposium on Mathematical Statistics*, Berkeley, CA, Vol. 1, pp. 697–715.

Ord, J. K. (1975). Estimation methods for models of spatial interaction. *Journal of the American Statistical Association*, 70(349), 120–126.

Ornstein, M. (1984). Interlocking directorates in Canada: Intercorporate or class alliance? *Administrative Science Quarterly*, 29(2), 210–231.

Park, J., & Newman, M. E. J. (2004). General methods of statistical physics – Statistical mechanics of networks. *Physical Review C*, 70(6), 66117.

Parkhe, A., Wasserman, S., & Ralston, D. A. (2006). New frontiers in network theory development. *Academy Of Management Review*, 31(3), 560–568.

Pattison, P. E., & Robins, G. L. (2004). Building models for social space: Neighbourhood-based models for social networks and affiliation structures. *Mathematics and Social Sciences*, 42(168), 11–29.

Pattison, P. E., Robins, G. L., & Kashima, Y. (2008). Psychology of social networks. In S. Durlauf & L. Blume (Eds.), *The new Palgrave dictionary of economics* (2nd ed., pp. 718–721). Basingstoke, UK: Palgrave Macmillan.

Pattison, P. E., Robins, G. L., Snijders, T. A. B., & Wang, P. (2011a). *A hierarchy of dependence assumptions for exponential random graph models for social networks*. Unpublished working paper. Psychological Sciences, University of Melbourne, Melbourne, Victoria, Australia.

Pattison, P. E., Robins, G. L., Snijders, T. A. B., & Wang, P. (2011b). *Conditional estimation of exponential random graph models from snowball sampling designs*. Unpublished working paper. Psychological Sciences, University of Melbourne, Melbourne, Victoria, Australia.

Pattison, P. E., Robins, G. L., Snijders, T. A. B., & Wang, P. (2012). *Conditional estimation of exponential random graph models from snowball sampling designs*. Technical report. Psychological Sciences, University of Melbourne, Melbourne, Victoria, Australia.

Pattison, P., & Robins, G. (2002). Neighbourhood-based models for social networks. *Sociological Methodology*, 32, 301–337.

Pattison, P., & Robins, G. L. (2002). Neighbourhood-based models for social networks. *Sociological Methodology*, 32, 301–337.

Pattison, P., & Wasserman, S. (1999). Logit models and logistic regressions for social networks: II. Multivariate relations. *British Journal of Mathematical and Statistical Psychology*, 52, 169–193.

Pattison, P., Wasserman, S., Robins, G. L., & Kanfer, A. M. (2000). Statistical evaluation of algebraic constraints for social networks. *Journal of Mathematical Psychology*, 44(4), 536–568.

Pattison. (1993). *Algebraic models for social networks*. Cambridge: Cambridge University Press.

Paxton, P., & Moody, J. (2003). Structure and sentiment: Explaining emotional attachment to group. *Social Psychology Quarterly*, 66(1), 34–47.

Pfeffer, J., & Salancik, G. R. (1978). *The external control of organizations*. New York: Harper & Row.

Podolny, J. M. (1994). Market uncertainty and the social character of economic exchange. *Administrative Science Quarterly*, 39(3), 458–483.

Podolny, J. M. (2001). Networks as the pipes and prisms of the market. *American Journal of Sociology*, 107, 33–60.

Podolny, J. M., Stuart, T. E., & Hannan, M. H. (1996). Networks, knowledge, and niches: Competition in the worldwide semiconductor industry, 1984–1991. *American Journal of Sociology*, 102, 659–689.

Poteat, V. P., Espelage, D. L., & Green, H. D., Jr. (2007). The socialization of dominance: Peer group contextual effects on homophobic and dominance attitudes. *Journal of Personality and Social Psychology*, 92(6), 1040–1050.

Powell, W. W., White, D. R., Koput, K. W., & Owen-Smith, J. (2005). Network dynamics and field evolution: The growth of inter-organizational collaboration in the life sciences. *American Journal of Sociology*, 110(4), 1132–1205.

Preciado, P., Snijders, T. A. B., Burk, W. J., Stattin, H., & Kerr, M. (2012). Does proximity matter? Distance dependence of adolescent friendships. *Social Networks*, 34(1), 18–31.

Prell, C. (2011). *Social network analysis: History, theory and methodology*. Thousand Oaks, CA: Sage.

Prentice, D. A., & Miller, D. T. (1993). Pluralistic ignorance and alcohol-use on campus – Some consequences of misperceiving the social norm. *Journal of Personality and Social Psychology*, 64(2), 243–256.

Putnam, R. D. (2000). *Bowling alone: The collapse and revival of American community*. New York: Simon & Schuster.

Ramakrishnan, U., & Cerisola, M. (2004). *Regional economic disparities in Australia*. IMF Working Paper No. WP/04/144. Asia and Pacific Department, International Monetary Fund.

Rank, O., Robins, G., & Pattison, P. (2010). Structural logic of intraorganizational network. *Organizational Science*, 21(3), 745–764.

Rapoport, A. (1953). Spread of information through a population with a sociostructural bias: I. Assumption of transitivity. *Bulletin of Mathematical Biophysics*, 15(4), 523–533.

Rapoport, A. (1957). Contributions to the theory of random and biased nets. *Bulletin of Mathematical Biophysics*, 19(4), 257–277.

Rennolls, K. (1995). $p^{1/2}$. Paper presented at the International Conference on Social Networks, London.

Rivera, M. T., Soderstrom, S. B., & Uzzi, B. (2010). Dynamics of dyads in social networks: Assortative, relational, and proximity mechanisms. *Annual Review of Sociology*, 36, 91–115.

Robbins, H., & Monro, S. (1951). A stochastic approximation method. *Annals of Mathematical Statistics*, 22, 400–407.

Robins, G. L, & Pattison, P. (2005). Interdependencies and social processes: Generalized dependence structures. In P. J. Carrington, J. Scott, & S. Wasserman (Eds.), *Models and methods in social network analysis* (pp. 192–214). Cambridge: Cambridge University Press.

Robins, G. L., & Alexander, M. (2004). Small worlds among interlocking directors: Network structure and distance in bipartite graphs. *Computational and Mathematical Organization Theory*, 10(1), 69–94.

Robins, G. L., and Morris, M. (2007), Advances in Exponential Random Graph (*p**) Models, *Social Networks*, 29, 169–172 .

Robins, G. L., Elliott, P., & Pattison, P. E. (2001). Network models for social selection processes. *Social Networks*, 23(1), 1–30.

Robins, G. L., Pattison, P. E., & Elliott, P. (2001). Network models for social influence processes. *Psychometrika*, 66(2), 161–189.

Robins, G. L., Pattison, P. E., & Wang, P. (2009). Closure, connectivity and degree distributions: Exponential random graph (*p**) models for directed social networks. *Social Networks*, 31(2), 105–117.

Robins, G. L., Pattison, P. E., & Wasserman, S. (1999). Logit models and logistic regressions for social networks: III. Valued relations. *Psychometrika*, 64(3), 371–394.

Robins, G. L., Pattison, P. E., Snijders, T. A. B., & Wang, P. (2009). *Activity closure and brokerage in social network models*. Paper presented at the Northwestern Institute on Complex Systems (NICO) Complexity Conference, Evanston, IL, September 1–3.

Robins, G. L., Pattison, P., & Woolcock, J. (2004). Missing data in networks: Exponential random graph (*p**) models for networks with non-respondents. *Social Networks*, 26, 257–283.

Robins, G. L., Pattison, P., & Woolcock, J. (2005). Small and other worlds: Global network structures from local processes. *American Journal of Sociology*, 110(4), 894–936.

Robins, G.L, Snijders, T. A. B., Wang, P., Handcock, M.S, & Pattison, P. (2007). Recent developments in exponential random graph (*p**) models for social networks. *Social Networks, Special Section: Advances in Exponential Random Graph (p*) Models*, 29(2), 192–215.

Rousseau, D. M., Sitkin, S. B., Burt, R. S., & Camerer, C. (1998). Not so different after all: A cross-discipline view of trust. *Academy of Management Review*, 23(3), 393–404.

Rubin, R. S., Bartels, L. K., & Bommer, W. H. (2002). Are leaders smarter or do they just seem that way? Exploring perceived intellectual competence and leadership emergence. *Social Behavior and Personality*, 30(2), 105–118.

Sander, L., Warren, C., Sokolov, I., Simon, C., & Koopman, J. (2002). Percolation on heterogeneous networks as a model for epidemics. *Mathematical Biosciences*, 180(1–2), 293–305.

Schweinberger, M. (2009). *A stochastic blockmodel extension of ERGMs*. Paper presented at the XXX International Sunbelt Social Network Conference, Trento, Italy, June 29–July 4.

Schweinberger, M. (2011). Instability, sensitivity, and degeneracy of discrete exponential families. *Journal of the American Statistical Association*. 106(496), 1361–1370.

Schweinberger, M., & Snijders, T. A. B. (2003). Settings in social networks: A measurement model. *Sociological Methodology*, 33(1), 307–341.

Schweinberger, M., & Snijders, T. A. B. (2007). Markov models for digraph panel data: Monte Carlo-based derivative estimation. *Computational Statistics and Data Analysis*, 51(9), 4465–4483.

Scott, J. (1997). *Corporate business and capitalist classes*. Oxford: Oxford University Press.

Scott, J. (2000). *Social network analysis: A handbook* (2nd ed.). Thousand Oaks, CA: Sage.

Scott, J., & Griff, C. (1984). *Directors of industry: The British corporate network*. Cambridge: Polity Press.

Simmel, G. (1950). *The sociology of Georg Simmel*. New York: Free Press.

Simmel, G. (1955). *Conflict and the web of group-affiliations*. New York: Free Press.

Skvoretz, J., & Agneessens, F. (2009). *Clustering in two-mode networks controlling for degree and actor-event-degree distributions. Proceedings of the Conference and Workshop on Two-Mode Social Analysis*, VU University Amsterdam, Amsterdam, The Netherlands.

Skvoretz, J., & Faust, K. (1999). Logit models for affiliation networks. *Sociological Methodology*, 29(1), 253–280.

Snijders, T. A. B. (1981a). The degree variance: An index of graph heterogeneity. *Social Networks*, 3(3), 163–174.

Snijders, T. A. B. (1981b). *Maximum value and null moments of the degree variance*. TW-report 229. Departments of Mathematics, University of Groningen.

Snijders, T. A. B. (1999). The transition probabilities of the reciprocity model. *Journal of Mathematical Sociology*, 23(4), 241–253.

Snijders, T. A. B. (2001). The statistical evaluation of social network dynamics. *Sociological Methodology*, 31, 361–395.

Snijders, T. A. B. (2002). Markov chain Monte Carlo estimation of exponential random graph models. *Journal of Social Structure*, 3(2), 1–40.

Snijders, T. A. B. (2006). Statistical methods for network dynamics. In S. R. Luchini et al. (Eds.), *Proceedings of the XLIII Scientific Meeting, Italian Statistical Society* (pp. 281–296). Padova, Italy: CLEUP.

Snijders, T. A. B. (2010a). Conditional marginalization for exponential random graph models. *Journal of Mathematical Sociology*, 34(4), 239–252.

Snijders, T. A. B. (2010b). *Models for dynamics of non-directed network*. Unpublished manuscript.

Snijders, T. A. B. (2011). Statistical models for social networks. *Annual Review of Sociology*, 37(1), 131–153.

Snijders, T. A. B., & Baerveldt, C. (2003). A multilevel network study of the effects of delinquent behavior on friendship evolution. *Journal of Mathematical Sociology*, 27(2–3), 123–151.

Snijders, T. A. B., & Bosker, R. J. (1999). *Multilevel analysis: An introduction to basic and advanced multilevel modeling*. London: Sage.

Snijders, T. A. B., & van Duijn, M. (1997). Simulation for statistical inference in dynamic network models. In R. Conte, R. Hegselmann, & P. Terna (Eds.), *Simulating social phenomena* (pp. 493–512). Berlin: Springer.

Snijders, T. A. B., & Van Duijn, M. A. J. (2002). Conditional maximum likelihood estimation under various specifications of exponential random graph models. In J. Hagberg (Ed.), *Contributions to social network analysis, information theory, and other topics in statistics. A festschrift in honour of Ove Frank* (pp. 117–134). Stockholm: Department of Statictics, Stockholm University.

Snijders, T. A. B., Koskinen, J. H., & Schweinberger, M. (2010). Maximum likelihood estimation for social network dynamics. *Annals of Applied Statistics*, 4(2), 567–588.

Snijders, T. A. B., Pattison, P. E., Robins, G. L., & Handcock, M. (2006). New specifications for exponential random graph models. *Sociological Methodology*, 36(1), 99–153.

Snijders, T. A. B., Steglich, C. E. G., & Schweinberger, M. (2007). Modeling the co-evolution of networks and behavior. In K. van Montfort, H. Oud, & A. Satorra (Eds.), *Longitudinal models in the behavioral and related sciences* (pp. 41–71). Berlin: Lawrence Erlbaum.

Snijders, T. A. B., Steglich, C. E. G., Schweinberger, M., & Huisman, M. (2005). Manual for SIENA version 2.1. Available from http://stat.gamma.rug.nl/sie_man31.pdf.

Snijders, T. A. B., van de Bunt, G. G., & Steglich, C. E. G. (2010). Introduction to stochastic actor-based models for network dynamics. *Social Networks*, 32(1), 44–60.

Sorenson, O., & Stuart, T. E. (2008). Bringing the context back in: Settings and the search for syndicate partners in venture capital investing. *Administrative Science Quarterly*, 53(2), 266–294.

Sparrowe, R. T., & Liden, R. C. (2005). Two routes to influence: Integrating leader-member exchange and social network perspectives. *Administrative Science Quarterly*, 50(4), 505–535.

Stearns, L. B., & Mizruchi, M. S. (1986). Broken-tie reconstitution and the functions of interorganizational interlocks: A reexamination. *Administrative Science Quarterly*, 31(4), 522–538.

Steglich, C. E. G., Snijders, T. A. B., & West, P. (2006). Applying SIENA: An illustrative analysis of the co-evolution of adolescents' friendship networks, taste in music, and alcohol consumption. *Methodology: European Journal of Research Methods for the Behavioral and Social Sciences*, 2, 48–56.

Steglich, C. E. G., Snijders, T. A. B., & Pearson, M. (2010). Dynamic networks and behavior: Separating selection from influence. In T. F. Liao (Ed.), *Sociological methodology* (vol. 40, issue 1, pp. 329–393). Boston: John Wiley & Sons.

Stokes, J., Fuehrer, A., & Childs, L. (1980). Gender differences in self-disclosure to various target persons. *Journal of Counseling Psychology*, 27(2), 192–198.

Strauss, D. (1986). On a general class of models for interaction. *SIAM Review*, 28(4), 513–527.

Strauss, D., & Ikeda, M. (1990). Pseudolikelihood estimation for social networks. *Journal of the American Statistical Association*, 85(409), 204–212.

Sweezy, P. M. (1953). Interest groups in the American economy. In P. M. Sweezy (Ed.), *The present as history: Essays and reviews on capitalism and socialism*. New York: Monthly Review Press.

Swidler, A. (1998). Culture and social action. In P. Smith (Ed.), *The new American cultural sociology* (pp. 171–187). Cambridge: Cambridge University Press.

Tajfel, H., & Turner, J. C. (1979). An integrative theory of intergroup conflict. In W. G. Austin & S. Worchel (Eds.), *The social psychology of intergroup relations* (pp. 33–47). Monterey, CA: Brooks/Cole.

Thompson, S., & Frank, O. (2000). Model-based estimation with link-tracing sampling designs. *Survey Methodology*, 26(1), 87–98.

Tierney, L. (1994). Markov chains for exploring posterior distributions. *Annals of Statistics*, 22(4), 1701–1762.

Topa, G. (2001). Social interactions, local spillovers and unemployment. *Review of Economic Studies*, 68(2), 261–295.

Turner, J. C., Hogg, M. A., Oakes, P. J., Reicher, S. D., & Wetherell, M. S. (1987). *Rediscovering the social group: A self-categorization theory*. Oxford: Blackwell.

Tversky, A., & Kahneman, D. (1974). Judgment under uncertainty: Heuristics and biases. *Science*, 185(4157), 1124–1131.

Useem, M. (1984). *The inner circle: Large corporations and the rise of business political activity in the U.S. and U.K.* Oxford: Oxford University Press.

Uzzi, B. (1996). The sources and consequences of embeddedness for the economic performance of organizations: The network effect. *American Sociological Review*, 61(4), 674–698.

Valente, W. (1995). *Network models of the diffusion of innovations*. Cresskill, NJ: Hampton Press.

van Duijn, M. A. J., & Vermunt, J. K. (2006). What is special about social network analysis? *Methodology: European Journal of Research Methods for the Behavioral and Social Sciences*, 2(1), 2–6.

van Duijn, M. A. J., Snijders, T. A. B., & Zijlstra, B. (2004). A random effects model with covariates for directed graphs. *Statistica Neerlandica*, 58(2), 234–254.

van Duijn, M. A. J., Zeggelink, E. P. H., Huisman, M., Stokman, F. N., & Wasseur, F. W. (2003). Evolution of sociology freshmen into a friendship network. *Journal of Mathematical Sociology*, 27(2), 153–191.

Wahba, J., & Zenou, Y. (2005). Density, social networks and job search methods: Theory and application to Egypt. *Journal of Development Economics*, 78(2), 443–473.

Wang, P., Pattison, P., & Robins, G. (in press). Exponential random graph model specifications for bipartite networks – A dependence hierarchy. *Social Networks*.

Wang, P., Robins, G. L., & Pattison, P. E. (2009). PNet: Program for the simulation and estimation of p^* exponential random graph models. Available from http://www.sna.unimelb.edu.au/.

Wang, P., Sharpe, K., Robins, G. L., & Pattison, P. E. (2009). Exponential random graph (p^*) models for affiliation networks. *Social Networks*, 31(1), 12–25.

Wasserman, S. (1979). A stochastic model for directed graphs with transition rates determined by reciprocity. In K. F. Schuessler (Ed.), *Sociological Methodology 1980*. San Francisco: Jossey-Bass. 392–412.

Wasserman, S. (1980). Analyzing social networks as stochastic processes. *Journal of the American Statistical Association*, 75(370), 280–294.

Wasserman, S., & Faust, K. (1994). *Social network analysis: Methods and applications*. Cambridge: Cambridge University Press.

Wasserman, S., & Pattison, P. (1996). Logit models and logistic regressions for social networks .1. An introduction to Markov graphs and p*. *Psychometrika*, 61(3), 401–425.

Watson, D., Clark, L. A., & Tellegen, A. (1988). Development and validation of brief measures of positive and negative affect: The PANAS scale. *Journal of Personality and Social Psychology*, 54(6), 1063–1070.

Watts, D. J. (1999). Networks, dynamics, and the small-world phenomenon. *American Journal of Sociology*, 105(2), 493–527.

Watts, D. J., & Strogatz, S. H. (1998). Collective dynamics of "small-world" networks. *Nature*, 393(6684), 440–442.

Webster, C. M. (1995). Detecting context-based constraints in social perception. *Journal of Quantitative Anthropology*, 5(4), 285–303.

Wellman, B., Salaff, J., Dimitrova, D., Garton, L., Gulia, M., & Haythornthwaite, C. (1996). Computer networks as social networks: Collaborative work, telework, and virtual community. *Annual Review of Sociology*, 22(1), 213–238.

White, H. (1992). *Identity and control: A structural theory of social action*. Princeton, NJ: Princeton University Press.

White, H. C. (2008). *Identity and control: How social formations emerge* (2nd ed.). Princeton, NJ: Princeton University Press.

White, H. C., Boorman, S. A., & Breiger, R. L. (1976). Social structure from multiple networks. I. Blockmodels of roles and positions. *American Journal of Sociology*, 81(4), 730–780.

Whittington, K., Powell, W., & Owen-Smith, J. (2009). Networks, propinquity and innovation in knowledge-intensive industries. *Administrative Science Quarterly*, 54(1), 90–122.

Wikipedia. (2012). *Observable universe*. Retrieved from http://en.wikipedia.org/wiki/Observable_universe.

Wilson, W. (1987). *The truly disadvantaged: The inner city, the underclass and public policy*. Chicago: The University of Chicago Press.

Wong, G. Y. (1987). Bayesian models for directed graphs. *Journal of the American Statistical Association*, 82(397), 140–148.

Yukl, G. (2010). *Leadership in organizations* (7th ed.). Upper Saddle River, NJ: Pearson.

Yule, G. U. (1925). A mathematical theory of evolution, based on the conclusions of Dr. J. C. Willis, F.R.S. *Philosophical Transactions of the Royal Society of London, Series B, Containing Papers of a Biological Character*, 213(402–410), 21–87.

Zalensky, M. D., & Graen, G. B. (1987). Exchange theory in leadership research. In A. Kiser & G. Reber Wanderer (Eds.), *Handbook of leadership* (pp. 714–727). Stuttgart, Germany: CE Paeschel Verlag.

Zeitlin, M. (1974). Corporate ownership and control: The large corporation and the capitalist class. *American Journal of Sociology*, 79(5), 1073–1119.

Zhao, Y. (2007). *Multiple networks in organizations*. Unpublished PhD thesis. University of Melbourne, Melbourne, Victoria, Australia.

Zweigenhaft, R. L., & Domhoff, G. W. (2006). *Diversity in the power elite*. Lanham, MD: Rowman & Littlefield.

Index

2-in-star, 22, 25, 67–68, 118, 175, 182, 184, 253, 254–255
2-out-star, 17, 22, 25, 118, 175, 182–184, 253–256
2-paths, 22, 25, 43–44, 54, 58, 64, 67, 69–72, 73, 85, 87, 107, 111, 118–119, 124–126, 137, 157, 174–175, 182, 184, 194, 203, 207, 253, 256, 296–297
activity, 24–26, 42, 95
activity closure, 73, 203–212, 222
activity spread, 43, 69, 174–175, 195, 207
actor-relation effects, 26–27, 46, 93, 176, 183, 194, 199, 207, 209, 211, 232, 234, 248, 252, 256–258, 268–269
　heterophily, 43, 177–178, 194–195, 198, 199, 232, 234. *See also* homophily
　homophily, 11, 17–18, 21, 26–27, 37, 39, 43, 45, 91, 93–98, 126–127, 177–178, 183, 189, 194, 195, 196, 197, 199, 203, 204, 208, 250, 252, 254, 256, 257, 290
　receiver effects, 24, 26, 45, 60, 95, 178, 195, 197–198, 221, 232, 234, 252, 254–256
　sender effects, 24, 26, 45, 95, 183, 197, 198, 254–255, 258
Akaike information criterion (AIC), 159
alternating-in-star, 68–69, 174, 184, 207. *See also* popularity spread.
alternating-out-star. *See* activity spread
alternating star, 65–67, 119, 171–174, 184, 275

alternating triangle, 69–73, 118, 142–145, 152–153, 168–172, 174–175, 183–184, 275
alternating 2-path, 71–72, 125, 174–175
alters, 108, 163, 183, 275, 281, 283
analysis of variance (ANOVA), 21
attributes
　actor attributes, 10, 12, 13, 15, 17, 21, 24, 26–27, 36, 38–39, 74, 91–93, 103–106, 119, 124, 125, 193, 214, 224, 237–247, 261, 275
　binary, 43, 45, 93–98, 125–126, 177, 178, 195, 210, 216, 263
　categorical, 15, 43, 45, 93, 94, 96, 120, 127–128, 177–178, 194
　continuous, 15, 43, 45, 94–98, 119, 125–128, 177, 194, 195, 232
　dyadic, 95, 120, 275
Autologistic actor attribute models (ALAAM), 15, 102–114, 237–247

balance theory, 17
Bayesian inference, 14, 67, 148
Bayesian information criterion (BIC), 159
Bernoulli assumption, 56, 79, 128
Bernoulli model, 58–59, 83–84, 116, 122, 160, 176, 178, 292, 295
bipartite networks, 2, 120–129, 260–271
bridges, 137, 256
brokerage, 17, 24, 26, 75, 207, 294
burn-in, 145, 146, 148, 151, 154, 155, 168, 181

centrality, 9, 17, 23, 25, 42, 62–63, 66–67,
    69, 85, 123, 126, 171–173, 175, 191,
    197, 201, 221, 224, 231, 281
  in-degree, 18, 25, 42, 67, 69, 175, 210,
    231
  out-degree, 18, 25, 42, 67–69, 74, 154,
    193, 221, 224, 231
change statistic, 54–55, 97, 133, 146, 156
cliques, 25, 69, 81–84, 85–88, 90, 169,
    170, 171, 173, 295–297
closure theories, 75
clustering, 25, 62, 65, 113, 117, 118, 121,
    123, 129, 182–183, 194, 239, 246,
    252, 254–256, 279, 288, 290, 298
cohesive subgroups, 25
conditional estimation, 154, 163–165, 243,
    299
convergence, 153–154, 166, 175, 178,
    179, 181, 219, 221, 267, 275, 277,
    280, 297
convergence statistic, 153, 154, 166,
    176–179, 181
covariate effects, 28, 93, 96, 105, 109,
    112, 244
cross-network effects, 116–120, 224
cyclic closure, 43, 44, 74, 175, 204–205,
    207, 209, 212, 222, 252–253
cyclic triad, 25–26, 175, 182, 252–256

degeneracy. *See* near degeneracy
density, 42, 51, 64, 66, 85, 122, 154, 168,
    174, 184, 217–218, 235, 274, 275,
    277, 278, 280, 289
dependence
  dependence graph, 77–90, 106
  dyadic independence (aka dyad
    dependence), 12, 13, 20, 59–60, 68,
    208, 292
  independent attribute assumption,
    106–107, 109
  indirect dependent attribute assumption,
    108
  Markov dependence, 20, 52, 57, 58, 60,
    65, 68–69, 79–80, 85–88, 122, 292
  network covariate dependence
    assumption, 109
  network-dependent assumption, 107
  partial conditional independence
    assumption, 57, 107
  realization-dependent models, 57, 289
  social circuit dependence, 21, 57–58, 69,
    80, 87–88, 116, 119, 165, 292

directed acyclic graph (DAG), 106
direct network-attribute assumption,
    107–108
directed network, 22, 23, 25, 26, 33, 38,
    52, 60, 72, 95–97, 99, 116, 117–119,
    133, 138, 206, 215, 252
distribution of graphs, 30, 33–34, 56, 141,
    142, 165
dyadic covariates, 21, 23, 28, 53–54,
    91–93, 98–99, 113, 136, 288

entrainment, 28, 39, 43, 99, 117, 119–120,
    177–178, 214, 215, 216, 220, 221,
    222, 224–225
ERGM
  Theory, 10–12, 16
  Definition, 1, 9–10
  Equation, 55
  History of, 12–14
  Software, 2–3, 13–14, 106, 116, 121,
    179, 245, 252, 261
  Estimation. *See* estimation
  Goodness of fit. *See* goodness of fit
    (GOF)
  Directed network. *See* directed network
  Simulation. *See* simulation
  Nondirected network. *See* nondirected
    network
  Purely structural effects. *See* purely
    structural effects
  Actor-relation effects. *See* actor-relation
    effects
  Significant effects. *See* significant effects
ERGM theory, 10–12, 16
estimation, 2, 13–14, 34–35, 87, 100, 106,
    135–136, 141, 142, 147, 148, 151,
    153–156, 158, 162, 174–179
exchange, 117, 120, 213, 215, 216,
    218–224
exogenous variables, 10, 23, 24, 27, 28,
    43, 90, 106, 108, 112, 246, 290, 298
exponential random graph model (ERGM),
    See ERGM

gain factor, 151, 152, 154
general transitivity, 74, 174, 222
generalized exchange, 44, 68, 175, 205,
    209, 211, 252, 254, 255, 256
geometrically weighted degree (GWD),
    65–66
geometrically weighted dyadwise shared
    partner (GWDSP), 71

geometrically weighted edgewise shared partner (GWESP), 71

geospatial effects, 91, 99–101, 113, 244, 245, 247

Geyer-Thompson algorithm, 149

goodness of fit, 139, 141, 165–166, 167, 175, 177, 179–185, 193, 231–232, 277

  approximate Bayesian goodness of fit, 166

Hammersley-Clifford theorem, 82, 85, 90

Hamming distance, 155

heterophily. *See* actor-relation effects

high degree nodes, 62, 63, 66, 123, 171, 173, 184, 197, 267

history of ERGM, 12–14

homogeneity assumption, 35–36, 83, 86–88, 292, 299, 300

homophily. *See* actor-relation effects

importance sampling, 149, 151, 152, 154

independent observations, 21, 34, 52, 59

likelihood ratio test, 159, 160, 165

Local Indicators of Spatial Association (LISA), 239

logistic regression, 6, 34, 52–54, 58, 59, 86, 97, 98, 105–107, 108, 109, 112

log-linear model, 12, 13, 52, 77

longitudinal ERGM, 15, 252–259

longitudinal models, 2, 130–140, 251

Markov
  Markov chain Monte Carlo, 15, 142
  Markov chain Monte Carlo maximum likelihood estimation, 243, 300
  Markov dependence, 20, 52, 57, 58, 60, 65, 68–69, 79, 80, 85–88, 122, 292
  Markov effects, 170, 295
  Markov random graph model, 13, 60, 85, 161

maximum likelihood estimation, 13, 35, 67, 122, 141, 147, 155, 162, 243, 289, 300

Metropolis algorithm, 146, 151, 163

missing data, 14, 162–164, 299

moment equation, 136, 147–149, 155

multiple connectivity, 43, 175, 194, 207, 231, 275, 277–278

multiple triangulation, 25, 70

multiplication factor, 150, 151, 154, 162, 177, 181

multivariate analysis (analysis of multiple networks), 13, 115–120, 213–225, 275, 280–282

mutual ties, 9, 39, 176, 218

near degeneracy, 13, 136, 160–162, 176, 219, 289, 295–296, 300

network configurations, 1, 9, 11, 12, 17–19, 21, 22, 27–28, 30, 34, 54–56, 58, 59, 60–63, 67–70, 72, 73, 75–76, 82–90, 105, 118, 174, 184, 194, 219, 290, 294

network self-organization, 10–11, 23–27, 38, 91, 179, 183

network statistic, 9, 30, 31, 82, 290, 291

network tie-variables, 49–51, 52, 55–60, 75, 77–79, 86–88, 93, 104, 116, 122–124, 132, 133, 136, 295

non-directed network. *See* undirected network

normalizing constant, 9, 82, 146, 159, 160

ordinal ties, 14

p^* models, 13

p_1 model, 12

parameter estimates, 41–44, 135, 151, 155, 161, 162, 176, 197, 199, 210, 233, 245, 298

  negative, 41, 42, 43, 44, 53, 63, 64, 67, 71, 96, 105, 171–173, 175, 195, 210, 211

  positive, 35, 41–45, 54, 55, 62–63, 66, 71, 95–96, 105, 123, 125, 171–173, 177, 195

partially observed data. *See* missing data

path closure, 17, 20, 44, 72–73, 178, 204, 207–208. *See also* transitivity.

phase transition, 64, 65, 123, 169

PNet. *see* software

popularity closure, 74, 204, 207, 209, 211–212, 220–222

popularity effects, 17–18, 23, 26, 42, 69, 96, 118. *See also* popularity spread.

popularity spread, 69, 174, 175, 195

probability distribution, 30, 55, 82, 89, 105, 132, 133, 136, 148, 162

pseudolikelihood estimation, 13

purely structural effects (endogenous), 23, 43, 45, 183, 194

Quadratic Assignment Procedure (QAP), 115, 191, 215, 218, 221–222, 224, 277

random graphs, 30–32
random variables, 78, 104
receiver effects. *See* actor-relation effects
reciprocity, 1, 11, 16, 18, 20, 21, 24, 29, 32, 35–36, 37, 42, 60, 68, 137, 176, 179, 183, 191, 194, 197, 199, 202, 203, 208, 219, 221, 224, 231, 233, 235, 252, 254–256, 299
Robbins-Monro algorithm, 151–154

score test, 158–159, 165, 166
sender effects. *See* actor-relation effects
SIENA. *See* software
simple connectivity, 43, 175, 196. *See also* 2-paths
simple random graphs, 31
simulation, 4, 35, 52, 74, 122, 133, 135, 141, 142, 144, 145, 146, 147, 151, 155, 158, 162, 167–173, 255
snowball sampling, 14, 15, 162, 164, 165, 239, 243, 299
social circuit effects, 119, 175
social identity theory (SIT), 190, 227
social influence, 4, 5, 13, 15, 16, 88–90, 92, 102–104, 108, 114, 201, 244, 245, 246, 283. *See also* social processes: contagion and diffusion.
social processes
  contagion, 103, 108, 111, 112, 245, 247
  diffusion, 16, 102–105, 109, 211, 212, 272
  multiple, 10, 11, 21–23
  nested, 21
social selection, 4, 13, 16, 27, 88, 91–101, 104, 114, 119, 121, 124, 127, 189–191, 193, 201, 228, 248, 250, 252, 255–257, 258, 264
software
  PNet, 2, 14, 38, 93, 106, 116, 121, 125, 129, 149, 151, 162, 165–166, 167, 175, 177, 179, 181, 183, 193–194, 207, 216, 231, 245, 252, 261

SIENA, 2, 14, 149, 259
statnet, 2, 14, 71–72, 96, 149, 150, 151, 154, 162, 166, 175, 178, 179, 181, 183
standard errors of the estimates, 154
stationary distribution, 134, 135, 145
statnet. *see* software
stochastic actor-oriented models, 136, 138–139, 259. *See also* software: SIENA.
stochastic approximation, 149, 151
stochastic blockmodel, 298–299
structural equivalence, 4, 112, 203, 208, 211
structural holes, 17, 73
structural zeroes (fixing ties), 154, 231, 232
sufficient statistics, 82, 86, 87, 148, 159, 295

thinning, 146, 150, 181
tie-based models, 9, 137, 139
tie-variables. *See* network tie-variables
transitive triad, 22, 23, 25, 26, 30, 31–33, 35, 44, 68, 74, 177, 182–183, 252–256. *See also* transitivity.
transitivity, 1, 11, 13, 20, 22, 25, 33, 35, 43, 44, 68, 74, 136, 179, 191, 236, 257, 262, 283
  general transitivity, 74, 174, 222
triads, 12, 17, 22, 31, 33, 38, 65, 99, 137, 175, 205, 207, 209, 283, 290. *See also* transitive triads.
two-mode networks, 120–129, 260–271. *See also* bipartite networks.

undirected networks, 14, 25–26, 49, 77, 83, 94–95, 97, 99, 116–118, 133, 138, 168, 174, 242, 275, 288

Wald test, 157–158, 165, 166
weak ties, 17, 249–250, 257
within-network effects, 116–118, 215, 219, 280

Name Index

Abbott, A., 11, 238
Aberg, Y., 238
Agneessens, F., 121, 124
Ahmadjian, C., 202
Airoldi, E. M., 298
Akaike, H., 159
Akerlof, G. A., 238
Albert, R., 17, 23, 262
Alexander, M., 121, 260
Alliger, G. M., 227
Allport, F. H., 190
Altman, I., 249
Anselin, L., 102
Atchade, Y. F., 148

Baddeley, A., 57, 293
Baerveldt, C., 189
Baker, W. E., 203
Bales, R. F., 226
Barabási, A. L., 17, 23, 262
Batagelj, V., 120
Baum, J. A. C., 203
Bavelas, A., 17
Beaman, L. A., 238
Bearman, P., 205
Bernard, H. R., 272, 273, 274, 277
Bernardo, J. M., 148
Besag, J., 82, 100, 111
Bian, Y., 108
Bill, A., 237, 238, 239
Blau, P. M., 16
Blei, D. M., 298
Boase, J., 249
Bollobás, B., 56
Bond, M., 260, 263

Boneva, B., 250
Bono, J. E., 227, 228
Borgatti, S., 273
Bosker, R. J., 52
Bothner, M. S., 204, 211
Box, G. P., 148
Brandes, U., 139
Brass, D. J., 140
Breiger, R. L., 11, 115, 120, 260
Brock, W. A., 108
Burda, Z., 161
Burk, W. J., 101
Burris, V., 263
Burt, R. S., 17, 26, 103, 112, 203, 207,
    249, 294
Butts, C. T., 75, 100, 139, 149

Caimo, A., 2, 148, 149
Camerer, C., 203
Carlson, W. L., 51
Carson, J. B., 228, 229
Cartwright, D., 17
Casciaro, T., 189
Cashman, J., 236
Centola, D., 190
Cerisola, M., 237
Chase, I., 212
Cheshire, P., 237
Chib, S., 144
Childs, L., 257
Chuang, Y.-T., 203
Clark, L. A., 230
Cliff, A. D., 102
Cohen, S., 230
Coleman, J. S., 203, 261, 270

Collet, J., 205
Conley, T., 238
Connell, R. W., 192, 228
Conrey, F., 108
Contractor, N. S., 11, 13, 21
Cook, J. M., 17, 91, 250
Cooley, C. H., 260
Corander, J., 13, 68, 147
Cozby, P. C., 249
Crossland, C., 283
Crouch, B., 13, 147

Dahmström, K., 13, 147
Dahmström, P., 13, 147
Dansereau, F., 236
Daraganova, G., 49, 77, 91, 100, 101, 102,
        106, 108, 165, 237, 240, 288
Davies, M., 103
Davis, J. A., 25
Dawid, A. P., 57
de Klepper, M., 248, 250
de Nooy, W., 6
de Solla Price, D., 23
DeGroot, M. H., 103
Dekker, D., 115
Denrell, J., 108
Devader, C. L., 227, 228
Diaconis, P., 148
DiMaggio, P. J., 203, 211
Dindia, K., 249
Domhoff, G. W., 261
Dooley, P. C., 261
Doreian, P., 102, 103, 120
Dukers-Muijrers, N., 129
Durlauf, S., 103, 104, 108, 238

Eden, D., 227
Edling, C., 124, 127, 129, 139
Ekeh, P., 205
Elliott, P., 13, 89, 93, 95, 103, 106, 107,
        248, 288
Emerson, R., 261
Emirbayer, M., 26, 138, 189, 287
Epstein, J. L., 103
Erbring, L., 102, 103
Erdös, P., 12, 292
Espelage, D. L., 192
Everett, M., 273

Faust, K., 6, 13, 25, 31, 88, 120,
        122
Ferligoj, A., 120

Festinger, L., 190
Fienberg, S., 59
Fitch, R., 261
Freeman, L., 17, 191, 273, 282, 283
French, J. R. P., 103
Friedkin, N. E., 103, 108
Friel, N., 2, 148, 149
Frohlich, D., 250
Frosh, S., 201
Fuehrer, A., 257

Gargiulo, M., 202, 203, 209
Gerhardt, M. W., 227, 228
Gerlach, M., 202
Geyer, C. J., 149
Gile, K., 162, 163, 164, 299
Goktepe, J. R., 226
Goodman, L. A., 239
Goodreau, S. M., 3, 14, 15, 149, 150, 154,
        159, 160, 165, 166, 288, 297
Goodwin, J., 26, 138, 189
Gould, R. V., 103
Graen, G., 236
Granovetter, M. S., 17, 238, 249, 257,
        262
Green, H. D., Jr., 192
Greenberg, E., 144
Griff, C., 261
Guastello, S. J., 228
Gulati, R., 202, 203, 209

Hagberg, J., 25, 62
Häggström, O., 161
Hallen, B. L., 202
Handcock, M. S., 2, 11, 13, 14, 62, 65, 67,
        68, 146, 147, 148, 149, 151, 158,
        159, 160, 161, 162, 163, 164,
        165, 288, 289, 290, 297, 298,
        299
Hannan, M. H., 4, 204
Hanneman, R. A., 6
Harary, F., 17, 62, 103
Harrigan, N., 260, 262, 263
Hastings, W. K., 135, 144, 146
Hays, R. B., 248
Haythornthwaite, C., 249
Heckman, R., 228
Hedström, P., 18, 238
Heider, F., 17
Hoebe, C., 129
Hoff, P. D., 11, 298
Hogg, M. A., 190, 200, 227

Holland, P. W., 12, 59, 62, 67, 88, 131, 183, 262, 290, 292
Horrigan, J. B., 249
Huisman, M., 162
Hunter, D. R., 2, 3, 14, 66, 67, 146, 147, 148, 149, 158, 159, 160, 165, 237, 288, 290, 297, 300

Ibarra, H., 214, 250
Igarashi, T., 248, 249, 250, 258
Ihlanfeldt, K. R., 237
Ikeda, M., 147
Ingram, P., 211
Ito, M., 249

Jackson, M., 103, 287
Janis, I. L., 189
Jennings, H., 12, 31
Johnsen, E. C., 103
Johnsen, T. E., 249
Joinson, A. N., 250
Jonasson, J., 161
Jourard, S. M., 249
Judge, T. A., 227, 228
Jurkiewicz, J., 161

Kahneman, D., 273
Kalish, Y., 189, 226
Kamarck, T., 230
Kandel, D. B., 103
Kapferer, B., xix, 142, 143
Karasawa, M., 251
Karlberg, M., 62
Karoński, M., 56
Kenis, P., 213
Kerr, M., 101
Kilduff, M., 26, 189, 283
Killworth, P. D., 272, 273
Kirkpatrick, S., 227, 228
Kleinberg, J. M., 100
Knoke, D., 6, 213
Koehly, L. M., 283
Koenig, T., 261
Kolaczyk, E. D., 6
Kolm, A. S., 238
Koopman, J., 103
Koput, K. W., 210
Koskinen, J., 49, 67, 77, 124, 127, 129, 130, 139, 141, 148, 155, 160, 162, 163, 166, 174, 299
Kossinets, G., 163
Krackhardt, D., 26, 115, 189, 215, 283

Kraut, R., 250
Krzywicki, A., 161

Langan, E., 249
Lartillot, N., 148
Latané, B., 100
Laumann, P., 202, 203, 211
Lauritzen, S. L., 78, 82
Lawler, E. J., 258
Lazega, E., 129, 140, 205, 214, 252
Leenders, R., 102, 137
Lehmann, E. L., 147
Leinhardt, S., 12, 59, 62, 67, 88, 131, 183, 262, 290, 292
Lerner, J., 139
Leviatan, U., 227
Levine, J. H., 261
Liden, R. C., 236
Lincoln, J., 202
Lindenberg, S., 191, 200
Lindley, D. V., 148
Ling, R., 249
Lizardo, O., 256
Locke, E., 227, 228
Lomi, A., 202, 206
Lord, R. G., 226, 227, 228, 235
Lubbers, M. J., 15, 174, 231
Luria, G., 226, 229
Lusher, D., 9, 16, 29, 37, 167, 189, 191, 192

Mace, M. L., 261
Macy, M., 190
Maher, K. J., 227
Manski, C. F., 103
Marrone, J. A., 228
Marsden, P. V., 108, 202, 203, 211, 272
Mason, W., 108
Matsuda, M., 249
McPherson, M., 17, 91, 189, 250
Mehra, A., 228, 235
Mens, G., 108
Mercken, L., 129
Mermelstein, R., 230
Merton, R. K., 17
Metropolis, N., 135, 144, 146, 151, 156, 163
Meyers, L. A., 103
Miller, D. T., 190, 192
Mills, C. W., 261
Milo, R., 202
Mintz, B., 261

Misiolek, N. I., 228
Mitchell, B., 237, 239
Mizruchi, M. S., 261
Möller, J., 57, 293
Molm, L., 205
Monastiriotis, V., 237
Monge, P. R., 11, 13, 21
Monro, S., xix, 151, 152, 153, 179, 181
Moody, J., 250, 258
Moreno, J., 12, 31
Morris, M., 2, 3, 67, 146, 149
Mrvar, A., 6
Murray, I., 148

Nadel, S. F., 17
Neubert, M. J., 226, 234
Newbold, P., 51
Newcomb, T. M., 248, 257
Newman, M. E. J., 25, 62, 161
Niekamp, A., 129
Nohria, N., 213
Norris, J. R., 131, 134
Nowicki, K., 298

Oakes, P. J., 189, 190, 250
Okabe, D., 249
Oppenheimer, M., 261
Opsahl, T., 121
Orchard, T., 162
Ord, J. K., 102
Ornstein, M., 261
Owen-Smith, J., 208
Oxley, D., 248

Pallotti, F., 202, 206
Park, J., 25, 62, 161
Parkhe, A., 26
Pattison, P., 2, 4, 5, 12, 13, 14, 57, 65, 67,
        68, 69, 72, 73, 74, 75, 81, 82, 87,
        89, 93, 95, 100, 103, 106, 107,
        113, 115, 116, 120, 121, 122,
        123, 124, 129, 148, 161, 162,
        163, 164, 165, 179, 182, 183,
        193, 202, 205, 214, 216, 232,
        236, 237, 245, 248, 252, 260,
        261, 262, 267, 283, 287, 288,
        289, 291, 292, 293, 294, 295,
        299, 300, 301
Paxton, P., 250, 258
Pearson, M., 191
Pfeffer, J., 261
Podolny, J. M., 203, 204

Poteat, V. P., 192
Powell, W. W., 208, 210
Preciado, P., 101
Prell, C., 6
Prentice, D. A., 190, 192
Putnam, R. D., 249, 262, 270

Quandt, J., 249
Quintane, E., 272

Raftery, A. E., 11, 298
Rainie, L., 249
Ralston, D. A., 26
Ramakrishnan, U., 237
Rank, O., 213, 214
Rapoport, A., 12
Reicher, S. D., 189, 190, 250
Rennolls, K., 13
Renyi, A., 12, 292
Riddle, M., 6
Rivera, M. T., 287
Robbins, H., xix, 151, 152, 153, 179, 181
Robert, C., 148
Robertson, B., 228, 235
Robins, G., 2, 4, 9, 13, 14, 16, 29, 37, 57,
        65, 67, 68, 69, 72, 73, 74, 75, 81,
        82, 87, 89, 91, 93, 95, 100, 102,
        103, 106, 107, 113, 120, 121,
        122, 123, 124, 129, 148, 161,
        162, 163, 165, 167, 179, 182,
        183, 189, 193, 202, 203, 207,
        212, 214, 216, 232, 236, 245,
        248, 252, 260, 261, 262, 267,
        287, 288, 289, 291, 292, 293,
        294, 295, 299, 300, 301
Roose, H., 121
Rosenbluth, A. W., 144
Rosenbluth, M. N., 144
Rousseau, D. M., 203
Rowley, T. J., 203
Rubin, R. S., 227

Sahlstein, E. M., 249
Sailer, L., 272
Salancik, G. R., 261
Sander, L., 103
Schaefer, D., 205
Schneier, C. E., 226
Schwartz, M., 261
Schweinberger, M., 11, 155, 156, 236,
        298, 300
Scott, J., 6, 261

Sheppard, S., 237
Shipilov, A. V., 203
Simmel, G., 17, 260
Sjoquist, D. L., 237
Skvoretz, J., 13, 120, 121, 122
Sleebos, E., 248, 250
Smith, A. F. M., 148
Smith, E., 108
Smith-Lovin, L., 17, 91, 250
Snijders, T. A. B., 5, 11, 13, 14, 15, 19, 25, 52, 59, 60, 62, 65, 66, 67, 68, 70, 72, 75, 87, 101, 114, 115, 123, 130, 136, 137, 138, 139, 140, 141, 146, 147, 151, 155, 156, 160, 161, 163, 164, 174, 184, 189, 203, 231, 236, 239, 259, 287, 288, 289, 290, 292, 293, 294, 295, 297, 298
Soderstrom, S. B., 287
Sonquist, J., 261
Sorenson, O., 203
Sparrowe, R. T., 236
Stattin, H., 101
Stearns, L. B., 261
Steglich, C., 114, 136, 139, 140, 236, 259, 289
Stenberg, S. Å., 174
Stokes, J., 257
Strauss, D., 13, 56, 57, 62, 66, 68, 77, 78, 81, 82, 85, 86, 88, 147, 158, 262, 290, 292, 295
Stuart, T. E., 203, 204
Swedberg, R., 18
Sweezy, P. M., 261
Swidler, A., 200

Taggar, S., 226, 234
Tajfel, H., 189, 190
Takai, J., 249
Tantrum, J. M., 11
Taylor, D. A., 249
Tellegen, A., 230
Teller, A. H., 144
Teller, E., 144
Terry, D. J., 190
Tesluk, P. E., 228
Teuter, K., 102
Thompson, E., 149
Thompson, S., 162, 163
Thorne, B., 51
Tiao, G. C., 148
Tierney, L., 144

Timmerman, L., 249
Topa, G., 238
Torjman, A., 229
Trachtenberg, F., 13, 147
Tsai, W. P., 140
Turner, J. C., 189, 190, 250
Tversky, A., 273

Useem, M., 261, 263
Uzzi, B., 203, 209, 287

Valente, W., 103
van de Bunt, G., 114, 136, 139, 250, 259, 289
van Duijn, M. A. J., 6, 11, 13, 60, 138, 184, 248, 250, 257, 258, 259
van Knippenberg, D., 227
Vermunt, J. K., 6

Waege, H., 121
Wahba, J., 238
Wang, P., 2, 14, 69, 73, 74, 75, 102, 115, 120, 121, 122, 123, 124, 129, 179, 182, 183, 193, 216, 232, 236, 245, 252, 256, 260, 261, 262, 267, 288, 291, 293, 294, 295, 300
Wasserman, S., 6, 13, 25, 26, 31, 59, 88, 115, 116, 137, 147, 262, 301
Wasseur, F. W., 248, 250, 257, 258, 259
Watson, D., 230
Watts, D. J., 29, 262
Watts, M., 100, 101, 288
Webster, C. M., 273
Wellman, B., 249, 250
West, P., 259
Wetherell, M. S., 189, 190, 250
White, D. R., 102, 210
White, H., 11, 17, 19, 29, 115, 189, 210, 249
White, K. M., 190, 200
Whittington, K., 208, 210
Willer, R., 190
Wilson, W., 238
Wong, G. Y., 60
Woodbury, M. A., 162
Woolcock, J., 68, 87, 161, 162, 165

Xing, E. P., 11, 298

Yang, S., 6

Ylvisaker, D., 148
Yoon, J., 258
Yoshida, T., 248, 249
Young, A. A., 102, 103, 238
Young, H., 102, 103, 238
Yue, L. Q., 211
Yukl, G., 226, 235

Zalensky, M. D., 236
Zeitlin, M., 261
Zenou, Y., 238
Zhao, Y., 213, 215
Zhou, Z., 256
Zijlstra, B., 11, 60
Zweigenhaft, R. L., 261